Jon E. Lewis is the author and editor of numerous books on military history including *The Mammoth Book of Life Before the Mast, The Mammoth Book of War Diaries and Letters, Eye-Witness D-Day, The Mammoth Book of True War Stories, The Mammoth Book of How It Happened World War I* and *The Mammoth Book of How It Happened World War II.*

D0726365

WITHDRAWN

Stroud College LRC

Also available

The Mammoth Book of Awesome Comic Fantasy
The Mammoth Book of Best New Erotica 3
The Mammoth Book of Best New Horror 14
The Mammoth Book of Climbing Adventures
The Mammoth Book of Comic Crime
The Mammoth Book of Egyptian Whodunnits
The Mammoth Book of Elite Forces
The Mammoth Book of Endurance and Adventure
The Mammoth Book of Explorers
The Mammoth Book of Eyewitness America
The Mammoth Book of Eyewitness Battles
The Mammoth Book of Eyewitness Everest
The Mammoth Book of Fantasy
The Mammoth Book of Fighter Pilots
The Mammoth Book of Future Cops
The Mammoth Book of Great Detective Stories
The Mammoth Book of Haunted House Stories
The Mammoth Book of Heroes
The Mammoth Book of Heroic and Outrageous Women
The Mammoth Book of Historical Whodunnits
The Mammoth Book of Humor
The Mammoth Book of Illustrated Crime
The Mammoth Book of Journalism
The Mammoth Book of Legal Thrillers
The Mammoth Book of Literary Anecdotes
The Mammoth Book of Locked-Room Mysteries and Impossible Crimes
The Mammoth Book of Maneaters
The Mammoth Book of Men O'War
The Mammoth Book of Mountain Disasters
The Mammoth Book of Murder and Science
The Mammoth Book of Native Americans
The Mammoth Book of Private Eye Stories
The Mammoth Book of Prophecies
The Mammoth Book of Pulp Action
The Mammoth Book of Roaring Twenties Whodunnits
The Mammoth Book of Roman Whodunnits
The Mammoth Book of Science Fiction
The Mammoth Book of Sea Battles
The Mammoth Book of Sex, Drugs and Rock 'n' Roll
The Mammoth Book of Short Erotic Novels
The Mammoth Book of Tales from the Road
The Mammoth Book of the Titanic
The Mammoth Book of UFOs
The Mammoth Book of Vampires
The Mammoth Book of Vampire Stories by Women
The Mammoth Book of War Correspondents
The Mammoth Book of Women Who Kill

The Mammoth Book of
HOW IT HAPPENED
TRAFALGAR

**Over 50 first-hand accounts
of the greatest sea battle in history**

Edited by
JON E. LEWIS

CARROLL & GRAF PUBLISHERS
New York

TS4814   940·27

Carroll & Graf Publishers
An imprint of Avalon Publishing Group, Inc.
245 W. 17th Street
New York
NY 10011–5300
www.carrollandgraf.com

AVALON
publishing group incorporated

First published in the UK by Robinson,
an imprint of Constable & Robinson Ltd 2005

First Carroll & Graf edition 2005

Collection and editorial material copyright © J. Lewis-Stempel 2005

All rights reserved. No part of this publication
may be reproduced in any form or by any means
without the prior permission of the publisher.

ISBN 9781841198187

Printed and bound in the EU

For the usual crew: Penny, Tristram and Freda

CONTENTS

Part Two: The Long Watch: Nelson and the Napoleonic War, 16 May 1803–20 October 1805   123

Part Three: England's Glory The Battle of Trafalgar, 21 October 1805   153

Part Four: Aftermath   207

CHRONOLOGY OF THE AGE OF FIGHTING SAIL, 1758–1815

1758	Horatio Nelson born (29 September), Burnham Thorpe, Norfolk
1759	Keel of HMS *Victory* laid down at Old Single Dock, Chatham
1770	Nelson rated midshipman in *Raisonnable*
1773	Nelson serves in expedition to the Arctic
1775–83	**War of American Independence**
1777	Nelson passes lieutenant's examination
1778	Nelson appointed master of the brig *Badger*, Carribbean theatre
1779	Nelson made post-captain; Spain declares war on Britain
1780	Nelson commands naval force in San Juan expedition; Rodney destroys Spanish squadron in Battle of Cape St Vincent
1781	Battle of Dogger Bank (5 August); Battle of Chesapeake Bay (5 September)
1782	Battle of St Kitts (25–6 January); Battle of the Saintes (12 April)
1787	Nelson marries creole heiress Fanny Nisbet (11 March) with Prince William in attendance
1788	Nelson unemployed in Norfolk
1793–1802	**French Revolutionary Wars**
1793	Nelson re-engaged by Admiralty; Allied occupation of Toulon, part of French fleet destroyed; Nelson meets Emma Hamilton for first time, Naples (August)
1794	Howe beats Villaret-Joyeuse in Battle of Glorious First of June off Ushant; Nelson loses right eye in bombardment off Corsica (12 July)
1796	Nelson promoted commodore; Spain declares war on Britain
1797	Jervis and Nelson beat Cordova's fleet in Battle of Cape St Vincent (14 February); Nelson promoted rear-admiral of the Blue; naval mutinies at Nore and Spithead (April–August); Nelson loses arm at

	the Battle of Tenerife (24–5 July); defeat of the Dutch fleet by British in Battle of Camperdown (11 October)
1798	Nelson destroys Brueys' fleet in battle of the Nile (August); Nelson created Baron Nelson of the Nile; evacuates Hamiltons and royal family from Naples (December)
1799	Nelson promoted rear-admiral of the Red; created Duke of Bronte
1800	Nelson takes seat in house of Lords
1801	Nelson promoted vice-admiral of the Blue; Horatia born; Battle of Copenhagen (2 April); Nelson created Viscount Nelson of the Nile and Burnham Thorpe; Nelson attacks Boulogne flotilla (15 August)
1802	Peace of Amiens
1803–15	**Napoleonic Wars**
1803	Nelson appointed commander-in-chief in the Mediterranean; Nelson hoists his flag in HMS *Victory*
1805	Calder forces Villeneuve back to Spain in battle of Finistere (22 June); Nelson killed in decisive defeat of Villeneuve's allied fleet in Battle of Trafalgar (21 October 1805); Battle of Cape Ortegal (4 November)
1806	State funeral of Nelson in St Paul's Cathedral, London; Boulogne attacked by Congreve; rockets fired from British boats
1807	Bombardment of Copenhagen
1809	Battle of Aix Roads (10–11 April); ill-fated British Walcheren expedition (28 July–23 December)
1811	Battle of Lissa secures British command of Adriatic
1812–15	**War of 1812**
1812	HMS *Guerriere* captured by USS *Constitution*
1813	HMS *Shannon* captures USS *Chesapeake*
1814	British amphibious forces capture Washington (24–5 August)
1814	Treaty of Ghent
1815	Treaty of Vienna

CHRONOLOGY OF THE BATTLE OF TRAFALGAR, 21 OCTOBER 1805 (TIMES APPROXIMATE)

0600	Fleets sight each other at approx 8–10 miles distance
0622	*Victory* makes signal "Prepare for battle"
0800	Combined Fleet wears
1000	Combined Fleet completes wearing
1115	Villeneuve signals "Open fire as soon as enemy is within range"
1156	*Victory* makes signal "England expects every man to do his duty"
1158	*Victory* makes signal "Engage the enemy more closely"
1200	*Fougueux* opens fire on *Royal Sovereign*
1204	*Royal Sovereign* cuts enemy line and fires upon *Santa-Ana*
1213	*Belleisle* cuts enemy line
1230	*Victory* engages *Bucentaure*
1259	*Victory* cuts enemy line
1300	*Téméraire* cuts enemy line
1308	*Victory* engages *Redoutable*
1310	*Victory* and *Redoutable* locked together
1325	Nelson shot
1330	Villeneuve signals for van of Combined Fleet to wear together
1340	*Téméraire* rakes *Redoutable*'s deck hitting nearly 200 men assembled for the boarding of *Victory*
1400	*Bucentaure* and *San-Juan-Nepomuceno* surrender
1410	*Téméraire* takes *Bucentaure*
1415	*Santa Ana* surrenders to *Royal Sovereign*
1430	Allied rear effectively destroyed
1500	*Bellerophon* takes *Monarca, Colossus* takes *Swiftsure* and *Bahama*
1530	*San-Augustino* surrenders to *Leviathan*

1600   *Defiance* takes *Aigle*, *Achille* takes *Berwick*, *Intrépide* strikes her colours
1630   Nelson dies, *Intrépide* taken by *Orion*, *Achille* set afire by *Prince*
1715   *Neptuno* taken by *Minotaur*
1745   *Achille* blows up
1730   *Santisima* taken by *Prince*

"Engage the enemy more closely"

Admiral Lord Nelson, Trafalgar,
11.58 a.m., 21 October 1805

INTRODUCTION

"England Expects That Every Man Will Do His Duty"

Thus fluttered Nelson's signal flags as his ships closed in on the Franco-Spanish fleet off Cadiz, Spain, in the leaden late morning of 21 October 1805. Nelson's showy exhortation has entered legend but it was the next and last signal run up by the English commander, at 12.20 p.m. as the fleets reached shooting distance, that was the key to the man and his victories:

"Engage the enemy more closely."

Horatio Nelson, the vicar's boy from Norfolk and a gentleman barely, was a ruthless English patriot. Other, more aristocratic, English naval commanders sometimes seemed content to pursue the Napoleonic war in a manner akin to fox-hunting – as sport. Nelson, by contrast, not only wanted to beat the French in seafights, but he wanted their "annihilation".

Nelson's single-minded purpose inspired confidence in his officers, his "band of brothers", whom he wined and dined and befriended, and into whom he instilled his beliefs and his tactics. From the captains, the Nelsonian will to win trickled down to the men. Wrote one ordinary seaman of Nelson, "Men adored him and in fighting under him, every man thought himself sure of success".

Nelson's battle plan at Trafalgar was novel: it was to attack in two columns, approaching bow on, and was designed to force a close-quarters mêlée in which the English could maximize their superior ship-handling and firepower.

There is a sense in which the Battle of Trafalgar was over before the first cannonade was loosed off. The Franco-Spanish Combined Fleet had nothing about it to match the Nelsonian personality or the highly trained capabilities of England's sailors. The French had been blown out of the water by Nelson before, most spectacularly at the Battle of the Nile. Off the coast of Spain on that Autumn morning 200 years ago, the French knew what fate awaited them. They were sailing to a salt-water Armageddon.

Villeneuve, the Franco-Spanish commander, was competent but uninspiring. Some of his officers considered him a coward, although his caution was well-founded: French crews were overly populated by delinquent landsmen, who tended to be seasick out of sight of land. Despite everything, the French and Spanish fought determinedly at Trafalgar, and their fleet out-numbered the English fleet by 33 ships of the line to 27. It was a battle not a massacre.

The most conspicuous English casualty was, of course, Nelson himself, mortally felled by a musket ball. To die at the moment of his greatest achievement had something of Greek myth or Shakespearean epic about it. Before Trafalgar, Nelson had been an English hero; after Trafalgar, he became the nation's first superstar. People cried publicly in the streets on hearing of his death; only the demise of Diana, Princess of Wales, almost 200 years later, would cause a similar show of grief.

The personal tragedy of Nelson, while central to the story of Trafalgar, should not distract from the battle's wider impor-tance. The last great fleet action of the age of sail, Trafalgar forced Napoleon to abandon his planned invasion of England. Obliged to use the sea like fugitives, the French were, further-more, unable to protect their colonies or enforce Napoleon's blockade of British trade.

Something more than French sea power was sunk at Tra-falgar; so was the whole of Napoleon's dark ambition for a trans-continental military dictatorship. By contrast, the British sailed from Trafalgar as the undisputed ruler of the world's waves and set on a compass bearing that would lead them to establish the world's greatest ever empire (and not a few democracies).

Trafalgar, in other words, was one of a handful of truly decisive battles in history. Over the course of a fatal 5 hours in the afternoon of 21 October 1805, the direction of human affairs changed course.

For the better.

Part One

Prelude

Nelson and the War of the French Revolution,
1793–1801

INTRODUCTION

Cometh the hour, cometh the man. At a little after midday on 21 October 1805, off the wild coast of Cadiz, an English admiral led his "band of brothers" into battle against a combined French-Spanish fleet under Villeneuve. The destiny of nations rested on the outcome. The admiral fell in the action but he did not fail in it; the victory of the Royal Navy at Trafalgar definitively established English superiority at sea over the old Gallic enemy. It did more. Trafalgar set England fair to become the greatest power in the history of the world.

That admiral was, of course, Horatio Nelson. On 21 October 1805 Nelson equalled, surpassed even, the task of the hour. That he did so was somewhat the result of innate personal courage and willpower – he had both qualities in abundance – and it was somewhat more the result of preparation. A life's worth of it. Everything of Nelson's existence, even from boyhood, seemed but training for that encounter at Cape Trafalgar on a blustery autumn day in 1805.

Horatio Nelson was born on 29 September 1758 at Burnham Thorpe in Norfolk, England, where his father was rector. At least according to the later accounts of his family and friends, he was a singularly brave child; at Paston School, so the famous anecdote goes, he scrumped pears from the headmaster's orchard in dead of night "because every other boy was afraid [to do it]". Nelson's courage did not stem from any physical grandeur.

He was always slight of build; even when adult, he stood a mere 5 foot 6 inches in his stockings. Given Nelson's frailty, it came as some surprise to his uncle, Maurice Suckling, RN, Captain of the HMS *Raisonnable*, when the twelve-year-old Nelson wrote asking to be taken to sea. "What has poor Horatio done, who is so weak," replied Suckling, "that he above all the rest [of Horatio's siblings] should be sent to rough it out at sea? But let him come; and the first time we go into action, a cannon ball may knock off his head and provide for him at once." In the eighteenth century, it was commonplace for middle sons of the middle class to settle upon a career as naval officer, though these aspirants were given no special training. Midshipman Nelson was effectively a deckhand, literally "learning the ropes" along-side the seamen. His time "up forrard" engendered a sympathy with the common sailor which never left him. After a year and half, spent on his uncle's guardship in the Medway and cross-Atlantic runs in a West Indiaman, Nelson cajoled his way into a Royal Naval expedition to the North Pole, and afterwards served in the East Indies. There, following a near-fatal attack of malaria, he sank into depression, "impressed with a feeling that I should never rise in my profession". But as his ship neared home, Nelson had vision of a "radiant orb . . . [and] A sudden glow of patriotism was kindled in me and presented my King and Country as my patron".

Nelson's new and conscious conception of himself as a "hero" was only confirmed when the *Dolphin* arrived in England and he was greeted with the wholly unexpected news that uncle Maurice had been appointed Comptroller of the Navy. Advancement in the Georgian navy depended on ability – and rather more on patronage. Nelson now had a most powerful patron, one who wasted no time in promoting his eighteen-year-old nephew lieutenant. On 10 April 1777, Nelson was appointed to the frigate *Lowestoffe*, which enabled him to take a token role in the American War of Independence, when he led the boarding party which seized an American merchantman. Thereafter, Nelson's progress up the career rigging was relent-less; he transferred to the *Bristol* in September 1778 as first lieutenant, to the brig *Badger* as commander three months later, becoming post-captain in command of the *Hinchinbrooke* on 11

June 1779, five days before Spain declared war on Britain as her contribution to the War of Independence. As commander of the naval force in the expedition against San Juan in Nicaragua (a Spanish possession), Nelson acquitted himself well, and in 1781 he commissioned the frigate *Albemarle* and joined the squadron under Lord Hood on the North American Station. It was here that Nelson was first acquainted with Prince William (later King William IV), who was midshipman on Hood's flagship.

A PORTRAIT OF NELSON AS POST-CAPTAIN, NEW YORK, November 1782

Midshipman Prince William[1]

Nelson was twenty-four at the time of this encounter.

I was then a Midshipman on board the *Barfleur*, lying in the Narrows off Staten Island, and had the watch on deck, when Captain Nelson of the *Albemarle*, came in his barge alongside, who appeared to be the meerest boy of a captain I ever beheld; and his dress was worthy of attention. He had on a full laced uniform; his lank unpowdered hair was tied in a stiff Hessian tail, of an extraordinary length; the old fashioned flaps of his waistcoat added to the general quaintness of his figure, and produced an appearance which particularly attracted my notice; for I had never seen anything like it before, nor could I imagine who he was, nor what he came about. My doubts were however, removed when Lord Hood introduced me to him. There was something irresistibly pleasing in his address and conversation; and an enthusiasm when speaking on professional subjects, that showed he was no common being.

After service on the North American Station, Nelson got his heart's desire, a transfer to the West Indies, where the chance "for glory" was greater. There, following the termination of the War of Independence, he enforced the Navigation Acts against the Americans with a vigour that made him a talking point among the English colonists.

NELSON IN THE WEST INDIES: A WOMAN'S VIEW, 1785

Anonymous[2]

The author of this letter writes to her neighbour, Fanny Nisbet.

We have at last seen the Captain of the *Boreas* of whom so much has been said. He came up just before dinner, much heated, and was very silent; yet seemed, according to the old adage, to think the more. He declined drinking any wine; but after dinner, when the President, as usual, gave the following toasts, the King, the Queen and Royal Family, and Lord Hood, this strange man regularly filled his glass, and observed that these were always bumper toasts with him; which having drank, he uniformly passed the bottle, and relapsed into his former taciturnity. It was impossible, during this visit, for any of us to make out his real character; there was such a reserve and sternness in his behaviour, with occasional sallies, though very transient, of a superior mind. Being placed by him, I endeavoured to rouse his attention by showing him all the civilities in my power; but I drew out little more than Yes and No. If you, Fanny, had been there, we think you would have made something of him; for you have been in the habit of attending to these odd sort of people.

Frances "Fanny" Nisbet, the attractive Creole widow of a sugar planter, soon had her chance to "make something of him", when Nelson and she met on 11 May 1785. Nelson, a serial romantic, fell in love instantly and by August was requesting the permission of her uncle, John Richardson Herbert, President of Nevis, for Fanny's hand in marriage.

A LOVE LETTER, 19 August 1785

Horatio Nelson[3]

To Fanny Nisbet. His infatuation with her did not prevent Nelson from misspelling her name but then his spelling was never very accurate.

My dear Mrs Nisbit,
    To say how anxious I have been, and am, to receive a line from Mr Herbert, would be far beyond the descriptive

powers of my pen. Most fervently do I hope his answer will be of such a tendency as to convey real pleasure, not only to myself, but also to you. For most sincerely do I love you, and I think that my affection is not only founded upon the principles of reason but also upon the basis of mutual attachment. Indeed, My charming Fanny, did [I] possess a Million, my greatest pride and pleasure would be to share it with you; and as to living in a Cottage with you, I should esteem it superior to living in a palace with any other I have yet met with.

My age is enough to make me seriously reflect upon what I have offered, and commonsense tells me what a Good choice I have made. The more I weigh you in my mind, the more reason I find to admire both your head and heart . . .

My temper you know as well as myself, for by longer acquaintance you will find I possess not the Art of concealing it. My situation and family I have not endeavoured to concial.

Don't think me rude by this entering into a correspondence with you.

Frances Nisbet and Horatio Nelson were married on 11 March 1787. She came complete with her son, Josiah, whom Nelson always treated with great affection. Among the guests at the wedding was Prince William.

Soon after the marriage, Nelson and his new wife journeyed to England (Nelson, en route, suffering a malady which almost did for him) which the *Boreas* reached in July 1787. With no prospect of war, and after having disjointed the collective nose of the Admiralty by his friendship with the troublesome Prince William, Nelson was put on half-pay. For five long years, Nelson disconsolately played country squire at his father's Norfolk house.

Not until January 1793, when the whiff of war with revolutionary France was in the air, was Nelson recalled to the colours and given command of a ship, the *Agamemnon*, a sixty-four. Hostilities opened on 1 February. Shortly afterwards, Nelson was dispatched on a goodwill mission to Naples, the Italian kingdom allied with Britain against republican France. In Naples, Nelson was cheerfully aided by the

British ambassador, Sir William Hamilton, whose beautiful young second wife, Emma, a former courtesan, beguiled many – including Goethe – with her after-dinner dancing and theatrical entertainments.

On leaving Naples for Sardinia, the *Agamemnon* had a "little brush" with the enemy, leaving both herself and a French frigate severely damaged. After repairs, the *Agamemnon* was dispatched in January 1794 to Corsica to attack the fortress of Bastia. "The expedition," wrote Nelson, "is almost a child of my own, and I have no fears about the final issue. It will be a victory."

It was, whereupon Nelson joined the siege of Calvi, with guns from the *Agamemnon* unloaded and dragged up hills into position. On 12 July, Nelson was hit in the eye by stone fragments after a cannon shot landed nearby. He made light of the wound, writing to Fanny of "a very slight scratch towards my right eye", but in truth the damage caused permanent loss of sight. The Corsican interlude left Nelson more than blinded in the eye; it left him disenchanted, for (as he saw it) his labours at Bastia and Calvi were insufficiently unsung by his superiors. He wrote to his uncle, Maurice Suckling, complaining:

> My diligence is not mentioned . . . It is known that, for two months, I blockaded Bastia with a Squadron: only sixty sacks of flour got into the Town. At San Fiorenzo and Calvi, for two months before, nothing got in, and four French frigates could not get out and are now ours . . . Others . . . are handsomely mentioned. *Such things are.* I have got upon a subject near to my heart, which is full when I think of the treatment I have received. Every man who had a considerable share in the reduction has got some place or other – I, only I, am without reward. Nothing but my anxious endeavours to serve my country makes me bear up against it; but I sometimes am ready to give all up . . . But never mind, some day I'll have a *Gazette* of my own.[4]

Nelson's resentment was not improved by the news that while he was on Mediterranean duty, the Royal Navy had scored its first considerable success at sea over the revolutionary French, in the Battle of Ushant, forever afterwards known to the British as the Glorious First of June.

THE GLORIOUS FIRST OF JUNE, 30 May–1 June 1794

Midshipman William Dillon, HMS Defence[5]

To cover the arrival of a grain shipment from America, the French government sent the Brest fleet into the Atlantic, where they were pursued by twenty-five ships of the Royal Navy under the command of Lord Howe. The French admiral, Villaret-Joyeuse, several times resisted battle, but his line was eventually broken through by "Black Dick" Howe 450 miles west of Ushant.

On the morning of May 28, having strong breezes and hazy weather, the fleet being on the starboard tack, about 8 o'clock the signal was made from the flying squadron that a strange fleet was in sight, some distance to windward, which proved to be the enemy we had been so anxiously looking for. His ships were not, by appearance, in any regular order of sailing. Lord Howe made the signal to prepare for battle, and for the flying squadron to chace and engage the enemy. So soon as those signals were displayed to our ships, a state of excitement was manifested totally beyond my powers of description. No one thought of anything else than to exert himself to his utmost ability in overcoming the enemy. It was also very satisfactory to observe the change of disposition in the ship's company of the *Defence*. All animation and alacrity pervaded these men: no more sulky looks. The enemy was near, and all hands were determined to support their captain. The ships when near each other were cheered by their crews in succession. Death or Victory was evidently the prevailing feeling.

The enemy's fleet did not alter its course upon seeing us: therefore it neared. But unluckily the wind, increasing to a gale, obliged us to reef the topsails, and our progress was in consequence much delayed. Our Captain exerted himself in a wonderful manner, determined to set a noble example to all under his command. Whilst we were in chace, a splinter netting was fitted over the quarter deck to receive the blocks that might be shot away aloft, and a cask of water was hoisted into the main top, to be prepared for fire. The enemy, having closed us to about eight miles, hauled to the wind (in the western quarter). The whole of our fleet being in chace, the order of sailing was no longer an object. About 4 o'clock in the afternoon the wind moderated a little. Just at this time we noticed one of the advanced squadron, under Rear Admiral Pasley, firing upon the enemy's rear. Some of our sails were split, but luckily held on. At 7 o'clock our ships were closing, and brought the French to action about 8 o'clock. The engagement was followed up with great spirit, but moderated, and finally ceased, as night came on. The wind had lulled, and as total darkness prevailed, all further operations were at an end. Every ship in the British fleet carried distinguishing lights, to prevent mistakes with the enemy's, and the night was passed in watching each other's motions, as well as it could be done.

At daylight on the 29th, the two fleets were on opposite tacks, and the leading ship of our van, the *Caesar* of 80 guns, exchanged shots with the rear of the French. But our opponents had contrived to keep the weather gage. We soon tacked, to place ourselves upon a line with our adversaries. We now missed the *Audacious*, 74. It was evident she had parted from us during the night. Her absence reduced our number to 25 sail of the line. In counting the enemy's fleet, we made out 26 of the line. It was afterwards ascertained that the *Audacious* had parted company in attempting to take possession of the *Revolutionnaire*, a French three decker that had been disabled by the fire of our ships on the previous evening; but, failing to do so, fell in the next morning with a squadron of enemy, and was obliged to run off to prevent being captured: and, finally, instead of trying to rejoin our fleet, put into Plymouth.

We had a commanding breeze this day, but as our opponents kept well to windward, we could not close with them. However, about 10 o'clock, the enemy's van gradually edged down towards ours, and they began a distant engagement before 11 o'clock. Lord Howe then made the signal for the *Caesar*, the leading ship, to tack and cut through the French rear. But this signal not being obeyed disconcerted his Lordship, who was completely at a loss in not having his plan of attack carried into effect. Meanwhile the firing on both sides was kept up with determined spirit. The signal mentioned was repeated several times, but the *Caesar* kept on her course. At length Lord Howe tacked, in the *Queen Charlotte*, and those ships near followed the example. When he thought that he should succeed in the desired object, he made the signal for a general chace. That signal left every captain at liberty to follow his own plan in bringing his ship into action, and the line of battle was no longer in force. Consequently every ship was trying to attack the enemy in the best way that offered. However, this signal was entirely annulled by the sudden visitation of a violent squall of wind, accompanied by a thick mist with rain, during which no object could be distinguished at 100 yards' distance. Such an unexpected event brought the English fleet into a state of disorder. When the mist cleared away, scarcely any two ships were on the same tack, and many were near running on board each other. Nothing but confusion was visible in our fleet, whilst the enemy's line was in perfect order. Had the enemy availed himself of the opportunity thus offered, not intentionally, of attacking our broken line, who knows what might have been the result?

Every British officer was aware of our critical position: therefore no time was lost in forming the line as well as it could be done. Lord Howe had cut through the enemy's line at the 5th ship from his rear. Many ships had followed, and, at last, it came to our turn. At the opening that had been made in the enemy's line lay a large French 80-gun ship, *l'Indomptable*. All her topmasts had been shot away, and she was motionless. But she kept up a most spirited fire as we passed her. The *Orion*, 74, had taken a position on her lee quarter, and we concluded that she would be taken. However, whilst all these operations were going on, the French admiral noticed the dangerous situation of the ship mentioned, as well as of another, *le Tyrannicide*, also disabled. He wore his fleet, and by that means rescued them.

So soon as we had passed through the French rear, we attempted to tack, but failed; then were obliged to wear. In performing that evolution we nearly ran on board of another ship, as several of ours were rather crowded, and too close together to admit of forming the line without risk. Nevertheless, with care and good management we extricated ourselves from all these difficulties; and, having finally brought to the wind on the starboard tack, we became exposed to the attack of a large

French three decker. The shot from him flew about us like hailstones. As yet we had not any man hurt, but our sails and rigging were much injured. At this critical moment the *Defence* lay over so much that our quarter deck was open to the enemy's fire, our opponents pelting away without intermission. Presently one of his shot struck the upper part of the quarter deck bulwark, on the larboard side, killed one man and wounded nine. One or two shots passed so close to the captain that I thought he was hit. He clapped both hands upon his thighs with some emotion: then, recovering himself, he took out of his pocket a piece of biscuit and began eating it as if nothing had happened. He had evidently been shook by the wind of the shot. He had on a cocked hat, and kept walking the deck, cheering up the seamen with the greatest coolness.

I had never seen a man killed before. It was a most trying scene. A splinter struck him in the crown of the head, and when he fell the blood and brains came out, flowing over the deck. The captain went over, and, taking the poor fellow by the hand, pronounced him dead. The others, who were wounded, were taken below to the Surgeon. Just at that moment, a volley of shot assailed the poop, cut away the main brace, and made sad havoc there. Some of the men could not help showing symptoms of alarm: which the captain noticing, he instantly went up, and, calling the seamen together, led them to set the brace to rights. At this instant Twysden made his appearance, and explained to the captain that our guns from the main deck had no effect upon the three decker. To prove this, he waited till the smoke had cleared away, then went down and, giving one of the guns the utmost elevation, fired it. The shot only reached halfway to the Frenchman. Consequently our firing was useless. Under these circumstances our guns were kept quiet. We were in a most trying situation, receiving the enemy's fire without being able to return the compliment. But, luckily, one of our three deckers, the *Glory*, noticing the danger to which we were exposed, closed upon us and, directing his broadsides upon our adversary, drew off his attention. This act of the *Glory*'s gave us a little breathing time, by which we were enabled to set the ship to rights.

I was quartered on the lower deck under Lieut. Beecher. He

had the command of the seven foremost guns, and three of them in the bow were under mine. As we could not use the guns below, I availed myself of that circumstance to attend on the quarter deck, to witness all that was passing. Never having been before present in an action of the kind, my curiosity and anxiety were beyond all bounds. The danger to which I exposed myself had not the slightest influence over me. Owing to that desire I saw more than most of the mids, who kept to their stations, and I can now relate what I really did see. The result of this action, which had fallen sharply upon a few of our ships, was the obtaining of the weather gage: an advantage of considerable importance, as it enabled the British admiral to direct his attack upon the enemy when it suited his convenience. The two ships that suffered most in our fleet were the *Royal George*, 100 guns, Admiral Sir Alexander Hood, and the *Queen*, 98, Sir Alan Gardner. The sails of both those ships were literally torn into shreds. There they lay, perfectly motionless, the eyes of the whole fleet turned upon them, whilst their crews were occupied in unbending and replacing their useless sails. *L'Indomptable* and *le Tyrannicide*, two deckers, bore the brunt of the action on the side of France, as those ships lay exactly in that part of their line where ours cut through. In due time both fleets were formed in the order of battle, and, about 5 o'clock, all again in as complete a condition as circumstances would permit. The French ships appeared to have suffered more than ours, as several had lost topmasts and yards, whereas on our side nothing of the kind was discernible.

At this season of the year we could reckon upon daylight till past 8 o'clock. We had, therefore, plenty of time to renew the action. Why that was not done astonished all hands on board the English fleet. Lord Howe had obtained, by clever tactics, the position most desirable for his operations, and we all expected the signal would be made to renew the battle. But this was not the case. It was the custom with the French to wait the attack, instead of being the aggressors. They were under easy sail to leeward of us, on the larboard tack, evidently anticipating our closing upon them. Lord Howe, it seems, was not satisfied that the enemy had shown a resolution to fight, and not evade us. Under that impression, he determined to take his time. By that decision we had two or three days of more anxiety, previous to our having an opportunity of bringing affairs to a conclusion. The night was passed in tolerable quietness.

On the morning of the 30th we had foggy weather. Our fleet not being in very good order, the signals were made from Lord Howe's ship to form in line of battle. The *Caesar* happened at that moment to be close to us, pumping out quantities of water, the effect of the shot she had received below. We heard that one of her guns had burst on the previous day, by which 18 men were killed and wounded. The fog partially clearing away, the enemy was seen to leeward. The admiral instantly made the signal to prepare for action, upon which the *Caesar* threw out the signal of inability to do so. Our fleet formed in line of battle as well as circumstances would allow, but the hazy weather rendered our evolutions uncertain, and there did not appear any probability, that day, of any more fighting. Finally, the fog becoming thicker, we lost sight of the French, so that we could not close upon the enemy.

The morning of the 31st was still misty, with favourable symptoms of its clearing away, the wind in the S.W. quarter. In the afternoon, the fog disappearing, we beheld the enemy some distance to leeward. We prepared for action, and made sail to close upon him. By 7 o'clock we had reached within five miles of the French fleet. The weather became fine, and we enjoyed one of the most splendid sights ever witnessed – the two fleets close to each other in line of battle, only waiting for the signal to commence the work of destruction, the repeating frigates of the two nations within gunshot. However, all passed off in quietness. Lord Howe, having placed his fleet in an exact line with that of the enemy, he drew off for the night, which we passed in extreme anxiety. We could not reckon on more than six hours of darkness, and therefore concluded that we should commence operations with the dawn. Very few of the *Defence*'s took off any clothing, and the hammocks were not piped down. Our whole thoughts hung upon the approaching event. As to your humble servant, being rather fatigued, I preferred, it being a beautiful starlight night, to remain on deck. I selected one of the topsail halyard tubs on the forecastle, and coiled myself as well as I could inside of it, where I took a snooze which I enjoyed, and felt more refreshed when awoke by the tars than I should have done had I gone to bed: at least I thought so. I felt an elasticity beyond expression.

Rising then from my tub, I beheld the enemy about 10 miles off to leeward, on the starboard tack. There was a fine breeze and lovely weather. It was Sunday, and I thought the Captain would not have much time for prayers, as the work in hand would be of a very different nature. Lord Howe drew up the fleet in capital order. He made several changes in the disposition of the ships, to render every part of his line equal. The *Defence* was the seventh ship in the van. When his Lordship had completed his arrangements for attacking the enemy, he made the signal for the different divisions, that is the van, centre and rear, to engage the opposite divisions of the French: then for each ship in the English line to pass through the enemy and attack his opponent to leeward. Next, the fleet was hove to, that the crews might have their breakfasts. This was going to work in a regular methodical manner. His Lordship knew that John Bull did not like fighting with an empty stomach; but it was a sorry meal, scarcely deserving the name. We had not had much time for a fire in the range for cooking since the 28th of last month. All the tables and conveniences were stowed below; all the partitions taken down; nothing to be seen on the decks but powder, shot, ramrods and instruments of destruction. Whilst the ship's Company were making the best of the time allowed for refreshment, the Captain collected most of his officers in the cabin, where a short prayer suitable to the occasion was offered to the Almighty for protection against the impending event. The half hour having elapsed, up went the signal for the fleet to bear down and bring the enemy to action, it being then near 9 o'clock. What an awful moment! How shall I describe it? A scene of magnificence and importance, not of common occurrence, and not often equalled on the ocean – upwards of 50 sail of the line viewing each other, and preparing to pour out their thunder destructive of the human species, which would decide the fate of either fleet, and probably that of the nation.

Our Captain went round the ship and spoke to all the men at

their guns in terms of encouragement, to fight for their country.
The replies he received were gratifying in the highest degree.
The noblest feelings of patriotism were proclaimed, with expressions of the warmest enthusiasm: in short, a determination
to conquer prevailed throughout the ship – and, I may as well
say, throughout the British fleet. As we neared the French up
went our colours –

> High o'er the poop the flattering winds unfurl'd
> Th' imperial Flag that rules the watery world.

The *Defence*, being a good sailer, made rapid speed through the
waves, going under double reefed topsails with a commanding
breeze. Twysden, noticing that we had advanced too far
beyond our line, hastened on to the quarter deck to point
out to his Captain, with becoming respect, that he was exposing
his ship to the utmost danger by going on singlehanded without
support, and that he ran the risk of being either sunk or totally
disabled. The maintopgallant sail had been set by us, the only
ship in the line to have done so. In fact, when the signal had
been made to bear down, the ship came before the wind, and
the Captain, anxious to obey orders, was striving to commence
the action as soon as he could. Lord Howe had observed this
action of Capt. Gambier's, and mentioned it to the officers near
him, saying, "Look at the *Defence*. See how nobly she is going
into action!" His Lordship then turning round and casting his
eyes over the fleet, said, "I believe I cannot make any more
signals. Every ship has had instructions what to do"; then,
shutting his signal book, left the poop to take his chance on the
quarter deck. Lieut. Twysden prevailed on his Captain to take
in the maintopgallant sail, but the ship still proceeded, and
extended her distance beyond the British line. Then the mizen
topsail was braced aback, by which more wind filled the
maintopsail. Therefore, instead of retarding her motion, it
was accelerated. The lieutenant mentioned this, but the Captain would not make any more reduction of sail. He said, "I am
acting in obedience to the admiral's signal. Fill the mizen
topsail-again. It may probably be thought that I have no wish
to do so if I shorten sail." This last reply quieted Twysden. As I

happened to be present at that particular moment, I heard every word that passed. The mizen topsail was braced round to receive the wind, and our whole attention was then directed to the ship in the enemy's line – the 7th – that we were to engage.

The French fleet had their maintopsails to the mast, and were waiting for our attack. Shortly after 9 o'clock we were getting very near to our opponents. Up went their lower deck ports, out came the guns, and the fire on us commenced from several of the enemy's van ships. Twysden then went to his quarters on the main deck, and your humble servant went below to his station. We retained our fire till in the act of passing under the Frenchman's stern, then, throwing all our topsails aback, luffed up and poured in a most destructive broadside. We heard most distinctly our shot striking the hull of the enemy. The carved work over his stern was shattered to pieces. Then, ranging up alongside of him within half pistol shot distance, our fire was kept up with the most determined spirit. When we had measured our length with that of our adversary, we backed the maintopsail. In that position the action was maintained for some time. We had instructions below to lower the ports whilst loading the guns, that the enemy's musketry might not tell upon our men, and also to fire with a slight elevation, as the upper deck guns would be depressed a few degrees, thus making a cross fire upon the Frenchman. After the two or three first broadsides, I became anxious to have a good view of the ship we were engaging. To effect this object, I requested the men at the foremost gun to allow me a few seconds, when the port was hauled up, to look out from it. They complied with my wishes. The gun being loaded, I took my station in the centre of the port; which being held up, I beheld our antagonist firing away at us in quick succession. The ship was painted a dark red, as most of the enemy's fleet were, to denote (as previously mentioned) their sanguinary feelings against their adversaries. I had not enjoyed the sight long – only a few seconds – when a rolling sea came in and completely covered me. The tars, noticing this, instantly let down the port, but I got a regular soaking for my curiosity. The men cheered me, and laughingly said, "We hope, Sir, you will not receive further injury. It is rather warm work here below: the salt water will keep you cool."

One of these; John Polly, of very short stature, remarked that he was so small the shot would all pass over him. The words had not been long out of his mouth when a shot cut his head right in two, leaving the tip of each ear remaining on the lower part of the cheek. His sudden death created a sensation among his comrades, but the excitement of the moment soon changed those impressions to others of exertion. There was no withdrawing from our situation, and the only alternative was to face the danger with becoming firmness. The head of this unfortunate seaman was cut so horizontally that anyone looking at it would have supposed it had been done by the blow of an axe. His body was committed to the deep.

The action was kept up with the utmost determination. At $\frac{1}{2}$ past 10 our mizen mast was shot away, and our ship drifted to leeward. Several of my men were wounded. Holmes, the Captain of one of the guns, a powerful fine fellow, had his arm carried away close to the shoulder. By this time it was evident that the French were getting the worst of it, as we were obliged to go over to the starboard side to defend ourselves against an enemy's ship. At $\frac{1}{2}$ past 11 the main mast came down on the starboard side of the poop with a terrible crash. This information was conveyed to us below by some of the seamen who had been in the tops. As they could no longer be useful in consequence of two of the masts being shot away, they were ordered down to the guns. They reported the upper end of the quarter deck to be dreadfully shattered. The lower deck was at times so completely filled with smoke that we could scarcely distinguish each other, and the guns were so heated that, when fired, they nearly kicked the upper deck beams. The metal became so hot that, fearing some accident, we reduced the quantity of powder, allowing also more time to elapse between the loading and firing of them.

One of the Captains of my guns was a Swede, by name John West. I noticed his backwardness, but before I could take any steps in his behalf, we had to change sides, a ship engaging us on our left. We had not been long occupied with her when we were called over to the right. After firing a broadside, John Lee, second captain of West's gun, told me that he had deserted his quarters. "Why didn't you knock him down?" I asked. "I did,

Sir," was the reply, "with this handspike," showing it to me. However, West had absconded, and I was too much taken up with the pressing events of the moment to look after him. The ship we were engaging was very close, and the shot from him did us considerable injury. One of my guns was dismounted. This disaster created some confusion, more especially as the ship, from the loss of her masts, was rolling deeply; and we had considerable difficulty in securing the gun. Whilst we were occupied about this job, Lieut. Beecher thought that he observed a disinclination on the part of the seamen to exert themselves. All of a sudden he drew his sword from the scabbard, and began flourishing it about with threats that he would cut the first man down that did not do his duty. The tars were rather astonished at this proceeding of their officer as, hitherto, he had approved of their conduct. They had been fighting hard for upwards of two hours, and naturally were fatigued. They explained their anxiety to do their best. This pacified the heroic lieutenant. He sheathed his sword, and the men went on at the guns as before.

Just as this scene terminated, two of the men were blown down from the wind of a shot from the ship we were engaging, and I was carried away with them by the shock. I thought myself killed, as I became senseless, being jammed between these men. So soon as the smoke cleared away, our companions noticed my situation. They came, lugged me out, and began rubbing my limbs. This brought me to my senses. They lifted me up, enquiring if I felt myself hurt. I called out for water to drink. They handed to me a bowl with water. When I drank of it, it was quite salt. There were some salt bags hanging up close by, belonging to the men of that particular mess. These had been shot down, and had impregnated the water placed there to be used as required by those that were thirsty. Recovering myself, I felt considerable pain in my head and shoulders. My left cheek was cut by a splinter and bled profusely. I then examined the two men with whom I had been knocked down. In outward appearance they were dead; but as I did not consider myself a sufficient judge of these matters, I desired a couple of seamen to take them below to the surgeon. Whilst I was giving these directions, we were called over to the larboard side to repel the attack of an enemy. After a few broadsides he passed us. From him we received no injury at my quarters. Not long after, another Frenchman ranged up on the starboard side. Away we turned to, and pelted him as hard as we could. In crossing over I beheld the two wounded men still lying in the same position I had left them. Then, calling upon those to whom I had given orders to take the disabled men below, I insisted upon their immediately complying with my directions. They were then conveyed to the cockpit. After a few broadsides exchanged with our opponent, he made sail to leeward, and we had a few minutes' rest. This gave me an opportunity of looking out of the ports, but there was not much to be seen from that low situation. All that we could make out, in our conjectures, led us to believe that the action was nearly over. We could plainly at times distinguish the French ships sailing off and forming to leeward, engaging our ships as they passed by.

We had not long been quiet, when we received orders from the quarter deck for all hands to lie down, as an enemy three decker was coming to rake us. This ship closed gradually upon us with only her foremast standing, the sail of which enabled him to make way at a very slow pace. This was, to me, the most awful part of the battle. We could not defend ourselves from the stern, and here was an immense overpowering ship of upwards of 100 guns going to pour in her broadside into the weakest and most exposed part of our ship. It was a moment of extreme anxiety, as there was a chance of our being sunk. As he neared us there was an appearance of intending to board, and the boarders were called to repulse the attempt. But when he altered his course to rake, we were again ordered to lie down. We waited the coming event with a silent suspense not easily described. At length the enemy in passing across our stern, to our astonishment, only fired a few random shot, which brought down our disabled foremast. We were now completely dismasted and quite unmanageable. The three decker, ranging up on our larboard side, gave us an opportunity of sending some well directed shot into him. In watching the motions of this ship, I noticed that the Frenchmen, in many instances, loaded their guns from the outside. One man I distinctly saw riding upon a lower deck gun, loading it. He was stripped from the waist upwards, and had we been sufficiently near, our marines could have picked him off with their muskets. This three decker soon got out of range, leaving us free of further molestation.

It was past 12 o'clock, and I concluded the fighting part of our duty to be at an end. My clothes were still damp: my shoes, to which I had small buckles, were covered with blood; my face and hands smutched with powder and blood. At my quarters I had 14 men killed and wounded (if I included myself I should say 15); and a gun. I now ascertained that no part of the lower deck had suffered so much as mine. On my way aft I shook hands with other mids who had escaped. Of these I shall never forget Ritchie. He was in his shirt upwards, with a bandage round his head. These were all bloody, and I thought he had been hurt. On my inquiring of him if it were the case, he gave me a hearty shake by the hand, telling me he was strong and hearty, and ready to continue the action when required. The bloody spots on his linen were occasioned by his having assisted some wounded men below. He gave the strongest symptoms of a bold and daring spirit, and had it not been for the bloody marks upon him, one might have supposed he had been at a merry and jovial party instead of a destructive battle. The next person I came in contact with was one of my messmates, Consitt. He also had taken off his coat and waistcoat, and his linen too was all bloody, which led me to suppose that he had been injured. However, upon enquiry, I found that he was safe and sound. In a few words he gave me an interesting account of what had been going on upon the quarter deck, as he was one of the Captain's aides-de-camp. He had been sent down to the lower deck to ascertain its state and condition. Among the informations received from him, he stated that the *Royal Sovereign*, one of our three deckers, had fired into us and wounded some of our men. Upon further inquiry his assertion turned out to be true.

I now hastened up to the quarter deck. In attempting to do so I was prevented by the splinter netting which, from its lying across the quarter deck under the mainmast, had turned the place into a sort of cage. There was no getting on it until the netting had been cut away. Whilst on the ladder, Mr. Hawtayne, the clergyman, came to me. From my appearance he thought that I had been seriously injured, but I soon set his mind at rest on that subject. Leaving him, I at length reached the poop, where I met my Captain. He noticed me very kindly, and in replying to his questions I related to him what had happened at my quarters. Whilst in conversation with him, the second lieutenant, Mr. Dickson, began firing some of the starboard main deck guns. He was drunk. By this rash act he set the ship on fire, as the fore-topsail was lying over the side. But in due time the fire was extinguished, and our alarms at an end.

The cannonade of the hostile fleets had lulled the wind, but the swell of the sea was still paramount, and our ship, without sails or masts to balance her motion, laboured in a most annoying manner. The first object that attracted my notice on the quarter deck was the immense quantity of the enemy's musket shot lying there. On the starboard side, which had at the commencement of the action been the lee one, they were at least three or four tier deep, and the rest of the deck completely covered with them. How could it be possible, thought I, for anyone to escape being hit where so many thousand instruments of death had fallen? But so it was; and the Captain, with many of those around him, came off without injury. The only officers of the ship that were killed were the master, Webster, and the boatswain, Mr. Fitzpatrick Lieut. Boycott of the 2nd Regiment, Queen's, was severely wounded. He was a remarkably fine young man. The effect of his wounds obliged him to quit the ship upon our arrival at Spithead, to the regret of all who knew him. Looking around me, I saw the *Queen*, 98, some distance to leeward of us, still engaged with the enemy's ships which had formed a line on the starboard tack. That ship had lost her main mast, but it soon became evident that she would rejoin us, and there was no apprehension on her account. But the *Brunswick*, 74, was to leeward of the French, and we were uneasy about her fate. She had lost her mizen mast. By one o'clock all firing was at an end.

The next thing to be done was to attend to the disabled ships. We made the signal for assistance from the stump of our mizen mast. In clearing away the lumber on the poop, a marine was found stowed away under the hen coops. Those who lugged him out thought him dead. However, he soon came to life. This was the Fugleman of that Corps, one of the finest limbed men I ever beheld, and the most perfect in his exercise. All hands laughed at him when they saw he had not been hurt. He was, also, like my friend West, a foreigner.

There was no walking the quarter deck till the small shot had been cleared away. The next object of consequence was to get rid of the main mast, which with some difficulty was finally rolled overboard. The quantity of damaged spars, with rigging, that was floating about gave proofs of the severity of the contest in which we had been engaged. The *Queen Charlotte*, Lord Howe's flagship, passed close to leeward of us. She had lost all her topmasts, which prevented his following the French admiral. We gave his Lordship three hearty cheers, at which moment, we were afterwards told, Lord Howe observed, "If every ship of the fleet had followed Capt. Gambier's example, the result of this action would have been very different from what it is." The flagship having stood on a little while longer, signals were made to form on the starboard tack. While these things were passing, an opinion existed on board of us that the action would be renewed, as it became clear that the French were fairly beaten.

But that signal was not made. There were 14 sail of the line dismasted, 12 French and 2 English – ourselves and the *Marlborough*, 74, Capt. the Hon. George Berkeley. Capt. Gambier, giving me his spy glass (which had been hit by a shot) desired me to let him know the number of ships in the British fleet with topgallant yards across; and as Mr. Twysden overheard that order, he said he would assist me in the counting. We accordingly set to work, and after a strict examination, twice repeated, we made out 18 sail of the line in our fleet with topgallant yards across, and in appearance fit to go into battle. We had 7 disabled ships; the French more than 12. What astonished us most at this critical moment was the want of instructions. No signal had as yet been made to take possession of the enemy's disabled ships. Capt. Troubridge, who had been captured in the *Castor*, already mentioned, was a prisoner of war on board the *Sanspareil*, 80. He was quite lost at this apparent inactivity. Had that signal been made at the close of the action, we might with ease have captured their 12 disabled ships; instead of which upwards of an hour was allowed to elapse

before such a signal was thrown out. In that hour 5 French ships
contrived to slip through our line under their spritsails, and join
their own to leeward, leaving 7 with us, which were then taken
possession of. I hardly know how to restrain my feelings on this
subject even now, 26 years after the event. Had Lord Howe
been a younger man, there is every probability – I ought to say
no doubt—but the action would have been renewed. We were
200 miles away from the land, with plenty of sea room for
evolutions. His Lordship was clever at naval tactics: therefore,
had the French been brought to action that afternoon, the
result would have been the most splendid victory ever achieved
on the ocean over our enemy. On our way into port, the many
officers that visited the *Defence* expressed the same opinions as I
have herewith written down.

Many years afterwards, I heard from the best authority that
the Captain of the fleet, Sir Roger Curtis, who had been
selected by Lord Howe to assist him in his naval duties, when
consulted by his Lordship after the action, replied, "You have
gained a victory. Now make sure of it. If you renew the action,
who knows what may be the result? Make sure of what you have
got. Your Lordship is tired. You had better take some rest, and
I will manage the other matters for you." Lord Howe accordingly went below, to bed I believe, leaving the Captain of the
fleet to make signals as he thought necessary.

To return to the *Defence*: whilst we were hard at work in
clearing the wreck, the *Invincible*, 74, the Hon. Capt. Thomas
Pakenham, came up and hailed us. These two Captains were
very intimate. "Jemmy," said Capt. Pakenham, "whom the
Lord loveth He chasteneth" – in allusion to the shattered
condition we were in. Our Captain made a suitable reply, then
asked if he had lost many men: to which question he answered,
"Damn me if I know. They won't tell me, for fear I should stop
their grog." A few more words passed, when Capt. Pakenham
sent an officer on board to inquire if any help was required. I
shall never forget that gentleman. When he came alongside he
was dressed in a Guernsey jacket with a welch wig, and had not
the slightest appearance of an officer, as all the boat's crew were
similarly attired. When he reached the quarter deck, we ascertained by the buttons on his smalls that he was a lieutenant –

McGuire. He was presented to the Captain, to whom he said he had been sent to offer us assistance. Capt. Gambier naturally put many questions to him relating to the action. His replies were delivered with many oaths, which so disgusted our chief that he turned his back and left him. The lieutenant then, very quietly folding his arms, seated himself on the stump of the main mast; but as none of the *Defence*'s seemed inclined to take further notice of him after his rudeness, he left the ship. Capt. Pakenham, it seems, had given directions that his officers and Ship's Company, all Irish, should all be dressed alike: of which Mr. McGuire was a specimen. The Hon. Thos. Pakenham, brother to Lord Longford, was a regular character, and established a discipline on board the *Invincible* in direct opposition to the established rules of the Navy. But as I shall have to bring him again into notice, I take my leave of the Honourable Captain for the present.

We had scarcely done with the *Invincible* when the *Phaeton* Frigate, Capt. George Bentinck, came to take us in tow. This ship had been commanded by Sir Andrew Douglas. Several of my messmates of the *Alcide* were on board her, from whom I received many hearty congratulations at having escaped with my life. I little thought then that I should command that frigate. It is not many months since I paid her off. She was, without exception, one of the best sea boats I have ever had my foot on board. Whilst the frigate was taking us in tow, up came another line of battle ship, the *Valiant* (I believe Capt. Pringle). Her Captain overloaded ours with compliments upon the noble example he had shown to the whole fleet and among other sayings he insisted that we had sunk an enemy's ship. This we could not make out. However, it was for a long time the general opinion that we had sent a French 74 to the bottom. But time set this matter at rest. The ship we engaged in breaking the line was called *l'Eole*. She arrived safe at Brest: consequently, she could not have been sunk by us.

So soon as the Surgeon could make his report, it appeared that we had 91 men killed and wounded on this day: altogether, in the two actions of May 29 and June 1, 20 killed and 80 wounded. One of our Mates, Mr. Elliot, was severely wounded in the thigh by a grape shot. He was in the first instance moved into the Captain's cabin, where I saw him resting on a sofa in great agony, until he could be taken below to the doctor. He had served in the American War, and was a very superior young man. The havoc on board us was terrific. Two of the ports on the larboard side of the main deck were knocked into one by the shot. Only one shot penetrated between wind and water. It came into the bread room on the larboard side and smashed some of the lanterns there, without any serious injury to the ship. The spars upon our booms were sadly cut up. One of our boats, smashed to atoms, was thrown overboard, and, I am sorry to say, many other things were cast into the sea that might have been turned to account. My duty, I thought, was to obey orders, and not to point out the acts of wastefulness I witnessed. No doubt there were many similar ones on board of the other ships. The expense in refitting the fleet must have been immense.

The number of men thrown overboard that were killed, without ceremony, and the sad wrecks around us taught those who, like myself, had not before witnessed similar scenes that war was the greatest scourge of mankind. The first leisure I had, I went to see the Captain of my gun, who had lost his arm. He was in good spirits, and when I told him we had gained the victory, he replied, "Then I don't mind the loss of my arm. I am satisfied." Leaving him, I met a young man who had lost a part of his arm. When I spoke to him he was quite cheerful, not seeming to mind his misfortune. He was eating a piece of buttered biscuit as if nothing had happened. It was a very gratifying circumstance to witness so many acts of heroic bravery that were displayed on board our ship. Patriotic sentences were uttered that would have done honour to the noblest minds: yet these were expressed by the humblest class of men.

Meanwhile, in the Mediterranean, Nelson at least had the consolation of two successful brushes with the French fleet off Toulon in the summer of 1795, though he considered that the British could have done better with a harder-nosed commander-in-chief than Vice-Admiral Hotham. Hotham's replacement, Hyde Parker, Nelson also found wanting, but in November 1795 the veteran Sir John Jervis was sent out as commander of the Mediterranean fleet. "The moment I knew of your arrival," Nelson told Jervis later, "I felt perfectly at ease." It was a meeting of single-minds; Jervis was as purposeful in warfare as Nelson himself. Under Jervis, Nelson's star began to wax. On 11 June 1796, Nelson left the battered *Agamemnon* and transferred his commodore's broad pendant to the *Captain*, a seventy-four. His first job in her was, however, distasteful; it was to oversee the British evacuation of Corsica, the island he had helped conquer only two years before.

THE EVACUATION OF CORSICA, October 1796

M.C.[6]

The author was a seaman under Nelson's command.

In consequence of the war with Spain [Spain declared war on Britain on 8 October 1796] orders were received that Corsica was immediately to be given up, and the fleet were to quit the Mediterranean. Nelson was paralyzed. This intelligence was so contrary to the orders he had received from Admiral Jervis that he knew not how to act. He immediately sent a despatch to the admiral, and loudly lamented the present orders, which he openly characterized as disgraceful to the honour of England. His chagrin was too great to be concealed from his officers or crew, and in the bitterness of his disappointment he remarked, "The Ministers at home do not seem to know the capabilities of our fleet. I frankly declare I never beheld one in point of officers and men equal to that under Sir John Jervis, who is a commander-in-chief fully capable of increasing the glory of England."

Sir John Jervis was as much chagrined as Nelson, and although the bluff sailor concealed his feelings from those around him, yet the whole fleet were well aware that he was prepared to act very differently. However, much as we all regretted it, there was no help. The orders had arrived, and must be obeyed.

On the 13th of October, Captain Nelson was close in with Bastia by daylight, in the *Diadem*, Captain Towry; and, before it came to anchor, Nelson, accompanied by his boat's crew, went on shore to visit the viceroy, who was rejoiced to see him, and requested that his valuable papers might immediately be sent on board by our boat, for it was impossible to foresee how long they might be safe on shore at Bastia.

We went to the viceroy's house, and got all the valuables safe into the boat, which we took on board ship, and then returned with a further supply of boats and men. It now appeared that the Corsicans had taken up arms, and that a committee of thirty had seized and detained all the property of the English, and that a plan had been laid to seize the person of the viceroy. General de Burgh also reported to Captain Nelson, that, from the number of armed Corsicans, there was little or no prospect of saving either stores, cannon, or provisions. But Nelson, whose decision was promptitude itself, ordered the citadel gate to be shut, in order to prevent any more armed Corsicans from entering, and gave immediate orders to moor his ships opposite the town. The merchants and owners likewise informed him that even their trunks of clothes were refused them, and that they would be complete beggars unless he could help them. A privateer had been moored across the mole-head by the Corsicans, which would not even allow a transport boat to pass. Nelson requested them to remain easy, and assured them that he would soon find means to relieve them.

At this time, while our boat's crew were waiting on shore, we observed several armed Corsicans making towards the citadel, who seemed struck with surprise when they found the gate closed upon them. We could not refrain from laughing at their disappointment; which provoked them to such a degree, that one fellow had the temerity to present his piece at us, exclaiming, "Brigands Anglais!" (rascally Englishmen!) intending to fire amongst us: but, unfortunately for him, Archibald Menzies, our stroke-oar (whom we nicknamed "Scotch Hercules" on account of his immense strength), who was taking his cutty, or short pipe, comfortably near the gate, caught sight of this maneuver, and, rushing up to the dastard Corsican, gave him such a severe blow under the ear with his iron fist that he fell and completely rolled over in the dust with the force of the blow. His companions paused for a moment in surprise, as they eyed the tall gaunt figure of Archibald, but suddenly rushed in a body upon him; but Archibald, having torn up a wooden rail that ran along the road-side, laid about him with such fury that the cowardly Corsicans threw down their arms and ran for their lives; and before we could reach the spot, although we ran as quickly as we could, to assist our messmate, Archibald was master of the field, his assailants having all decamped except two unfortunate fellows whom he held fast in his iron gripe.

"Deil tak you!" exclaimed Archy,—"d'ye ken me? Never show your ugly walnut-coloured faces to a Briton again, unless you can behave like cannie men, or, by Saint Andrew! I'll batter your faces against each ither till ye shallna ken whether you be yourselves or no Get awa wi' ye, ye cursed black-nebs! I dinna like to swear, but I'll be d—d if I don't mak haggismeat o' ye, if I catch you here again."

Having let them loose, which he did with a kick behind, the fellows made swift work of it, and were soon out of sight. We collected the arms they had left, and stowed them safely in the boat.

Nelson having returned from the citadel, we quickly got on board in order to commence operations. The *Egmont*, Captain Sutton, had now arrived, and was ordered to moor the same as the *Diadem*. At noon, Captain Nelson made the signal for the boats manned and armed, and Captain Towry [of HMS *Diadem*] proceeded into the mole with them, in order to open the passage for all vessels which might choose to come out. Captain Towry had also received instructions from Nelson to take the first English vessel in tow which he met with; and, if the slightest molestation was offered, he was to send to the municipality in his (Nelson's) name, to tell them that if any obstruction was thrown in the way of getting any vessel out of the mole, or removing any of the property belonging to the English, he would instantly batter the town about their ears.

Now it has always been said, that the great John Duke of Marlborough created such terror and dismay among the enemies of England, by his rapid and surprising succession of victories, that he was in France held up as a bugbear; and nurses were accustomed to frighten refractory children into submission by telling them *Malbrouk would come and take them away*. The name of Nelson was not without its terrors among the Corsicans, and they never heard it without a feeling of fear; and I believe they would as soon have faced the devil himself as Nelson, as the sequel will show.

Captain Towry proceeded to the mole, when the privateer, which was moored across it, immediately pointed her guns at him, and at least an hundred guns were levelled from the mole-head. On observing this, Capt. Sutton immediately sent Nelson's message on shore, which threatened to batter down the town if a single shot was fired, and, taking out his watch, said he would give them a quarter-of-an-hour for a reply, which if not fully satisfactory the ships would instantly open their fire.

Nelson's name was enough, and more so when the Corsicans found that Towry and Sutton were not to be trifled with. The message acted like magic, for in a few minutes the people quitted the privateer; and those at the mole-head, even to the Corsican sentries, quitted the spot with the utmost precipitation, leaving the vessels to come out of the mole entirely unmolested.

We were now occasionally on shore as well as on board, according to circumstances; for it appeared the municipality were still bent on committing depredations whenever they could do so with impunity. Captain Nelson, therefore, made it his custom to remain where he could be easiest of access, in order that all persons who had complaints to make might do so with facility.

In the course of the day, the owner of a privateer came to complain that he had forty hogsheads of tobacco and other goods in the custom-house, which the municipality refused to deliver to him; whereupon Captain Nelson told him to go to the Committee of Thirty, and say that he (Nelson) had sent for the goods, which, if not instantly delivered, he would fire upon the town. The owner not liking to go alone, Nelson sent a midshipman, with half-a-dozen men as a kind of convoy, among whom was Archibald Menzies. The owner delivered the message, and the Committee seemed to hint at requiring time to consider; but the midshipman said he could brook no delay; whereupon Archibald, who could contain himself no longer, burst out with, "Hoot awa' wi' ye, and your dally dirty ways; ye ken this gentleman is our officer, and we canna stand here waiting for your decision. Ye ken, if ye dinna give up the goods this instant, our Captain will give your dirty town such a belabouring, that he'll nae leave one stane upon the t'other. So come awa' wi' ye, mister merchant." Archy's speech decided the controversy; the Corsicans did not like the threats of Captain Nelson, nor did they like the looks of the man that uttered them. They all turned as pale as death; and, without uttering a single word, delivered up the keys to the merchant, who returned with the boat's crew to Nelson, and acquainted him with the result of his errand; who took immediate means to put the owner in possession of his property.

One would have supposed that the Corsicans had received sufficient proofs that the English would not be trifled with; but they still obstinately clung to their desire to annoy the British merchants, for, in the evening, they made an attempt to get duty paid for some wine which was about to be embarked by a British merchant. However, Captain Nelson sent a message to them, declaring, that if any more complaints were made to him, however slight their nature, he should, without any further notice, pay them such a visit as they would have cause to repent. This was conclusive; the Committee saw that further attempts at opposition would be likely to draw down destruction on them, and they therefore gave up their system of annoyance; and from that moment not an armed man was to be seen in the streets of Bastia.

The viceroy was taken on board our ship that night, and was consequently placed out of danger. Nelson landed his troops on the 15th, early in the morning; who took post at the viceroy's house, which covered the spot where the embarkation took place. General de Burgh also furnished another hundred men for the same purpose, part of which kept post in the citadel. One hundred seamen were also sent on shore to complete the embarkation. One of our men met with a strange adventure. John Thompson, while ashore, heard the wailings of a female, and other persons' voices speaking peremptorily. Jack, conceiving he had a right to interfere if anything was going wrong, listened awhile, and soon found that his assistance would be required. The door opened, and four rough-looking fellows pulled a couple of chests into the street.

"Avast! you saffron-faced swabs," cried Jack, as he placed himself in front of them; "What are you going to be after with the lady's cargo, eh?" "*Contrabande! contrabande! choses prohibées!*" exclaimed the Corsicans. "Chose be d—d," cried Jack; "none of your nonsense with me. Let the lady have her goods, or by the honour of my Commander, I'll spoil your daylights!" "*Non intendo, non intendo!*" exclaimed the Corsicans, (meaning, we don't understand you.) But Jack mistook the meaning of the word, and exclaimed, "Not intend it! Yes, but you *did* intend it, you lying swab, and you would have DONE it too, if I had not been here to prevent you." The Corsicans paused a little; but seeing that Thompson was quite alone, and they were four in number, they determined on attacking and overpowering him; consequently two of them advanced, but Jack Thompson knocked them down with his fists; the others then advanced, but at this moment an unexpected reinforcement arrived; for the hostess observing the unequal attack of the cowardly Corsicans, rushed to the spot, followed by her stable-boy, and seizing a broomstick, while the stable-boy presented a pitchfork, they laid about them with such spirit that they proved a powerful reinforcement to Jack Thompson. Others of the Corsican breed joined their rascally companions, and Jack Thompson and his two auxiliaries would doubtless have been defeated; but the timely arrival of half-a-dozen of our crew struck the Corsicans with such terror that they made a precipitate retreat, and left Jack Thompson and his confederates in possession of the prize. The husband of the hostess wore a wooden leg, and therefore could not join in the active part of the fray; he, however, proved of signal service, and acted occasionally as a flanking battery; for, having seated himself on one of the tubs, he pulled off his wooden leg, and every Corsican who happened to come within his reach during the scuffle, received a hearty thump with it from the old gentleman, who, at every blow, roared out, "*Viva Inglesi. Bono Inglesi!*" The hostess and her *caro marito* (as she termed her husband) insisted on our partaking of some refreshment; and so pleased were they with our presence, that I believe, if we could have emptied one of their brandy casks, we should have been welcome. Having regaled ourselves, we assisted them to remove their property to a place of safety.

We now went heartily to work in removing provisions, cannon, gunpowder, and various stores, besides a vast quantity of baggage and household articles; for the poor emigrants could not afford to leave any things behind them. There were many novel scenes exhibited in Bastia at this time. Whole families might be seen moving along with their little stock of goods under the protection of British sailors or soldiers, while their enemies could do no more than look on with envy and vexation, and see themselves deprived of their intended plunder.

Our sailors had plenty of opportunities of displaying their gallantry; for it was nothing uncommon to see two or three of our ship's crew marching along with a female under each arm, convoying them safely to the place of embarkation. Here you might see a group of men conveying a lot of furniture, while the family were carrying the lighter articles, such as band-boxes, bundles, and such-like gear. Our carpenter's second mate was an Irishman, and a merry fellow he was; but he was rather ill-favoured in his appearance. He had somewhat of a squint about his eyes, rather a flat nose, and a wide mouth, and he passed by the cognomen of the "Munster Beauty." Poor Pat Macguire! he was as able a seaman as ever sailed in the fleet; and whenever he committed a blunder it was on the right side: he lived long enough to see much service, for I think it was in the battle of Trafalgar that a grape-shot signed his death-warrant.

Pat Macguire had charge of the removal of the domestic part of the goods, and proud enough he was of the berth, and well pleased into the bargain; for Pat was always fond of being in ladies' company, and here he was surrounded by all ranks. Old and young, rich and poor – all came to consult Pat as to the manner in which they were to proceed.

Some of our strongest men, who were employed in removing the cannon and other cumbersome materials, took good care to jeer Pat Macguire in his enviable employment. One would say, "There's Mister Macguire, the lady's man – pretty, delicate creature – he's obliged to be stationed here to look after the gowns and petticoats, because our work is too hard for him."

Old Jack Townsend (the grumbler) would say, "What can

you expect of an Irishman? – They never were able seamen; they're of no use on board, unless it be to act as washerwomen."

"A bull, a bull!" cried Pat Macguire; "who ever heard of a man-washerwoman? Now, look you, Master Townsend, it's no use your jibing and jeering after that fashion, because ye see the Captain has picked me out for this especial service, because I was one of the most polite and best-behaved of the crew. And let me tell you that there's neither man, woman, nor child, that sails on the salt sea, that knows how to accommodate the ladies better, or half so well, as an Irishman. So, roll that up as a quid and chew it, Master Townsend, if you plase."

"Ugh!" said old Townsend, "that's all you're good for. I dare say the Captain will give you a new berth aboard – he'll make you head nurse to the women." "Och, good luck to him!" cried Pat; "I wish he may. Hurrah, old Jack! Pat Macguire's just the boy for a nursery-maid."

Had our time not been too much occupied, we should have derived much amusement by setting old Townsend and Pat Macguire on the high ropes, but our duty was rather hard, and time was running short, and, therefore, there was no other jeering except a little occasional shy fighting between these two, whose opinions differed as widely as the east and west winds.

Pat Macguire was also a bit of a politician and occasionally made some very shrewd remarks. When the despatch arrived which ordered us to evacuate Corsica, it caused much murmuring in the fleet, particularly among those who had seen good service under Sir John Jervis; and this gave Pat Macguire an opportunity of giving his opinion on the state of parties. One of the sailors having asked who it was that caused such orders to be given, Pat replied, "Sure, it was the Parliament."

"Then," said one of the topmen, "the Parliament never sailed under Admiral Jervis, nor fought as we have done." Whereupon Pat Macguire, with a look of the most signal contempt, exclaimed –

"'Sblood, man, d'ye take the Parliament for a man or a woman? The Parliament, I'd have you to know, is a great many people mustered together, and they settle the affairs of the nation by talking to each other."

"Talking to each other!" echoed the topman.

"Yes," continued Pat; "they talk till they talk the breath out of each other, and then it's put to the vote as to who spoke the longest and loudest, and that's the one as gains the day."

"And is that all they do?" inquired the topman.

"Yes, honey," replied Pat; "they talk and we execute."

Pat's logic was too learned to allow the topman to argue any further; and the Boatswain having piped to quarters put an end to the debate.

We had now worked without intermission till sunset on the 19th, and must have saved about two hundred thousand pounds' worth of stores, and other effects belonging to the emigrants.

The French had landed their troops at Cape Corse on the 18th, and on the following day they sent to the municipality to know if they intended to receive them as friends, because, if so, they required that the English should be prevented from embarking. Time would not allow us to save anything more, and, therefore, after having spiked all the guns, we quitted the citadel at midnight; but, from the wind blowing a gale, it was dawn of day before we all got on board. All the time these transactions were going on, we were observed by a mob of Corsicans, who lined the shore, and who had the mortification to witness every soul embark who chose to leave the island, without their daring to offer the least molestation.

Captain Nelson and General de Burgh were the last who left the spot; and as Nelson stepped into the boat, he coolly turned to the mob and said, "Now, John Corse, follow the natural bent of your detestable character – plunder and revenge!" We were soon on board, and in less than half an hour we showed our sterns to the island of Corsica.

Nelson "showed his stern" to Corsica on 29 January 1797, setting sail in the frigate *la Minerve* for a rendezvous with Jervis in the Atlantic. Putting in at Gibraltar, he exchanged some Spanish prisoners of war for two of his own lieutenants, Hardy and Culverhouse, and took on fresh supplies of water. So was put in motion Nelson's first act in the limelight, the Battle of Cape St Vincent.

THE BATTLE OF CAPE ST VINCENT: THE PASSENGER'S VIEW, 14 February 1797

Colonel John Drinkwater Bethune[7]

Bethune was a former aide to the British viceroy of Corsica. Here he not only describes the mighty confrontation off Cape St Vincent, but its preamble, when Nelson, getting underway from Gibraltar, refused to abandon Hardy, who was again in danger of being captured by the Spanish.

On the forenoon of the 11th of February, the *Minerve* got under weigh. She had scarcely cast round from her anchorage, when two of the three Spanish line-of-battle ships in the upper part of Gibraltar Bay were observed to be also in motion. It was soon evident that they had been watching the commodore's movements, and were prepared to pursue him as soon as the *Minerve* should take her departure from Gibraltar.

As the Spanish ships had a steady wind from the eastward over the Isthmus, whilst the *Minerve* was embarrassed with the eddies and baffling flaws, that usually prevail in an easterly wind, near the Rock, the Spaniards had for some time the advantage in pushing forwards in the bay. The *Minerve* was not, however, long in getting the steady breeze, and soon after got into the Straits, when the chace of the enemy became, as we afterwards heard, a most interesting "spectacle" to our friends of the garrison.

The *Minerve* was a captured ship from the French – taken in the Mediterranean in 1795, and considered to be a tolerably good sailer, particularly with the wind on her quarter. The Spanish ships were not equally good goers; one of them, the *Terrible*, was a first-rate sailer, well known to the British officers, Culverhouse and Hardy, who had been exchanged from her only the day before. Her consort was a dull sailing ship. Advancing into the Straits, the *Minerve* had the wind abaft, and after marking her progress with that of the enemy, it was evident that the headmost ship of the chace gained on the British frigate. No sooner was this point ascertained, than directions were given by Sir Gilbert Elliot to have certain parts of his public papers ready to be sunk, if necessary, at a moment's notice. The ship was cleared for action, and the position of the *Minerve* was now becoming every moment more and more interesting. At this period I was walking with Commodore Nelson, conversing on the probability of the enemy's engaging the *Minerve*, and his words, and manner of uttering them, made a strong impression on me. He said that he thought an engagement was very possible, as the headmost ship appeared to be a good sailer; but, continued he (looking up at his broad pendant), "before the Dons get hold of that bit of bunting I will have a struggle with them, and sooner than give up the frigate, I'll run her ashore."

Captain Cockburn, who had been taking a view of the chacing enemy, now joined the commodore, and observed that there was no doubt of the headmost ship gaining on the *Minerve*. At this moment dinner was announced, but before Nelson and his guests left the deck, orders were given to set the studding sails. At table I found myself seated next to Lieutenant Hardy, and was congratulating him on his late exchange from being a prisoner of war, when the sudden cry of a "man overboard," threw the dinner party into some disorder. The officers of the ship ran on deck: I, with others, ran to the stern windows to see if any thing could be observed of the unfortunate man; we had scarcely reached them before we noticed the lowering of the jolly boat, in which was my late neighbour Hardy, with a party of sailors; and before many seconds had elapsed, the current of the Straits (which runs strongly to the eastward) had carried the jolly boat far astern of the frigate, towards the Spanish ships. Of course the first object was to recover, if possible, the fallen man, but he was never seen again. Hardy soon made a signal to that effect, and the man was given up as lost. The attention of every person was now turned to the safety of Hardy and his boat's crew; their situation was extremely perilous, and their danger was every instant increasing from the fast sailing of the headmost ship of the chace, which, by this time had approached nearly within gun-shot of the *Minerve*. The jolly boat's crew pulled "might and main" to regain the frigate, but apparently made little progress against the current of the Straits. At this crisis, Nelson, casting an anxious look at the hazardous situation of Hardy and his companions, exclaimed, "By G— I'll not lose

Hardy! Back the mizen top-sail." No sooner said than done; the *Minerve*'s progress was retarded, leaving the current to carry her down towards Hardy and his party, who seeing this spirited manoeuvre to save them from returning to their old quarters on board the *Terrible*, naturally redoubled their exertions to rejoin the frigate. To the landsmen on board the *Minerve* an action now appeared to be inevitable; and so, it would appear, thought the enemy, who surprised and confounded by this daring manoeuvre of the commodore (being ignorant of the accident that led to it,) must have construed it into a direct challenge. Not conceiving, however, a Spanish ship of the line to be an equal match for a British frigate, with Nelson on board of her, the Captain of the *Terrible* suddenly shortened sail, in order to allow his consort to join him, and thus afforded time for the *Minerve* to drop down to the jolly-boat to take out Hardy and the crew; and the moment they were on board the frigate, orders were given again to make sail.

Being now under studding sails, and the widening of the Straits allowing the wind to be brought more on the *Minerve*'s quarter, the frigate soon regained the lost distance; and, in a short time, we had the satisfaction to observe, that the dastardly Don was left far in our wake; and at sunset, by steering further to the southward, we lost sight of him and his consort altogether.

What course the *Minerve* pursued after nightfall, I did not remark. The interesting incidents of the preceding day had afforded matter to occupy our attention; and we landsmen retired to rest, congratulating ourselves on what we could not but feel to have been a fortunate escape.

On the removal of the passengers from the *Romulus* into the *Minerve*, at Gibraltar, the crowded state of the latter frigate would not allow of other arrangements than of my having a cot slung alongside of that of the viceroy, in the after cabin. So situated, I was awakened in the night, by the opening of our cabin door, through which I saw, by the light burning in the fore cabin, some person enter, and on raising myself, I observed that it was Nelson. Seeing me awake, he enquired if Sir Gilbert was asleep, to which I replied in the affirmative. To my enquiry if any thing new had occurred, the commodore approached my cot, and told me that he had every reason to believe that the *Minerve* was at that very moment in the midst of the Spanish fleet. From their signals, he said that he knew it was not that of Sir John Jervis; that the night was foggy; that the *Minerve* was then between two very large ships within hail of each of them, and others were near on all sides; that he and Captain Cockburn had little doubt of the strangers being Spanish; that Captain Cockburn and his officers were all on the alert; and every cautionary direction given, particularly to watch the movements of the strange ships, and do as they did, &c., &c.

When Nelson had finished these details, I could not help observing that this was a verifying of the old adage, "out of the frying-pan into the fire," alluding to our escape of the day before. The commodore allowed that we had got into something like a scrape, but added that it was quite unavoidable, on account of the night and fog; nevertheless, he thought that, with address, we might extricate ourselves.

He remained for some time, making various observations on these strange ships, and then continued to the following effect:—If they did not belong to the Spanish grand fleet, he thought they must be a convoy, or detached squadron, proceeding to the West Indies (of which, it appears, he had received some previous information), and that, if the latter were the fact, they must be destined to strengthen the Spanish naval force in that quarter; in which case, it would be of the first moment that the British commander on the West India station should be early apprised of these movements of the enemy; a duty, he conceived he was called upon to undertake, instead of joining Sir John Jervis.

On hearing Nelson express these opinions, I could not avoid saying, "But what will you do with Sir Gilbert Elliot? It is of the greatest importance, owing to his recent interviews with the Italian states, that he should not only see Sir John Jervis, but reach England with the least possible delay." The commodore admitted the force of these remarks; but the other point, in his judgment, outweighed every other consideration: "but," said he, breaking off, "I'll go on deck, and see how things are going on." To awake Sir Gilbert in our present uncertainty could answer no good purpose; I therefore did not disturb him, but ruminated on this new and unlooked for occurrence, in the hope of devising some means of avoiding a trip to the West Indies, which, I thought would be at least an untoward conclusion of our Mediterranean campaign.

It soon occurred to me, that as we must pass near Madeira, in our way to the West Indies, the viceroy and his party might be landed on that island; or, if any neutral ship crossed our track, we might equally avail ourselves of a transfer to her, and obtain a passage to Lisbon, or perhaps to England.

This plan I had settled to my own satisfaction, when Nelson again appeared, and observed that the strange ships having been seen to tack, or wear, I forget which, the *Minerve* had followed their example; and that after having so done, directions were given for the frigate's edging away insensibly, and that Captain Cockburn and himself were inclined to think the *Minerve* was getting out of the thick of the fleet, and would soon cease to be embarrassed with them. After this gratifying communication, Nelson repeated his former opinions and intentions, and we were earnestly discussing the subject, when Sir G. Elliot was awakened by our conversation. He was then made acquainted with all that had been passing, with the commodore's suspicions regarding the strange ships, and with his conditional plan, to proceed immediately to the West Indies. After some general observations, and repeating his determination, if necessary, of carrying us to the West Indies, the commodore left the cabin again, and soon returned with the agreeable intelligence that the *Minerve* had, he trusted, got quit of the strange fleet. "We propose," added Nelson, "to stand on our present course during the night: at daybreak, we shall take another direction, which will enable us to fall in with the strange ships again, should they be on their way to the westward. I shall then ascertain the force of the convoy, or of the squadron, if it consist only of men-of-war; and should it then appear advisable, I shall start for the West Indies. Should we not fall in with any strange ships in the course which the *Minerve* will steer after daybreak, my conclusion is, that the fleet we have fallen in with must be the grand fleet of Spain; it will be then of the first importance that I join Sir John Jervis as soon as possible, in order that he may be informed of the enemy's fleet not having been yet able to get into Cadiz, and of their state on quitting Carthagena, of which Lieutenants Culverhouse and Hardy are able to give the latest and most minute accounts."

The commodore then left Sir Gilbert Elliot and me to our repose, if that were possible. After he had left the cabin, I asked Sir Gilbert what he thought of this new occurrence, and of the prospect of a trip to the West Indies. "It was another escape," he replied, "and as to the voyage to the West Indies, if the commodore considered the public service required that proceeding, he must submit to circumstances; he was only a passenger." This cool way of receiving and considering our present situation and prospects did not surprise me, well acquainted as I was with the viceroy's character. However, I made known to him the plan I had devised to avoid a visit to a tropical climate, of which he approved. Nothing further occurred until we all met at breakfast, when the incidents of the last twenty-four hours became the subject of conversation, and were fully discussed. I then learned that the *Minerve* was at that instant standing on the course which would soon confirm one of the two suspicions entertained by Nelson, regarding the strange ships seen during the past night. A good look out was naturally kept during the whole of the 12th of February, but no ships of any sort appearing, Nelson felt assured that the fleet with which the *Minerve* had been entangled the night before, was the Spanish grand fleet; and being more confirmed in this idea as the day advanced, he became very anxious to join Sir John Jervis's fleet, whose rendezvous, as fixed with the commodore, was not far from the place where we then were.

At daybreak, on the 13th of February, the weather was hazy, and as the *Minerve* was approaching the place of rendezvous, orders were given for keeping a good look out. In the forenoon a brig and cutter hove in sight, and soon after a larger sail, which, as the frigate neared, was discovered to be a ship of war. She proved to be the British frigate, the *Lively*, of thirty-two guns, an out-skirter of Sir John Jervis's fleet, which in a very short time the *Minerve* joined, not a little to the gratification of all parties.

On joining Sir John Jervis's fleet, the commodore, accompanied by the viceroy, repaired on board the flag-ship the *Victory* – the latter to confer with the admiral on political matters, the former to report in what manner he had executed his last orders, and to communicate all the naval intelligence he had gleaned in his late cruize, particularly of his being chaced by the enemy on leaving Gibraltar, and of his very recent nightly rencontre with the Spanish grand fleet. It was at this period that the capture of Lieutenants Culverhouse and Hardy, so much regretted at the time it took place, proved to be of the highest importance. The recaptured Spanish frigate, *Santa Sabina*, in which the above officers had been made prisoners, had returned to Carthagena, where the greatest part of the Spanish grand fleet was equipping for sea. These English officers had thus many favorable opportunities of noticing their state and condition, and having also sailed with the fleet when it left Carthagena for Cadiz, they had ample means of obtaining accurate knowledge of their numbers, equipment, and discipline. The information collected by Lieutenants Culverhouse and Hardy was of the greatest value, and being made known to the British admiral, was found to corroborate much of what he had learned from other quarters. Being also assured, not only by Nelson's intelligence, but by additional information brought by the *Bonne Citoyenne*, that the Spanish fleet was close at hand, Sir John Jervis, with that decision which was a prominent trait in his character, determined, notwithstanding the enemy's very superior force, to bring the Spaniards, if possible, to action.

No sooner was this decision taken, than the admiral's intentions were promulgated to his squadron, by throwing out the signal to prepare for action. Nelson, on rejoining the fleet, quitted the *Minerve*, and resumed the command of his regular ship, the *Captain*. Sir Gilbert Elliot and his party also left the *Minerve*, and were directed to repair on board the *Lively* frigate, commanded by Lord Garlies, who had orders to proceed with them immediately to England. But the viceroy could not bear the idea of leaving the British fleet at so critical and interesting a juncture. His Excellency's first request of Sir John Jervis was to be allowed to remain with the admiral as a volunteer on board of the *Victory*, until the issue of the approaching contest was known, which proposal Sir John positively refused; and all that the viceroy could obtain, was the admiral's assent that the *Lively* should not leave the British fleet until she could carry with her

the despatches conveying the result of the expected engagement.

This enabled me to be an eye-witness of the action of the 14th
of February, 1797, and the following letter to my father con-
tains the narrative of that battle, which, as already mentioned,
I published, on my arrival in England, in the spring of that
year.

On board the Lively *Frigate,*
off the Island of Scilly, February 27, 1797.

ONCE MORE, MY DEAR SIR, I am in sight of Old England, the land
of rational liberty; and the pleasure of revisiting my native
country, after an absence of six years, is not a little increased by
the satisfaction of being on board a frigate that is the messenger
of great and important news – a splendid and decisive victory –
a victory unparalleled in the annals of our naval history.

Admiral Sir John Jervis, with fifteen sail of the line and four
frigates, has defeated the Spanish Grand fleet, consisting of
twenty-seven ships of the line and ten frigates, and captured
four sail of the line, two of which are of three decks.

This brilliant affair took place off Cape St. Vincent on the
14th of February, the anniversary of St. Valentine, who by this
glorious event has almost eclipsed his brother Crispian; and
henceforth we must say, with the poet:

> He that's outliv'd this day, and comes safe home,
> Will stand a tiptoe when the day is nam'd,
> And rouse him at the name of *Valentine*.

Captain Calder, Captain of the fleet under the command of
Sir John Jervis, bears home the admiral's dispatches and is now
on board the *Lively*. It is expected that he will land tomorrow;
and I purpose to avail myself of that opportunity, to transmit
you such an account of this splendid action, as I have been able
to arrange in the time that has elapsed since we separated from
the British fleet in Lagos Bay.

Before I enter on the detail of the proceedings of the important day which will certainly immortalize the name of

Jervis, and of his brave seconds, it is proper to state the relative force of the British and Spanish fleets.

The British fleet, or to use, I believe, a more correct term, the British squadron, consisted of fifteen sail of the line, four frigates, a sloop of war, and a cutter; viz., two of 100 guns, two of 98 guns, two of 90 guns – total, six three-deckers, eight of 74 guns, and one of 64 guns.

The Spanish fleet was composed of twenty-seven sail of the line, ten frigates, and one brig; viz., one of four decks, carrying 136 guns; six of three decks, each of 112 guns; two of 84 guns, and eighteen of 74 guns each.

The Spanish admiral had sailed from Carthagena the 4th February. On the 5th, he passed Gibraltar, leaving in that Bay three line-of-battle ships, supposed to be laden with military stores for the Spanish troops stationed before that garrison; two of which ships afterwards chaced Commodore Nelson, in the *Minerve*. The strong easterly gale that had been friendly for their getting out of the Mediterranean was, however, unpropitious to their gaining the Port of Cadiz.

On the night of the 11th, as I have before mentioned, they were fallen in with, off the mouth of the Straits, by the *Minerve*. And the evening of the day on which Commodore Nelson joined Sir John Jervis off Cape St. Vincent, we find their fleet driven farther to the westward; for a part of them were not only seen by the *Minerve*, before she joined the British fleet, but *la Bonne Citoyenne*, a British sloop of war, commanded by Captain Lindsay, arrived in the fleet the same evening with intelligence that not two hours before she had exchanged shots with one of the enemy's frigates, and that the enemy's fleet was not far distant.

Before sun-set in the evening of the 13th, the signal had been made for the British squadron to prepare for battle, and the ships were also directed to keep in close order during the night.

At daybreak on the 14th (St. Valentine's day) the British fleet was in complete order, formed in two divisions standing on a wind to the SSW. The morning was hazy. About half-past six o'clock, a.m., the *Culloden* made the signal for five sail in the SW by S quarter, which was soon after confirmed by the *Lively* and *Niger* frigates, and that the strange sail were by the wind on the starboard tack. The *Bonne Citoyenne* sloop of war, Captain Lindsay, was therefore directed to reconnoitre. At a quarter past eight o'clock, the squadron was ordered, by signal, to form in a close order; and in a few minutes afterwards the signal was repeated to prepare for battle.

About half-past nine o'clock, the *Culloden, Blenheim,* and *Prince George* were ordered to chace in the S by W quarter; which, upon the *Bonne Citoyenne*'s making a signal that she saw eight sail in that quarter, was afterwards strengthened by the *Irresistible, Colossus,* and *Orion.*

A little past ten o'clock, the *Minerve* frigate made the signal for twenty sail in the SW quarter, and a few minutes after, of eight sail in the S by W. Half an hour afterwards the *Bonne Citoyenne* made the signal that she could distinguish sixteen, and immediately afterwards twenty-five of the strange ships, to be of the line. The enemy's fleet were indeed become now visible to all the British squadron.

The ships first discovered by the *Culloden* were separated from their main body, which being to windward, were bearing down in some confusion, with a view of joining their separated ships. It appeared to have been the British admiral's intention, upon discovering the separated ships of the enemy's fleet, to have cut them off, if possible, before their main body could arrive to their assistance; and with this view, the fast sailing ships of his squadron were ordered to chace.

Assured now of the near position of their main body, he probably judged it most advisable to form his fleet into the line of battle, and the signal was made for their forming the line of battle a-head and a-stern as most convenient. A signal was made directing the squadron to steer SSW.

About twenty minutes past eleven o'clock, the admiral pointed out that the *Victory* (his flag-ship) would take her station next to the *Colossus.* Some variation in steering was afterwards directed, in order to let the rear ships close up. At twenty-six minutes past eleven o'clock, the admiral communicated his intention to pass through the enemy's line, hoisting his large flag and ensign, and soon after the signal was made to engage.

The British van by this time had approached the enemy; and

the distinction of leading the British line into action fell to the lot of the *Culloden*, commanded by Captain Troubridge. About half-past eleven o'clock, the firing commenced from the *Culloden* against the enemy's headmost ships to windward.

As the British squadron advanced, the action became more general; and it was soon apparent that the British admiral had accomplished his design of passing through the enemy's line.

The animated and regular fire of the British squadron was but feebly returned by the enemy's ships to windward, which, being frustrated in their attempts to join the separated ships, had been obliged to haul their wind on the larboard tack: those to leeward, and which were most effectually cut off from their main body, attempted also to form on their larboard tack, apparently with a determination of either passing through, or to leeward, of our line and joining their friends; but the warm reception they met with from the centre ships of our squadron soon obliged them to put about; and excepting one, the whole sought safety in flight, and did not again appear in the action until the close of the day.

The single ship just mentioned persevered in passing to leeward of the British line but was so covered with smoke that her intention was not discovered until she had reached the rear, when she was not permitted to pass without notice, but received the fire of our sternmost ships; and as she luffed round the rear, the *Lively* and other frigates had also the honor of exchanging with this two-decker several broadsides.

Sir John Jervis, having effected his first purpose, now directed his whole attention to the enemy's main body to windward, consisting at this time of eighteen sail of the line. At eight minutes past twelve, the signal therefore was made for the British fleet to tack in succession, and soon after he made the signal for again passing the enemy's line.

The Spanish admiral's plan seemed to be to join his ships to leeward, by wearing round the rear of our line; and the ships which had passed and exchanged shots with our squadron had actually borne up with this view.

This design, however, was frustrated by the timely opposition of Commodore Nelson, whose place in the rear of the British line afforded him an opportunity of observing this maneuver, and of penetrating the Spanish admiral's intention. His ship, the *Captain*, had no sooner passed the rear of the enemy's ships that were to windward, than he ordered her to wear, and stood on the other tack towards the enemy.

In executing this bold and decisive maneuver, the commodore reached the sixth ship from the enemy's rear, which was the Spanish admiral's own ship, the *Santisima Trinidad*, of 136 guns, a ship of four decks, and said to be the largest in the world. Notwithstanding the inequality of force, the commodore instantly engaged this colossal opponent, and for a considerable time had to contend not only with her, but with her seconds a-head and a-stern, of three decks each. While he maintained this unequal combat, which we viewed with admiration mixed with anxiety, his friends were flying to his support; and the enemy's attention was soon directed to the *Culloden*, Captain Troubridge, and in a short time after to the *Blenheim*, of 90 guns, Captain Frederick, who opportunely came to their assistance.

The intrepid conduct of the commodore staggered the Spanish admiral, who already appeared to waver in pursuing his intention of joining the ships cut off by the British fleet, when the *Culloden*'s arrival, and Captain Troubridge's spirited support of the *Captain*, together with the approach of the *Blenheim*, followed by Rear-Admiral Parker, with the *Prince George*, *Orion*, *Irresistible*, and *Diadem*, not far distant, determined the Spanish admiral to change his design altogether, and to make the signal for the ships of his main body to haul their wind, and make sail on the larboard tack.

Advantage was now apparent in favor of the British squadron, and not a moment was lost in improving it. As the ships of Rear-Admiral Parker's division approached the enemy's ships, in support of the *Captain* and her gallant seconds, the *Blenheim* and *Culloden*, the cannonade became more animated and impressive. The superiority of the British fire over that of the enemy, and its effects on the enemy's hulls and sails, were so evident that we in the frigate no longer hesitated to pronounce a glorious termination of the contest.

The British squadron at this time was formed in two divisions, both on the larboard tack; their situation was as follows: Rear-Admiral Parker, with the *Blenheim*, *Culloden*, *Prince George*, the rear-admiral's ship, *Captain*, *Orion*, *Irresistible*, composed one division, which was engaged with the enemy's rear. Sir John Jervis, with the other division, consisting of the *Excellent*, *Victory*, *Barfleur*, *Namur*, *Egmont*, *Goliath*, and *Britannia*, was pressing forward in support of his advanced squadron, but had not yet approached the real scene of action.

The *Colossus* having, in the early part of the day, unfortunately lost her fore-yard and fore-top-sail-yard, was obliged, in consequence of these losses, to fall to leeward, and the *Minerve's* signal was made to take her in tow, which was, however, handsomely declined by Captain Murray when the *Minerve* had come within hail in execution of her orders.

While the British advanced division warmly pressed the enemy's centre and rear, the admiral meditated, with his division, a co-operation, which must effectually compel some of them to surrender.

In the confusion of their retreat, several of the enemy's ships had doubled on each other, and in the rear they were three or four deep. It was therefore the British admiral's design to reach the weathermost of these ships, then bear up, and rake them all in succession with the seven ships composing his division. His object afterwards was to pass on to the support of his van division, which, from the length of time they had been engaged, he judged might be in want of it. The casual position, however, of the rear ships of his van division, prevented his executing this plan: the admiral, therefore, ordered the *Excellent*, the leading ship of his own division, to bear up; and, with the *Victory*, he himself passed to leeward of the enemy's rearmost and leeward-most ships, which, though almost silenced in their fire, continued obstinately to resist the animated attacks of all their opponents.

Captain Collingwood, in the *Excellent* in obedience to the admiral's orders, passed between the two rearmost ships of the enemy's line, giving to the one most to windward, a seventy-four, so effectual a broadside that, with what she had received before, her captain was induced to submit. The *Excellent* afterwards bore down on the ship to leeward, a three-decker; but observing the *Orion* engaged with her, and the *Victory* approaching her, he threw into her only a few discharges of musketry and passed on to the support of the *Captain*, at that time warmly engaged with a three-decker carrying a flag. His interference here was opportune, as the continual and long fire of the *Captain* had almost expended the ammunition she had at hand, and the loss of her fore-top-mast, and other injuries she had received in her rigging, had rendered her nearly ungovernable.

The Spanish three-decker had lost her mizenmast; and before the *Excellent* arrived in her proper station to open on this ship, the three-decker dropped astern aboard of, and became entangled with, a Spanish two-decker that was her second: thus doubled on each other, the *Excellent* gave the two ships her fire, and then moved forwards to assist the headmost ships in their attack on the Spanish admiral and the other ships of the enemy's centre.

Meanwhile, Sir John Jervis, disappointed in his plan of raking the enemy's rear ships, and having directed, as before observed, the *Excellent* to bear up, ordered the *Victory* to be placed on the lee-quarter of the rearmost ship of the enemy, a three-decker, and having, by signal, ordered the *Irresistible* and *Diadem* to suspend their firing, threw into the three-decker so powerful a discharge that her commander, seeing the *Barfleur*, carrying Vice-Admiral the Hon. W. Waldegrave's flag, ready to second the *Victory*, thought proper to strike to the British chief. Two of the enemy's ships had now surrendered, and the *Lively* frigate and *Diadem* had orders to secure the prizes. The next that fell were the two with which Commodore Nelson was engaged.

While Captain Collingwood so nobly stepped in to his assistance, as has been mentioned before, Captain R. W. Miller, the commodore's captain, was enabled to replenish his lockers with shot and prepare for a renewal of the fight: no sooner, therefore, had the *Excellent* passed on than the gallant commodore renewed the battle.

The three-decker with which he was before engaged having fallen aboard her second, that ship, of 84 guns, became now the Captain's opponent. To her Commodore Nelson directed a vigorous fire; nor was it feebly returned, as the loss of the *Captain* evinced, near twenty men being killed and wounded in a very few minutes. It was now that the various damages already sustained by that ship through the long and arduous conflict which she had maintained, appearing to render a continuance of the contest in the usual way precarious, or perhaps impossible; and the commodore not bearing to part with an enemy of whom he had assured himself, he instantly resolved on a bold and decisive measure, and determined, whatever might be the event, to attempt his opponent sword in hand. The boarders were summoned and orders given to lay the *Captain* on board the enemy.

Fortune favors the brave; nor on this occasion was she unmindful of her favorite. Captain Miller so judiciously directed the course of the *Captain* that she was laid aboard the starboard quarter of the 84 gun ship, her spritsail yard passing over the enemy's poop, and hooking her mizen shrouds; and the word to board being given, the officers and seamen destined for this duty, headed by Lieutenant Berry, together with the detachment of the 69th regiment, commanded by Lieutenant Pearson, then doing duty as marines on board the *Captain*, passed with rapidity on board the enemy's ship; and in a short time the *San Nicolas* was in the possession of her intrepid assailants. The commodore's impatience would not permit him to remain an inactive spectator of this event. He knew the attempt was hazardous; and his presence, he thought, might contribute to its success. He therefore accompanied the party in this attack, passing from the fore chains of his own ship into the enemy's quarter gallery, and thence through the cabin to the quarter-deck, where he arrived in time to receive the sword of the dying commander, who was mortally wounded by the boarders. For a few minutes after the officers had submitted, the crew below were firing their lower-deck guns: this irregularity, however, was soon corrected, and measures taken for the security of the conquest. But this labor was no sooner achieved, than he found himself engaged in another and more arduous one. The stern of the three-decker, his former opponent, was directly amidships on the weather-beam of the *San Nicolas*; and, from her poop and galleries, the enemy sorely annoyed, with musketry, the British on board the *San Nicolas*. The commodore was not long in resolving on the conduct to be observed upon this momentous occasion. The alternative that presented itself, was to quit the prize, or advance. Confident in the bravery of his seamen, he determined on the latter. Directing therefore an additional number of men to be sent from the *Captain*, on board the *San Nicolas*, the undaunted commodore headed himself the assailants in this new attack, and success crowned the enterprise. Such, indeed, was the panic occasioned by his preceding conduct that the British no sooner appeared on the quarter-deck of their new opponent than the Commandant advanced, and asking for the British commanding officer, dropped on one knee and presented to him his sword; making, at the same time, an excuse for the Spanish admiral's not appearing, as he was dangerously wounded. For a moment Commodore Nelson could scarcely persuade himself of this second instance of good fortune; he therefore ordered the Spanish Commandant, who had the rank of a brigadier, to assemble the officers on the quarter-deck, and direct steps to be taken instantly for communicating to the crew the surrender of the ship. All the officers immediately appeared, and the commodore found the surrender of the *San Josef* ascertained, by each of them delivering to him his sword.

The coxswain of Nelson's barge had attended him throughout this perilous adventure. To his charge the commodore gave the swords of the Spanish officers as he received them; and the jolly tar, as they were delivered to him, tucked these honorable trophies under his arm, with all the sang-froid imaginable.

It was at this moment also that an honest Jack Tar, an old acquaintance of Nelson's, came up to him in the fullness of his heart, and excusing the liberty he was taking, asked to shake him by the hand, to congratulate him upon seeing him safe on the quarter-deck of a Spanish three-decker.

This new conquest had scarcely submitted, and the commodore returned on board the *San Nicolas*, when the latter ship was discovered to be on fire in two places. At the first moment appearances were alarming; but presence of mind and resources were not wanting to the British officers in this emergency. The firemen were immediately ordered from the *Captain*; and proper means being taken, the fires were soon got under.

A signal was now made by the *Captain* for boats to assist in separating her from her prizes; and as the *Captain* was incapable of further service until refitted, the commodore hoisted his pendant, for the moment, on board the *Minerve* frigate, and in the evening removed it to the *Irresistible*, Captain Martin.

Four of the enemy's ships were now in [the] possession of the British squadron (two of three decks, the *Salvador del Mondo* and the *San Josef*, of 112 guns each; one of 84, the *San Nicolas*; and the *San Ysidro*, of 74 guns;) and the van of the British line still continued to press hard the *Santisima Trinidad* and others in the rear of the enemy's flying fleet. The approach, however, of the enemy's ships which had been separated from their main body in the morning, two new ships also bearing down from to windward, and two of the enemy's flying ships wearing to support their chief, at that time severely pressed, add to which, the closing of the day – these circumstances, but more particularly the lateness of the hour, while the prizes were not yet properly secured, determined the British admiral to bring to. The headmost of the enemy's approaching ships (in all nine in number, two of which were of three decks) had indeed advanced to fire on the *Britannia*, in which Vice-Admiral Thompson carried his flag, and the sternmost ships of the rear-division, which were fortunately, at this period, in a situation to keep the enemy in check. The *Victory* likewise, with the *Barfleur* and *Namur*, had formed to cover the prizes. The British admiral, therefore, a little before four o'clock, p.m., made the preparative, and soon after the signal for the British fleet to bring to. The enemy's fresh ships, on approaching, opened a fire on our covering ships; but, though both fresh, and so superior in numbers, they contented themselves with the noise of a few irregular broadsides, leaving their captured friends, and seeming too happy to be allowed to escape with their discomfited chief, and his disabled companions, to think of molesting our squadron in bringing to on the starboard tack.

The frigates having orders to take in charge the prizes not already taken possession of, the four were soon secured as well as circumstances permitted; and the *Captain* having suffered very considerably in her masts and rigging, the *Minerve* was ordered to take her in tow.

At the close of the evening, the British fleet was again formed in most admirable line of battle, on a wind with their heads of the southward, and the *Niger* frigate ordered to look out during the night.

The close of the day, before the four prizes were secured, undoubtedly saved the Spanish admiral's flag from falling into the hands of the victors. The *Santisima Trinidad*, in which he carried it, had been so much the object of attention that the ship was a perfect wreck when the action ceased. Many indeed aver that she actually struck both her flag and ensign, hoisting a flag as a signal of submission; but as she continued her course, and afterwards hoisted a Spanish jack, others doubt this circumstance. It is however, a truth that her fire had been silent for some time before this event is reported to have occurred.

The loss of the enemy in this engagement must have been very considerable. The fire of the British squadron was, throughout the action, superior in the proportion of five or six to one; and if we were to judge from the number of killed and wounded found on board the prizes, their casualties must greatly exceed the numbers that have been usually computed. Almost all their wounded that had lost limbs died for want of assistance; and many others, who were wounded in other parts, were found dead in the holds.

The loss of the British squadron, in killed and wounded, amounted to exactly three hundred: moderate indeed, when compared with that of the enemy, and considering the duration of the action! But the expenditure of ammunition was, I am told, beyond any recent example. The *Culloden* expended, it is said, 170 barrels of powder; the *Captain*, 146; and the *Blenheim*, 180; other ships expended in the same proportion. It is not unworthy of remark also that not a single gun in the British squadron burst in this action.

The *Captain* fired more shot than are usually given to a ship of her rate, at her first equipment in England; and it was observed, that when shot or grape were wanting on board this ship for the carronades, the tars substituted in their place nine-pounds shot, seven of which were frequently discharged at one time, and then at so short a distance that every shot of the seven must have had effect.

If I may be permitted to hazard an opinion, the whole

squadron have gained immortal honor; for the victory of the 14th of February stands, in all its circumstances, first and unparalleled in naval history.

Thus, my dear Sir, you have the most interesting particulars of this brilliant affair. I have other anecdotes in store; which I reserve until we meet to talk over this, as well as other occurrences, that have happened since we parted. I cannot, however, conclude my letter without remarking, for your satisfaction, knowing you to be a particular man, that the time mentioned in the narrative is taken from the minutes kept on board the *Victory*. Some difference occurs between them and those kept on board other ships; but I have thought proper to follow the former, conceiving them to be the most correct. In the hope of our meeting in a few days, I remain.

MY DEAR SIR, & C.
J. DRINKWATER.

A Meeting with Nelson

On the morning of the 15th, Sir Gilbert Elliot proceeded to offer to the British admiral his congratulations on the success of the previous day. Lord Garlies of course accompanied him. I was to have been of this party and another person. My friends kindly offered to make room for me, but as this could not be done without occasioning great inconvenience to the whole party, I reluctantly gave up the intention of accompanying them.

My disappointment, however, was amply made up by what took place immediately after the *Lively*'s barge had left the frigate. A boat was seen approaching the *Lively* on the opposite side, and I heard with surprise, and no little pleasure, that Nelson was on board of her. Seeing me on the quarter-deck, the commodore immediately approached me, offering his hand, which I seized with a most cordial grasp, expressing, at the same time, my high admiration of the gallant conduct of the *Captain* on the preceding day, and my warmest congratulations on the success of the battle.

"Where is Sir Gilbert?" was his first inquiry. "Gone with Lord Garlies to the *Victory*," was my reply. "I hoped," he rejoined, "to have caught him before he saw the admiral, but come below with me," and he led the way to the cabin.

Seated alone with the commodore, I renewed in the most expressive terms, my congratulations on his safety from the perils of such a fight, and on the very distinguished part he had personally taken in the action, of which many particulars had by this time reached the *Lively*. He received my compliments with great modesty, though evidently with great satisfaction. I then remarked that, as the *Lively* would bear the glorious news to England, I should feel much obliged by his giving me as many particulars of the proceedings of his ship, the *Captain*, and of his own conduct in the capture of the two ships, as he was disposed to communicate. Our intimacy was such that I felt no difficulty in drawing from him these details; and this circumstance will be an apology for my making these remarks with such great freedom. I observed to him that the position of the *Captain* appeared to all of us in the *Lively* to be for a long time most extraordinary and unaccountable. We had expected every instant to see the ship annihilated by the overpowering force to which she was singly opposed. In the animation of conversation, I went so far as to ask, "How came you, commodore, to get into that singular and perilous situation?" He good-naturedly replied, "I'll tell you how it happened. The admiral's intention, I saw, was to cut off the detached squadron of eight sail and afterwards attack the main body, weakened by this separation. Observing, however, as our squadron advanced and became engaged with the enemy's ships, that the main body of the enemy were pushing to join their friends to leeward, by passing in the rear of our squadron, I thought, unless by some prompt and extraordinary measure, the main body could be diverted from this course, until Sir John (at that time in action in the *Victory*) could see their plan, his well arranged designs on the enemy would be frustrated. I therefore ordered the *Captain* to wear, and passing the rear of our squadron, directed Captain Miller to steer for the centre of the enemy's fleet, where was their admiral-in-chief, seconded by two three-deckers, hoping by this proceeding to confound them, and, if possible, make them change their course (as he did), and thus afford Sir John Jervis time to see their movements, and take measures to follow up his original intention." I do not say that Nelson expressed himself in exactly the above words, but his statement was to the same effect.*

In compliance with my request, he then gave me the details of his boarding the *St Nicholas*, and afterwards the *St Josef*, which are given in the original Narrative, adding the following particulars: "I saw (and then he spoke with increased animation) that from the disabled state of the *Captain*, and the effective attack of the approaching British ships, I was likely to have my beaten opponent taken from me; I therefore decided to board the *St Nicholas*, which I had chiefly fought and considered to be my prize. Orders were given to lay the *Captain* aboard of her: the spritsail-yard passed into her mizen rigging. Lieutenant Berry with the ship's boarders, and Captain Pearson with the 69th regiment (acting as marines on board the *Captain*), soon got possession of the enemy's ship. Assisted by one of the sailors, I got from the fore-chains into the quarter-gallery through the window, and thence through the cabin to the quarter-deck, where I found my gallant friends already triumphant." He then gave me the details of the extraordinary circumstances attending his afterwards getting possession of the *St Josef*. Of course, my high admiration of his conduct was often expressed, as he proceeded, in giving me these very interesting particulars, of

* I have since often heard Commodore Nelson's conduct, in the above transaction, variously commented on. According to the strict rules of discipline, some persons say the *Captain* should not have quitted the British line-of-battle without orders. The strength of Sir John Jervis's squadron lay in its compactness, and the loss of one ship, from any cause, where the numbers opposed to each other were so disproportionate, might have defeated the British admiral's maneuvers, and even have endangered the safety of the whole. Others have remarked, and apparently with good grounds, that when Nelson saw the necessity of some immediate and bold measure to disconcert the enemy, and had decided on the step he took, he should not have gone alone, but have taken with his own 74, all the ships in his rear; and if we may judge from results, and the success of one ship, there can be no doubt that the attack of the *Captain*, supported by two or three others, must have been more effective, and the victory of the day would, in that case, have been more complete. In these comments there seems to be reason and good sense; but in warfare, circumstances must often arise which baffle principles, and customary modes of proceeding. Nelson, no doubt, saw the conduct of the Spanish admiral in its true light: his decision and boldness astonished and confounded the enemy, who were thus taken by surprise, and unprepared for such singular resolution. The measure succeeded, and to this movement, hazardous as it was, may chiefly be attributed the success of the day.

which I made pencil notes on a scrap of paper I found at hand; and these communications from my gallant friend were the more valuable from their being made before he had seen any other officer of the fleet, except Captain G. Martin, of the *Irresistible*, to which ship he had repaired for refreshment and repose, until the *Captain*, his own ship, almost a wreck in her rigging, &c., could be put into manageable order.

Towards the conclusion of this interesting interview, I repeated my cordial felicitations at his personal safety, after such very perilous achievements. I then adverted to the honors that must attend such distinguished services. "The admiral," I observed, "of course will be made a peer, and his seconds in command noticed accordingly. As for you, commodore," I continued, "they will make you a baronet." The word was scarcely uttered, when placing his hand on my arm, and looking me most expressively in the face, he said, "No, no: if they want to mark my services, it must not be in that manner." "Oh!" said I, interrupting him, "you wish to be made a Knight of the Bath," for I could not imagine that his ambition, at that time, led him to expect a peerage. My supposition proved to be correct, for he instantly answered me, "Yes; if my services have been of any value, let them be noticed in a way that the public may know me – or them." I cannot distinctly remember which of these terms was used, but, from his manner, I could have no doubt of his meaning, that he wished to bear about his person some honorary distinction, to attract the public eye, and mark his professional services.

This casual discovery of Nelson's peculiar feelings on this subject was not forgotten, or without consequences. As was expected, his Majesty, in reward for Nelson's distinguished conduct, had intended to create him a baronet. Sir Gilbert Elliot, who took a warm interest in Nelson's welfare, called on me in London to impart this news; when I made known to him the purport of my conversation on board the *Lively*, and suggested that it was advisable to make this circumstance known to the government. Sir Gilbert saw the matter in the same light. He lost no time in communicating what had passed on this subject to some member of the cabinet, Lord Spencer, I believe, who was then at the head of the Admiralty Board, and his lordship took steps to meet Nelson's wishes, in the manner most likely to gratify his feelings, by obtaining for him, instead of a baronetcy, the Order of the Bath, although, for that purpose, it was necessary to make him an extra knight.

What I had noticed in the above interview with Nelson, agreed perfectly with the opinion I formed from all I observed during our subsequent acquaintance. The attainment of public honours, and an ambition to be distinguished above his fellows, were his master passions. His conduct was constantly actuated by these predominant feelings. It will account for the personal gratification he invariably evinced at receiving the many decorative honors presented to him by almost every power in Europe in amity with Great Britain; but, in reference to such distinctions, it may be observed, that if such pre-eminent talents as those of this most extraordinary man could be so cheaply purchased, the English nation, and indeed Europe, situated as she then was, had only to approve and applaud his moderation.

When Nelson quitted the *Lively*, he went on board the *Victory* to receive from his gallant Chief, Sir John Jervis, and from his friend, Sir Gilbert Elliot, those congratulations and commendations which he so highly merited.

Homecoming

There being little wind on the 15th of February, both fleets, as has been already remarked, remained almost becalmed in sight of each other. That of the enemy appeared in great disorder; the British squadron was concentrated. On the 16th, the British squadron was still off Cape St. Vincent, which, on account of the adverse wind, and the disabled state of the prizes, the squadron could not weather. If they could have passed to the westward of the Cape, it was thought the admiral would have proceeded to Lisbon.

During the day, some movements of the enemy indicating an intention of approaching the British squadron, Sir John, closely attentive to their proceedings, ordered the frigates to assemble round the *Victory*, to be at hand to act towards the prizes (which, in case of a renewal of hostilities, might embarrass him) in such manner as circumstances might point out.

Various reports were in circulation regarding their disposal

in case of another action. Amongst other measures, it was
rumoured that it had been suggested to run the four prizes
ashore on the coast of Portugal, and to leave the Spanish crews
to shift for themselves. All conjecture on this head was, however,
removed in the afternoon: finding it not practicable to get
round Cape St. Vincent, the admiral made the signal to bear
away for Lagos Bay, a few leagues to leeward, where the
squadron and the prizes came to anchor in the evening.*

On the 17th, despatches were sent off by land to Lisbon,
giving information of the late victory. In the course of the day,
intelligence reached Sir John, through an American trader,
that a large three-decker, supposed to be the *Santisima Trinidad*,
had been seen off Cape St Mary's, in distress, with an English
frigate hovering round her. Two frigates were in consequence
detached to bring her in, or to destroy her; but although the
disabled ship proved to be the ship in question, her crew at
length contrived to get her into port.

The 18th of February proved to be calm, but a fine day. The
Spanish fleet had now approached Cape St Vincent, off which
they were seen, in number, twenty-two ships of the line,

---

* On the fleet's assembling in Lagos Bay, the admiral communicated, in general
orders, his thanks to the admirals and officers of the squadron under his command,
in the following terms:

VICTORY, *LAGOS BAY*,
February 16, 1797.

SIR,

No language I am possessed of can convey the high sense I entertain of the
exemplary conduct of the flag-officers, captains, officers, seamen, marines, and
soldiers, embarked on board every ship of the squadron I have the honor to
command, present at the vigorous and successful attack made upon the fleet of
Spain on the 14th inst. The signal advantage obtained by His Majesty's arms on
that day is entirely owing to their determined valor and discipline; and I request
you will accept yourself and give my thanks and approbation to those composing
the crew of the ship under your command.

I AM, SIR,
YOUR MOST HUMBLE SERVANT,
J. JERVIS.
OF H.M. SHIP—.

Considering how distinguished had been the services of some of the commanders of
the fleet in the action of the 14th, it was thought extraordinary at the time, that not
the least notice, by name, was taken of any of these officers in the preceding circular
communication to the squadron.

manoeuvring, as well as they were able, to form a line-of-battle.

Arrangements having by this time been made with the Portuguese authorities at Lagos, for the reception of the Spanish prisoners of war, they were landed this day, to the number of about 2,300 men, and commenced their march to the eastward for the Spanish frontier. In the afternoon, a large Spanish frigate that had hugged the shore, under cover of a small headland, forming the western point of the Bay of Lagos, suddenly appeared, almost within shot of the British squadron. The *Lively*'s signal was made to slip and chace, but the enemy no sooner saw his danger, than he hauled his wind, and, crowding all sail, stood for the Spanish fleet, then drawing off from the land, and the *Lively's* signal was annulled. At night, two of the British frigates were chaced into the anchorage of the fleet by one of the enemy's line-of-battle ships. On Sunday, the 19th of February, Captain Robert Calder, captain of the fleet, came on board the *Lively*, with the admiral's despatches, of which he was to be the bearer to England. About noon, the *Lively* got under way, and the wind having become favorable, and blowing fresh, she soon doubled Cape St Vincent, seeing nothing of the Spanish fleet, and before night-fall, had left the British squadron far behind.

The *Lively* lay her course towards England until the 23rd of February, when the wind changed to the eastward. On the 25th, she had got into soundings, but the adverse easterly wind prevented her advancing up the Channel. By the 28th, the *Lively* had weathered the Scilly Islands, and passed to the northward, between those islands and the Lands End. There being little prospect of any change of wind, and Captain Calder being very impatient to reach London with his good news, he desired Lord Garlies to put him on shore at St Ive's, where he landed, giving express orders that no letters, nor any other person except himself and servant should be allowed to land. Some idea was then entertained that the *Lively* might make for Milford Haven, but our good fortune interposed to defeat this project, which, had it been carried into effect, might have brought the frigate into contact with a French flying squadron, then hovering off the coast of South

Wales, and which had landed a body of troops near Fish-guard. It was luckily decided to return to the English Channel, where the frigate contrived to contend for some days against a stiff Levanter, until she had got abreast of the Eddystone, when seeing little prospect of any alteration in the wind, and anxious to get on shore, Sir Gilbert Elliot requested Lord Garlies to land him and his party at Plymouth; and, in a few hours after our course was changed, I had the satisfaction (which is only to be felt and understood by those who have been absent long on foreign service) of finding myself once more in old England.

We landed on Sunday, the 5th of March. Being the messengers of such glorious news as the defeat of the Spanish grand fleet, the rumour of which, it was concluded, would have already reached Plymouth, we anticipated a most joyful reception. We expected, on our reaching the shore, that the *Lively*'s arrival would have been hailed with the customary congratulations and rejoicings; but the people who received us, did not even enquire whence she came. Not a word nor a sign of welcome met our landing. Captain Calder had kept his good news so secret, that not a whisper of it had reached Plymouth, where, not a little to our surprise, we saw nothing but long faces and desponding looks in all classes.

We were not, however, long in learning the cause of this appearance and behaviour. Before we could tell them our gratifying intelligence, they announced to us the news (which had reached them that morning from the metropolis) of the shutting up of the National Bank of England, and the general *suspension of cash payments*. The union of the Spanish with the French fleets, they added, was considered as certain. Some flying squadrons of the latter were then known to be in the Irish channel, and the usual alarm of invasion universally prevailed. Nothing but England's disgrace and downfall was foretold and talked of throughout the kingdom.

After listening to these discouraging details for some time, we availed ourselves of the first favorable opening to relieve them of some of their apprehensions. Immediate invasion, we said, was not to be looked for. Sir John Jervis had retarded, if not entirely defeated that measure; and we then made known the particulars of the glorious Battle of St Valentine's day. For some time they would scarcely give our statements credit; and even when at length the fact was forced on their belief, such was the panic then prevailing that we could only collect at Plymouth, from the admiral, the general, and other friends, fifteen guineas in gold, towards enabling the viceroy, and his party of six individuals, and their servants, to pay their travelling expenses to the metropolis.

A grateful Britain made Jervis Earl St Vincent, and Nelson at last got the honour he thought his due: he was created a Knight of the Order of the Bath. His promotion to rear-admiral was also forthcoming.

The euphoria of victory at Cape St Vincent, however, did nothing to stem the anger rumbling through the lower ranks of the Royal Navy over low pay and conditions. At Spithead and the Nore, the British Grand Fleet burst into mutiny (*see* Appendix IV). Reinforcements joining Jervis brought discontent with them, and rebellions aboard the *Marlborough* and *St George* were only quashed when Jervis insisted that the ring leaders were hung by their shipmates. As encouragement, he surrounded the ships with the remainder of the fleet, with orders to fire. Sensing also that rebellion was afoot in the *Theseus*, he ordered Nelson to transfer to her. Nelson impressed the men by his firmness, but also his fairness; when Jervis insisted that two of the *Theseus*'s crew were "shamming" mental illness, Nelson interceded on their behalf. A little later, the lower deck wrote him an anonymous note: "Success attend Admiral Nelson God bless Captain Miller. We are happy and comfortable and will shed every drop of blood in our veins to support them, and the name of *Theseus* shall be immortalized as high as *Captain's* ship's company."

The men of the *Theseus* were as good as their word. They bled plenty for Nelson.

After joining the blockade of Cadiz, where he was involved in hand-to-hand fighting, Nelson was ordered to: "proceed with the ships . . . under [his] command . . . with the utmost expedition to the Island of Tenerife and there make dispositions for taking possession of the town of Santa Cruz by a sudden and vigorous assault. In case of success, you are authorized to lay a heavy contribution on the inhabitants of the Town and adjacent district, if they do not put you in possession of the whole cargo of *El Principe d'Asturias . . .* and all the treasure belonging to the Crown of Spain."

Santa Cruz was to be taken by a surprise attack by troops landing at night. Unfortunately a gale prevented the boats getting to shore, and alarm guns were fired in the town. Ignoring the cautions of the – soldiers in his command, Nelson his eyes on the twin prizes of glory and silver – then ordered a second assault on the port, which was driven back.

TENERIFE: THE SECOND ASSAULT, 24–5 July 1797

Captain Thomas Troubridge[8]

From the darkness of the night, I did not immediately hit the Mole, the spot appointed to land at, but pushed on shore under the enemy's battery, close to the southward of the Citadel. Captain Waller landed at the same instant, and two or three other boats. The surf was so high, many put back: the boats were full of water in an instant, and stove against the rocks, and most of the ammunition in the men's pouches wet. As soon as I had collected a few men, I immediately pushed, with Captain Waller, for the Square, the place of rendezvous, in hopes of there meeting you [Nelson] and the remainder of the people, and waited about an hour, during which time I sent a Sergeant with two gentlemen of the Town, to summons the Citadel. I fear the Sergeant was shot on his way, as I heard nothing of him afterwards.

The ladders being all lost in the surf, or not to be found, no immediate attempt could be made on the Citadel. I therefore marched to join Captains Hood and Miller, who, I had intelligence, had made good their landing to the SW of the place I did, with a body of men. I endeavoured then to procure some intelligence of you, and the rest of the officers, without success. By day-break, we had collected about 80 Marines, 80 Pikemen, and 180 small-arm Seamen. These, I found, were all that were alive that had made good their landing. With this force, having procured some ammunition from the Spanish prisoners we had made, we were marching to try what could be done with the Citadel without ladders; but found the whole of the streets commanded by field-pieces, and upwards of 8,000 Spaniards and 100 French under arms, approaching by every avenue. As the boats were all stove, and I saw no possibility of getting more men on shore – the ammunition wet, and no provisions – I sent Captain Hood with a Flag of Truce to the Governor, to say I was prepared to burn the Town, which I should immediately put in force if he approached one inch further; and, at the same time, I desired Captain Hood to say it would be done with regret, as I had no wish to injure the inhabitants; that if he would come to my terms, I was ready to treat, which he readily agreed to: a copy of which I had the honour to send you by Captain Waller, which, I hope, will meet your approbation, and appear highly honourable.

From the small body of men, and the greater part being pike and small-arm seamen, which can be only called irregulars, with very little ammunition in the pouches but what was wet in the surf at landing, I could not expect to succeed in any attempt upon the enemy, whose superior strength I have before mentioned. The Spanish Officers assure me they expected us, and were perfectly prepared with all the batteries, and the number of men I have before mentioned under arms: with the great disadvantage of a rocky coast, high surf, and in the face of forty pieces of cannon, though we were not successful, will show what an Englishman is equal to.

Despite his high rank, Nelson personally led a landing party in the second wave. As he stepped on to the Mole, his right arm was shattered by grapeshot above the elbow. Nelson's stepson, Josiah, who was with him, bound the wound with silk handkerchiefs.

SANTA CRUZ: NELSON LOSES AN ARM, 25 July 1797

Midshipman William Hoste, HMS Theseus[9]

At 1.00 a.m. commenced one of the heaviest cannonading I ever was witness to from the town upon our boats, likewise a very heavy fire of musketry, which continued without intermission for the space of four hours. At 2.00, Admiral Lord Nelson returned on board, being dreadfully wounded in the right arm with a grape-shot. I leave you to judge of my situation when I beheld our boat approach with him, who I may say has been a second father to me, his right arm dangling by his side, while with the other he helped himself to jump up the ship's side, and with a spirit that astonished everyone, told the surgeon to get his instruments ready, for he knew he must lose his arm, and that the sooner it was off the better. He underwent the amputation with the same firmness and courage that have always marked his character, and I am happy to say is now in a fair way of recovery.

Tenerife was a disaster; 148 officers and men were killed in the night assault of 24–5 July. Nelson became engulfed in a sense of failure, as a leader of men and as the lightning rod of his own destiny.

"USELESS TO MY COUNTRY": NELSON IN DESPAIR, 27 July 1797

Admiral Sir Horatio Nelson[10]

A letter to Earl St Vincent

> I am become a burthen to my friends, and useless to my Country; but by my letter wrote the 24th, you will perceive my anxiety for the promotion of my son-in-law, Josiah Nisbet. When I leave your command, I become dead to the World; I go hence, and am no more seen. If from poor Bowen's loss, you will think it proper to oblige me, I rest confident you will do it; the boy is under obligations to me, but he repaid me by bringing me from the Mole of Santa Cruz. I hope you will be able to give me a frigate, to convey the remains of my carcass to England.

St Vincent replied with generosity:

> My dear Admiral, Mortals cannot command success; you and your Companions have certainly deserved it, by the greatest degree of heroism and perseverance that ever was exhibited. I grieve for the loss of your arm and for the fate of poor Bowen and Gibson, with the other brave men who fell so gallantly. I hope you and Captain Fremantle are

doing well; the *Seahorse* shall waft you to England the
moment her wants are supplied. Your Son-in-law is Captain of the *Dolphin* Hospital-ship, [he had promoted Josiah
Master and Commander] and all other wishes you may
favour me with shall be fulfilled, as far as is consistent with
what I owe to some valuable Officers in the *Ville de Paris*.
. . . Give my love to Mrs Fremantle. I will salute her and
bow to your stump to-morrow morning, if you will give me
leave.[11]

Vincent did more for his protege than issue him kind private words.
He promoted Josiah – a mere seventeen – master and commander.
More, in his dispatch to the Admiralty, which was published in the
London Gazette, Vincent declared the siege of "Tenerife to be an affair in
which his majesty's arms have acquired a very great degree of lustre".
Tenerife was a defeat, but it had dash and derring. With a sleight of
pen, Vincent turned Tenerife from an unmitigated disaster to an
heroic failure. Nelson's fame increased exponentially.

After four and half years at sea, Nelson arrived in England in
early September, to be reunited with Fanny. He was a physical
wreck: his hair was white, many of his teeth were missing, he had
lost sight in his right eye and his amputed stump of an arm was
infected. None of this decreased Fanny's devotion to him; likewise,
none of the bodily losses and infirmities decreased Nelson's devotion
to his ultimate love: his own life on the ocean waves. Much of his
recuperation was spent courting men in high Admiralty places with
a view to getting back to sea as soon as possible. He was given the
Vanguard, and by April 1798 was sailing to the Mediterranean to
ascertain the destination of the French invasion force being assembled by Napoleon in Toulon.

THE NILE CAMPAIGN: THE COMMANDER'S REPORT, 1 May–31 July 1798

Admiral Sir Horatio Nelson[12]

To Lady Nelson   Lisbon, *1st May, 1798*
   I joined the Fleet yesterday, and found Lord St. Vincent
everything I wished him; and his friends in England have done
me justice for my zeal and affection towards him. I have my

fears that he will not be much longer in this Command, for I believe he has written to be superseded, which I am sincerely sorry for. It will considerably take from my pleasure in serving here; but I will hope for the best. The Dons have, I find, long expected my return with Bomb-vessels, Gunboats, and every proper implement for the destruction of Cadiz and their Fleet. They have prepared three floating batteries to lie outside their walls, to prevent the fancied attack; and, lo, the mountain has brought forth a mouse: – I am arrived with a single Ship, and without the means of annoying them. The Admiral probably is going to detach me with a small Squadron; not on any fighting expedition, therefore do not be surprised if it should be some little time before you hear from me again. I direct this to our Cottage, where I hope you will fix yourself in comfort and I pray that it may very soon please God to give us Peace. England will not be invaded this summer. Buonaparte is gone back to Italy, where 80,000 men are embarking for some expedition. With every kind wish that a fond heart can frame, believe me, as ever, your most affectionate husband.

HORATIO NELSON

To the Captains of the *Orion*,
Alexander and _Vanguard_ Gibraltar Bay, *7th May, 1798*

It being of the very greatest importance that the Squadron should not be separated, it is my positive orders that no temptation is to induce a Line-of-Battle Ship to separate from me, except the almost certainty of bringing a Line-of-Battle Ship of the Enemy to Action; but in common chaces, if the weather is such as to risk separation, or the approach of night, it is my directions you leave off the chace, and rejoin me, even without waiting the signal of Recall, unless I make the signal to continue the pursuit, by No. 104, page 30, S.B.

HORATIO NELSON[13]

To Lord St Vincent *Vanguard*, off Cape Sicie,
May 17th, 1798

My Lord,

This morning, the *Terpsichore* captured a small French Corvette, of six guns and sixty-five men, which came out of Toulon at

11 o'clock, last night. From the general report of Vessels
spoke, you will observe the uniformity of the reports – viz.,
that an expedition is preparing to sail from Toulon. We have
separately examined the crew of this Corvette, and, from the
whole, I believe the following may be depended on as near the
truth – that Buonaparte arrived at Toulon last Friday and has
examined the troops which are daily embarking in the numerous transports; that Vessels with troops frequently arrive
from Marseilles; it is not generally believed that Buonaparte is
to embark, but no one knows to what place the Armament is
destined. Fifteen Sail of the Line are apparently ready for sea,
but nineteen are in the harbour, and yet it is said only six Sail
of the Line are to sail with the transports now ready; that
about 12,000 men are embarked; their cavalry arrived at
Toulon, but I cannot learn that any are yet embarked.
Reports say they are to sail in a few days, and others that
they will not sail for a fortnight. This Corvette was bound to
the westward, I believe, with dispatches, but the Commander
denies it.

The Admiral Brueys has his Flag in *l'Orient*, 120 guns; *le
Formidable* and *Spartanade*, of 80 guns, are also Flag-ships. The
Venetian Ships are considered as very bad in every respect,
but I do not learn that the Fleet is deficient in either men or
stores. All this information is but little more than you knew
when I left you, but, still, knowing that late information of the
state of the Enemy's Fleet is desirable, I send an intelligent
young man, Mr Charles Harford, who has just served his
Time, with this letter, and I beg leave to recommend him to
your notice. You may rely, my Lord, that I shall act as
occasions may offer, to the best of my abilities, in following up
your ideas for the honour of His Majesty's Arms, and the
advantage of our Country, and believe me, your Lordship's
obedient Servant,

HORATIO NELSON

I saw three French Frigates this afternoon, but as they did not
see the Squadron, I am in hopes of getting near them. The
Squadron is as I wish them.[14]

Vanguard, Island of St Peter's,
in Sardinia, *May 24th, 1798*

My dearest Fanny*,

I ought not to call what has happened to the *Vanguard* by the cold name of accident: I believe firmly, that it was the Almighty's goodness, to check my consummate vanity. I hope it has made me a better Officer, as I feel confident it has made me a better Man. I kiss with all humility the rod.

Figure to yourself a vain man, on Sunday evening at sun-set, walking in his cabin with a Squadron about him, who looked up to their Chief to lead them to glory, and in whom this Chief placed the firmest reliance, that the proudest Ships, in equal numbers belonging to France, would have bowed their Flags; and with a very rich Prize lying by him. Figure to yourself this proud, conceited man, when the sun rose on Monday morning, his Ship dismasted, his Fleet dispersed, and himself in such distress, that the meanest Frigate out of France would have been a very unwelcome guest. But it has pleased Almighty God to bring us into a safe Port, where, although we are refused the rights of humanity, yet the *Vanguard* will in two days get to sea again, as an English Man-of-War.

The exertions of Sir James Saumarez, in the *Orion*, and Captain A. Ball, in the *Alexander*, have been wonderful; if the Ship had been in England, months would have been taken to send her to sea: here, my operations will not be delayed four days, and I shall join the rest of my Fleet on the rendezvous.

If this letter gets to you, be so good as to write a line to Lord Spencer, telling him that the *Vanguard* is fitted tolerably for sea, and that what has happened will not retard my operations. We are all health and good humour: tell Lady Saumarez Sir James never was in better health. With kind love to my Father, believe me ever your affectionate husband,

HORATIO NELSON

I have wrote to Lord S. by another, but I still wish you to write a line to say we are all well, for yours may arrive and his Lordship's miscarry.

* His wife, Lady Frances.

P.S. Mr Thomas Meek, who was recommended by Mr Hussey and my brother Suckling, was killed, and several seamen were wounded.[15]

To Lord St Vincent   *Vanguard*, Island of St. Peter's,
                                           in Sardinia, *May 24th, 1798*

My Lord,

I am sorry to be obliged to inform you of the accidents which have happened to the *Vanguard*. On Saturday, May the 19th, it blew strong from the NW. On Sunday it moderated so much, as to enable us to get our top-gallant masts and yards aloft. After dark it began to blow strong; but as the Ship was prepared for a gale, my mind was easy. At half-past one a.m. on Monday, the main-top-mast went over the side, as did soon afterwards the mizen-mast. As it was impossible for any night-signal to be seen, I had hopes we should be quiet till day-light, when I determined to wear, and scud before the gale; but about half-past three the foremast went in three pieces, and the bowsprit was found to be sprung in three places. When the day broke, we were fortunately enabled to wear the Ship with a remnant of the spirit-sail. The *Orion, Alexander*, and *Emerald* wore with us; but the *Terpsichore, Bonne Citoyenne*, and a French Smyrna ship, continued to lay to under bare poles. Our situation was 25 leagues south of the Islands of Hieres; and as we were laying with our head to the NB, had we not wore, which was hardly to be expected, the Ship must have drifted to Corsica. The gale blew very hard all the day, and the ship laboured most exceedingly. In the evening, being in latitude 40° 50′ N, I determined to steer for Oristan Bay, in the Island of Sardinia: during the night, the *Emerald* parted company, for what reason I am at present unacquainted with. Being unable to get into Oristan, the *Alexander* took us in tow, and by Captain Ball's unremitting attention to our distress, and by Sir James Saumarez's exertions and ability in finding out the Island of St Peter's, and the proper anchorage, the *Vanguard* was, on May the 23rd, at noon, brought safely to an anchor into the harbour of St Peter's.

I have the honour to be, &c.

                                        HORATIO NELSON[16]

To the Viceroy of Sardinia   His Britannic Majesty's Ship
Vanguard, At Anchor, off the Island
of St Peter's, *26th May, 1798*
Sir,

Having, by a gale of wind sustained some trifling damage, I
anchored a small part of his Majesty's Fleet, under my orders,
off this Island, and was surprised to hear, by an Officer sent by
the Governor, that admittance was to be refused to the Flag of
his Britannic Majesty into this Port. When I reflect that my
most gracious Sovereign is the oldest, (I believe,) and certainly
the most faithful, Ally which his Majesty of Sardinia ever had, I
could feel the sorrow which it must have been to his Majesty to
have given such an order, and also for your Excellency, who has
to direct its execution. I cannot but look at Africa's shore, where
the followers of Mahomet are performing the part of the good
Samaritan, which I look for in vain at St Peter's, where it is said
the Christian Religion is professed. May I request the favour of
your Excellency to forward one Letter for his Britannic Majesty's Minister at Turin, and the other for his Britannic Majesty's
Consul at Leghorn. May God Almighty bless your Excellency is
the sincere wish of your most obedient servant.

HORATIO NELSON[17]

To Lord St. Vincent   *31st May, 1798*
My dear Lord,

My pride was too great for man; but I trust my friends will
think that I bore my chastisement like a man. It has pleased
God to assist us with his favour, and here I am again off Toulon.

I am, &c.

HORATIO NELSON[18]

A week later, Captain Troubridge brought the following orders to
Nelson from Lord St Vincent: "In pursuance of instructions I have
received from the Lords Commissioners of the Admiralty, to employ a
squadron of His Majesty's Ships within the Mediterranean, under the
command of a discreet Officer (copies of which are enclosed and of
papers necessary for your guidance) in conformity thereto, I do hereby
authorize and require You, on being joined by the Ships named in the
margin [*Culloden, Goliath, Minotaur, Defence, Bellerophon, Majestic,*

Audacious, Zealous, Swiftsure, Theseus] to take them and their captains
under your command, in addition to those already with you, and to
proceed with them in quest of the Armament preparing by the Enemy
at Toulon and Genoa . . . On falling in with said Armament, or any
part thereof, you are to use your utmost endeavours to take, sink, burn
or destroy it . . ." This was an unparalleled commission for such a
junior admiral, but both the First Lord of the Admiralty, Earl
Spencer, and Vincent concurred that Nelson – and only Nelson –
was the man for the task. (When Sir John Orde, a flag officer senior to
Nelson, complained that he had been slighted by the detachment of
Nelson and not himself "on a service of the greatest national importance", Vincent peremptorily ordered him to England.) Effectively, Nelson was now the master of the Mediterranean. And his own
destiny.

To Lord St Vincent   *June 11th*
The *Mutine*, Captain Hardy, joined me on the 5th, at day-light,
with the flattering account of the honour you intended me of
commanding such a Fleet. *Mutine* fell in with *Alcmene*, off
Barcelona on the 2nd. Hope had taken all my Frigates off
the rendezvous, on the presumption that the *Vanguard*; from her
disabled state, must return to an Arsenal. I joined dear Troubridge with the reinforcement of ten Sail of the Line, and the
Leander on the 7th in the evening: it has been nearly calm ever
since, which grieves me sorely. The French have a long start but
I hope they will rendezvous in Telamon bay, for the 12,000 men
from Genoa in 100 Sail of Vessels, escorted by a Frigate, had not
put to sea on the 2nd, nor were all the troops embarked. You
may be assured I will fight them the moment I can reach their
Fleet, be they at anchor, or under sail, I am, &c.

                                        HORATIO NELSON[19]

To Lord St Vincent   *12th of June, 1798*
As I see no immediate prospect of a Letter, I shall continue my
private one in form of a Diary, which may not be unpleasant to
refer to: therefore to begin. Being so close to the Enemy, I take
the liberty of keeping *Orion* for a few days. Owing to want of
wind, I did not pass Cape Corse until this morning; at four we
were becalmed. The moment we had passed, I sent the *Mutine*

to look into Telamon Bay, which, as all the French troops had not left Genoa on the 6th, I thought a probable place for the rendezvous of a large Fleet; and went with the Squadron between Monte Christi, and Giulio, keeping the Continent close on board.

13th of June: *Mutine* joined; nothing in Telamon Bay. I then ran the Fleet between Plenosa and Elba, and Monte Christi; and on the 14th at noon, at now off Civita Vecchia; spoke a Tunisian cruiser, who reported he had spoke a Greek, on the 10th, who told him, that on the 4th, he had passed through the French Fleet, of about 200 Sail, as he thought, off the NW end of Sicily, steering to the eastward. Am in anxious expectation of meeting with Dispatch-boats, Neapolitan cruisers, &c., with letters for me from Naples giving me information.

15th of June: Off the Ponza Islands; my hopes of information were vain. Not finding a Cruiser, I shall send Troubridge into Naples, in the *Mutine*, to talk with Sir William Hamilton and General Acton. Troubridge possesses my full confidence, and has been my honoured acquaintance of twenty-five years' standing. I only beg that your Lordship will believe, I shall endeavour to prove myself worthy of your selection of me for this highly honourable Command. Not a moment shall be lost in pursuing the Enemy. I am, &c.

HORATIO NELSON[20]

To Earl Spencer *Vanguard*, off the Island of
Ponza, *15th June, 1798*

My Lord,

Not having received orders from my Commander-in-Chief to correspond with the Secretary of the Admiralty, I do not feel myself at perfect liberty to do it, unless on extraordinary occasions, when I shall send copies of my Letters to Lord St Vincent; but as your Lordships must be anxious to hear of us, I take the liberty of acquainting you that Captain Troubridge joined on the 7th, but it was the 12th before we passed Cape Corse. The last account I had of the French Fleet, was from a Tunisian Cruiser, who saw them on the 4th, off Trapani, in Sicily, steering to the eastward. If they pass Sicily, I shall believe they are going on their scheme of possessing Alexandria, and getting troops to India – a plan concerted with Tippoo Saib, by no means so difficult as might at first view be imagined; but be they bound to the Antipodes, your Lordship may rely that I will not lose a moment in bringing them to Action, and endeavour to destroy their Transports. I shall send Captain Troubridge on shore to talk with General Acton, and I hope the King of Naples will send me some Frigates; for mine parted company on the 20th of May, and have not joined me since. The whole Squadron is remarkably healthy, and perfectly equal to meet the French Fleet. As I send this before I receive accounts from Naples, it is not in my power to say anything more of the Enemy, for I shall make sail and pass the Faro of Messina the moment Captain Troubridge returns.

Highly honoured as I feel with this very important command, I beg you will believe that I shall endeavour to approve myself worthy of it, and that I am, with the highest respect,

Your Lordship's most obedient servant,

HORATIO NELSON

I have taken the liberty of enclosing a letter for Lady Nelson, which I beg your Lordship will have the goodness to order to be sent to her.[21]

To Lord St Vincent *Vanguard*, off the Islands of Ponza,
June 15th, 1798

My Lord,

I have the honour to acquaint you of my arrival here with the whole Line-of-Battle Ships, the Fifty, and Brig, all in the most perfect health. I am sending Captain Troubridge in the *Mutine* to see Sir William Hamilton [Sir William Hamilton, British ambassador to Naples, husband of Emma Hamilton.] and General Acton, and to get accounts of the French Fleet. I shall lay with the Squadron off Ischia till Captain Troubridge's return, when not a moment shall be lost in pursuing the Enemy, and bringing them to Action. With the highest respect, believe me, your Lordship's most obedient servant,

HORATIO NELSON[22]

To Sir William Hamilton   *Vanguard*, off the Faro of
                                      Messina, *June 20th, 1798*

My dear Sir,

I have thought so much, and heard so much, of the French, since I left Naples, that I should feel culpable, was I for a moment to delay expressing my sentiments on the present situation of the Kingdom of the Two Sicilies. I trust it will be received as I mean it – as proof of the lively interest I take in the fate of their Sicilian Majesties. I shall begin by supposing myself commanding a Fleet attending an Army which is to invade Sicily. If the General asked if Malta would not be a most useful place for the depot of stores, &c., &c., my answer would be, if you can take Malta, it secures the safety of the Fleet, Transports, stores, &c., and insures your safe retreat should that be necessary; for if even a superior Fleet of the Enemy should arrive, before one week passes, they will be blown to leeward, and you may pass with safety. This would be my opinion. There can be no doubt but the French know as well as you and I do, that their Sicilian Majesties called for our help to save them, (even this is crime enough with the French). Here we are, and are ready, and will shed our blood in preventing the French from ill-treating them. On the arrival of the King's Fleet I find plenty of good will towards us, with every hatred towards the French; but no assistance for us – no hostility to the French. On the contrary, the French Minister is allowed to send off Vessels to inform the Fleet of my arrival, force, and destination, that instead of my surprising them, they may be prepared for resistance. But this being past, I shall endeavour briefly to state what in my opinion is now best to be done, and what Naples ought to do, if it is earnestly wished to save Sicily. I shall suppose the French not advanced since the last accounts, but still on Gozo and Comino, the Fleet anchored between them. By the communication from Naples, they will be formed in the strongest position, with Batteries and Gun-boats to flank them. We shall doubtless injure them, but our loss must be great; and I do not expect to force them from the anchorage, without Fire-ships, Bomb-vessels, and Gun-boats when one hour would either destroy or drive them out. If our Fleet is crippled, the blockade ends; if not, it will be continued, by attention, and sending two Ships at a time to Sicily to get refreshments, for the summer, at least; but whenever this Fleet may be drawn away, and the Ministry find what has passed at Naples – *no co-operation*, although we are come to their assistance – who can say that the Fleet will be kept in these seas? I have said and repeat it, *Malta is the direct road to Sicily*. It has been, and may be yet in the King of Naples' power, by giving me help of every kind, directly to destroy this Armament, and force the Army to unconditional submission. Naples must soon find us masts, yards, stores, ammunition, &c., &c., Will not this be a declaration of War against the French? Therefore why delay sending help, if it is only six Gunboats at a time. But not a moment must be lost – it can never be regained. I recollect General Acton, in his letter to you calling for our help, says, "Will the King and Ministry wish to see these fine Countries in the hands of the French?" the answer is, No; and we have sent the means of preventing it. It may now be asked – will the Ministry of their Sicilian Majesties permit these fine Countries to fall into the hands of the French? This will assuredly happen if they do not co-operate with us. If I have wrote my mind too freely, I trust it will be excused. The importance of the subject called for my opinion. I have given it like an honest man, and shall wish to stand or fall with it.

I am, dear Sir, with the highest respect, &c.

HORATIO NELSON[23]

To George Baldwin, Consul at Alexandria

Vanguard, at Sea, *26th June, 1798*

Sir,

The French having possessed themselves of Malta, on Friday, the 15th of this month, the next day, the whole Fleet, consisting of sixteen Sail of the Line, Frigates, Bomb-vessels, &c. and near three hundred Transports, left the Island. I only heard this unpleasant news on the 22nd, off Cape Passaro. As Sicily was not their object, and the wind blew fresh from the westward, from the time they sailed, it was clear that their destination was to the eastward; and I think their object is, to possess themselves of some Port in Egypt, and to fix themselves at the head of the Red Sea, in order to get a formidable Army into India; and, in concert with Tippoo Saib, to drive us, if possible, from India. But I have reason to believe, from not seeing a Vessel, that they have heard of my coming up the Mediterranean, and are got safe into Corfu. But still I am most exceedingly anxious to know from you if any reports or preparations have been made in Egypt for them; or any Vessels prepared in the Red Sea, to carry them to India, where, from the prevailing winds at this season, they would soon arrive; or any other information you would be good enough to give me, I shall hold myself much obliged.

I am, Sir, &c.
HORATIO NELSON[24]

To Sir William Hamilton   *Vanguard*, Syracuse,

July 20th, 1798

My dear Sir,

It is an old saying, "the Devil's children have the Devil's luck." I cannot find, or to this moment learn, beyond vague conjecture where the French Fleet are gone to. All my ill fortune, hitherto, has proceeded from want of Frigates. Off Cape Passaro, on the 22nd of June, at daylight, I saw two Frigates, which were supposed to be French, and it has been said since that a Line of Battle Ship was to leeward of them, with the riches of Malta on board, but it was the destruction of the Enemy, not riches for myself, that I was seeking. These would have fallen to me if I had had Frigates, but except the Ship of the Line, I regard not all the riches in this world. From every information off Malta I believed they were gone to Egypt. Therefore, on the 28th, I was communicating with Alexandria in Egypt, where I found the Turks preparing to resist them, but know nothing beyond report. From thence I stretched over the Coast of Caramania, where not meeting a Vessel that could give me information, I became distressed for the Kingdom of the Two Sicilies, and having gone a round of 600 leagues at this season of the year (with a single Ship) with an expedition incredible, here I am as ignorant of the situation of the Enemy as I was twenty-seven days ago. I sincerely hope, that the Dispatches which I understand are at Cape Passaro, will give me full information. I shall be able for nine or ten weeks longer to keep the Fleet on active service, when we shall want provisions and stores. I send a paper on that subject herewith. Mr Littledale is, I suppose, sent up by the Admiral to victual us, and I hope he will do it cheaper than any other person; but if I find out that he charges more than the fair price, and has not the provisions of the very best quality, I will not take them; for, as no Fleet has more fag than this, nothing but the best food and greatest attention can keep them healthy. At this moment, we have not one sick man in the Fleet. In about six days I shall sail from hence, and if I hear nothing more from the French, I shall go to the Archipelago where if they are gone towards Constantinople I shall hear of them. I shall go to Cyprus, and if they are gone to Alexandretta, or any other part of Syria or Egypt, I shall get information. You will, I am sure, and so will our Country, easily conceive what has passed in my anxious mind, but I have this comfort, that I have no fault to accuse myself of. This bears me up, and this only. I send you a Paper, in which a letter is fixed for different places, which I may leave at any place, and except those who have the key, none can tell where I am gone to.

July 21st: The Messenger has returned from Cape Passaro, and says, that your letters for me are returned to Naples. What a situation am I placed in! As yet, I can learn nothing of the Enemy; therefore I have no conjecture but that they are gone to Syria, and at Cyprus I hope to hear of them. If they were gone westward, I reply that every place in Sicily would have information for us, for it is news too important to leave me one moment in doubt about. I have no Frigate, nor a sign of one. The masts, yards, &c., for the *Vanguard* will, I hope, be prepared directly; for should the French be so strongly secured in Port that I cannot get at them, I shall immediately shift my Flag into some other Ship, and send the *Vanguard* to Naples to be refitted; for hardly any other person but myself would have continued on service so long in such a wretched state. I want to send a great number of Papers to Lord St Vincent, but I dare not trust any person here to carry them even to Naples. Pray send a copy of my letter to Lord Spencer. He must be very anxious to hear of this Fleet. I have taken the liberty to trouble your Excellency with a letter for Lady Nelson: Pray forward it for me, and

believe me, with the greatest respect, your most obedient
Servant,

HORATIO NELSON[25]

To Lady Nelson   Syracuse, *July 20th, 1798*
I have not been able to find the French Fleet, to my great
mortification, or the event I can scarcely doubt. We have been
off Malta, to Alexandria in Egypt, Syria, into Asia, and are
returned here without success: however, no person will say that
it has been for want of activity. I yet live in hopes of meeting
these fellows; but it would have been my delight to have tried
Buonaparte on a wind, for he commands the Fleet, as well as the
Army. Glory is my object, and that alone. God Almighty bless
you.

HORATIO NELSON[26]

To the Commanders of any of His Majesty's Ships
Vanguard, Syracuse, *22nd July, 1798*
Sir,
Resting with the greatest confidence that had the French
Fleet proceeded to the westward from Malta, that his Majesty's
Minister at Naples would have taken care to have lodged
information for me in every Port in Sicily, knowing I was gone
to the eastward, I now acquaint you that I shall steer direct for
the Island of Cyprus, and hope in Syria to find the French Fleet.
I am, &c.

HORATIO NELSON

Having received some vague information of the Enemy, I
shall steer to the north of Candia, and probably send a Ship to
Milo, and if the Enemy are not in those seas, I shall pass on for
Cyprus, Syria, and Egypt.[27]

To the Right Hon. Sir William Hamilton, K.B.
Vanguard, Syracuse, *July 22, 1708*
My dear Sir,
I have had so much said about the King of Naples' orders
only to admit three or four of the Ships of our Fleet into his
Ports, that I am astonished. I understood that private orders, at

least, would have been given for our free admission. If we are to
be refused supplies, pray send me by many Vessels an account,
that I may in good time take the King's Fleet to Gibraltar. Our
treatment is scandalous for a great Nation to put up with, and
the King's Flag is insulted at every Friendly Port we look at. I
am, with the greatest respect, &c.,

HORATIO NELSON[28]

You will observe that I feel as a Public man, and write as
such. I have no complaint to make of private attention, quite
the contrary. Every body of persons have been on board to offer
me civilities.

To Sir William and Lady Hamilton   *22nd July, 1708*

My dear Friends,
    Thanks to your exertions, we have victualled and watered:
and surely watering at the Fountain of Arethusa, we must have
victory. We shall sail with the first breeze, and be assured I will
return either crowned with laurel, or covered with cypress.[29]

To the Right Honourable Sir William Hamilton, K.B.

Vanguard, Syracuse, *23rd July, 1708*

My dear Sir,
    The Fleet is unmoored, and the moment the wind comes off
the land, shall go out of this delightful harbour, where our
present wants have been most amply supplied, and where every
attention has been paid to us; but I have been tormented by no
private orders being given to the Governor for our admission. I
have only to hope that I shall still find the French Fleet, and be
able to get at them: the event then will be in the hands of
Providence, of whose goodness none can doubt. I beg my best
respects to Lady Hamilton, and believe me ever your faithful

HORATIO NELSON.

No Frigates! – to which has been, and may again, be attributed the loss of the French Fleet.[30]

At 4.00 p.m. on the afternoon of 1 August 1798, the British finally
found their prey – the French fleet, consisting of thirteen ships of the

line and four frigates, moored in line of battle in Aboukir Bay, just
north-east of Alexandria. Although Nelson had no reliable charts, he
decided to attack immediately, before Admiral Brueys could slip away
in the approaching darkness. Arising from his table, Nelson is reputed
to have told the officers gathered to share a meal with him, "Before this
time tomorrow I shall have gained a peerage or Westminster Abbey".

THE BATTLE OF THE NILE: THE MIDSHIPMAN'S VIEW, 1 August 1798

Midshipman the Hon. George Elliot, HMS Goliath[31]

The *Goliath*, captained by Foley (to whom some attribute the daring
plan to slip through the shallow shore side of the French line), led the
British squadron into battle.

I, as signal-midshipman, was sweeping round the horizon
ahead with my glass from the royal-yard, when I discovered
the French fleet at anchor in Aboukir Bay. The *Zealous* was so
close to us that, had I hailed the deck, they must have heard me.
I therefore slid down by the backstay and reported what I had
seen. We instantly made the signal, but the under-toggle of the
upper flag at the main came off, breaking the stop, and the
lower flag came down. The compass-signal, however, was clear
at the peak; but before we could recover our flag, *Zealous* made
the signal for the enemy's fleet; whether from seeing our
compass-signal or not I never heard. But we thus lost the little
credit of first signalling the enemy, which, as signal-midshipman, rather affected me. . . .

When we were nearly within gunshot, standing as A.D.C.
close to Captain Foley, I heard him say to the Master that he
wished he could get inside the leading ship of the enemy's line
(the *Guerrier*). I immediately looked for the buoy or her
anchor, and saw it apparently at the usual distance of a
cable's length – i.e. 200 yards – which I reported. They both
looked at it, and agreed there was room to pass between the
ship and her anchor (the danger was the ship being close up to
the edge of the shoal), and it was decided to do it. The Master
then had orders to go forward and drop the anchor the
moment it was a ship's breadth inside the French ship, so

that we should not actually swing on board of her. All this was exactly executed.

I also heard Foley say he should not be surprised to find the Frenchman unprepared for action on the inner side; and as we passed her bow I saw he was right. Her lower-deck guns were not run out, and there was lumber, such as bags and boxes, on the upper-deck ports, which I reported with no small pleasure. We first fired a broadside into the bow. Not a shot could miss at the distance. The *Zealous* did the same, and in less than a quarter of an hour this ship was a perfect wreck, without a mast, or a broadside gun to fire.

The French captains were all on board their Admiral's ship, and did not expect us to come in that night. They had sent for their boats to return from the shore where they were procuring water. The senior officer of the van division, seeing us stand on under all sail, got anxious, and sent his own boat to hasten off the boats of his division without waiting to fill with water. She had not got back when we were getting very close, and as his own launch was passing the flag-ship, half-laden with water, he got into her, but she pulled up slowly against the fresh sea-breeze and did not reach his ship till we had passed her. I saw him waving his hat, and evidently calling to his ship, when still at a considerable distance. An officer was leaning against his ensign staff listening. At last this officer ran forward to the poop and down to the lower deck. We knew what was coming, and off went their whole broadside, but just too late to hit us, and passed harmlessly between us and *Zealous*, and before he could give a second broadside *Zealous* was past his range. We therefore both got up to our places without injury of any sort, and were able to take up the exact positions we wished, neither ship returning a single shot . . . *Zealous* exactly followed *Goliath*'s example, but the enemy being occupied, she furled her sails, and anchoring a little more to windward, veered into the place just left by the *Goliath*. From this moment the *Guerrier* never fired a shot, except from her stern guns; she had been practically destroyed in five minutes by her two opponents. As the *Goliath* passed her quarter the *Guerrier*'s foremast fell by the deck, and five minutes after the main and mizen fell, and also the main of the *Conquérant* . . . As the *Theseus* passed the *Goliath* in getting to her station, she gave her three tremendous cheers. Returned by the *Goliath*'s crew and an attempt made by the French to copy, but the effort was ridiculous, and caused shouts of laughter in our ships, loud enough to be heard by both sides. The French admitted that the enthusiastic cheers were very disheartening to them.

THE BATTLE OF THE NILE: THE CAPTAIN'S VIEW, 1 August 1798

Captain Sir Edward Berry, HMS Vanguard[32]

The *Vanguard* was Nelson's flagship.

The enemy appeared to be moored in a strong and compact Line of Battle, close in with the shore, their line describing an obtuse angle in its form, flanked by numerous Gun-boats, four Frigates, and a battery of guns and mortars, on an Island in their Van. This situation of the enemy seemed to secure to them the most decided advantages, as they had nothing to attend to but their artillery, in their superior skill in the use of which the French so much pride themselves, and to which indeed their splendid series of land victories are in a great measure to be imputed.

The position of the enemy presented the most formidable obstacles; but the Admiral viewed these with the eye of a seaman determined on attack, and it instantly struck his eager and penetrating mind, that where there was room for an enemy's ship to swing, there was room for one of ours to anchor. No further signal was necessary than those which had already been made. The Admiral's designs were as fully known to his whole squadron, as was his determination to conquer or perish in the attempt. The *Goliath* and *Zealous* had the honour to lead inside, and to receive the first fire from the van ships of the enemy . . . These two ships, with the *Orion*, *Audacious* and *Theseus*, took their stations inside of the enemy's line, and were immediately in close action. The *Vanguard* anchored the first on the outer side of the enemy, and was opposed within half pistol-shot to *le Spartiate*, the third in the enemy's line. In standing in, our leading ships were unavoidably obliged to receive into their

bows the whole fire of the broadsides of the French line; until
they could take their respective stations . . . At this time the
necessary number of our men were employed aloft in furling
sails, and on deck, in hauling the braces, etc., preparatory to
our casting anchor. As soon as this took place, a most animated
fire was opened from the *Vanguard*, which ship covered the
approach of those in the rear, which were following in a close
line. The *Minotaur, Defence, Bellerophon, Majestic, Swiftsure*, and
Alexander, came up in succession, and passing within hail of the
Vanguard, took their respective stations opposed to the enemy's
line . . . Captain Thompson, of the *Leander*, of 50 guns, . . .
advanced towards the enemy's line on the outside, and most
judiciously dropped his anchor athwart hause of *le Franklin*,
raking her with great success, the shot from the *Leander*'s
broadside which passed that ship all striking *l'Orient*, the
flag-ship of the French Commander-in-Chief.

The action commenced at sun-set which was at thirty-one
minutes past six p.m., with an ardour and vigour, which it is
impossible to describe. At about seven o'clock total darkness
had come on, but the whole hemisphere was, with intervals,
illuminated by the fire of the hostile fleets. Our ships, when
darkness came on, had all hoisted their distinguishing lights,
by a signal from the Admiral. The van ship of the enemy, *le
Guerrier*, was dismasted in less than twelve minutes, and, in ten
minutes after, the second ship, *Le Conquérant*, and the third, *le
Spartiate*, very nearly at the same moment were almost dismasted. *L'Aquilon* and *le Souverain Peuple*, the fourth and fifth
ships of the enemy's line, were taken possession of by the
British at half-past eight in the evening. Captain Berry, at that
hour, sent Lieutenant Galwey, of the *Vanguard*, with a party of
marines, to take possession of *le Spartiate*, and that officer
returned by the boat the French captain's sword, which
Captain Berry immediately delivered to the Admiral, who
was then below, in consequence of the severe wound which he
had received in the head during the heat of the attack. At this
time it appeared that victory had already declared itself in our
favour, for although *l'Orient, l'Heureux*, and *Tonnant* were not
taken possession of, they were considered as completely in our
power, which pleasing intelligence Captain Berry had likewise

the satisfaction of communicating in person to the Admiral. At ten minutes after nine, a fire was observed on board *l'Orient*, the French admiral's ship, which seemed to proceed from the after part of the cabin, and which increased with great rapidity, presently involving the whole of the after part of the ship in flames. This circumstance Captain Berry immediately communicated to the Admiral, who, though suffering severely from his wound, came up on deck, where the first consideration that struck his mind was concern for the danger of so many lives, to save as many as possible of whom he ordered Captain Berry to make every practicable exertion. A boat, the only one that could swim, was instantly despatched from the *Vanguard*, and other ships that were in a condition to do so immediately followed the example; by which means, from the best possible information the lives of about seventy Frenchmen were saved. The light thrown by the fire of *l'Orient* upon the surrounding objects, enabled us to perceive with more certainty the situation of the two fleets, the colours of both being clearly distinguishable. The cannonading was partially kept up to leeward of the centre till about ten o'clock, when *l'Orient* blew up with a most tremendous explosion. An awful pause and death-like silence for about three minutes ensued, when the wreck of the masts, yards etc. which had been carried to a vast height, fell down into the water, and on board the surrounding ships. A port fire from *l'Orient* fell into the main royal of the *Alexander*, the fire occasioned by which was, however, extinguished in about two minutes, by the active exertions of Captain Ball.

After this awful scene, the firing was recommenced with the ships to leeward of the centre, till twenty minutes past ten, when there was a total cessation of firing for about ten minutes, after which it was revived till about three in the morning when it again ceased . . . The whole of the 2nd was employed in securing the French ships that had struck . . . The Admiral, knowing that the wounded of his own ships had been well taken care of, bent his first attention to those of the enemy. He established a truce with the Commandant of Aboukir, and through him made a communication to the Commandant of Alexandria, that it was his intention to allow all the wounded Frenchmen to be taken ashore to proper hospitals.

THE BATTLE OF THE NILE: GUNNER JOHN NICHOL IN ACTION, 1 August 1798

John Nichol[33]

Nichol was one of *Goliath*'s gun crew.

The sun was just setting as we went into the bay, and a red and fiery sun it was. I would, if I had had my choice, have been on deck; there I would have seen what was passing, and the time would not have hung so heavy; but every man does his duty with spirit, whether his station be in the slaughter-house or in the magazine. (The seamen call the lower deck, near the mainmast, "the slaughter-house", as it is amidships, and the enemy aim their fire principally at the body of the ship.) My station was in the powder-magazine with the gunner. As we entered the bay we stripped to our trousers, opened our ports, cleared, and every ship we passed gave them a broadside and three cheers. Any information we got was from the boys and women who carried the powder. They behaved as well as the men, and got a present for their bravery from the Grand Signior. When the French Admiral's ship blew up, the *Goliath* got such a shake we thought the after-part of her had blown up until the boys told us what it was. They brought us every now and then the cheering news of another French ship having struck, and we answered the cheers on deck with heartfelt joy. In the heat of the action, a shot came right into the magazine, but did no harm, as the carpenters plugged it up, and stopped the water that was rushing in. I was much indebted to the gunner's wife, who gave her husband and me a drink of wine every now and then, which lessened our fatigue much. There were some of the women wounded, and one woman belonging to Leith died of her wounds, and was buried on a small island in the bay. One woman bore a son in the heat of the action; she belonged to Edinburgh.

When we ceased firing, I went on deck to view the state of the fleets, and an awful sight it was. The whole bay was covered with dead bodies, mangled, wounded, and scorched, not a bit of clothes on them except their trousers. There were a number of French, belonging to the French Admiral's ship, the *l'Orient*, who had swam to the *Goliath*, and were cowering under her forecastle. Poor fellows! They were brought on board, and Captain Foley ordered them down to the steward's room, to get provisions and clothing. One thing I observed in these Frenchmen quite different from anything I had before observed. In the American War, when we took a French ship, the *Duc de Chartres*, the prisoners were as merry as if they had taken us, only saying, "Fortune de guerre – you take me today, I take you tomorrow". Those we now had on board were thankful for our kindness, but were sullen and downcast as if each had lost a ship of his own.

. . . The only incidents I heard of are two. One lad who was stationed by a salt-box, on which he sat to give out cartridges, and keep the lid close – it is a trying berth – when asked for a cartridge, he gave none, yet he sat upright; his eyes were open. One of the men gave him a push; he fell all his length on the deck. There was not a blemish on his body, yet he was quite dead, and was thrown overboard. The other, a lad who had the match in his hand to fire his gun. In the act of applying it, a shot took off his arm; it hung by a small piece of skin. The match fell to the deck. He looked to his arm, and seeing what had happened, seized the match in his left hand, and fired off the gun before he went to the cockpit to have it dressed. They were in our mess, or I might never have heard of it. Two of the mess were killed, and I knew not of it until the day after. Thus terminated the glorious first of August, the busiest night in my life.

"SO DISPROPORTIONED A STRUGGLE": A FRENCH OFFICER AT THE BATTLE OF THE NILE, 1 August 1798

Rear-Admiral Blanquet[34]

The 1st of August, wind N.N.W., light breezes and fine weather. The second division of the Fleet sent a party of men on shore, to dig wells. Every Ship in the Fleet sent twenty-five men to

protect the workmen from the continual attacks of the Bedouins
and vagabonds of the Country.

At two o'clock in the afternoon, the *Heureux* made the Signal
for 12 Sail, W.N.W., which we could easily distinguish from
the mast-head to be Ships of War. The signal was then made
for all the boats, workmen, and guards to repair on board of
their respective Ships, which was only obeyed by a small
number. At 3 o'clock, the Admiral not having any doubt
but the Ships in sight were the Enemy, he ordered the
hammocks to be stowed for Action, and directed the *Alert*
and *Railleur Brig*, Sloops of War, to reconnoitre the Enemy,
which we soon perceived were steering for Bequier Bay under a
crowd of canvas, but without observing any order of sailing. At
four o'clock, saw over the Fort of Aboukir, two Ships, apparently working to join the Squadron: without doubt they had
been sent to look into the Ports at Alexandria. We likewise saw
a Brig with the 12 Ships. In two hours there were 14 Ships of
the Line in sight, and a Brig.

The English Fleet was soon off the Island of Bequier. The
Brig *Alert* then began to put the Admiral's orders into execution viz., to stand toward the Enemy until nearly within gun-
shot, and then to manœuvre and endeavour to draw them
toward the outer shoal lying off that Island. But the English
Admiral, without doubt, had experienced Pilots on board, as
he did not pay any attention to the Brig's track, but allowed
her to go away: he hauled well round all the dangers. At four
o'clock, a small Country-boat dispatched from Alexandria to
Rosetta, voluntarily bore down to the English Brig, which took
possession of her, notwithstanding the repeated efforts of the
Alert to prevent it, by firing a great many shot at the Boat. At
five o'clock, the Enemy came to the wind in succession. This
manœuvre convinced us that they intended attacking us that
evening. The Admiral got the top-gallant-yards across, but
soon after made the signal that he intended engaging the
Enemy at anchor – convinced, without doubt, that he had not
seamen enough to engage under sail; for he wanted at least 200
good seamen for each Ship. After this signal, each Ship ought
to have sent a stream-cable to the Ship astern of her, and to
have made a hawser fast to the cable about twenty fathoms in

the water, and passed the opposite side to that intended as a spring. This was not generally executed. Orders were then given to let go another bower-anchor, and the broadsides of the Ships were brought to bear upon the Enemy. Having the Ships' heads S.E. from the Island of Bequier, forming a Line about 1300 fathoms N.W. and S.E., distant from each other 80 fathoms, each with an anchor out, in the S.S.E. At a quarter past five, one of the Enemy's Ships that was steering to get to windward of the headmost of her Line, ran on the reef, E.N.E. of the Island. She had immediate assistance from the Brig, and got afloat in the morning. The Battery on the Island opened a fire on the Enemy, and the shells fell ahead of the second Ship in the Line. At half-past five, the headmost Ships of our Line, being within gun-shot of the English, the Admiral made the signal to engage, which was not obeyed until the Enemy were within pistol-shot and just doubling us. The Action then became very warm. The *Conquerant* began the fire then *le Guerrier*, *le Spartiate*, *l'Aquilon*, *le Peuple Souverain*, and *le Franklin*. At 6 o'clock, the *Sérieuse* Frigate and the *Hercule* bomb cut their cables, and got under weigh, to avoid the Enemy's fire. They got on shore. The *Sérieuse* caught fire, and had part of her mast burnt. The *Artemise* was obliged to get under weigh and likewise got on shore. These two Frigates sent their Ships' companies on board of the different Line-of-Battle Ships. The Sloops of War, two Bombs, and several Transports that were with the Fleet, were more successful, as they got under weigh, and reached the anchorage under the protection of the Fort of Aboukir.

All the Van were attacked on both sides by the Enemy, who ranged close along our Line. They had each an anchor out astern which facilitated their motions, and enabled them to place themselves in the most advantageous position. At a quarter past 6, the *Franklin* opened her fire upon the Enemy from the starboard side: at three-quarters past 6, she was engaged on both sides. The *l'Orient* at the same time began firing her starboard guns, and at 7 o'clock, the *Tonnant* opened her fire. All the Ships, from the *Guerrier* to the *Tonnant*, were now engaged against a superior force: this only redoubled the ardour of the French who kept up a very heavy and regular fire. At 8 o'clock at night, the Ship which was engaging *l'Orient*, on the starboard quarter, notwithstanding her advantageous position, was dismasted and so roughly treated, that she cut her cables, and drove rather far from the Line. This event gave the *Franklin* hopes that *l'Orient* would now be able to assist her by attacking one of the Ships opposed to her; but, at this very moment, the two Ships that had been perceived astern of the Fleet, and were quite fresh, steered right for the centre. One of them anchored on *l'Orient*'s starboard bow, and the other cut the Line, astern of the *l'Orient*, and anchored on her larboard quarter. The Action in this part then became extremely warm. Admiral de Brueys, who at this time had been slightly wounded, in the head and arm, very soon received a shot in the belly, which almost cut him in two. He desired not to be carried below, but to be left to die upon deck. He only lived a quarter of an hour. Rear Admiral Blanquet, [who] as well as his Aide-de-camp, were unacquainted with this melancholy event, (until the Action was nearly over,) received a severe wound in the face which knocked him down. He was carried off the deck, senseless. At a quarter past eight, the *Peuple Souverain* drove to leeward of the Line, and anchored a cable's length abreast of *l'Orient*. It was not known what unfortunate event occasioned it. The vacant space she made placed the *Franklin* in a most unfortunate position, and it became very critical, by the manœuvre of one of the Enemy's fresh Ships, which had been to the assistance of the Ship on shore. She anchored athwart the *Franklin*'s bows, and commenced a very heavy raking fire. Notwithstanding the dreadful situation of the Ships in the centre, they continually kept up a very heavy fire. At half-past 8 o'clock, the Action was general, from the *Guerrier* to the *Mercure*, and the two Fleets engaged.

The death of Admiral de Brueys, and the severe wounds of Rear-Admiral Blanquet, must have deeply affected the people who fought under them, but it added to their ardour for revenge, and the Action continued on both sides with great obstinacy. At 9 o'clock the Ships in the Van slackened their fire, and soon after totally ceased; and, with infinite sorrow, we supposed that they had surrendered. They were dismasted very soon after the Action began, and so much damaged, that it is to be presumed that they could not hold out any longer against an Enemy so superior by her advantageous position, in placing several Ships against one. At a quarter past 9 o'clock, *l'Orient* caught fire in the cabin; it soon afterwards broke out upon the poop. Every effort was made to extinguish it, but without effect, and very soon it was so considerable, that there were not any hopes of saving the Ship.

At half-past 9, Citizen Gillet, Capitaine de Pavillon of the *Franklin*, was very severely wounded, and carried off the deck. At three-quarters past 9, the arm-chest, filled with musket-cartridges, blew up, and set fire to several places on the poop and quarter-deck, but was fortunately extinguished. Her situation, however, was still very desperate; surrounded by Enemies, and only 80 fathoms to wind-ward of *l'Orient*, (entirely on fire,) there could not be any other expectation than falling a prey either to the Enemy or the flames. At 10 o'clock, the main and mizen-masts fell, and all the guns on the main deck were dismounted. At a quarter past 10, the *Tonnant* cut her cable, to avoid the fire from *l'Orient*. The English Ship that was on *l'Orient*'s larboard quarter, so soon as she had done firing at her, brought her broadside upon the *Tonnant*'s bow, and kept up a very heavy raking fire. The *Heureux* and *Mercure* conceived that they ought likewise to cut their cables. This manœuvre created so much confusion among the Rear Ships, that they fired into each other, and did considerable damage.

The *Tonnant* anchored ahead of the *Guillaume Tell*, *Généreux*, and *Timoleon*; the other two Ships got on shore. The Ship that had engaged the *Tonnant* on her bow, cut her cables; all her rigging and sails were cut to pieces, and she drove down, and anchored astern of the English Ship that had been engaging the *Heureux* and *Mercure*, before they changed their position. Those of the *Etat Major* and Ship's company of *l'Orient* who had escaped death, convinced of the impossibility of extinguishing the fire, (which had got down to the middle-gun deck,) endeavoured to save themselves. Rear-Admiral Ganteaume saved himself in a boat, and went on board of the Salamine, and from thence to Aboukir and Alexandria. The Adjutant-General Motard, although badly wounded, swam to the Ship nearest *l'Orient*, which proved to be English. Commodore Casabianca and his son, only ten years old, who during the Action gave proofs of bravery and intelligence far above his age, were not so fortunate. They were in the water, upon the wreck of *l'Orient*'s mast, (not being able to swim,) seeking each other, until three-quarters past 10, when the Ship blew up, and put an end to their hopes and fears. The explosion was dreadful, and spread the fire all round to a considerable distance. The Franklin's decks were with red-hot pincers, pieces of timber, and rope, on fire. She was on fire the fourth time, but luckily got it under. Immediately after the tremendous explosion, the Action ceased everywhere, and was succeeded by the most profound silence. The sky was obscured by thick clouds of black smoke, which seemed to threaten the destruction of the two Fleets. It was a quarter of an hour before the Ships' crews recovered from the kind of stupor they were thrown into. Towards 11 o'clock, the *Franklin*, anxious to preserve the trust confided to her, recommenced the Action with a few of her lower-deck guns; all the rest were dismounted, two-thirds of her Ship's company being killed or wounded, and those who remained much fatigued. She was surrounded by Enemy's Ships, some of which were within pistol-shot, and who mowed down the men every broadside. At half-past 11 o'clock, having only three lower-deck guns that could defend the honour of the Flag, it became necessary to put an end to so disproportioned a struggle; and Citizen Martinet, Captain of a Frigate, ordered the Colours to be struck.

The Action in the Rear of the Fleet was very trifling, until three-quarters past 11 o'clock, when it became very warm. Three of the Enemy's Ships were engaging them, and two were very near. The *Tonnant*, already badly treated, [which] was the nearest to the Ships engaged, returned a very brisk fire. About 3 o'clock in the morning, she was dismasted, and obliged to cut her cable a second time, and not having any more anchors left, she drove on shore. The *Guillaume Tell, le Généreux*, and *le Timoleon*, shifted their berth, and anchored further down, out of gun-shot. These Vessels were not much damaged. At half-past 3 o'clock the Action ceased throughout the Line. Early in the morning, the Frigate, *la Justice*, got under weigh, and made small tacks to keep near the *Guillaume Tell*, and at nine o'clock anchored, an English Ship having got under weigh, and making short tacks, to prevent her getting away. At 6 o'clock, two English Ships joined those which had been engaging the Rear, and began firing on the *Heureux* and *Mercure*, which were aground. The former soon struck, and the latter followed her example, as they could not bring their broadsides to bear upon the Enemy. At a quarter past seven, the Ship's crew of the *Artemise* Frigate quitted her, and set her on fire. At 8 o'clock she blew up. The Enemy, without doubt, had received great damage in their masts and yards, as they did not get under weigh to attack the remains of the French Fleet. The French flag was flying on board of four Ships of the Line and two Frigates. This Division made the most of their time, and at three-quarters past 11, *le Guillaume Tell*, *le Généreux*, *la Diane*, and *la Justice*, were under weigh, and formed in Line of Battle. The English Ship that was under sail, stood towards her Fleet, fearing that she might be cut off; two other Enemy's Ships were immediately under weigh to assist her. At noon, the *Timoleon*, which probably was not in a state to put to sea, steered right for the shore, under her foresail, and as soon as she struck the ground, her foremast fell. The French Division joined the Enemy's Ships, which ranged along their Line, on opposite tacks, within pistol-shot, and received their broadsides, which she returned. They then each continued their route. The Division was in sight at Sunset.

Nothing remarkable passed during the night of the 2nd.

The 3rd of August. In the morning the French colours were flying in the *Tonnant* and *Timoleon*. The English Admiral sent a Cartel to the former, to know if she had struck, and upon being answered in the negative, he directed two Ships to go against her. When they got within gun-shot of her, she struck, it being impossible to defend her any longer. The *Timoleon* was aground, too near in for any Ship to approach her. In the night of the 2nd instant, they sent the greatest part of their Ship's company on shore, and at noon the next day they quitted her, and set her on fire.

Thus ends the Journal of the 1st, 2nd, and 3rd days of

August, which will ever be remembered with the deepest sorrow by those Frenchmen who possess good hearts, and by all those true Republicans who have survived this melancholy disaster.

Despite being wounded, Nelson started composing his victory dispatches – he always had his eye on publicity, but also on due praise to his men – even as the battle still sounded around him.

"ALMIGHTY GOD HAS BLESSED HIS MAJESTY'S ARMS IN THE LATE BATTLE": THE BRITISH COMMANDER REPORTS ON THE BATTLE OF THE NILE AND ITS AFTERMATH, 2 August–16 September 1798

Admiral Sir Horatio Nelson

To the Respective Captains of the Squadron

Vanguard, off the Mouth of the Nile,
2nd August, 1798

Almighty God having blessed His Majesty's Arms with Victory, the Admiral intends returning Public Thanksgiving for the same at two o'clock this day; and he recommends every Ship doing the same as soon as convenient.

HORATIO NELSON[35]

To the Captains of the Ships of the Squadron

Vanguard, off the Mouth of the Nile,
2nd day of August, 1798

The Admiral most heartily congratulates the Captains, Officers, Seamen, and Marines of the Squadron he has the honour to command, on the event of the late Action; and he desires they will accept his most sincere and cordial Thanks for their very gallant behaviour in this glorious Battle. It must strike forcibly every British Seaman, how superior their conduct is, when in discipline and good order, to the riotous behaviour of the lawless Frenchmen.

The Squadron may be assured the Admiral will not fail, with his Dispatches, to represent their truly meritorious conduct in the strongest terms to the Commander-in-Chief.

HORATIO NELSON[36]

On 3 August, the captains of the Squadron met on board the *Orion*, the ship of Sir James Saumarez, the second in command, and wrote the following message to their leader:

> The Captains of the Squadron under the Orders of Rear-Admiral Sir Horatio Nelson, K.B., desirous of testifying the high sense they entertain of his prompt decision and intrepid conduct in the Attack of the French Fleet, in Bequier Road, off the Nile, the 1st of August, 1798, request his acceptance of a Sword; and, as a further proof of their esteem and regard, hope that he will permit his Portrait to be taken, and hung up in the Room belonging to the Egyptian Club, now established in commemoration of that glorious day.
>
> Dated on board of His Majesty's Ship *Orion*, this 3rd of August, 1798

Jas. Saumarez	D. Gould
T. Troubridge	Th. Foley
H.D. Darby	R. Willett Miller
Tho. Louis	Ben. Hallowell
John Peyton	E. Barry
Alex. John Ball	T.M. Hardy
Sam. Hood	

To the Captains of His Majesty's Ships off the Nile

Vanguard, August 3rd, 1798

Gentlemen,

I feel most sensibly the very distinguished honour you have conferred upon me by your Address of this day. My prompt decision was the natural consequence of having such Captains under my command, and I thank God I can say, that in the Battle the conduct of every Officer was equal. I accept, as a particular mark of your esteem, the Sword you have done me the honour to offer, and will direct my Picture to be painted the first opportunity, for the purpose you mention.

I have the honour to be, Gentlemen,

With the highest respect, your most obliged,

HORATIO NELSON[37]

To Lord St Vincent

Vanguard, off the Mouth of the Nile,
3rd August, 1798

My Lord,

Almighty God has blessed his Majesty's Arms in the late Battle, by a great Victory over the Fleet of the Enemy, who I attacked at sunset on the 1st of August, off the Mouth of the Nile. The Enemy were moored in a strong Line of Battle for defending the entrance of the Bay, (of Shoals,) flanked by numerous Gun-boats, four Frigates, and a Battery of Guns and Mortars on an Island in their Van; but nothing could withstand the Squadron your Lordship did me the honour to place under my command. Their high state of discipline is well known to you, and with the judgment of the Captains, together with their valour, and that of the Officers and Men of every description, it was absolutely irresistible. Could anything from my pen add to the character of the Captains, I would write it with pleasure, but that is impossible.

I have to regret the loss of Captain Westcott of the *Majestic*, who was killed early in the Action; but the Ship was continued to be so well fought by her First Lieutenant, Mr Cuthbert, that I have given him an order to command her till your Lordship's pleasure is known.

The Ships of the Enemy, all but their two rear Ships, are nearly dismasted: and those two, with two Frigates, I am sorry to say, made their escape; nor was it, I assure you, in my power to prevent them. Captain Hood most handsomely endeavoured to do it, but I had no Ship in a condition to support the *Zealous*, and I was obliged to call her in.

The support and assistance I have received from Captain Berry cannot be sufficiently expressed. I was wounded in the head, and obliged to be carried off the deck; but the service suffered no loss by that event; Captain Berry was fully equal to the important service then going on, and to him I must beg leave to refer you for every information relative to this Victory. He will present you with the Flag of the Second in Command, that of the Commander-in-Chief being burnt in *L'Orient*.

Herewith I transmit you Lists of the Killed and Wounded,

and the Lines of Battle of ourselves and the French. I have the honour to be, my Lord, your Lordship's most obedient Servant,

HORATIO NELSON[38]

To the Lord Mayor of London

Vanguard, Mouth of the Nile,
8th August, 1798

My Lord,

Having the honour of being a Freeman of the City of London, I take the liberty of sending to your Lordship, the Sword of the Commanding French Admiral, Monsieur Blanquet, who survived after the Battle of the first, off the Nile; and request, that the City of London will honour me by the acceptance of it, as a remembrance, that Britannia still rules the Waves, which, that She may for ever do, is the fervent prayer of your Lordship's most obedient Servant,

HORATIO NELSON[39]

To Earl Spencer, First Lord of the Admiralty

Mouth of the Nile, *9th August, 1798*

My Lord,

Was I to die this moment, "Want of Frigates" would be found stamped on my heart. No words of mine can express what I have, and not be left without Ships, for each Prize takes a Ship of the Line to man her, and attend to her wants. This you will believe, when I tell you that only two masts are standing, out of nine Sail of the Line. *L'Orient* certainly struck her colours, and did not fire a shot for a quarter of an hour before, unfortunately for us, she took fire; but although we suffer, our Country is equally benefited. She had on board near six hundred thousand pounds sterling; so says the Adjutant-General of the Fleet, who was saved out of her, and although he does not say she struck her colours, yet he allows that all resistance on her part was in vain. Admiral Brueys was killed early in the battle, and from the commencement of the fight, declared all was lost. They moored in a strong position in a Line of Battle, with Gun-boats, Bomb-Vessels, Frigates, and a gun and mortar Battery on an Island in their Van, but my band of friends was irresistible. The French Army is in possession of Alexandria, Aboukir, Rosetta,

Damietta, and Cairo; and Buonaparte writes that he is sending a detachment to take possession of Suez and Fayoum.

By the intercepted letters from the Army (for we took the Vessel with Buonaparte's courier) they are grievously disappointed, the Country between their Posts completely hostile. I have little doubt but that Army will be destroyed by plague, pestilence, and famine, and battle and murder, which that it may soon be, God grant. The Turks will soon send an Army into Syria, and as for the present, we block them up by sea, they must soon experience great distress. I hope to find, on my arrival at Naples, that the Emperor and many other Powers are at war with the French, for until they are reduced there can be no peace in this world. The Admiral having sent up Mr Littledale, the victualling of the Fleet does not rest with me.

7th September

I feel so much recovered, that it is probable I shall not go home at present. The Turks have seized all French Ships in the Levant, in consequence of the taking a Turkish sixty-gun Ship at Alexandria, and seizing all Turkish property. This was done on the 14th of August. I shall always receive pleasure in hearing from you, both as a public and private man; and believe me, dear Sir, &c.

HORATIO NELSON[40]

To Earl Spencer

Vanguard, 7th September, 1798

My Lord,

On the 15th August, I received Earl St Vincent's most secret Orders and Letters. As not a moment was to be lost, I determined to destroy the three Prizes (*Guerrier, Heureux,* and *Mercure,*) which had not sailed with Sir James Saumarez, and they were set on fire on the 18th. I rest assured that they will be paid for, and have held out that assurance to the Squadron; for if an Admiral is, after a victory, only to look after the captured ships, and not distressing the Enemy, very dearly indeed does the Nation pay for the Prizes, and I trust that £60,000 will be deemed a very moderate sum; and I am bold to say, when the services, time, and men, with the expense of fitting those three Ships for a voyage to England is valued, that Government will save nearly as much as they are valued at. I rejoice, in the present instance, that a particular regard for my own interest cannot be supposed to actuate me, for if the moderate sum of £60,000 is paid, my share can only be £625, while if it is not paid, I have defrauded the Commander-in-Chief and the other Classes, of the sums set off against them:

Commander-in-Chief	£3,750	0	0
Junior Admirals, each	625	0	0
Captains, each	1,000	0	0
Lieutenants' Class, each	75	0	0
Warrant Officers, each	50	0	0
Petty Officers, each	11	0	0
Seamen and Marines, each	2	4	1

Your Lordship will do me the justice to say, that pay for Prizes, in many instances, (it is not a new idea of mine,) would be not only an amazing saving to the State, without taking into calculation what the Nation loses by the attention of Admirals to the property of the Captors, an attention absolutely necessary as a recommence for the exertions of the Officers and men. An Admiral may be amply rewarded by his feelings and the approbation of his superiors, but what reward have the inferior Officers and men but the value of the Prizes? If an Admiral takes that from them, on any consideration, he cannot expect to be well supported. However, I trust, as in all other instances, if, to serve the State, any persons or bodies of men suffer losses, it is amply made up to them; and in this I rest confident my brave associates will not be disappointed. I have the honour to be, &c.

HORATIO NELSON[41]

DISPOSITION OF THE FLEET UNDER MY COMMAND

Vanguard, 13th September, 1798

Vanguard – Wants new masts and bowsprit, but shall defer getting them till I know the situation of [:]

Culloden – To be careened at Naples.

Alexander – When her masts are reduced and secured, to be sent down the Mediterranean, unless particularly wanted for a month or six weeks.

Goliath – Ordered to be sent from Alexandria the moment the *Lion* arrives. Main-mast bad.

Zealous	
Swiftsure	Ordered to cruise off Alexandria
Emerald	as long as they
Alcmene	can with propriety.
Seahorse	
La Fortune	

Thalia – Joined me this morning.

Terpsichore – Sent by Captain Dixon to Naples, and from thence to join the Commander-in-Chief. (Parted company 20th May).

Transfer – Never joined. Reported to be gone to Cyprus.

Lion – Joined Captain Hood off Alexandria, the 25th August.

Mutine – Going down with Dispatches.

Bonne Citoyenne – Gone to Naples.

Earl St. Vincent – With Captain Retalick, to join the Portuguese Squadron.

Portuguese Squadron – Returning from Alexandria, and requested to block up Malta.

Minotaur	Ordered, when Sir James
	Saumarez gets between Sardinia
Audacious	and Minorca, to join me at Naples.
Orion	
Defence	
Bellerophon	On their passage to Gibraltar with the Prizes.
Theseus	
Majestic	

Flora, Cutter – Gone to Alexandria.

HORATIO NELSON[42]

Began at Sea,
September 16th, 1798

My dearest Fanny,

It is hardly possible for me to know where to begin. My head is almost turned by letters already and what am I not to expect when I get on shore. Noise enough to distract me. My head is healed and I am better.

The Kingdom of the two Sicilies are mad with joy from the throne to the peasant all are alike. From Lady Hamilton's letter the situation of the Queen was truly pitiable. I only hope I shall not have to be witness to a renewal of it. I give you Lady Hamilton's words. "How shall I describe the transports of the Queen? Tis not possible. She fainted, cried, kissed her husband, her children, walked frantic about the room, cried, kissed and embraced every person near here exclaiming 'Oh, brave Nelson; Oh God bless and protect our brave deliverer! Oh Nelson, Nelson, what do we not owe you! Oh victor, saviour of Italy! Oh that my swollen heart could not tell him personally what we owe to him.'" You may judge of the rest, but my head will not allow to tell you half. So much for that.

My fag without success would have had no effect. But blessed be God for his goodness to me. I have your letters of May 22nd, June 11th and July 16th. The box you were so good as to send me with places, seal etc. if sent by *l'Aigle* is lost but never mind that, I feel equally your kindness. Do not send any more. What is likely to go on here time only can shew. I am sure I cannot guess, but as the French have only one regular ship of the line, tis not likely I shall see any more fighting. As to Round Wood if the place or neighbourhood is not to your satisfaction, I hope the country will put me in a situation of choosing another, but my dear Fanny unless you can game, and talk scandal, that is lies, most probably your company will never be coveted by country town tabbies. Young people have more goodness than old cats. I put Hoste into a sloop of war. I hope Lord St Vincent will allow him to remain in her. His father is under no obligation to me. If he writes stuff tell him so. All must go to Earl St Vincent I have not power to make a cook. The Queen of Naples has given Hoste a very elegant ring value at least £500 sterling. So much for being a messenger of good news. Sir James Saumarez is on his passage home, so that Lady Saumarez will have the pleasure of his company this winter. Had his wound been very little deeper it would have done his business but as it is, he is not the worse. Josiah is in the *Bonne Citoyenne*. I see no prospect of his being made post. I wish he was as great a favourite of Lord St Vincent's as I wish him, but that is not my fault. However, I hope he will do well in time. He is young and will not endeavour to make him agreeable for his interest or comfort.[43]

A HERO'S WELCOME: NELSON ARRIVES IN NAPLES, 22 September 1798

Admiral Sir Horatio Nelson[44]

The *Vanguard*, somewhat theatrically described as a "wreck" by Nelson, was put in at Naples for repair work in the Posillipo yards. He already had some inkling of his likely reception in the city, from the excited correspondence of Emma Hamilton. It was during this heady visit to Naples that he began his infatuation with Emma Hamilton – a tremor of which can be detected in this injudicious letter to his wife. Emma Hamilton was not quite the beauty of yore, but as Sir Gilbert noted of the contemporary Emma: "Her face is beautiful. She is all Nature, and yet all Art; that is to say her manners are perfectly unpolished, of course very easy, though not with the ease of good breeding, but of a barmaid; excessively good-humoured and wishing to please and be admired by all ages and sorts of persons that come in her way . . ." Nelson was overhelmed by her vitality, her willingness to flatter and to please.

To Fanny Nelson

September 25th. – The poor wretched *Vanguard* arrived here on the 22nd. I must endeavour to convey to you something of what passed, but if it was so affecting to those only who are united in bonds of friendship what must it be to my dearest wife. My friends say everything which is most dear to me in this world. Sir William and Lady Hamilton came out to sea attended by numerous boats with emblems etc. My most respectable friends had really been laid up and seriously ill, first from anxiety and then from joy. It was imprudently told Lady Hamilton in a moment. The effect was a shot. She fell apparently dead and is not yet perfectly recovered from severe bruises. Alongside my honoured friends came, the scene in the boat appeared terribly affecting. Up flew her ladyship and exclaiming: "Oh God is it possible," fell into my arms more dead than alive. Tears however soon set matters to rights, when alongside came the King. The scene was in its way affecting. He took me by the hand, calling me his deliverer and preserver, with every other expression of kindness. In short all Naples calls me "Nostra Liberatore" for the scene with the lower classes was truly affecting. I hope one day to have the pleasure of

introducing you to Lady Hamilton. She is one of the very best
women in this world. How few could have made the turn she has.
She is an honour to her sex and a proof that even reputation may
be regained, but I own it requires a great soul. Her kindness with
Sir William to me is more than I can express. I am in their house,
and I may now tell you it required all the kindness of my friends to
set me up. Her ladyship, if Josiah was to stay, would make
something of him and with all his bluntness I am sure he likes
Lady Hamilton more than any female. She would fashion him in
6 months in spite of himself. I believe Lady Hamilton intends
writing you.

   May God Almighty bless you, my dearest Fanny, and give us in
due time a happy meeting. Should the King give me a peerage* I
believe I scarcely need state the propriety of your going to court.
Don't mind the expense. Money is trash. Again God Almighty
bless you.

Ever your most affectionate,
HORATIO NELSON

You cannot write to Naples by common post. The Admiralty or
Secretary of State is the only way.

Nor can Lady Nelson fail to have been alarmed by her husband's
missive of 28 September.

To Lady Nelson   *28 September 1778*
The preparations of Lady Hamilton, for celebrating my birth-
day to-morrow, are enough to fill me with vanity; every ribbon,
every button, has "Nelson," &c. The whole service is marked
"H.N. Glorious 1st of August!" Songs and Sonnetti are numerous beyond what I ever could deserve. I send the additional†
verse to God save the King, as I know you will sing it

---

* Nelson was made Baron Nelson of the Nile, and Parliament voted him a pension
of £2,000 per annum.
† "Join we in great Nelson's name,
First on the rolls of Fame
   Him let us sing.
Spread we his fame around,
Honour of British ground,
Who made Nile's shore's resound,
   God save the King."

with pleasure. I cannot move on foot, or in a carriage, for the kindness of the populace; but good Lady H. preserves all the papers as the highest treat for you. The Queen yesterday, being still ill, sent her favourite son to visit, and bring me a letter from Her of gratitude and thanks.—Miserable accounts of Le Guillaume Tell. I trust God Almighty will yet put her into the hands of our King. His all-powerful hand has gone with us to the Battle, protected us, and still continues destroying the unbelievers: All glory be to God! The more I think, the more I hear, the greater is my astonishment at the extent and good consequences of our Victory.   Yours, &c.

HORATIO NELSON[45]

As well as enjoying the charms of Lady Hamilton, Nelson let himself be unduly influenced by her ambassadorial husband, who conjured up the idea that the Neopolitans – aided by Nelson – should eject the "ragamuffin" French from the portion of Italy they occupied. Sir William Hamilton and Admiral Nelson got their way and their war. On 23 November the Neopolitan army marched northwards to Rome, whilst Nelson sailed with a squadron to Leghorn, to cut off the retreating French. A week later the Neopolitans entered Rome. And a week after that, the French re-entered Rome and then proceeded to invade Naples itself. On 21 December Nelson was obliged to evacuate the King and Queen of Naples, their family, and the Hamiltons. So much for trouncing the French army in Italy.

THE EVACUATION OF NAPLES, 21 December 1798

Admiral Lord Nelson[46]

To Admiral the Earl of St. Vincent, K.B.

Palermo, *December 28th, 1798*

My Lord,

On the 22nd, I wrote a line to Commodore Duckworth, telling him, that the Royal Family of the Two Sicilies were safely embarked on board the Vanguard, and requested him to take the first opportunity of acquainting your Lordship of this event. For many days previous to the embarkation it was not difficult to foresee that such a thing might happen, I therefore sent for the Goliath from off Malta, and for Captain Troubridge in the Culloden, and his Squadron from the north and west Coast of Italy, the *Vanguard* being the only Ship in Naples Bay. On the 14th, the Marquis de Niza, with three of the Portuguese Squadron, arrived from Leghorn, as did Captain Hope in the *Alcmene* from Egypt: from this time, the danger for the personal safety of their Sicilian Majesties was daily increasing, and new treasons were found out, even to the Minister of War. The whole correspondence relative to this important business was carried on with the greatest address by Lady Hamilton and the Queen, who being constantly in the habits of correspondence, no one could suspect. It would have been highly imprudent in either Sir William Hamilton or myself to have gone to Court, as we knew that all our movements were watched, and even an idea by the Jacobins of arresting our persons as a hostage (as they foolishly imagined) against the attack of Naples, should the French get possession of it.

Lady Hamilton, from this time to the 21st, every night received the jewels of the Royal Family, &c. &c., and such clothes as might be necessary for the very large party to embark, to the amount, I am confident, of full two millions five hundred thousand pounds sterling. On the 18th, General Mack wrote that he had no prospect of stopping the progress of the French, and entreated their Majesties to think of retiring from Naples with their august Family as expeditiously as possible. All the Neapolitan Navy were now taken out of the Mole, consisting of three Sail of the Line and three Frigates: the seamen from the two Sail of the Line in the Bay left their Ships and went on shore: a party of English seamen with Officers were sent from the *Vanguard* to assist in navigating them to a place of safety. From the 18th, various plans were formed for the removal of the Royal Family from the palace to the water-side; on the 19th, I received a note from General Acton, saying, that the King approved of my plan for their embarkation; this day, the 20th and 21st, very large assemblies of people were in commotion, and several people were killed, and one dragged by the legs to the palace. The mob by the 20th were very unruly, and insisted the Royal Family should not leave Naples; however, they were pacified by the King and Queen speaking to them.

On the 21st, at half-past 8 p.m. three Barges with myself and Captain Hope, landed at a corner of the Arsenal. I went into the palace and brought out the whole Royal Family, put them into the Boats, and at half-past nine they were all safely on board the *Vanguard*, when I gave immediate notice to all British Merchants that their persons would be received on board every and any Ship in the Squadron, their effects of value being before embarked in the three English transports who were partly unloaded, and I had directed that all the condemned provisions should be thrown overboard, in order to make room for their effects. Sir William Hamilton had also directed two Vessels to be hired for the accommodation of the French emigrants, and provisions were supplied from our Victuallers; in short, everything had been done for the comfort of all persons embarked.

I did not forget in these important moments that it was my duty not to leave the chance of any Ships of War falling into the hands of the French, therefore, every preparation was made for burning them before I sailed; but the reasons given me by their Sicilian Majesties, induced me not to burn them till the last moment. I, therefore, directed the Marquis de Niza to remove all the Neapolitan Ships outside the Squadron under his command, and if it was possible, to equip some of them with jury masts and send them to Messina; and whenever the French advanced near Naples, or the people revolted against their legitimate Government, immediately to destroy the Ships of War, and to join me at Palermo, leaving one or two Ships to cruize between Capri and Ischia in order to prevent the entrance of any English Ship into the Bay of Naples. On the 23rd, at 7 p.m., the *Vanguard*, *Sannite*, and *Archimedes*, with about twenty sail of Vessels left the Bay of Naples; the next day it blew harder than I ever experienced since I have been at sea. Your Lordship will believe that my anxiety was not lessened by the great charge that was with me, but not a word of uneasiness escaped the lips of any of the Royal Family. On the 25th, at 9 a.m., Prince Albert, their Majesties' youngest child, having eat a hearty breakfast, was taken ill, and at 7 p.m. died in the arms of Lady Hamilton; and here it is my duty to tell your Lordship the obligations which the whole Royal Family as well as myself are under on this trying occasion to her Ladyship. They necessarily came on board without a bed, nor could the least preparation be made for their reception. Lady Hamilton provided her own beds, linen, &c., and became *their slave*, for except one man, no person belonging to Royalty assisted the Royal Family, nor did her Ladyship enter a bed the whole time they were on board. Good Sir William also made every sacrifice for the comfort of the august Family embarked with him. I must not omit to state the kindness of Captain Hardy and every Officer in the *Vanguard*, all of whom readily gave their beds for the convenience of the numerous persons attending the Royal Family.

At 3 p.m., being in sight of Palermo, his Sicilian Majesty's Royal Standard was hoisted at the main-top gallant-mast head of the *Vanguard*, which was kept flying there till his Majesty got into the *Vanguard*'s barge, when it was struck in the Ship and hoisted in the Barge, and every proper honour paid to it from the Ship. As soon as his Majesty set his foot on shore, it was struck from the Barge. The *Vanguard* anchored at 2 a.m. of the 26th; at 5, I attended her Majesty and all the Princesses on shore; her Majesty being so much affected by the death of Prince Albert that she could not bear to go on shore in a public manner. At 9 a.m., his Majesty went on shore, and was received with the loudest acclamations and apparent joy. I have the honour to be, &c.

NELSON.

At Palermo, Nelson alternated between despair at his health and lust for Emma Hamilton.

"YOUR OWN FAITHFUL NELSON WHO LIVES ONLY FOR HIS EMMA": A LOVE LETTER TO EMMA HAMILTON, January 1799

Admiral Lord Nelson[47]

I can neither Eat or Sleep for thinking of You my dearest love, I never touch even pudding You know the reason. No I would Starve sooner. My only hope is to find You

have Equally kept Your Promises to Me . . . but I rest
perfectly confident in the reallity of Your love and that
You would die sooner than be false in the smallest thing to
Your Own faithful Nelson who lives only for his Emma
. . . I shall run Mad . . . In one of my dreams I thought I
was at a large Table You was not present. Sitting between
a Princess who I detest and another. They both tried to
Seduce Me and the first wanted to take those liberties with
Me which no Woman in this World but Yourself ever did.
The consequence was I knocked her down and in the
moment of bustle You came in and, taking Me to Your
embrace wispered "I love nothing but You My Nelson." I
kissed You fervently And we enjoy'd the height of love. Ah
Emma I pour out my Soul to You . . . no love is like Mine
towards You.

There was another demand on Nelson's attention. The kingdom of
Naples had slid into anarchy, then into French protection as the puppet
Parthenopean republic. This was a horror not to be borne by the
decidedly English and irredeemably royalist Nelson, who determined to
orchestrate the city's retaking on behalf of the Neopolitan king and
queen. Accordingly, he blockaded the city, seized outlying islands,
including Capri, and ordered the extirpation of "Jacobins" wherever
they were found.

Then, in June 1799, the French withdrew most of their forces from
Naples, to stem Austrian successes in the north of Italy, leaving the
hapless city disputed by, *inter alia*, a Russian expeditionary force, a
Calabrian rabble led by Cardinal Ruffo (supposedly pro-monarchy),
the Neopolitan nobilty, and republicans, who holed up in the seafront
fortresses of Nuovo and Uovo. To defuse a looming bloody crisis, Ruffo
and the Royal Navy's man on the spot, Captain Foote, agreed a treaty
with the republicans which allowed them to surrender the castles and
embark for Toulon or stay in Naples unmolested. And then on 24 June
Nelson sailed into the Bay of Naples with his squadron and moored in
line of battle. What occurred next is the most controversial incident in
his career. Disliking the treaty with the rebels Nelson, with the king's
backing, lured the rebels from their fortress on to barges, supposedly
bound for Toulon – and took them prisoner. One hundred and sixty-

two of them were executed, most famously Francesco Caracciola, duca di Brienza, a Neopolitan admiral who had gone over to the republicans, hung from the foreyard arm of HMS *Minerva*.

The whole incident left a bad taste. Nelson firstly annulled a treaty, then took advantage of it to imprison the rebels. For abetting such a dubious transaction Sir William Hamilton was recalled by the British government. Nelson was a bigger fish, and was left alone, but the Naples business tainted his reputation.

For the record, Nelson's intercession at Naples was effective. The throne was restored to the Bourbons. A grateful King Ferdinand created Nelson "Duke of Bronte". Nelson's own account of the Neopolitan affair is below.

NAPLES RETAKEN, June 1799

Admiral Lord Nelson[48]

To Vice-Admiral Lord Keith, K.B.

Bay of Naples, *June 27th, 1799*

My dear Lord,

Having detailed my proceedings to the 16th of June, by the *Telegraph* brig, I have now to go on with my movements.

On the 17th the Alexander and Goliath joined me from off Malta; leaving to look out in that quarter, three Sloops of War; – the force with me was now fifteen Sail of two-decked Ships, English, and three Portuguese, with a Fire-ship and Cutter. On the 20th, the *Swallow*, Portuguese corvette, brought me your Lordship's dispatch of the 17th, acquainting me of the near approach of the Squadron under Sir Alan Gardner, and that Lord Keith was going in search of the French fleet. As I had now no prospect of being in a situation to go in search of the Enemy's fleet, which at least is twenty-five Sail of the Line, and might be reinforced with two Venetian ships, although I was firmly resolved they should not pass me without a battle, which would so cripple them that they might be unable to proceed on any distant service, I determined to offer myself for the service of Naples, where I knew the French fleet intended going. With this determination I pushed for Palermo, and on the 21st I went on shore for two hours, saw their Majesties and General Acton, who repeated to me what the General had wrote, (but which I had not received,) to request that I would instantly go into the Bay of Naples to endeavour to bring His Sicilian Majesty's affairs in that City to a happy conclusion.

I lost not one moment in complying with the request, and arrived in the Bay of Naples on the 24th, where I saw a Flag of Truce flying on board His Majesty's Ship *Seahorse*, Captain Foote, and also on the Castles of Uovo and Nuovo. Having on the passage received letters informing [me] that an infamous Armistice was entered into with the Rebels in those Castles, to which Captain Foote had put his name, I instantly made the signal to annul the Truce, being determined never to give my approbation to any terms with Rebels, but that of unconditional submission. The Fleet was anchored in a close line of battle, N.W. by N. and S.E. by S., from the Mole head one and a-half mile distant, flanked by twenty-two Gun and Mortar boats, which I recalled from Procida. I sent Captains Troubridge and Ball instantly to the Cardinal Vicar-General, to represent to his Eminence my opinion of the infamous terms entered into with the Rebels, and also two papers which I enclose. His Eminence said he would send no papers, that if I pleased I might break the Armistice, for that he was tired of his situation. Captain Troubridge then asked his Eminence this plain question: "If Lord Nelson breaks the Armistice, will your Eminence assist him in his attack on the Castles?" His answer was clear, "I will neither assist him with men or guns." After much communication, his Eminence desired to come on board to speak with me on his situation. I used every argument in my power to convince him that the Treaty and Armistice was at an end by the arrival of the Fleet; but an Admiral is no match in talking with a Cardinal. I therefore gave him my opinion in writing – viz, "Rear-Admiral Lord Nelson, who arrived in the Bay of Naples on the 24th June with the British Fleet, found a Treaty entered into with the Rebels, which he is of opinion ought not to be carried into execution without the approbation of His Sicilian Majesty, Earl St. Vincent, – Lord Keith."

Under this opinion the Rebels came out of the Castles, which was instantly occupied by the Marines of the Squadron. On the 27th Captains Troubridge and Ball, with 1300 men, landed from the Ships, united with 500 Russians and a body of Royalists, half of whose *Officers* are, I have every reason to believe, *Rebels*, – cowards they have already proved themselves. Our batteries are open on St. Elmo, and a few days will, I hope, reduce it. The *Alexander* and another are just going to resume their station off Malta, which I am confident will very soon surrender, now all hopes of relief are cut off. I shall not fail to keep up a constant communication with your Lordship, and have the honour to be, with the greatest respect, your most obedient faithful Servant,

Nelson

Carracciolo was executed on board H. S. Majesty's Ship *Minerva*, on the 29th June.

The century was ending, as was Nelson's long sojourn in the Mediterranean. The Admiralty disliked his scandalous dalliance with Emma, who was now carrying his child, his tendency to believe himself above orders, and the reports of his ill health. He was requested back to England. Striking his flag, Nelson journeyed back with the Hamiltons, taking a land route to see the sights.

In England, he made a triumphal progress into London, was mobbed in the Strand, although high society turned its back on Emma Hamilton. After a dire attempt to persuade Fanny to accept Emma as his friend and not his mistress, Nelson and his wife separated. At the end of January 1801, Emma gave birth to Nelson's daughter, Horatia, who was passed off – to avoid more scandal – as Horatia Thompson and whisked off to be wet-nursed. Almost simultaneously, Nelson was assigned to the Baltic expedition, which was intended to force the Danes – in a classic piece of British gunboat diplomacy – to adhere to the Royal Navy's trade blockade of France. Leading the expedition was Sir Hyde Parker, who at the age of sixty-one had just married a girl of eighteen (Hyde Parker's "*sheet* anchor" as *The Morning Post* called her); to Nelson's voiced disappointment, Parker seemed more interested in his young bride than in besting the Danes. Eventually, the British set sail and dawdled to Copenhagen. Nelson, impatient as always, wanted a quick, bold attack (because "the boldest measures are the safest"), while Parker dithered. At length, persuaded by Nelson's energy and enthusiasm (and his own drought of offensive notions), Parker allowed Nelson to lead an attack with shallow draft ships through the channel in front of

Copenhagen, which would then blast a hole in the Danish defences through which bombs could be rained down on the Citadel. Although Nelson conceded that the Danish defences – which consisted of shore batteries, ships and moored hulks – looked formidable "to those who are children at war", it was his judgement that "with the sail of the line I think I can annihilate them". Nelson had trained his crews to fire a broadside a minute. The Danish, he calculated, could not hope to match such a rate in a stand-up fight.

COPENHAGEN: NELSON PREPARES FOR BATTLE, 1–2 April 1801

Colonel Stewart[49]

The author commanded the troops with the Baltic expedition.

On board the *Elephant*, the night of the 1st of April was an important one. As soon as the Fleet was at anchor, the gallant Nelson sat down to table with a large party of his comrades in arms. He was in the highest spirits, and drank to a leading wind, and to the success of the ensuing day. Captains Foley, Hardy, Fremantle, Riou, Inman, his Lordship's second-in-command, Admiral Graves, and a few others to whom he was particularly attached, were of this interesting party; from which every man separated with feelings of admiration for their great leader, and with anxious impatience to follow him to the approaching battle. The signal to prepare for action had been made early in the evening. All the captains retired to their respective ships, Riou excepted, who with Lord Nelson and Foley arranged the order of battle, and those instructions that were to be issued to each ship on the succeeding day. These three officers retired between nine and ten, to the after-cabin, and drew up those orders that have been generally published . . . From the previous fatigue of this day, and of the two preceding, Lord Nelson was so much exhausted while dictating his instructions, that it was recommended to him by us all, and indeed, insisted upon by his old servant, Allen, who assumed much command on these occasions, that he should go to his cot. It was placed on the floor, but from it he still continued to dictate . . . The orders were completed about one o'clock, when half a dozen clerks in the foremost cabin proceeded to transcribe them. Lord Nelson's impatience again showed itself; for instead of sleeping undisturbedly, as he might have done, he was every half hour calling from his cot to these clerks to hasten their work, for that the wind was becoming fair: he was constantly receiving a report of this during the night. Their work being finished about six in the morning, his Lordship, who was previously up and dressed, breakfasted, and about seven made the signal for all captains. The instructions were given to each by eight o'clock . . .

The action began at 10.05 a.m., and it took nearly an hour and a half for the British ships to get in position. Soon, a thousand guns were engaged in a gargantuan artillery duel. By 1.00 p.m. the battle had reached crisis point, and with several of Nelson's ships in evident distress, the bystanding Parker decided that the fire was "too hot for Nelson to oppose".

COPENHAGEN: NELSON TURNS A BLIND EYE, 2 April 1801

Colonel Stewart[50]

Lord Nelson was at this time, as he had been during the whole action, walking the starboard side of the quarter-deck; sometimes much animated, and at others heroically fine in his observations. A shot through the mainmast knocked a few splinters about us. He observed to me, with a smile, "It is warm work, and this day may be the last to any of us at a moment"; and then stopping short at the gangway, he used an expression never to be erased from my memory, and said with emotion, "but mark you, I would not be elsewhere for thousands". When the signal, No. 39* was made, the Signal Lieutenant reported it to him. He continued his walk, and did not appear to take notice of it. The Lieutenant meeting his Lordship at the next turn asked, whether he should repeat it. Lord Nelson answered, "No, acknowledge it". On the Officer returning to the poop, his Lordship called after him, "Is No. 16† still hoisted?" The Lieutenant answering in the affirmative,

* To discontinue the action
†"For close action" which had been flying from the beginning.

Lord Nelson said, "Mind you keep it so". He now walked the deck considerably agitated, which was always known by his moving the stump of his right arm. After a turn or two, he said to me, in a quick manner, "Do you know what's shown on board of the Commander-in-Chief, No. 39?" On asking him what that meant, he answered, "Why, to leave off action". "Leave off action!" he repeated, and then added, with a shrug, "Now, damn me if I do". He also observed, I believe, to Captain Foley, "You know, Foley, I have only one eye – I have a right to be blind sometimes"; and then with an archness peculiar to his character, putting the glass to his blind eye, exclaimed, "I really do not see the signal". This remarkable signal was, therefore, only acknowledged on board the *Elephant*, not repeated. Admiral Graves did the latter, not being able to distinguish the *Elephant*'s conduct: either by a fortunate acci- dent, or intentionally, No. 16 was not displaced. The squadron of frigates obeyed the signal, and hauled off. That brave officer, Captain Riou, was killed by a raking shot, when the *Amazon* showed her stern to the *Trekoner*. He was sitting on a gun, was encouraging his men, and had been wounded in the head by a splinter. He had expressed himself grieved at being thus obliged to retreat, and nobly observed, "What will Nelson think of us?" His clerk was killed by his side; and by another shot, several of the Marines, while hauling on the main-brace, shared the same fate. Riou then exclaimed, "Come then, my boys, let us die all together!" The words were scarcely uttered, when the fatal shot severed him in two. . . .

The action now continued with unabated vigour. About 2 p.m. the greater part of the Danish line had ceased to fire; some of the lighter ships were adrift, and the carnage on board of the enemy, who reinforced their crews from the shore, was dreadful. The taking possession of such ships as had struck was, however, attended with difficulty; partly by reason of the batteries on Anak Island protecting them, and partly because an irregular fire was made on our boats, as they approached, from the ships themselves. The *Dannebrog* acted in this manner, and fired at our boat, although that ship was not only on fire and had struck, but the Commodore, Fischer, had removed his Pendant, and had deserted her. A renewed attack on her by the

Elephant and *Glatton*, for a quarter of an hour, completely silenced and disabled the *Dannebrog* . . . On our smoke clearing away, the *Dannebrog* was found to be drifting in flames before the wind, spreading terror throughout the enemy's line. The usual lamen-table scene then ensued; and our boats rowed in every direction, to save the crew, who were throwing themselves from her at every port-hole; few, however, were left unwounded in her after our last broadsides, or could be saved. She drifted to lee-ward, and about half-past three blew up . . . After the *Dannebrog* was adrift, and had ceased to fire, the action was found to be over, along the whole of the line astern of us; but not so with the ships ahead and with the Crown batteries. Whether from ignorance of the custom of war, or from confusion on board the Prizes, our boats were, as before mentioned, repulsed from the ships themselves, or fired at from Anak Island. Lord Nelson naturally lost temper at this, and observed: "That he must either send on shore, and stop this irregular proceeding, or send in our fire-ships and burn them." He accordingly retired into the stern galley, and wrote, with great dispatch, that well-known letter addressed to the Crown Prince, with the address, – "To the Brothers of Englishmen, the brave Danes" etc.: and this letter was conveyed on shore through the contending fleets.

COPENHAGEN: THE VIEW FROM HMS *DEFIANCE*, 2 August 1801

Rear-Admiral Thomas Graves[51]
[*Graves was Nelson's second-in-command.*]

Almost a thousand British sailors were killed or wounded at Copenhagen in Nelson's "no manoeuvring . . . downright fighting" onslaught on Copenhagen. But Denmark left the Armed Neutrality. And Nelson was awarded a viscountcy.

To John Graves

Defiance, off the town of Copenhagen, *April 3rd, 1801*.

Dear Brother, – Yesterday an awful day for the town of Copenhagen. Eleven sail of our ships under the command of Lord Nelson, under whom I served that day, attacked the floating batteries, ships, gun-vessels, and their works on shore, which lasted five hours, with as many hard blows and as much obstinacy as has been ever known, and with great loss on both sides, but finally ended in the complete overthrow of their outer defence. We have now eleven sail of their vessels in our possession. Two ran on shore, one sank, and one was blown up in the action. It was, certainly, a most gallant defence, and words cannot speak too high of the boldness of the attack, considering all the difficulties we had to struggle with, and their great superiority in number and weight of guns. I think we were playing a losing game in attacking stone walls, and I fear we shall not have much to boast of when it is known what our ships suffered, and the little impression we made on their navy. Lord Nelson tells me I shall be made a Baronet, but I shall only ask for justice being done to my two brothers. Lord Nelson was appointed to command this attack, and he asked for me to serve with him; if not, you might depend on my not staying behind when anything was to be done. I think yesterday must prove that the enterprise of the British is invincible. Our loss in killed and wounded was only *ninety*. Lord Nelson's ship not thirty, but the *Monarch* that was next to us in the attack, and not so much exposed to the great Crown Battery, lost between two and three hundred men killed and wounded. Boys escaped unhurt. *I am told* the battle of the Nile was nothing to this. I am happy that my flag was not a month hoisted before I got into action, and into the hottest one that has happened the whole of the war. Considering the disadvantages of navigation, the approach to the enemy, their vast number of guns and mortars on both land and sea, I do not think there ever was a bolder attack. Some of our ships did not get into action, which made those who did feel it the hotter. In short, it was worthy of our gallant and enterprising little Hero of the Nile. Nothing can exceed his spirit. Sir Hyde made the signal to discontinue the action before we had been at it two hours, supposing that our ships would all be destroyed. But our little Hero gloriously said, "I will not move till we are crowned with victory, or that the Commander-in-Chief sends an officer to order me away." And he was right, for if we had discontinued the action before the enemy struck, we should have all got aground and have been destroyed. As it was, both Lord Nelson's ship and the *Defiance* got aground in coming off. Lord Nelson sent for me at the close of the action, and it was beautiful to see how the shot beat the water all round us in the boat. Give my love to my dear daughter. She has ever the most ardent prayers for her happiness. The destruction amongst the enemy is dreadful. One of the ships that was towed into the fleet yesterday had between two and three hundred dead on her decks, besides what they had thrown overboard.

My dear Brother,
Your most affectionate friend,
THOS. GRAVES.

Landing in England, Nelson visited the naval hospital where some of the wounded from Copenhagen were recovering. One of the doctors, recorded an exchange between Nelson and a patient:

Nelson: "Well, Jack what's the matter with you?"
Sailor: "Lost my arm, your honour."
Nelson: [glancing down at his empty sleeve before turning again to the sailor]: "Well, Jack then you and I are spoiled for fishermen; cheer up, my brave fellow."

Small wonder that his men loved him. Before leaving Nelson distributed guineas to the nurses.

After a holiday with Emma Hamilton, Nelson was recalled to his duties, commanding a squadron in the Channel to defend the nation against the invasion force being assembled by Napoleon. Quickly tiring of such patrolling, he put forward plans for an attack on the French ships moored at Boulogne. It was rash, it was ill-conceived— and it ended in utter failure. It cannot have helped that Nelson was "preoccupied with the distant fair Emma, Good Emma, Great Emma, Virtuous Emma" and finding a suitable love-nest rather than the raid on the French port.

At length, Nelson did find a satisfactory house, Merton Place in Surrey, which he bought for £9,000. Emma moved in, along with her acquiesecent, cuckolded husband. Among the visitors was Lord Minto.

NELSON AT HOME, MERTON PLACE, Christmas 1801

Lord Minto[52]

I went to Lord Nelson's on Saturday to dinner and returned today in the forenoon. The whole establishment and way of life is such to make me angry as well as melancholy; but I cannot alter it and I do not think myself obliged or at liberty to quarrel with him for his weakness, though nothing shall ever induce me to give the smallest countenance to Lady Hamilton. She looks ultimately to the chance of marriage, as Sir W. will not be long in her way and she probably indulges a hope that she may survive Lady Nelson; in the meanwhile she and Sir William and the whole set of them are living with him at his expense. She is in high looks, but more immense than ever. Not only the rooms, but the whole house, staircase and all, are covered with nothing but pictures of her and him, of all sizes and sorts, and representations of his naval actions, coats of arms, pieces of plate in his honour, the flagstaff of *l'Orient*, etc. – an excess of vanity which counteracts its purpose. If it was Lady H.'s house there might be a pretence for it; to make his own a mere looking-glass to view himself all day is bad taste. [John] Braham, the celebrated Jew Singer, performed with Lady H. She is horrid, but he entertained in spite of her.

It was to Merton that Nelson retired during the Peace of Amiens.

Rarely has an international treaty been so misnamed; Napoleon had not the slightest inclination of forgoing his long struggle with the "nation of shopkeepers", but he needed time to rebuild his war machine. No sooner was the treaty signed, than he ordered massive expansion of the French navy. He also, against treaty obligations, acquired the Austrian Netherlands and her Channel ports. Seeing that the wind of war was brewing up, the British determined on pre-emptive action. On 16 May 1803, Britain declared war on France.

Part Two

The Long Watch

Nelson and the Napoleonic War,
16 May 1803 – 20 October 1805

INTRODUCTION

After eighteen months of playing country squire at Merton, Nelson hoisted his flag on HMS *Victory* on 18 May. He had reached the summit of his ambition: he was Commander-in-Chief of the Mediterranean fleet. Moreover, the *Victory* was arguably the finest ship in the Royal Navy. Certainly she was the largest, with 104 guns and a crew of 850. Under full sail, her canvas covered 4 acres.

He proceeded to Toulon, to keep watch on the French fleet there. As ever, Emma was large in his thoughts, and missives to her flew from his pen.

> My dearest beloved to say that I think of you by day night and all day and all night but too faintly expresses my feelings of love and affection towards you ... I am incapable of wronging you in thought word or deed no not all the wealth of Peru could buy me for one moment it is all yours ... and certainly from the first moment of our happy dear enchanting blessed meeting the thoughts of such happiness my dearest my beloved makes the blood fly into my head ... Ever for ever I am yours only yours even beyond this world, Nelson & Bronte for Ever for Ever your own Nelson.[1]

Horatia also received numerous letters from her "most affectionate father".

My dear Horatia

I feel very much pleased by your kind letter and for your present of a lock of your beautiful hair. I am very glad to hear that you are so good and mind everything which your governess Miss Connor and dear Lady Hamilton tell you, I send you a lock of my hair and a pound note to buy a locket to put it in and I give you leave to wear it when you are dressed and behave well, and I send you another to buy some little thing for Mary and your governess.

As I am sure that for the world you would not tell a story, it must have slipt my memory that I promised you a Watch therefore I have sent to Naples to get one and I will send it home as soon as it arrives – the Dog I never could have promised as we have no Dogs on board ship, Only I beg my dear Horatia be obedient and you will ever be sure of the affection of NELSON & BRONTE.[2]

Meanwhile, the watch over Toulon was arduous and monotonous. One midshipman later recalled:

THE WATCH OVER TOULON, 1803–4

Midshipman W. Lovell[3]

Whilst off Naples official notice reached us of the declaration of war against France, and we proceeded immediately off Toulon, where, in the course of a short time, Lord Nelson arrived in a frigate, and took the command of the fleet in the Mediterranean. His lordship's flagship (the *Victory*) joined us in a few weeks, having on her passage out captured a French frigate, and some merchant vessels. We continued to cruise in the Gulf of Lyons from June, 1803, until the 24th of July, 1804, without ever going into any port to refit. It is true that occasionally the whole fleet ran from the heavy gales of the Gulf of Lyons, and took shelter in various outlandish places in Sardinia, where we could get wood and water, such as at Agincourt sound – amongst the Magdalen islands . . . There was a small village seven or eight miles off, at one of the Magdalen islands, where some few got their linen washed, but most of us in the fleet were put to our shifts to get that necessary comfort (clean linen) accomplished.

These long cruises used to put our wits sadly to the test for an appearance of a bit of white linen above our black cravats, particularly when we had to answer the signal for a midshipman on board the flagship.

Soap was almost – indeed, I might say, quite – as scarce an article as clean shirts and stockings. It was a common thing in those days of real hard service to turn shirts and stockings inside out, and make them do a little more duty . . .

. . . Our noble and gallant chief used to manage to get us fresh beef twice a week – that is to say, so many live bullocks were embarked on board each ship, and we killed them as we wanted them – by which means, with the assistance of oranges that were procured occasionally, a few cases of scurvy occurred in the fleet, notwithstanding our long stay at sea. But as for articles of luxury – tea, potatoes, soap, and other sea stores for our messes – we had none.

The inhabitants of Sardinia were as wild as their country; the mountaineers and lowlanders generally were engaged in a kind of petty war with each other. Both parties always went armed, and murders frequently took place. At one of the anchorages in the straits, another mid and myself were attending a watering party – one of these fellows rode down with a bag of cheese, made of goat's or sheep's milk, for sale; he was armed with a long gun and pistols, and we had no firearms with us. Some dispute in the bargaining, for want of understanding each other's language, arose; the Sard very coolly mounted his horse, and taking up his cheeses, rode off a short distance, and fired at us; the ball passed through the sleeve of the mate's coat, and near my head . . .

Our long Cruise of near fourteen months off Toulon, amidst nothing but gales of wind, and heavy storms of most terrific thunder and lightning, met with no reward in the shape of prize-money.

Lovell at least was young and fit. His commander endured numerous bouts of ill-health and complained that his "shatter'd carcass is in the worst plight of the whole fleet".

I have had a sort of rheumatic fever. I am now better of that but have violent pain in my side and night sweats . . . the pain in my heart and spasms I have not had for some time now [possibly, he thought, as a result of the camphor and opium his doctor prescribed] . . . the constant anxiety I have experienced has shook my weak frame and my rings will hardly keep upon my fingers. What gives me more [concern than anything] is that I can every month perceive a visible (if I may be allowed the expression) loss of sight. A few years must, as I have always predicted, render me blind. I have often heard that blind people are cheerful, but I think I shall take it to heart.[4]

Nelson's pitiable health was exacerbated by his ceaseless industry and his carelessness for his physical well-being.

A PORTRAIT OF NELSON'S WAY OF LIFE ABOARD HMS *VICTORY*, 1803–5

Dr Beatty, surgeon aboard HMS Victory[5]

His Lordship used a great deal of exercise, generally walking on deck six or seven hours in the day. He always rose early, for the most part shortly after daybreak. He breakfasted in summer about six, and at seven in winter; and if not occupied in reading or writing despatches, or examining into the details of the Fleet, he walked on the quarter-deck the greater part of the forenoon; going down to his cabin occasionally to commit to paper such incidents or reflections as occurred to him during that time, and as might be hereafter useful to the service of his country. He dined generally about half-past two o'clock. At his table there were seldom less than eight or nine persons, consisting of the different officers of the ship . . . At dinner he was alike affable and attentive to every one; he ate very sparingly himself; the liver and wing of a fowl, and a small plate of macaroni, in general composing his meal, during which he occasionally took a glass of champagne. He never exceeded four glasses of wine after dinner, and seldom drank three; and even those were diluted with either Bristol or common water.

   . . . He possessed such a wonderful activity of mind, as even prevented him from taking ordinary repose, seldom enjoying two hours of uninterrupted sleep; and on several occasions he did not quit the deck during the whole night. At these times he took no pains to protect himself from the effects of wet, or the night air, wearing only a thin great coat; and he has frequently, after having his clothes wet through with rain, refused to have them changed, saying that the leather waistcoat which he wore over his flannel one would secure him from complaint. He seldom wore boots, and was consequently very liable to have his feet wet. When this occurred he has often been known to go down to his cabin, throw off his shoes, and walk on the carpet in his stockings for the purpose of drying the feet of them. He chose rather to adopt this uncomfortable expedient, than to give his servants the trouble of assisting him to put on fresh stockings; which, from his having only one hand, he could not himself conveniently effect.

Nelson took rather better care of his men than he did himself. He wrote:

> The great thing in all military service is health. You will agree with me that it is easier for an officer to keep men healthy than for a physician to cure them. Situated as this fleet has been without a friendly port where we could get all things necessary for us, yet I have, by changing the cruizing ground, not allowed the sameness of prospect to satiate the mind – sometimes by looking at Toulon, Villefranche, Barcelona and Rosas; then running around Minorca, Majorca, Sardinia and Corsica; and two or three times anchoring for a few days and sending a ship to the last place for onions, which I find the best thing that can be given to seamen; having always good mutton for the sick, cattle when we can get them, and plenty of fresh water . . .[6]

Alas, it was during such an excursion, in March 1805, that Villeneuve escaped from Toulon and slipped out of the Mediterranean to Cadiz. Villeneuve's movement was part of a master plan by Napoleon to draw the British blockading squadrons out to the West Indies, leaving the Channel free for the French army to cross and invade England. At Cadiz Villeneuve picked up more French ships and six Spanish ships of the line (Spain having recently declared war on Britain), and set off across the Atlantic.

So elaborate was Napoleon's plan that it at least had the merit of the unexpected. Nelson initially searched the Mediterranean for Villeneuve, before intelligence reached him that the Frenchman was bound for the West Indies. At this, Nelson set off in hot pursuit, only to arrive in the West Indies to disover that Villeneuve had left to return to Europe. A brig carrying Nelson's dispatches caught up with the French, and reported its course to the Admiralty on 8 July, allowing the First Lord to send a squadron under Calder to intercept the French off Finistere. Calder, though, lacked the will of Nelson, and after confused fighting in thick fog, broke off the engagement. Villeneuve scuttled off to hide in Cadiz. There he licked his wounds and tended his fears his men were undertrained, underfed and unhealthy (he had 1,700 on the sick list). He also had an emperor who was no naval strategist, despite the Napoleonic grand plan, the Channel was still protected by the British, for Sir William Cornwallis – who did have something of Nelson's indomitable will about him – would not let the French out of Brest.

Nelson himself, meanwhile, landed back in Gibraltar, having crossed the Atlantic twice ("an effort such as never was realised in former times, nor I doubt will ever be repeated by any other Admiral", as one admirer described it) with his crews in fine fettle and equally fine spirits. Their Admiral, however, had sunk into one of his sloughs of depression. After more than two years away, Nelson determined to sail for home, the *Victory* anchoring at Spithead on 18 August 1805. Two days later he was at "dear, dear Merton" and in the arms of Emma. Friends and relatives thronged to see him, and the house was full of visitors for days. Whenever he appeared in public – and he was instantly recognizible, with his green shade over his eye, and his missing arm – John Bull huzzahed. Lord Minto met Nelson "in a mob in Piccadilly". "It is really quite affecting," Minto told his wife, "to see the wonder and admiration, and love and respect of the whole world [towards Nelson]; and the genuine expression of all these sentiments at once, from gentle and simple, the moment he is seen. It is beyond anything represented in a play or in a poem of fame".

Another vignette of Nelson and his fans comes from his old friend, Sir J. Theophilus:

The crowd, which waited outside of Somerset House till the noble viscount came out, was very great. He was then very ill, and neither in look nor dress betokened the naval hero, having on a pair of drab-green breeches, and high black gaiters, a yellow waistcoat, and a plain blue coat, with a cocked hat, quite square, a large green shade over the eye, and a gold headed stick in his hand; yet the crowd ran before him and said, as he looked down, that he was then thinking of burning a fleet, &c. They gave his lordship repeated and hearty cheers; indeed the two pedestrians could hardly get to Salter's shop, so dense was the crowd . . . Lord Nelson said during the conversation . . . "I have still the coffin which that good fellow Hallowell made for me, on board your ship"; adding, "I always keep it in my cabin."[7]

It was on one of his trips to London that Nelson bought from Barrett, Corney and Corney, embroiderers to the crown, silver-embroidered stars of the orders of the Bath, the Crescent, St Joachim and St Ferdinand, to be sewn on to his coats.

He also met another figure who would become a military legend.

WELLINGTON MEETS NELSON, 10 September 1805

Arthur Wellesley, 1st Duke of Wellington[8]

I went to the Colonial Office in Downing Street and there I was shown into the little waiting-room on the right hand, where I found, also waiting to see the Secretary of State, a gentleman whom, from his likeness to his pictures and the loss of an arm, I immediately recognised as Lord Nelson. He could not know who I was, but he entered at once into conversation with me, if I can call it conversation, for it was almost all on his side and all about himself, and in, really, a style so vain and so silly as to surprise and almost disgust me. I suppose something that I happened to say may have made him guess that I was *somebody*, and he went out of the room for a moment, I have no doubt to ask the office-keeper who I was, for when he came back he was altogether a different man, both in manner and matter. All that I had thought a charlatan style had vanished, and he talked of the state of this country, and of the aspect and probabilities of affairs on the Continent with a good sense, and a knowledge of subjects both at home and abroad that surprised me . . . in fact he talked like an officer and a statesman. The Secretary of State kept us long waiting, and certainly, for the last half or three-quarters of an hour, I don't know that I ever had a conversation that interested me more. Now, if the Secretary of State had been punctual, and admitted Lord Nelson in the first quarter of an hour I should have had the same impression of a light and trivial character that other people have had.

By the time of this encounter with Wellington in the Colonial Office, Nelson had already had his orders to reassume command of the Mediterranean fleet. And beard Villeneuve in Cadiz.

In the gloom of the late evening of 13 September Nelson took his leave of Merton. Before climbing into the carriage, the Admiral knelt at the bedside of his sleeping four-year-old daughter and said a prayer for her. Emma, weeping, almost fainted as the carriage pulled away. As it rattled along English lanes in the night, Nelson composed a prayer for his private journal.

NELSON'S PRAYER, 13 September 1805

Admiral Lord Nelson[9]

Friday Night, 13th September
At half-past ten drove from dear dear Merton, where I left all which I hold dear in this world, to go to serve my King and Country. May the Great God whom I adore enable me to fulfil the expectations of my Country; and if it is His good pleasure that I should return, my thanks will never cease being offered up to the Throne of His Mercy. If it is His good providence to cut short my days upon earth, I bow with the greatest submission, relying that He will protect those so dear to me, that I may leave behind. – His will be done: Amen, Amen, Amen.

Nelson arrived at Portsmouth at six o'clock on 14 September. An enormous crowd had gathered to watch him embark, some crying, some praying for him, most cheering wildly. As his barge pushed off towards *Victory*, Nelson said to the ship's captain, Hardy, "I had their huzzas before – I have their hearts now!"

The *Victory* weighed anchor at 8.00 a.m. the next day, and made sail to the south-south-east to Cadiz, where Villeneuve was still holed up. Nelson's last campaign was rolling to its conclusion.

RENDEZVOUS WITH DESTINY: NELSON SAILS TO CADIZ, 15–28 September 1805

Admiral Lord Nelson

To Alexander Davison, Esq.

Victory, September 16th, 1805
Off Portland, Wind W.S.W.

My dear Davison,*

I regret most exceedingly, for many reasons, my not having had the pleasure of seeing you; but my fate is fixed, and I am gone, and beating down Channel with a foul wind. I am, my dear friend, so truly sensible of all your goodness to me, that I can only say, thanks, thanks. Therefore I will to business. I wish I could have been rich enough, with ease to myself, to have settled my Account with you; but as that is not done, I wish for my sake that you would have it closed, and receipts pass between us; and then I will give you a bond for the balance, as for money lent. Those bonds relative to Tucker, being all settled, should be returned to me. Be so good as to give them to Haslewood. If you and I live, no harm can happen; but should either of us drop, much confusion may arise to those we may leave behind. I have said enough. Haslewood will settle the Account with all legal exactness.

I have requested you to pay Chawner's account for work to be done in his line; and what is ordered, viz. the kitchen, ante-room, and for altering the dining-room, which you would have been provoked to see spoiled. The alteration will cost three times as much as if it had been done at first. However, Chawner

* Nelson's agent

now knows all my plans and wishes. Poor blind Mrs. Nelson I have given 150*l*. to pay her debts, and I intend to pay her house-rent in future, in addition to the 200*l*. a year, which I take will be about 40*l*. a year. I wished also to have seen you respecting my Proxy, for as it passed through your hands without an immediate communication with Lord Moira, so it should have returned that way. I ever was against giving my Proxy to any man, and now I have it again, it will probably never be given again. Lord Moira made me break my intention; and as very few can equal our friend for honour and independence, it is not very likely that I shall give it, without strong reasons, again. With every good wish; believe me ever, my dear Davison, your most obliged and faithful friend,

NELSON AND BRONTE

I have settled Chawner's account for all which has been hitherto done at Merton.[10]

Victory, off Plymouth, *September 17th [1805]*.
Nine o'Clock in the Morning, Blowing fresh
at W.S.W., dead foul wind.

I sent, my own dearest Emma, a letter for you, last night, in a Torbay Boat, and gave the man a guinea to put it in the Post-Office. We have had a nasty blowing night, and it looks very dirty. I am now signalising the Ships at Plymouth to join me; but I rather doubt their ability to get to sea. However, I have got clear of Portland, and have Cawsand Bay and Torbay under the lee. I intreat, my dear Emma, that you will cheer up; and we will look forward to many, many happy years, and be surrounded by our children's children. God Almighty can, when he pleases, remove the impediment. My heart and soul is with you and Horatia. I got this line ready in case a Boat should get alongside. For ever, ever, I am yours, most devotedly,

NELSON AND BRONTE

Mr. Rose said he would write to Mr. Bolton, if I was sailed; but I have forgot to give him the direction: but I will send it to-day. I think I shall succeed very soon, if not at this moment.

Wednesday, *September 18th*, off the Lizard.
I had no opportunity of sending your letter yesterday, nor do I see any prospect at present. The *Ajax* and *Thunderer* are joining; but it is nearly calm, with a swell from the Westward. Perseverance has got us thus far; and the same will, I dare say, get us on. Thomas seems to do very well, and content. Tell Mr. Lancaster that I have no doubt that his son will do very well. God bless you, my own Emma! I am giving my letters to Blackwood, to put on board the first Vessel he meets going to England or Ireland. Once more, heavens bless you!

Ever, for ever, your
NELSON AND BRONTE[11]

VICTORY'S LOG AND SIGNAL LOG

28th September, p.m. At 6, in steering sails, joined the Fleet off Cadiz under the command of Vice-Admiral Collingwood, consisting of twenty-three Sail of the Line, and six sail of the Line in shore. At 8, St. Sebastian's Light-house bore E.b.N distant five or six leagues.

PRIVATE DIARY

Sunday, September 28th, 1805
Fresh breezes at N.N.W. At daylight bore up, and made sail. At nine saw the Ætna cruising. At noon saw eighteen sail. Nearly calm. In the evening joined the Fleet under Vice-Admiral Collingwood. Saw the Enemy's Fleet in Cadiz, amounting to thirty-five or thirty-six Sail of the Line.

Sunday, September 29th
Fine weather. Gave out the necessary orders for the Fleet. Sent *Euryalus* to watch the Enemy with the *Hydra* off Cadiz.[12]

[This was Nelson's forty-seventh birthday]

To Unknown   *Victory*, off Cadiz, *October 3rd, 1805*
The reception I met with on joining the Fleet caused the sweetest sensation of my life. The Officers who came on board to welcome my return, forgot my rank as Commander-in-Chief in the enthusiasm with which they greeted me. As soon as these

emotions were past, I laid before them the Plan I had previously arranged for attacking the Enemy; and it was not only my pleasure to find it generally approved, but clearly perceived and understood. The Enemy are still in Port, but something must be immediately done to provoke or lure them to a Battle. My duty to my Country demands it, and the hopes centered in me, I hope in God, will be realised. In less than a fortnight expect to hear from me, or of me, for who can foresee the fate of Battle? Put up your prayers for my success, and may God protect all my friends!

I am, & c.,

NELSON AND BRONTE[13]

"IT WAS LIKE AN ELECTRIC SHOCK": THE ADMIRAL EXPLAINS THE "NELSON TOUCH", 29 September 1805

Admiral Lord Nelson

"The Nelson Touch" was the Admiral's revolutionary tactic to annhilate the enemy by attacking in two columns, one of which would cut the Combined Fleet's line about midway along (and stand off the the van), while the second column overwhelmed their rear. Its simplicity was its virtue, for numerous fleet actions had gone awry from overcomplicated instructions. In the operation of the "Nelson Touch" at Trafalgar, Nelson led the centre column in the *Victory*, Collingwood the second column in the 100-gun *Royal Sovereign*. In the letter to Emma below, Nelson describes the reception the exposition of the "Nelson Touch" received from his captains. First, though, is a perennial complaint about his health.

To Lady Hamilton   *Victory, October 1st, 1805*

My dearest Emma,

It is a relief to me, to take up the pen, and write you a line; for I have had, about four o'clock this morning, one of my dreadful spasms, which has almost enervated me. It is very odd; I was hardly ever better than yesterday. Fremantle stayed with me till eight o'clock, and I slept uncommonly well; but was awoke with this disorder. My opinion of its effect, some one day, has never altered. However, it is entirely gone off, and I am only quite weak. The good people of England will not believe that rest of body and mind is necessary for me! But perhaps this spasm may not come again these six months. I had been writing seven hours yesterday; perhaps that had some hand in bringing it upon me.

I joined the Fleet late on the evening of the 28th of September, but could not communicate with them until the next morning. I believe my arrival was most welcome, not only to the Commander of the Fleet, but also to every individual in it; and, when I came to explain to them the "*Nelson touch*," it was like an electric shock. Some shed tears, all approved – "It was new – it was singular – it was simple!"; and, from Admirals downwards, it was repeated – "It must succeed, if ever they will allow us to get at them! You are, my Lord, surrounded by friends whom you inspire with confidence." Some may be Judas's; but the majority are certainly much pleased with my commanding them.[14]

CADIZ: THE BLOCKADE, 29 September–18 October 1803

Admiral Lord Nelson

To Sir John Acton   *30th September, 1805*
My dear Sir John,
    After being only twenty-five days in England, I find myself again in the command of the Mediterranean Fleet. I only hope that I may be able, in a small degree, to fulfil the expectations of my Country. . . . I hear the French have two or three Sail of the Line at Toulon, two Frigates and a Corvette. In England they have not the smallest idea of such a force. If it be so, they must send more Ships; for although it is natural to look to the Russians to prevent those Ships from doing any harm to the Eastward of Toulon, yet I can answer for nothing but what is committed to the charge of English Ships. I was so little a while in England, and only three times with the Minister, that I hardly entered into any business but my own. I hope both Austria and Russia have begun; and, if the War comes into Italy, I have proposed such a co-operation on the part of England, that I am confident three months may, if all parties are agreed, free Italy and Piedmont; but we must all put our

shoulders to the wheel. The Combined Fleet in Cadiz is thirty-five, or thirty-six Sail of the Line, and eight at Carthagena. I have twenty-three Sail of the Line; and six occasionally at Gibraltar, and to have an eye upon the Ships at Carthagena. The French have made an exchange of an old French 74 for the *Santa Anna*, a Spanish First-rate. Be assured I am your Excellency's most faithful friend,

NELSON AND BRONTE[15]

To Alexander Davison, Esq. *Victory, [about 30th September, 1805.]*

Day by day, my dear friend, I am expecting the Fleet to put to sea – every day, hour, and moment; and you may rely that, if it is within the power of man to get at them, that it shall be done; and I am sure that all my brethren look to that day as the finish of our laborious cruise. The event no man can say exactly; but I must think, or render great injustice to those under me, that, let the Battle be when it may, it will never have been surpassed. My shattered frame, if I survive that day, will require rest, and that is all I shall ask for. If I fall on such a glorious occasion, it shall be my pride to take care that my friends shall not blush for me. These things are in the hands of a wise and just Providence, and His will be done! I have got some trifle, thank God, to leave to those I hold most dear, and I have taken care not to neglect it. Do not think I am low-spirited on this account, or fancy anything is to happen to me; quite the contrary – my mind is calm, and I have only to think of destroying our inveterate foe. I have two Frigates gone for more information, and we all hope for a meeting with the Enemy. Nothing can be finer than the Fleet under my command. Whatever be the event, believe me ever, my dear Davison, your much obliged and sincere friend,

NELSON AND BRONTE[16]

To Vice-Admiral Collingwood. *Victory, September 30th, 1805*

My dear Coll.,

I had rather that all the Ships burnt a blue-light, or false fire; for it must often happen that the cause of wearing is change of wind, and often a very confused sea, and Ships may be very anxious, from various circumstances, to be assured that her neighbour astern has wore, as the Line from the above circumstances would be entirely broke. It is perfectly understood that, unless in very fine weather, or extraordinary circumstances, the Fleet will not be directed to wear in succession. We have found the comfort of blue-lights and false fires in the Mediterranean, where the wind changes so often. I am writing to every part of the Mediterranean, and if *Thunder* defers her appearance till to-morrow, I shall be ready for her, and she shall go to Sardinia, Palermo, from whence my letters for Malta will go express to Girgenti, and from thence to Malta in a Sparanero. If the weather is fine, perhaps you will come on board to-morrow. If the weather suits I will ask you to dinner: our party will not be so numerous as yesterday and to-day. Captain Rotheram, of course.

The *Pickle Schooner* was off St. Vincent on Sunday looking for a Ship on that station. She was seven days from Plymouth.

Ever yours most faithfully,
NELSON AND BRONTE[17]

To William Marsden, Esq., Admiralty

Victory, off Cadiz, *2nd October, 1805*

Sir,

You will please to acquaint the Lords Commissioners of the Admiralty that I arrived off here on the evening of the 28th ult., where I found Vice-Admiral Collingwood with the Fleet, and on the morning following I took the Command from the Vice-Admiral, and received from him the several unexecuted Orders, &c. The Ships are getting short in their water and provisions: I shall, therefore, send Rear-Admiral Louis with six Sail of the Line immediately to Gibraltar and Tetuan to complete in everything; and the moment he returns, I shall send others to those places, in order that the Fleet may be all prepared for service before the winter sets in. The *Zealous* having come out from England with a bad mainmast, which has been found, upon survey, to be sprung, and decayed in several places, is just ordered to Gibraltar to get a new one, and otherwise completed for immediate service. The *Endymion* must also go into

Gibraltar, having this day joined the Fleet with her mainmast badly sprung. As I have had no Return from Rear-Admiral Knight, respecting the Disposition of His Majesty's Ships within the Mediterranean, and that of the Fleet off here being nearly the same as made in Vice-Admiral Collingwood's last Return, I shall not send their Lordships a Disposition of the Fleet at this time, being anxious to send the *Nimble Cutter* to England with the dispatches from Vice-Admiral Collingwood and Sir Robert Calder, which I detained in the *Nautilus*, off Cape St. Vincent, on her way home.

The Fleet is in very fair condition and good humour, and their Lordships may be assured that every exertion of mine shall be used to keep it so, and in a state to meet the Combined Fleet in Cadiz whenever they come out. Their force is about thirty-six Sail of the Line, apparently ready for sea, with a number of Frigates and Corvettes, &c. It is said that there is a great scarcity of provisions at Cadiz, and if Government strictly enforce the prohibition of provisions from the environs of that place, in any bottoms whatever, the Enemy must soon be in distress, and consequently be forced to come out: otherwise, the blockade of Cadiz is perfectly nugatory. The *Pickle Schooner* joined the Fleet from Plymouth yesterday.

I am, Sir, &c.,
NELSON AND BRONTE[18]

To Richard Ford, Esq., Agent Victualler Afloat

Victory, October 2nd, 1805

Dear Sir,

As I hear that Mr. Cutforth, the Agent Victualler at Gibraltar, is very much indisposed, so as probably to render him unable to go over to Tetuan, to settle several things with the Governor and English Vice-Consul at that place, I have therefore to desire that you will go to Gibraltar; and should Mr Cutforth not be able to proceed to Tetuan, that you will carry my instructions to Mr Cutforth into execution, marking to the Governor or Vice-Consul, that whatever I may allow for the guards, or any other purpose, is from myself, and not to be considered as a general tax; and you will consult with Mr Cutforth upon the best mode of keeping these gentry in good humour, and that the Fleet may get liberal supplies without any further trouble.

I have the firmest reliance upon your abilities and zeal that this matter will be well terminated; and although no man wishes to be more economical of the Public money than myself, yet in our present state, and with the sort of people with whom we have to manage these matters, care must be taken not to be *penny wise* and *pounds* foolish. I need not say more, but that I am sure I shall be content with whatever you do; and I am, with great esteem, dear Sir, &c.,

NELSON AND BRONTE[19]

You must not be many hours at Gibraltar, but ask Admiral Knight for a conveyance to Tetuan; for Admiral Louis, with a Squadron, will leave the Fleet this day.

N. AND B

To Captain Duff, HMS *Mars* *4th October, 1805*

As the Enemy's Fleets may be hourly expected to put to sea from Cadiz, I have to desire that you will keep, with the *Mars*, *Defence*, and *Colossus*, from three to four leagues between the Fleet and Cadiz, in order that I may get the information from the Frigates stationed off that Port, as expeditiously as possible. Distant Signals to be used, when Flags, from the state of the weather, may not readily be distinguished in their colours. If the Enemy be out, or coming out, fire guns by day or night, in order to draw my attention. In thick weather, the Ships are to close within signal of the *Victory*: one of the Ships to be placed to windward, or rather to the Eastward of the other two, to extend the distance of seeing; and I have desired Captain Blackwood to throw a Frigate to the Westward of Cadiz, for the purpose of an easy and early communication.

I am, &c.,

NELSON AND BRONTE[20]

To Captain The Hon. Henry Blackwood, HMS *Euryalus*

Victory, October 4th, 1805,

Cadiz, East 17 leagues

My dear Sir,

I have received from Rear-Admiral Louis, your information

respecting the intended movements of the Enemy, which strengthens my conviction that you estimate, as I do, the importance of not letting these rogues escape us without a fair fight, which I pant for by day, and dream of by night. I am momentarily expecting the *Phœbe*, *Sirius*, *Naiad*, and *Niger*, from Gibraltar; two of them shall be with you directly as I get hold of them; and if you meet them, and there is any way of sending information and their dispatches from Gibraltar, keep *Naiad* and *Phœbe*. *Juno* is a fixture between Cape Spartel and Gibraltar; *Mars*, *Colossus*, and *Defence*, will be stationed four leagues East from the Fleet, and one of them advanced to the East towards Cadiz, and as near as possible in the latitude. The Fleet will be from sixteen to eighteen leagues West of Cadiz; therefore, if you throw a Frigate West from you, most probably, in fine weather, we shall communicate daily. In fresh breezes Easterly, I shall work up for Cadiz, never getting to the Northward of it; and in the event of hearing they are standing out of Cadiz, I shall carry a press of sail to the Southward towards Cape Spartel and Arrache, so that you will always know where to find me. I am writing out regular instructions for the Frigates under your orders, but I am confident you will not let these gentry slip through our fingers, and then we shall give a good account of them, although they may be very superior in numbers. The *Royal Sovereign* and *Defiance* were to sail after the 24th. Belleisle, too, is ordered here. I send you two papers; I stole them for you. Ever, my dear Blackwood, most faithfully your friend,

NELSON AND BRONTE[21]

To Viscount Castlereagh   *5th October, 1805*

I have only two Frigates to watch them, and not one with the Fleet. I am most exceedingly anxious for more eyes, and hope the Admiralty are hastening them to me. The last Fleet was lost to me for want of Frigates; God forbid this should.

I am, &c.,

NELSON AND BRONTE[22]

To William Marsden, Esq., Admiralty
[About the 5th October, 1805.]

I am sorry ever to trouble their Lordships with anything like a complaint of a want of Frigates and Sloops; but if the different services require them, and I have them not, those services must be neglected to be performed. I am taking all Frigates about me I possibly can; for if I were an Angel, and attending to all the other points of my Command, let the Enemy escape for want of the *eyes of the Fleet*, I should consider myself as most highly reprehensible. Never less than eight Frigates, and three good fast-sailing Brigs, should always be with the Fleet to watch Cadiz; and to carry Transports in and out to refit it, would take at least ten and four Brigs, to do that service well. At present I have only been able to collect two, which makes me very uneasy.

I am, &c.,
NELSON AND BRONTE[23]

To The Right Hon. George Rose
Victory, 16 leagues West from Cadiz,
October 6th, 1805

My dear Mr Rose,

Your two letters of September 17th [have arrived], and I feel much obliged by your kind intentions for my dear Mr Bolton, and I think Mr. Pitt will do what he can to oblige me. I verily believe the Country will soon be put to some expense for my account, either a Monument, or a new Pension and Honours; for I have not the very smallest doubt but that a very few days, almost hours, will put us in Battle; the success no man can ensure, but the fighting them, if they are to be got at, I pledge myself, and if the force arrives which is intended. I am *very, very, very* anxious for its arrival, for the thing will be done if a few more days elapse; and I want for the sake of our Country that it should be done so effectually as to have nothing to wish for; and what will signify the force the day after the Battle? It is, as Mr Pitt knows, annihilation that the Country wants, and not merely a splendid Victory of twenty-three to thirty-six, – honourable to the parties concerned, but absolutely useless in the extended scale to bring Buonaparte to his marrow-bones: numbers can only annihilate. I think, not for myself, but the Country, therefore I hope the Admiralty will send the fixt force as soon as possible, and Frigates, and Sloops of War, for I am very destitute. I do not mean this as any complaint, quite the contrary; I believe they are doing all they can, if interest does not interfere; therefore, if Mr. Pitt would hint to Lord Barham, that he shall be anxious until I get the force proposed, and plenty of Frigates and Sloops in order to watch them closely, it may be advantageous to the Country: you are at liberty to mention this to Mr. Pitt, but I would not wish it to go farther. I am ever, my dear Mr. Rose,

Your most obliged and faithful friend,

NELSON AND BRONTE

The Treasury should order me to land the money, 150,000 dollars in Spanish, in the Mediterranean. I mentioned it to Mr. Pitt, but I am ordered to land it in England, and the Ships are here.[24]

This memorandum codifies the "Nelson touch" which the Admiral propounded to his "band of brothers" in the *Victory*'s great cabin on the 29 September (*see* page 136).

(Secret)   *Victory*, off Cadiz, *9th October, 1805*
     Memorandum.

Thinking it almost impossible to bring a Fleet of forty Sail of the Line into a Line of Battle in variable winds, thick weather, and other circumstances which must occur, without such a loss of time that the opportunity would probably be lost of bringing the Enemy to Battle in such a manner as to make the business decisive, I have therefore made up my mind to keep the Fleet in that position of sailing (with the exception of the First and Second in Command) that the Order of Sailing is to be the Order of Battle, placing the Fleet in two Lines of sixteen Ships each, with an Advanced Squadron of eight of the fastest sailing Two-decked Ships, *which* will always make, if wanted, a Line of twenty-four Sail, on whichever Line the Commander-in-Chief may direct.

The Second in Command will, after my intentions are made known to him, have the entire direction of his Line to make the attack upon the Enemy, and to follow up the blow until they are captured or destroyed.

If the Enemy's Fleet should be seen to windward in Line of Battle, and that the two Lines and the Advanced Squadron can fetch them, they will probably be so extended that their Van could not succour their Rear.

I should therefore probably make the Second in Command's signal to lead through, about their twelfth Ship from their Rear, (or wherever he could fetch, if not able to get so far advanced); my Line would lead through about their Centre, and the Advanced Squadron to cut two or three or four Ships a-head of their Centre, so as to ensure getting at their Commander-in-Chief, on whom every effort must be made to capture.

The whole impression of the British Fleet must be to over-power from two or three Ships a-head of their Commander-in-Chief, supposed to be in the Centre, to the Rear of their Fleet. I will suppose twenty Sail of the Enemy's Line to be untouched, it must be some time before they could perform a manœuvre to bring their force compact to attack any part of the British Fleet engaged, or to succour their own Ships, which indeed would be impossible without mixing with the Ships engaged.

Something must be left to chance; nothing is sure in a Sea Fight beyond all others. Shot will carry away the masts and yards of friends as well as foes; but I look with confidence to a Victory before the Van of the Enemy could succour their Rear, and then that the British Fleet would most of them be ready to receive their twenty Sail of the Line, or to pursue them, should they endeavour to make off.

If the Van of the Enemy tacks, the Captured Ships must run to leeward of the British Fleet; if the Enemy wears, the British must place themselves between the Enemy and the Captured, and disabled British Ships; and should the Enemy close, I have no fears as to the result.

The Second in Command will in all possible things direct the movements of his Line, by keeping them as compact as the nature of the circumstances will admit. Captains are to look to their particular Line as their rallying point. But, in case Signals can neither be seen or perfectly understood, no Captain can do very wrong if he places his Ship alongside that of an Enemy.

Of the intended attack from to windward, the Enemy in Line of Battle ready to receive an attack,

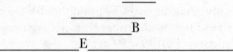

The divisions of the British Fleet will be brought nearly within gun shot of the Enemy's Centre. The signal will most probably then be made for the Lee Line to bear up together, to set all their sails, even steering sails, in order to get as quickly as possible to the Enemy's Line, and to cut through, beginning from the 12 Ship from the Enemy's Rear. Some Ships may not get through their exact place, but they will always be at hand to assist their friends; and if any are thrown round the Rear of the Enemy, they will effectually complete the business of twelve Sail of the Enemy.

Should the Enemy wear together, or bear up and sail large, still the twelve Ships composing, in the first position, the Enemy's Rear, are to be *the* object of attack of the Lee Line, unless otherwise directed from the Commander-in-Chief, which is scarcely to be expected, as the entire management of the Lee Line, after the intentions of the Commander-in-Chief, is [*are*] signified, is intended to be left to the judgment of the Admiral commanding that Line.

The remainder of the Enemy's Fleet, 34 Sail, are to be left to the management of the Commander-in-Chief, who will endeavour to take care that the movements of the Second in Command are as little interrupted as is possible.

NELSON AND BRONTE[25]

To The Respective Captains

Victory, off Cadiz, *10th October, 1805*

The Ships and Vessels of the Fleet under my command are directed not to show their Colours on joining, unless the Commander-in-Chief should show his.

NELSON AND BRONTE[26]

To The Respective Captains

Victory, off Cadiz, *10th October, 1805*

It is my particular directions that the Captains and Commanders of His Majesty's Ships and Vessels under my command, who may purchase bullocks, fresh beef, lemons, onions, or any other species of provisions or refreshments for their respective Companies, whether such purchase is for a particular Ship, or for the Fleet in general, and whether it is made by my order or otherwise, that a Voucher of the fresh beef, bullocks, &c., so procured for the individual Ship or Fleet, is transmitted to me, immediately the Ship making such purchase shall join the Fleet.

NELSON AND BRONTE[27]

To The Respective Captains

Victory, off Cadiz, *10th October, 1805*

It is my directions that whenever any men are sent to the Hospital, a statement of their case is sent with them, that the Medical Gentlemen belonging to the Hospital may know what has been done in order to remove the diseases.

NELSON AND BRONTE[28]

To The Respective Captains

Victory, off Cadiz, *10th October, 1805*

Having frequently known that onions have been purchased on account of Government when in Port, where the Pursers could and ought to purchase vegetables to put into the Ships' Companies' soup, and that the onions so purchased by Government for recruiting the health of the Ships' Companies, have been used for the benefit of the Purser, by putting these vegetables into the soup, which the Purser should be obliged to purchase when to be procured; it is, therefore, my positive directions, that the Pursers are obliged to purchase vegetables for the Ships' soup when it is possible to procure them; and that the Government onions are not used for the soup, if the Purser has the power of obtaining onions or other vegetables, as he is bound to do.

And it is my further directions, that whenever fresh provisions can be procured on reasonable terms, that it is purchased; but that onions, for the account of Government, are not purchased without my orders. Ships, absent for any length of time from me, are at liberty to purchase the gratuitous onions of Government for the recruiting the health of their Ships' Companies, who may have been long fed upon salt provisions.

NELSON AND BRONTE[29]

To Captain The Hon. Henry Blackwood, HMS *Euryalus*

Victory, October 10th, 1805. Cadiz, East, *13 Leagues*

My dear Blackwood,

Keep your five Frigates, *Weazle* and *Pickle*, and let me know every movement. I rely on you, that we can't miss getting hold of them, and I will give them such a shaking as they never yet experienced; at least I will lay down my life in the attempt. We are a very powerful Fleet, and not to be held cheap. I have told Parker, and do you direct Ships bringing information of their coming out, to fire guns every three minutes by the watch, and in the night to fire off rockets, if they have them, from the masthead. I have nothing more to say, than I hope they will sail to-night.

Ever yours most faithfully,

NELSON AND BRONTE[30]

On 18 October, Admiral Villeneuve of the Combined Fleet had a fit of bravery. What caused it was his discovery that Napoleon intended to supersede him with Admiral Rosily. Instead of this disgrace, Villeneuve decided to depart Cadiz and make a break for the Mediterranean. Villeneuve was no fool; in his last address to his fleet, he told them to beware of an enveloping attack on the rear.

At seven o'clock in the morning of 1 October the British frigate *Sirius*, waiting outside Cadiz, made the long-awaited signal 370: "The enemy's ships are coming out of port." Within 2 hours, the signal had been received by Nelson on *Victory* 50 miles away.

NELSON ORDERS THE CHASE, CADIZ, 9.30 a.m. 19 October 1805

Admiral Lord Nelson[31]

From Nelson's private journal:

October 19th

Fine weather, wind Easterly. At half-past nine, the Mars, being one of the look-out Ships, repeated the Signal, "that the Enemy was coming out of Port" – made the Signal for a "General Chase S.E."; wind at South, Cadiz bearing E.N.E. by compass, distant sixteen leagues. At three the *Colossus*, made the Signal, "that the Enemy's Fleet was at sea." In the evening directed the Fleet to observe my motions during the night, and for *Britannia*, *Prince*, and *Dreadnought*, they being heavy sailers, to take their stations as convenient; and for *Mars*, *Orion*, *Belleisle*, *Leviathan*, *Bellerophon*, and *Polyphemus*, to go ahead during the night, and to carry a light, standing for the Straits' Mouth.

NELSON'S LAST LETTER TO HIS DAUGHTER, HORATIA, 19 October 1805

Admiral Lord Nelson[32]

Victory, October 19th, 1805

My dearest Angel,

I was made happy by the pleasure of receiving your letter of September 19th, and I rejoice to hear that you are so very good a girl, and love my dear Lady Hamilton, who most dearly loves you. Give her a kiss for me. The Combined Fleets of the Enemy are now reported to be coming out of Cadiz; and therefore I answer your letter, my dearest Horatia, to mark to you that you are ever uppermost in my thoughts. I shall be sure of your prayers for my safety, conquest, and speedy return to dear Merton, and our dearest good Lady Hamilton. Be a good girl, mind what Miss Connor says to you. Receive, my dearest Horatia, the affectionate parental blessing of your Father,

NELSON AND BRONTE

NELSON'S LAST LETTER TO EMMA HAMILTON, 19 October 1805

Admiral Lord Nelson[33]

> *Victory, October 19th, 1805, Noon,*
> Cadiz, E.S.E., 16 Leagues

My dearest beloved Emma, the dear friend of my bosom. The signal has been made that the Enemy's Combined Fleet are coming out of Port. We have very little wind, so that I have no hopes of seeing them before to-morrow. May the God of Battles crown my endeavours with success; at all events, I will take care that my name shall ever be most dear to you and Horatia, both of whom I love as much as my own life. And as my last writing before the Battle will be to you, so I hope in God that I shall live to finish my letter after the Battle. May Heaven bless you prays your

NELSON AND BRONTE

Due to light breezes, only a very few of Villeneuve's fleet managed to clear Cadiz on the 19th, and it was not until the 20th that the Combined French and Spanish Fleet was able to properly assemble outside Cadiz and put to sea.

THE EVE OF BATTLE: THE COMBINED FLEET GETS UNDER SAIL, 20 October 1805

Captain Jean Lucas, the Redoutable[34]

Lucas would be one of the few French captains to be praised by Napoleon in the Battle of Trafalgar. The Combined Fleet composed eighteen ships of the line and fifteen Spanish.

On the 28th Vendémiaire An XIV (20th October, 1805)* the Combined Fleet got under sail to leave Cadiz Bay. The wind was southerly; light at first, afterwards fresh. The fleet comprised thirty-three sail of the Line, of which eighteen were

---

* The last day of December, 1805 (10th Nivose An XIV), saw the last of the Revolution Calendar, invented by Fabre d'Eglantine and Gilbert Romme. By order of Napoleon the Gregorian Calendar was restored on and after the 1st of January, 1806.

French, fifteen Spanish; with five frigates and two brigs, French. We were hardly outside when the wind shifted to the south-west and came on to blow strong. The admiral then ordered the fleet to reef sail, which was done, though some of the Spanish ships were so slow over it that they fell considerably to leeward. Some time was lost by that, but at length all worked back again, and then the fleet stood on, in no regular formation, heading to the west-north-west. The *Redoutable* was next astern to the Bucentaure, and a short distance off, when, towards noon, the flagship suddenly signalled "Man overboard!" I brought to at once, lowered a boat, picked the man up, and regained my station.

An hour after midday the wind shifted to the west, and the fleet went about all together. As soon as that was done, the Bucentaure signalled for the battle-squadron to form in three columns on the starboard tack, flagships in the centre of their divisions. In this order of sailing the *Redoutable*, as leader (*chef de file*) of the first division, should have been at the head of her column, and I manœuvred the ship to take that post.* All the afternoon, however, was spent without the fleet being able to get into the formation designated, although the admiral kept signalling repeatedly to ships to take station.

Towards seven in the evening the wind went down a little; but the sea was still rough, with a swell setting in from the south-west. The fleet was now steering to the south-south-west. I signalled at this time to the admiral that I could make out a fleet or squadron of the enemy to windward. They did not, to me, seem very far off. The ships of this squadron, as the evening went on, made a great many signals, showing for their purpose quite a remarkable display of coloured fires.

About nine o'clock at night the flagship made the general signal to the fleet to form in the order of battle at once (*promptement*), without regard to the stations of individual ships.

* According to the squadronal division of the French Fleet, the *Redoutable* belonged to Admiral Villeueuve's own group, which comprised the *Bucentaure*, *Neptune*, *Redoutable*, *Indomptable*, and *Héros*. Dumanoir's group comprised the *Formidable*, *Scipion*, *Intrépide*, *Duguay Trouin*, and *Mont Blanc*. Magon's group was formed of the *Algéçiras*, *Achille*, *Argonauta*, *Aigle*, and *Fougueux*, the fastest of the French ships; with the *Pluton*, *Swiftsure*, and *Berwick* added.

To carry out this evolution those ships most to leeward ought to have shown a light at each masthead, so as to mark their positions. Whether this was done I do not know: at any rate I was unable to see such lights. At that moment, indeed, we were all widely scattered. The ships of the battle squadron and those of the squadron of observation were all mixed up. Another cause of confusion was this. Nearly all the ships had answered the admiral's signals with flares, which made it impossible to tell which was the flagship. All I could do was to follow the motions of other ships near me which were closing on some to leeward.

Towards eleven I discovered myself close to Admiral Gravina, who, with four or five ships, was beginning to form his own line of battle. I was challenged and our name demanded, whereupon the Spanish admiral ordered me to take post in his line. I asked leave to lead it and he assented, whereupon I stood into station. The wind was in direction and force as before, and we were all still on the starboard tack.

The whole fleet was at this time cleared for action, in accordance with orders signalled from the *Bucentaure* earlier in the night. In the *Redoutable* we had, however, cleared for action immediately after leaving Cadiz, and everything had been kept since in readiness to go to quarters instantly. With the certainty of a battle next day, I retained but few men on deck during the night. I sent the greater number of the officers and crew to lie down, so that they might be as fresh as possible for the approaching fight.

The maneuvers of the Combined Fleet were shadowed closely by Blackwood in the frigate *Euryalus*, despite several attempts to run him off, and his reports back to Nelson allowed the Admiral to bring together the two fleets during the night of the 20th. He was positioned perfectly for battle the next day.

Part Three

England's Glory

The Battle of Trafalgar, 21 October 1805

253   269   863   261 471 958 220 374 4 21 19 24.

ENGLAND EXPECTS THAT EVERY MAN WILL DO HIS D U T Y.

INTRODUCTION

Daylight on the 21st revealed the fleets converging together like flocks of white seagulls, a little more than 7 leagues off the nearest land, Cape Trafalgar. Hampered by poor seamanship, the thirty-three ships of the line in the Combined French-Spanish fleet under Villeneuve were in a shapeless straggle over 3 miles of sea, bunched together in some places three abreast. The British were also out of formation – but not for long. At approximately 6.15 a.m. the *Victory* made signal Number 72: "Form the order of sailing in two columns". The Weather (left) column, headed by the *Victory*, comprised twelve ships and headed towards the centre of the Combined Fleet. To give maximum impact and firepower, behind the *Victory* (100 guns) were two other three-deckers: *Téméraire* (98 guns) and *Neptune* (98 guns). The Lee (right) column lead by Collingwood in the *Royal Sovereign* (100 guns) comprised fifteen ships and headed to "envelop the rear" of the Combined Fleet.

Such light wind meant that it took a great deal of time to close the 12-mile gap between the fleets, since most ships were making less than 3 knots. There was plenty of time for preparations.

THE MORNING OF TRAFALGAR: NELSON PREPARES HIS MEN FOR BATTLE, 6–8 a.m.

Dr William Beatty, HMS Victory[1]

Soon after daylight, Lord Nelson came upon deck; he was dressed as usual in his Admiral's frock-coat, bearing on the left breast four stars of different orders, which he always wore with his common apparel . . . He displayed excellent spirits, and expressed his pleasure at the prospect of giving a fatal blow to the naval power of France and Spain; and spoke with confidence of obtaining a signal victory, notwithstanding the inferiority of the British Fleet, declaring to Captain Hardy that he would not be contented with capturing less than twenty sail of the Line . . . The wind was now from the west, but the breezes were very light, with a long, heavy swell running. The signal being made for bearing down upon the enemy in two lines, the British Fleet set all possible sail. The Lee Line, consisting of thirteen ships, was led by Admiral Collingwood in the *Royal Sovereign*, and the Weather Line, composed of fourteen ships, by the Commander-in-Chief in the *Victory*.

His Lordship ascended the poop, to have a better view of both Lines of the British Fleet, and while there gave particular directions for taking down from his cabin the different fixtures . . .

Immediately after this he quitted the poop, and retired to his cabin for a few minutes.

There, Nelson composed the diary entry, prayer and codicil to his will below.

THE MORNING OF TRAFALGAR: NELSON'S LAST DIARY ENTRY AND WILL, 8.30 a.m.

Admiral Lord Nelson, HMS Victory[2]

PRIVATE DIARY

Monday, October 21st, 1805

At daylight saw the Enemy's Combined Fleet from East to E.S.E.; bore away; made the signal for Order of Sailing, and to

Prepare for Battle; the Enemy with their heads to the Southward: at seven the Enemy wearing in succession. May the Great
God, whom I worship, grant to my Country, and for the benefit
of Europe in general, a great and glorious Victory; and may no
misconduct in any one tarnish it; and may humanity after
Victory be the predominant feature in the British Fleet. For
myself, individually, I commit my life to Him who made me,
and may his blessing light upon my endeavours for serving my
Country faithfully. To Him I resign myself and the just cause
which is entrusted to me to defend. Amen. Amen. Amen.

CODICIL TO LORD NELSON'S WILL

October the twenty-first, one thousand eight hundred and
five, then in sight of the Combined Fleets of France and Spain,
distant about ten miles.

Whereas the eminent services of Emma Hamilton, widow of
the Right Honourable Sir William Hamilton, have been of the
very greatest service to our King and Country, to my knowledge, without her receiving any reward from either our King or
Country; – first, that she obtained the King of Spain's letter, in
1796, to his brother, the King of Naples, acquainting him of his
intention to declare War against England; from which Letter
the Ministry sent out orders to then Sir John Jervis, to strike a
stroke, if opportunity offered, against either the Arsenals of
Spain, or her Fleets. That neither of these was done is not the
fault of Lady Hamilton. The opportunity might have been
offered. Secondly, the British Fleet under my command, could
never have returned the second time to Egypt, had not Lady
Hamilton's influence with the Queen of Naples caused letters to
be wrote to the Governor of Syracuse, that he was to encourage
the Fleet being supplied with everything, should they put into
any Port in Sicily. We put into Syracuse, and received every
supply, went to Egypt, and destroyed the French Fleet. Could I
have rewarded these services I would not now call upon my
Country; but as that has not been in my power, I leave Emma
Lady Hamilton, therefore, a Legacy to my King and Country,
that they will give her an ample provision to maintain her rank
in life. I also leave to the beneficence of my Country my adopted
daughter, Horatia Nelson Thompson; and I desire she will use

in future the name of Nelson only. These are the only favours I ask of my King and Country at this moment when I am going to fight their Battle. May God bless my King and Country, and all those who I hold dear. My relations it is needless to mention: they will of course be amply provided for.

NELSON AND BRONTE[3]

Witness – Henry Blackwood.
            T.M. Hardy.

THE MORNING OF TRAFALGAR: THE SCENE BELOW DECKS ON HMS *AJAX*

Second-Lieutenant Ellis, Royal Marines[4]

I was sent below with orders, and was much struck with the preparations made by the bluejackets, the majority of whom were stripped to the waist; a handkerchief was tightly bound round their heads and over the ears, to deaden the noise of the cannon, many men being deaf for days after an action. The men were variously occupied; some were sharpening their cutlasses, others polishing the guns, as though an inspection were about to take place instead of a mortal combat, whilst three or four, as if in mere bravado, were dancing a horn-pipe; but all seemed deeply anxious to come to close-quarters with the enemy. Occasionally they would look out of the ports; and speculate as to the various ships of the enemy, many of which had been on former occasions engaged by our vessels . . .

THE MORNING OF TRAFALGAR AT 10.00 A.M.

Midshipman William Badcock, HMS Neptune[5]

The old *Neptune*, which never was a good sailor, took it into her head to sail better that morning than I ever remember to have seen her do before. About ten o'clock we got close to the *Victory*, and Captain Fremantle had intended to pass her and break the enemy's line, but poor Lord Nelson himself hailed us from the stern-walk of the *Victory*, and said, "*Neptune*, take in your studding-sails and drop astern; I shall break the line myself."

A signal was then made for the *Téméraire* (98) to take her station between us and the *Victory*, which consequently made us the third ship in the van of his lordship's column.

At this period the enemy were forming their double line in the shape of a crescent. It was a beautiful sight when their line was completed: their broadsides turned towards us, showing their iron teeth and now and then trying the range of a shot to ascertain the distance, that they might, the moment we came within point blank (about six hundred yards), open their fire upon our van ships – no doubt with the hope of dismantling some of our leading vessels before they could close and break their line. Some of them were painted like ourselves – with double yellow sides; some with a broad single red or yellow streak; others all black; and the noble *Santisima Trinidada* (138), with four distinct lines of red, with a white ribbon between them, made her seem to be a superb man-of-war, which indeed she was. Her appearance was imposing; her head splendidly ornamented with a colossal group of figures, painted white, representing, the Holy Trinity, from which she took her name. This magnificent ship was destined to be our opponent. She was lying-to under topsails, top-gallant sails, royals, jib, and span-ker; her courses were hauled up; and her lofty towering sails looked beautiful, peering through the smoke, as she awaited the onset. The flags of France and Spain, both handsome, che-quered the line, waving defiance to that of Britain.

Then, in our fleet, union-jacks and ensigns were made fast to the fore and fore-topmast-stays, as well as to the mizen rigging, besides one at the peak, in order that we might not mistake each other in the smoke, and to show the enemy of our determination to conquer. Towards eleven, our two lines were better formed, but still there existed long gaps in Vice-Admiral Collingwood's division. Lord Nelson's van was strong; three three-deckers (*Victory*, *Téméraire*, and *Neptune*), and four seventy-fours; their jib-booms nearly over the others' taffrails, the bands playing "God save the King," "Rule Britannia," and "Britons strike home."

THE MORNING OF TRAFALGAR: BRITISH GUN CREWS STAND BY FOR ACTION

C.R. Pemberton[6]

Everything was now in order, fires extinguished, fearnaught screens round the hatchways for passing powder from the magazines; shot racks drawn from under their peaceable coverings, and arranged ready for their work; guns cast loose, crowbars for pointing the guns lying at hand on the deck; tompions out all ready for a game of thunder . . . my friend the goat sent down to the cable tier – the captain's ducks and geese left in the coops, to cackle and quake and take their chance – the doctor's saws and knives and probes and bandages and tourniquets, all laid in order in the cockpit; and I devoutly hoping, as tempted by curiosity I looked at them, that I might be blown away all together, rather than that he should exercise his skill on my limbs or carcass. And every man and boy was mute as he stood at his station. Here and there might be seen one drawing the knot of his handkerchief, girt around his loins, or that of his head bandages; all grim in lip and glistening in eye . . . But don't you imagine, reader that I was not frightened in all this. Faith, there was something in the orderly stillness of lying there for half an hour with all this preparation for destruction and death that made me think might be worse places than the counting house after all. There was no noise, no laugh, no show of hilarity; yet was there some interjectorial jesting bandied about which called up grim smiles, but no laugh. Men, shirtless, with handkerchiefs bandaged tightly round their loins and heads, stood with naked brawny arms folded on their hairy and heaving chests, looking pale and stern, but still hushed; or glancing with a hot eye through ports . . . I felt a difficulty in swallowing.

MID-MORNING AT TRAFALGAR: THE VIEW OF THE FRENCH COMMANDER-IN-CHIEF

Admiral Pierre-Charles de Villeneuve, Bucentaure[7]

The enemy continued to steer for us under all sail, and at nine o'clock I was able to make out that their fleet was formed in two columns, of which one was heading directly for my flagship and the other toward the rear of the Combined Fleet. The wind was very light, the sea with a swell on, owing to which our formation in line was rendered very difficult to effect; but in the circumstances, considering the nature of the attack that I foresaw the enemy were about to make, the irregularity of our order did not seem a disadvantage, if each ship could have continued to keep to the wind, and close upon the ship next ahead.

I made a signal to the leading ships to keep as close as possible to the wind and to make all sail possible. At eleven o'clock I signalled to the rear squadron to keep closer to the wind and support the centre, which appeared to be the point on which the enemy now appeared to be directing his main attack. The enemy meanwhile came steadily on, though the wind was very light. They had their most powerful ships at the head of the columns.

Knowing from the barometer that there would be a storm that night, and desperate to achieve a decision before darkness, the British were hurrying into battle as fast as the conditions would allow. Even so the time dragged, and Nelson made a last round of the *Victory* to encourage her crew.

Previously to the commencement of the battle of Trafalgar, Lord Nelson went over the different decks of the *Victory*, saw and spoke to the different classes of seamen, encouraged them with his usual affability, and was much pleased at the manner in which the seamen had barricaded the hawse holes of the ship. All was perfect death-like silence, till just before the action began. Three cheers were given his Lordship as he ascended the quarter-deck ladder. He had been particular in recommending cool, steady firing, in preference to a hurrying fire, without aim or precision, and the event justified his Lordship's advice.[8]

As noon approached, the fleets had almost closed to shooting distance. The veritable master of morale, Nelson at 11.56 a.m. ordered that a signal should be sent.

NELSON SENDS THE SIGNAL "ENGLAND EXPECTS THAT EVERY MAN WILL DO HIS DUTY", 11.56 a.m.

Lieutenant George Brown, HMS Victory[9]

I was on the poop and quarter-deck whilst preparations for the fight were going on, and saw Lord Nelson, Captain Blackwood, and some other Captains of the frigates, in earnest conversation together, and a slip of paper in the hand of the former (which Captain Blackwood had looked at), yet I have no recollection that I ever saw it pass through other hands till it was given to Pasco, who, after referring to the telegraph signal book, took it back to his Lordship, and it was then that, I believe, the substitution of the words took place. I think (though not sure), the substitution was "expects" for the word "confides", the latter word not being in the telegraph book, and I think the word "England" had been previously substituted for "Nelson" for the same reason, at the suggestion of Captain Blackwood.

Collingwood in the *Royal Sovereign* could not see the point of the gesture. The men in the fleet could. Captain Blackwood was beside Nelson when the signal went up.

I was walking with him [Lord Nelson] on the poop when he said, "I'll now amuse the fleet with a signal", and he asked me if I did not think there was one yet wanting. I answered that I thought the whole of the Fleet seemed very clearly to understand what they were about, and to vie with each other who should first get nearest to the *Victory* or *Royal Sovereign*. These words were scarcely uttered when his last well known signal was made: "England expects every man will do his duty". The shout with which it was received throughout the fleet was truly sublime. "Now," said Lord Nelson, "I can do no more. We must trust to the Great Disposer of all Events, and the justice of our cause. I thank God for this great opportunity of doing my duty."[10]

Just minutes later, the battle commenced when the *Fougueux* opened fire on the approaching *Royal Sovereign* of Collingwood's Lee column.

THE FIRST SHOTS: *FOUGUEUX* ENGAGES *ROYAL SOVEREIGN*, 12.00 noon

Captain Pierre Servaux, Master of Arms, Fougueux[11]

The *Fougueux*, on board which I was master-at-arms, had for her immediate leader (*chef de file*) the Spanish man-of-war *Santa Ana*, of 110 guns. By bad handling that ship left a gap of at least a cable across, between herself and the next astern, ourselves; thus offering the enemy an easy passage through. It was just on this point that Admiral Collingwood directed his attack, as he advanced to break the line. It necessarily resulted that he crossed right in front of our bows, and so our first antagonist was Admiral Collingwood.

At a quarter past twelve o'clock* the *Fougueux*, a man-of-war of 74 guns, fired the first gun in the fleet. As she did so she hoisted her colours. She continued her cannonade, firing on the English flagship, which was a greatly superior vessel in size, height, guns and the number of the crew. Her main-deck and upper-deck guns, in fact, could fire right down on to our decks, and in that way all our upper-deck men employed in working the ship, and the infantry marksmen posted on the gangways, were without cover and entirely exposed. We had also, according to our bad habit in the French Navy, fired away over a hundred rounds from our big guns at long range before the English ship had practically snapped a gun lock. It was, indeed, not until we found ourselves side by side and yardarm to yardarm with the English flagship that she fired at all. Then she gave us a broadside from five and fifty guns and carronades, hurtling forth a storm of cannon balls, big and small, and musket-shot.

I thought the *Fougueux* was shattered to pieces – pulverized. The storm of projectiles that hurled themselves against and through the hull on the port side made the ship heel to starboard. Most of the sails and the rigging were cut to pieces, while the upper deck was swept clear of the greater number of the seamen working there, and of the soldier sharpshooters. Our gun-decks below had, however, suffered less severely. There,

* more probably 12.00 a.m.

not more than thirty men in all were put *hors de combat*. This preliminary greeting, rough and brutal as it was, did not dishearten our men. A well-maintained fire showed the English-men that we too had guns and could use them.

The English ship having come up to us, made to break the line between us and the *Santa Ana*. The Spanish ship, in fact, during our action with the English leader, had not fired a single shot. She had stolidly kept on and continued her course without shortening sail, thus giving an easy passage through to the enemy. After that, however, by the smart handling of our captain, we managed to come within our proper distance of her; as a fact, indeed, almost with our bowsprit over his poop. By this manœuvre we had the enemy's ship on the port quarter in such a way that whilst we could only receive a few shots from their stern guns, they were exposed to our whole broadside, raking the enemy, end-on, along all his decks. We soon saw the English vessel's mizen-mast go by the board, and then her rudder and steering gear were damaged, making the ship unmanageable. Her sails flapped loose in the wind, and her sheets and running rigging were cut to pieces by our hail of shot. For some time she ceased firing. We, for our part, now re-doubled our efforts and we next saw her maintopmast come down. At that moment the English ship hoisted two signal flags at the foremast. It made us think that she was calling for help. And we were not wrong. After a very little time two fresh English men-of-war came up and began to attack us; the one on the starboard quarter, the other at the stern. Under their fire, we held out for more than an hour, but they almost over-powered us with their terrible storm of round shot and a fusillade of bullets which carried death among our men.

Our mizen-mast was now shot by the board, while our spars were shot from the masts and were lying in wreckage along the sides of the ship. Then, too, fire broke out in the stern walk and the poop. We tried our best, in spite of the hail of shot, to put the fire out, and with hatchets to cut adrift the mass of wrecked top-hamper from the fallen masts and yards and cordage. It lay along the ship's sides by the gun-tiers and was endangering the ship and exposing her to the most imminent risk of destruction by fire. At this moment the captain ordered me to climb outboard and see if the wreckage of the mainsail was not in danger of being set on fire from the main-deck guns. I obeyed; but as I clambered from the gangway into the chains one of the enemy fired her whole starboard broadside. The din and concussion were fearful; so tremendous that I almost fell head-long into the sea. Blood gushed from my nose and ears, but it did not prevent my carrying out my duty. Then our mainmast fell. Happily it was shot through some ten or twelve feet above the deck and fell over to port. At once we cut away the shrouds to starboard; but it was with great difficulty that in the end we were able to clear ourselves.

Our fire was well maintained all this time: though the great superiority of the heavy guns of the English ships, and their very advantageous position, decimated our men in a fearful manner. More than half the crew had by this been struck down, killed or wounded. Then, at length, our last remaining mast went; falling forward on to the fore part of the ship. Our flag, however, was still flying. It was the only thing left above the deck.

ONE MAN'S BATTLE: SAM, HMS *ROYAL SOVEREIGN*

An undated letter home[12]

Royal Sovereign

Honoured Father,

This comes to tell you I am alive and hearty except three fingers; but that's not much, it might have been my head. I told brother Tom I should like to see a greadly battle, and I have seen one, and we have peppered the Combined rarely; and for the matter of that, they fought us pretty tightish for French and Spanish. Three of our mess are killed, and four more of us winged. But to tell you the truth of it, when the game began, I wished myself at Warnborough with my plough again; but when they had given us one duster, and I found myself snug and tight, I set to in good earnest, and thought no more about being killed than if were at Murrell Green Fair, and I was presently as busy and as black as a collier. How my fingers got knocked overboard I don't know, but off they are, and I never missed them till I wanted them. You see, by my writing, it was my left hand, so I can write to you and fight for my King yet. We have taken a rare parcel of ships, but the wind is so rough we cannot bring them home, else I should roll in money, so we are busy smashing 'em, and blowing 'em up wholesale.

Our dear Admiral Nelson is killed! so we have paid pretty sharply for licking 'em. I never sat eyes on him, for which I am both sorry and glad; for, to be sure, I should like to have seen him – but then, all the men in our ship who have seen him are such soft toads, they have done nothing but blast their eyes, and cry, ever since he was killed. God bless you! chaps that fought like the devil, sit down and cry like a wench. I am still in the *Royal Sovereign*, but the Admiral [Collingwood] has left her, for she is like a horse without a bridle, so he is in a frigate that he may be here and there and everywhere, for he's as *cute* as here and there one, and as bold as a lion, for all he can cry! – I saw his tears with my own eyes, when the boat hailed and said my lord was dead. So no more at present from your dutiful son,

SAM

HMS *BELLEROPHON* IN ACTION, 12.25–1.40 p.m.

The Log of the Bellerophon[13]

The *Bellerophon* was the fifth ship in Collingwood's (Lee) column, her log provides a succinct account of that column's early actions, and her own bloody engagement with the French *Aigle*.

12.10 Royal Sovereign opened fire on the enemy's centre. 12.13 answered 16 general. 12.20 *Royal Sovereign*, at the head of the larboard division, broke the enemy's line astern of a Spanish three-decker, and engaged her to leeward, being followed by the *Mars*, *Belleisle*, and *Tonnant*, who engaged their respective oponents. 12.25 opened our fire on the enemy. 12.28 *Victory*, at the head of the starboard division, opened her fire on the enemy. 12.30 engaging both sides in passing through the enemy's line, astern of a Spanish two-decker (*El Monarca*.) 12.35 fell on board the French two-deck ship *l'Aigle*, whilst hauling to the wind, our fore-yard locking with her main one, kept up a brisk fire both on her, on our starboard bow, and a Spanish two-decker (*El Monarca*) on the larboard bow, at the same time receiving and returning fire with a Spanish two-decker (*Bahama*) on the larboard quarter, and receiving the fire of a Spanish two-decker (*St. Juan Nepomuceno*) athwart our stern, and a French two-decker (*la Swiftsure*) on the starboard quarter: the action soon after became general. At one the main and mizen-top-masts fell over the starboard side, main-top-sail and top-gallant-sail caught fire. 1.5 the Master, and 1.11 the Captain fell, still foul of *l'Aigle*, and keeping up a brisk fire from the main and lower decks; quarter-deck, poop, and forecastle being nearly cleared by the enemy's musketry, chiefly from troops on board *l'Aigle*. 1.20 the jib-boom was shot away. 1.40 *l'Aigle* dropt astern under a raking fire from us as she fell off, our ship at this time quite unmanageable from braces, bowlines, &c. shot away.

A more personal view of the *Bellerophon*'s contest with the *Aigle* comes from an officer of the former ship.

. . . *l'Aigle* twice attempted to board us, and hove several grenades into our lower deck, which burst and wounded several of our people most dreadfully, she likewise set fire to our fore chains; our fire was so hot, that we soon drove them from the lower deck, after which our people took the coins out, and elevated their guns, so as to tear her decks and sides to pieces: when she got clear of us, she did not return a single shot whilst we raked her, her starboard quarter was entirely beaten in, and, as we afterwards learnt, 400 men *hors de combat*, so that she was an easy conquest for the *Defiance*, a fresh ship: we were well matched, she being the best manned ship in the Combined, and we in the British fleet. Unfortunately situated as we were, I have no doubt she would have struck, had we been able to follow and engage her for a quarter of an hour longer; but had, we been fairly alongside her, half an hour would have decided the contest; for I must say I was astonished at the coolness and undaunted bravery displayed by our gallant and veteran crew, when surrounded by five enemy's ships, and for a length of time unassisted by any of ours. Our loss, as might be expected, was considerable, and fell chiefly on our prime seamen, who were foremost in distinguishing themselves; twenty-eight, including the Captain, Master, and a Midshipman, were killed outright; and 127, including the Captain of Marines, who had eight balls in his body, and his right arm shot off, before he quitted the deck; Boatswain, and five Midshipmen, were badly wounded, and about forty more slightly, so as not to be incapable of duty; nineteen of the wounded had already died before we left Gibraltar. I consider myself as very fortunate in having escaped unhurt, as our class suffered so severely . . .[14]

As *Bellerophon*'s log indicates, some minutes after she went into action, the first ship of Nelson's (Weather) column opened fire. This was the *Victory* itself. Running down the Combined line from the north, she fired at several ships before pushing under the stern of Villeneuve's *Bucentaure*.

"EFFECTS THAT WERE MURDEROUS AND DESTRUCTIVE": UNDER FIRE FROM HMS *VICTORY*, 12.30 p.m.

Admiral Villeneuve, Bucentaure[15]

The port column, led by the *Victory*, with the flag of Admiral Nelson, came on in much the same way. She appeared as if she was aiming to break the line between the *Santisima Trinidad* and the bows of the Bucentaure. Whether, however, they found our line too well closed up at that point, or from some other reason, when they were almost within half pistol-shot – while we, for our part, prepared to board and had our grappling-irons ready for throwing – they swung off to starboard and passed astern of the *Bucentaure*. The *Redoutable* had the station of the *Neptune*, which had fallen to leeward, and she heroically fulfilled the duties of the second astern of the flagship. She ran on board the *Victory*, but the lightness of the wind had not prevented the *Victory* passing close under the stern of the *Bucentaure* and firing into us as she passed several treble-shotted broadsides, with effects that were murderous and destructive. At that moment I made the signal, "All ships not engaged owing to their stations, are to get into action as soon as possible!" It was impossible for me to see how things were going in the centre and rear of the fleet because of the dense smoke which enveloped us.

HMS *VICTORY* ENGAGES *BUCENTAURE* ... AND *REDOUTABLE*, 12.30–13.10 p.m.

Dr William Beatty, HMS Victory[16]

At fifty minutes past eleven, the enemy opened their fire on the commander in chief. They shewed great coolness in the commencement of the battle; for as the *Victory* approached their line, their ships lying immediately ahead of her and across her bows fired only one gun at a time, to ascertain whether she was yet within their range. This was frequently repeated by eight or nine of their ships, till at length a shot passed through the *Victory*'s main topgallant sail; the hole in which being discovered by the enemy, they immediately opened their broadsides, supporting an awful and tremendous fire.

In a very short time afterwards, Mr Scott, public secretary to the commander in chief, was killed by a cannon shot while in conversation with Captain Hardy. Lord Nelson being then near them; Captain Adair of the marines, with the assistance of a seaman, endeavoured to remove the body from his Lordship's sight: but he had already observed the fall of his secretary; and now said with anxiety, "Is that poor Scott that is gone?" and on being answered in the affirmative by Captain Adair, he replied, "Poor fellow!"

Lord Nelson and Captain Hardy walked the quarter deck in conversation for some time after this, while the enemy kept up an incessant raking fire.

A double-headed shot struck one of the parties of marines drawn up on the poop, and killed eight of them; when his Lordship, perceiving this, ordered Captain Adair to disperse his men round the ship, that they might not suffer so much from being together.

In a few minutes afterwards a shot struck the fore brace bits on the quarter deck, and passed between Lord Nelson and Captain Hardy; a splinter from the bits bruising Captain Hardy's foot, and tearing the buckle from his shoe. They both instantly stopped; and were observed by the officers on deck to survey each other with inquiring looks, each supposing the other to be wounded. His Lordship then smiled, and said: "This is too warm work, Hardy, to last long"; and declared that "through all the battles he had been in, he had never witnessed more cool courage than was displayed by the *Victory*'s crew on this occasion."

The *Victory* by this time, having approached close to the enemy's van, had suffered very severely without firing a single gun: she had lost about twenty men killed, and had about thirty wounded. Her mizzen topmast, and all her studding sails and their booms on both sides were shot away; the enemy's fire being chiefly directed at her rigging, with a view to disable her before she could close with them.

At four minutes past twelve o'clock, she opened her fire, from both sides of her decks, upon the enemy; when Captain Hardy represented to his Lordship, that "it appeared impracticable to pass through the enemy's line without going on board some one of their ships."

Lord Nelson answered, "I cannot help it: it does not signify which we run on board of; go on board which you please; take your choice."

At twenty minutes past twelve, the tiller ropes being shot away, Mr Atkinson, the master, was ordered below to get the helm put to port; which being done, the *Victory* was soon run on board the *Redoutable* of seventy-four guns.

For some 15 minutes, *Victory* and *Redoutable* blasted each other at point-blank range, the French preferring musketry from the tops, whilst the gun-crews of the *Victory* shot *Redoutable* to pieces. At approximately 1.25 p.m. the French got their man.

NELSON IS SHOT, HMS *VICTORY*, 1.25 p.m.

Dr William Beatty, HMS Victory[17]

It was from this ship (the *Redoutable*) that Lord Nelson received his mortal wound. About fifteen minutes past one o'clock, which was in the heat of the engagement, he was walking the middle of the quarter deck with Captain Hardy, and in the act of turning near the hatchway with his face towards the stern of the *Victory*, when the fatal ball was fired from the enemy's mizzen top; which, from the situation of the two ships (lying on board of each other), was brought just abaft, and rather below, the *Victory*'s main yard, and of course not more than fifteen yards distant from that part of the deck where his Lordship stood. The ball struck the epaulette on his left shoulder, and penetrated his chest. He fell with his face on the deck. Captain Hardy, who was on his right (the side furthest from the enemy) and [had] advanced some steps before his Lordship, on turning round, saw the serjeant major (Secker) of Marines with two seamen raising him from the deck; where he had fallen on the same spot on which, a little before, his secretary had breathed his last, with whose blood his Lordship's clothes were much soiled.

Captain Hardy expressed a hope that he was not severely wounded; to which the gallant chief replied: "They have done for me at last, Hardy."

"I hope not," answered Captain Hardy.

"Yes," replied his Lordship; "my backbone is shot through."

Captain Hardy ordered the seamen to carry the admiral to the cockpit; and now two incidents occurred strikingly characteristic of this great man, and strongly marking that energy and reflection which in his heroic mind rose superior even to the immediate consideration of his present awful condition. While the men were carrying him down the ladder from the middle deck, his Lordship observed that the tiller ropes were not yet replaced; and desired one of the midshipmen stationed there to go upon the quarter deck and remind Captain Hardy of that circumstance, and request that new ones should be immediately rove. Having delivered this order, he took his handkerchief from his pocket and covered his face with it, that he might be conveyed to the cockpit at this crisis unnoticed by the crew.

Several wounded officers, and about forty men, were likewise carried to the surgeon for assistance just at this time; and some others had breathed their last during their conveyance below. Among the latter were Lieutenant William Andrew Ram, and Mr Whipple, captain's clerk. The surgeon had just examined these two officers, and found that they were dead; when his attention was arrested by several of the wounded calling to him, "Mr Beatty, Lord Nelson is here: Mr Beatty, the admiral is wounded."

The surgeon now, on looking round, saw the handkerchief fall from his Lordship's face; when the stars on his coat, which also had been covered by it, appeared. Mr Burke the purser, and the surgeon, ran immediately to the assistance of his Lordship; and took him from the arms of the seamen who had carried him below. In conveying him to one of the midshipmen's berths, they stumbled; but recovered themselves without falling. Lord Nelson then inquired who were supporting him; and when the surgeon informed him, his Lordship replied, "Ah, Mr Beatty! you can do nothing for me. I have but a short time to live: my back is shot through."

The surgeon said, "he hoped the wound was not so dangerous as his Lordship imagined, and that he might still survive long to enjoy his glorious victory."

The Rev. Dr Scott, who had been absent in another part of the cockpit administering lemonade to the wounded, now came instantly to his Lordship; and in the anguish of grief wrung his hands, and said: "Alas, Beatty, how prophetic you were!" alluding to the apprehensions expressed by the surgeon for his Lordship's safety previous to the battle. His Lordship was laid upon a bed, stripped of his clothes, and covered with a sheet. While this was effecting, he said to Dr Scott, "Doctor, I told you so. Doctor, I am gone;" and after a short pause he added in a low voice, "I have to leave Lady Hamilton, and my adopted daughter Horatia, as a legacy to my country."

The surgeon then examined the wound, assuring his Lordship that he would not put him to much pain in endeavouring to discover the course of the ball; which he soon found had penetrated deep into the chest, and had probably lodged in the spine. This being explained to his Lordship, he replied, "he was confident his back was shot through." The back was then examined externally, but without any injury being perceived; on which his Lordship was requested by the surgeon to make him acquainted with all his sensations. He replied, that "he felt a gush of blood every minute within his breast: that he had no feeling in the lower part of his body: and that his breathing was difficult, and attended with very severe pain about that part of the spine where he was confident that the ball had struck; for," said he, "I felt it break my back."

It would be some two and half hours before Nelson died.

SERGEANT ROBERT GUILLEMARD SHOOTS ADMIRAL NELSON, 1.25 p.m.

Sergeant Robert Guillemard, Redoutable[18]

Guillemard, perched in *Redoutable*'s mizentop, claimed to have fired the shot which killed Nelson. English accounts declare that no one stationed in *Redoutable*'s mizentop left it alive.

All our top-men had been killed, when two sailors and four soldiers (of whom I was one) were ordered to occupy their posts in the tops. While we were going aloft, the balls and grape-shot showered around us, struck the masts and yards, knocked large splinters from them, and cut the rigging in pieces. One of my companions was wounded beside me, and fell from a height of thirty feet upon the deck, where he broke his neck.

When I reached the top, my first action was to take a view of the scene presented by the hostile fleets. For more than a league extended a thick cloud of smoke, above which were discernible a forest of masts and rigging, and the flags, the pendants, and the fire of the three nations. Thousands of flashes more or less near continually penetrated this cloud, and a rolling noise very like thunder, but much stronger arose from its bosom. The sea was calm, the wind light, and not very favourable to the execution of manoeuvers.

When the English top-men, who were only a few yards distant saw us appear, they directed a sharp fire upon us, which we returned*. A soldier of my company and a sailor were killed quite close to me; two others, who were wounded, were able to go below by the shrouds. Our opponents were, it seems, still worse handled than we, for I soon saw the English tops deserted, and none sent to supply the place of those who must have been

---

* *Victory* had no sharpshooters in her rigging.

killed or wounded by our balls. I then looked at the English vessel and our own. The smoke enveloping them was dissipated for a moment but returned thicker at each broadside. The two decks were covered with dead bodies which they had not time to throw overboard. I perceived Captain Lucas motionless at his post and several wounded officers still giving orders. On the poop of the English vessel was an officer covered with orders and with only one arm. From what I had heard of Nelson, I had no doubt that it was he. He was surrounded by several officers, to whom he seemed to be giving orders. At the moment I first perceived him, several of his sailors were wounded beside him by the fire of the *Redoutable*. As I had received no orders to go down, and saw myself forgotten in the tops, I thought it my duty to fire on the poop of the English vessel, which I saw quite exposed and close to me. I could even have taken aim at the men I saw, but I fired at hazard among the groups I saw of sailors and officers. All at once I saw great confusion on board the *Victory*: the men crowded round the officer whom I had taken for Nelson. He had just fallen, and was taken below, covered with a cloak. The agitation shown at this moment left me no doubt that I had judged rightly, and that it really was the English admiral.

Soon after Nelson was taken below, Captain Lucas on the *Redoutable* prepared his men to board the *Victory*. Their first attempt was parried by the *Victory*'s marines, and before the French could try again, they were interrupted by the arrival of HMS Téméraire.

BROADSIDE: HMS *TÉMÉRAIRE* ANNIHILATES THE *REDOUTABLE*, 1.35 p.m.

Captain Jean Lucas, Redoutable[19]

Admiral Nelson was killed by the firing of our musketry. Immediately after this the upper deck of the Victory became deserted, and she again ceased firing [according to British accounts, this was because they believed that *Redoutable* was seeking a surrender, since her guns were not firing: JEL], but it proved difficult to board her because of the motion of the two vessels, and the height of the Victory's upper tier and battery.

On that I gave the order to cut the supports of the main-yard so that it might serve as a bridge. At the same Midshipman Yon and four seamen sprang on board the Victory by means of her anchor, and we then knew that there was nobody left in the batteries. At that moment, when my brave fellows were hastening to follow, the three-decker *Téméraire*, which had seen that the *Victory* fought no longer and must without fail be taken (allait infailliblement être pris), came down, full sail, on our starboard side. We were immediately under the full fire of her artillery, discharged almost with muzzles touching.

It is impossible to describe the carnage produced by the murderous broadside of this ship. More than two hundred of our brave men were killed or wounded by it. I was wounded also at the same time, but not so seriously as to make me abandon my post. Not being able to undertake anything on the side of the *Victory*, I now ordered the rest of the crew to man the batteries on the other side and fire at the *Téméraire* with what guns the collision when she came alongside had not dismounted.

The order was carried out; but by this time we had been so weakened, and had so few guns left available, that the *Téméraire* replied to us with great advantage. A short time afterwards another ship, a two-decker, whose name I cannot recall, placed herself across the stern of the *Redoutable* and fired on us within pistol-shot. In less than half an hour our ship had been so fearfully mauled that she looked like little more than a heap of débris. Judging by appearances, no doubt, the *Téméraire* now hailed us to surrender and not prolong a useless resistance. My reply was instantly to order some soldiers who were near me to fire back; which they did with great alacrity. At the same moment almost, the mainmast of the *Redoutable* fell on board the English ship. The two topmasts of the *Téméraire* then came down, falling on board of us. Our whole poop was stove in, helm, rudder, and stern post all shattered to splinters, all the stern frame, and the decks shot through. All our own guns were either smashed or dismounted by the broadsides of the *Victory* and *Téméraire*. In addition, an 18-pounder gun on the lower deck, and a 32-pounder carronade on the forecastle had burst, killing and wounding a great many men. The hull itself was riddled, shot through from side to side: deck beams were shattered; port-lids torn away or knocked to pieces. Four of our six pumps were so damaged as to be useless. The quarter-deck ladders were broken, which rendered communication with the rest of the ship very difficult. Everywhere the decks were strewn with dead men, lying beneath the débris. Out of a crew of 634 men we had 522 *hors de combat*; of whom 300 were killed and 222 wounded – nearly all the officers among them. A number of the wounded were killed on the orlop deck below the water-line. Of the remaining 121, a large number were employed in the storerooms and magazines. The batteries and upper decks were practically abandoned – bare of men, and we were unable longer to offer any resistance. No one who had not seen the state of the *Redoutable* could ever form an idea of her awful condition. Really I know of nothing on board that had not been hit by shot.

"LAY HER HEAD FOR THE *BUCENTAURE!*": THE SOLO ATTACK OF *INTRÉPIDE*, 2.00 p.m.

Marquis Gicquel des Touches, Intrépide[20]

Under Rear-Admiral Dumanoir, the van of the Combined Fleet was merely a spectator to the early action, being stood off from the *Victory* by Nelson's steadily arriving supporters and a light wind which made it difficult to turn the French and Spanish ships around. There was also the matter of Dumanoir's own irresolution. One of his captains, Infernet, at least, was made of steelier stuff and determined to aid Villeneuve's flagship, the *Bucentaure*. This account of the *Intrépide*'s lone sail to glory is also notable for the prescience of des Touches's observation that Nelson's "method of engaging battle was contrary to ordinary prudence" (approaching bow on) but that "Nelson knew his own fleet – and ours."

Their fleet, divided into two columns, approached us before the wind, a breeze from the west, and led by the two vice-admirals, Nelson and Collingwood, whose flags flew at the head of each line in the three-deckers *Victory* and *Royal Sovereign*.

This method of engaging battle was contrary to ordinary prudence, for the British ships, reaching us one by one and at a

very slow speed, seemed bound to be overpowered in detail by
our superior forces; but Nelson knew his own fleet – and ours.

*   *   *   *   *   *

At the same moment that the Victory came into action with
the *Bucentaure* and the *Santisima Trinidad*, the column of Admiral
Collingwood engaged our rear division and the entire fleet
disappeared from our sight, blotted out by the smoke,

The leading division, however, although not a single British
ship threatened it, remained inactive. Our captain. Infernet,
with his eyes fixed on the *Formidable*, expected Admiral Dumanoir every moment to make the signal to go about and take part
in the battle. But no signal went up. Time passed, and the van
division slowly drew off from where the fighting was going on: it
became soon but too plain that its chief was keeping out of the
battle. Admiral Villeneuve, meanwhile, while he still had a
mast standing on which to hoist a signal, was ordering our ships
to put about and come into action. Undoubtedly, owing to the
lightness of the wind and the swell, the evolution was a slow and
difficult one; but it might at least have been attempted. I have
to admit, to the shame of the van division, that no effort was
made by them to obey Admiral Villeneuve's signals. And I saw
the *Mont Blanc*, the *Duguay Trouin*, and the *Scipion*, following in
the wake of the *Formidable* and drawing off slowly without
having received a single shot.

Happily Captain Infernet took another view of his duty, and
his honour. Although we were immediately under the orders of
M. Dumanoir, we had already made several unsuccessful
attempts to put about; but the wind had been entirely stilled
by the cannonading and the very heavy ground swell, presage
of an approaching storm, made it difficult for the ship to answer
the helm. In the end, though, after incessant efforts and by the
aid of the only boat we had available, we were able to wear
round, whereupon the captain called out in a resounding voice,
"Lou capo sur lou *Bucentaure*!" (Lay her head for the *Bucentaure*.)
It was now the hottest moment of the battle.

We could hardly make out, in the midst of the smoke and
confusion of the battle, the situation of our flagship, surrounded

as she was by the enemy, and having near her only the
Redoutable, a small 74, crushed by the overpowering mass of
the *Victory*, but still resisting with such heroism that they even
tried to carry by boarding Nelson's own ship. At all points the
British had the advantage of numbers over us. Not one of them
was idle, and the advantage of an attack from windward
permitted them to place themselves wherever their presence
was necessary – paying no heed to our ships to leeward. These
could not take part in the battle except from afar and must of
necessity succumb in detail and ineffectively. And more than
that. The enemy's superiority in gunnery was so great that, in a
very short time, our crews were decimated, whilst on the British
side the losses were comparatively trivial.

When at length we drew near where the *Bucentaure* and the
Redoutable lay, their masts had fallen, their fire was almost
silenced: yet the heroism of those on board kept up an unequal
and hopeless struggle, fighting against ships that were practically undamaged, from the ports of which broadside after
broadside flashed incessantly. It was into the thick of this fray
that our Captain Infernet led us. He wanted, he said, to rescue
Admiral Villeneuve and take him on board, and then to rally
round ourselves the ships that were still in a fit state to fight. It
was a reckless and forlorn hope, a mad enterprise; and he
himself could not doubt it. It was the pretext Infernet gave for
continuing the fight. He would not have it said that the *Intrépide*
had quitted the battle while she still could fight a gun or hoist a
sail. It was noble madness, but, though we knew it, we all
supported him with joyful alacrity: – and would that others had
imitated his example!

While the fighting raged around *Victory*, *Redoutable*, *Téméraire*, and the
Spanish four-decker *Santisima Trinidad* in the centre of the Combined
Fleet, Collingwood's column was, ship-by-ship, dealing destruction at
the rear. HMS *Revenge* was the eighth of Collingwood's column to go
into action, engaging at approximately 12.30 p.m.

THE AFTERNOON OF TRAFALGAR: WILLIAM ROBINSON IN ACTION ABOARD HMS *REVENGE*, 12.30–2.00 p.m.

William Robinson, HMS Revenge[21]

As we drew near, we discovered the enemy's line was formed with a Spanish ship between two French ones, nearly all through their line; as I suppose, to make them fight better; and it must be admitted that the Dons fought as well as the French in that battle; and, if praise was due for seamanship and valour, they were well entitled to an equal share. We now began to hear the enemy's cannon opening on the *Royal Sovereign*, commanded by Lord Collingwood, who commenced the action; and, a signal being made by the admiral to some of our senior captains to break the enemy's line at different points, it fell to our lot to cut off the five stern-most ships; and, while we were running down to them, of course we were favoured with several shots, and some of our men were wounded. Upon being thus pressed, many of our men thought it hard that the firing should be all on one side and became impatient to return the compliment: but our captain had given orders not to fire until we got close in with them, so that all our shots might tell; indeed, these were his words: "We shall want all our shot when we get close in: never mind their firing: when I fire a carronade from the quarter-deck, that will be a signal for you to begin, and I know you will do your duty as Englishmen." In a few minutes the gun was fired, and our ship bore in and broke the line, but we paid dear for our temerity, as those ships we had thrown into disorder turned round, and made an attempt to board. A Spanish three-decker ran her bowsprit over our poop, with a number of her crew on it, and, in her fore rigging, two or three hundred men were ready to follow; but they caught a Tartar, for their design was discovered, and our marines with their small arms, and the carronades on the poop, loaded with canister shot, swept them off so fast, some into the water and some on the decks, that they were glad to sheer off. While this was going on aft, we were engaged with a French two-deck ship on our starboard side, and on our larboard bow another, so that many of their shots must have struck their own ships and done severe execution. After being engaged about an hour, two other ships fortunately came up, received some of the fire intended for us, and we were now enabled to get at some of the shot-holes between wind and water and plug them up: this is a duty performed by the carpenter and his crew. We were now unable to work the ship, our yards, sails, and masts being disabled, and the braces completely shot away. In this condition we lay by the side of the enemy, firing away, and now and then we received a good raking from them, passing under our stern. This was a busy time with us, for we had not only to endeavour to repair our damage, but to keep to our duty. Often during the battle we could not see for the smoke whether we were firing at a foe or friend, and as to hearing, the noise of the guns had so completely made us deaf, that we were obliged to look only to the motions that were made.

At around 1.00 p.m., the first ships in the rear of the Combined Fleet began to surrender. Among them was Spanish *San-Juan-Nepomuceno*.

THE *SAN-JUAN-NEPOMUCENO* SURRENDERS, 2.00 p.m.

Anonymous member of the crew of San-Juan-Nepomuceno[22]

The *San-Juan-Nepomuceno* was at the end of the line. The *Royal Sovereign* and the *Santa Ana* opened fire and then all the ships in turn came into action. Five English vessels under Collingwood attacked our ship; two, however, passed on, and Churruca had only three to deal with.

We held out bravely against these odds till two in the afternoon, suffering terribly, though we dealt double havoc on the foe. Our leader seemed to have infused his heroic spirit into the crew and soldiers, and the ship was handled and her broadsides delivered with wonderful promptitude and accuracy. The new recruits learnt their lesson in courage in no more than a couple of hours' apprenticeship, and our defence struck the English with astonishment.

They were in fact forced to get assistance, and bring up no

less than six against one. The two ships that had at first sailed past us now returned, and the *Dreadnought* came alongside of us, with not more than half a pistol-shot between her and our stern.* You may imagine the fire of these six giants pouring balls and small shot into a vessel of 74 guns!

*   *   *   *   *   *

Churruca, meanwhile, who was the brain of all, directed the battle with gloomy calmness. Knowing that only care and skill could supply the place of strength, he economized our fire, trusting entirely to careful aim, and the consequence was that each ball did terrible havoc on the foe. He saw to everything, settled everything, and the shot flew round him and over his head without his ever once changing colour even.

*   *   *   *   *   *

It was not the will of God, however, that he should escape alive from that storm of fire. Seeing that no one could hit one of the enemy's ships which was battering us with impunity, he went down himself to judge of the line of fire and succeeded in dismasting her. He was returning to the quarter-deck when a cannon ball hit his right leg with such violence as almost to take it off, tearing it across the thigh in the most frightful manner. He fell to the ground, but the next moment he made an effort to raise himself, supporting himself on one arm. His face was as white as death, but he said, in a voice that was scarcely weaker than his ordinary tone: "It is nothing – go on firing!' " ["Esto no es nada. Siga el fuego!"]

He did all he could to conceal the terrible sufferings of his cruelly mangled frame. Nothing would induce him, it would seem, to quit the quarter-deck. At last he yielded to our entreaties and then he seemed to understand that he must give up the command. He called for Moyna, his second in command, but was told that he was dead. Then he called for the officer in command on the main deck. That officer, though

* About thirty yards.

himself seriously wounded, at once came to the quarter-deck and took command.

It was just before he went below that Churruca, in the midst of his agonies, gave the order that the flag should be nailed to the mast. The ship, he said, must never surrender so long as he breathed. ["Despues," says the account in the family papers, "pidió á los que vinieron en su ayuda que clavara la bandera y no se rindiera el buque mientras el tuviera un atomo de vidas."]

The delay, alas! could be but short. He was going fast. He never lost consciousness till the very end, nor did he complain of his sufferings. His sole anxiety was that the crew should not know how dangerous his wound was; that no one should be daunted or fail in his duty. He specially desired that the men should be thanked for their heroic courage. Then he spoke a few words to Ruiz de Apodoca, and after sending a farewell message to his poor young wife, whom he had married only a few days before he sailed, he fixed his thoughts on God, Whose name was ever on his lips. So with the calm resignation of a good man and the fortitude of a hero, Churruca passed away.

After he was gone, it was too quickly known, and the men lost heart. . . . Their courage was really worn out. It was but too plain that they must surrender. . . . A sudden paralysis seemed to seize on the crew; their grief at losing their beloved leader apparently overpowered the disgrace of surrender.

Quite half the *San Juan*'s crew were *hors de combat*, dead or wounded. Most of the guns were disabled. All the masts, except the main-mast, had gone by the board. The rudder was useless.

And yet, in this deplorable plight even, they made an attempt to follow the *Principe de Asturias*, which had given the signal to withdraw; but the *San Juan Nepomuceno* had received her death blow. She could neither sail nor steer.

ONE SHIP'S BATTLE: THE LOG OF HMS *BELLEISLE*, 21 October 1805

Belleisle was the second ship of Collingwood's Lee column to cut the enemy line.

At daylight saw the Enemy's Fleet bearing East, distant about nine miles, consisting of 33 Sail of the Line, 3 Frigates, and a Brig. At 4.40 answered the general signal to form the Order of Sailing. At 6 answered the general signal to bear up and sail large, and prepare for battle – threw overboard clearing the Ship for Action 7 butts, &c. – out all reefs and made sail bearing down on the Enemy. At 8 light airs – body of the Enemy S.E., six miles, forming in a line of battle – *Royal Sovereign* S.E. b. S. 1 mile – the Admiral made the *Britannia*, *Prince*, and *Dreadnought* signal to take station as most convenient – at 8.40 *Royal Sovereign* made signal for Larboard Division to make more sail. At 9 the Admiral made the general signal to alter one point to port – at 9.20 the *Royal Sovereign* made the *Belleisle*'s and *Tonnant*'s signal to exchange places in the Line of Battle, and the *Belleisle*'s signal to make more sail – set the royals and studding-sails – at 9.30 the *Royal Sovereign* made the *Belleisle*'s signal to bear S.W. of her – at 9.40 the *Royal Sovereign* made the *Belleisle*'s signal to alter course one point to starboard. At 11.50 the *Royal Sovereign* made the *Belleisle*'s signal to keep closer order – at 11.53 the Admiral made the general signal to prepare to anchor after close of day – at 11.55 the Enemy from centre to rear, opened their fire on the *Royal Sovereign* and *Belleisle*, which was returned by the *Royal Sovereign*, and the Admiral made the signal for close action. At noon, distant from the Enemy's Line three quarters of a mile, reserving all our fire, with all sail set to cut their Line. Distance from the *Royal Sovereign* two cables' length. Light airs, with a heavy swell. Cape Trafalgar, S.E. b. E. 5 leagues. P.M. Light airs and hazy, with a heavy swell. 0.4 *Royal Sovereign* cut the Enemy's Line astern of a Spanish three-decked Ship, bearing a Rear-Admiral's flag – 0.5 opened our fire on the Enemy – 0.13 set the Enemy's line astern of a French 80-gun Ship, second to the Spanish Rear-Admiral's Ship, at the same time keeping up a heavy fire on both sides – 0.40 our main-topmast was shot away.

At 1.0 a great Ship bore up to rake us, and a Ship on each side engaging us. At 1.10 the mizen-mast went six feet above the deck. At 1.20 the Enemy's Ship on our starboard side sheered off – at 1.30 the Enemy's Ship, which had laid itself athwart our stern, placed herself on our larboard quarter, at the same time a fresh Ship ranged up at our starboard side – kept up a heavy fire on them as we could get our guns to bear, the Ship being lately unmanageable, most of her rigging and sails being shot. At 2.10 the main-mast went by the board – at 2.30 an Enemy's Ship placed herself across our starboard bow – at 2.40 the foremast and bowsprit went by the board – still engaging three of the Enemy's Ships. 3.15 one of our Ships passed our bow and took the fire off one of the Enemy's Ships laying there. At 3.20 the Enemy's Ship, on our starboard side, was engaged by one of our Ships. At 3.25 the *Swiftsure* passed our stern, and cheered us, and commenced firing on the Enemy, and into the Enemy's Ship on our larboard quarter. Ceased firing, and turned the hands up to clear the wreck. Sent a boat and took possession of the Spanish 80-Gun Ship, *Argonaut*. The Action still continuing general, cut away the wreck fore and aft. At 4.15 the *Naiad* came down and took us in tow – sent a Lieutenant and a division of men to the prize – saw a French Ship of the Line take fire. At 5.10 the French Ship blew up – observed several of the Enemy's Ships had struck, and several of the Enemy's Ships making off to leeward, and 4 French Ships of the Line going off on the starboard tack. At 5.30 the Action ceased – people employed securing the guns, clearing and cleaning Ship, and variously employed. At 8 mustered the Ship's company found killed in battle, 2 Lieutenants, 1 Midshipman, and 31 Seamen and Marines; and 94 Seamen and Marines wounded.[23]

"OUR SIDES GRINDING SO MUCH AGAINST EACH OTHER THAT WE WERE OBLIGED TO FIRE THE LOWER-DECK GUNS WITHOUT RUNNING THEM OUT": THE VIEW FROM HMS *TONNANT*, 1.00–2.15 p.m.

Anonymous lieutenant, HMS Tonnant[24]

Part of Collingwood's Lee line *Tonnant* arrived in the fray, beating off the *Monarca* before settling down to a duel to the death with Rear-Admiral Magon's *Algeciras*.

A French ship of eighty guns, with an admiral's flag came up, and poured a raking broadside into our stern which killed and wounded forty petty officers and men, nearly cut the rudder in two, and shattered the whole of the stern with the quarter galleries. She then, in the most gallant manner, locked her bowsprit in our starboard main shrouds and attempted to board us with the greater part of her officers and ship's company. She had riflemen in her tops, who did great execution. Our poop was soon cleared and our gallant captain shot through the left thigh and obliged to be carried below. During this time we were not idle. We gave it to her most gloriously with the starboard and main deckers, and turned the forecastle gun, loaded with grape, on the gentleman who wished to give us a fraternal hug. The marines kept up a warm destructive fire on the boarders. Only one man made good his footing on our quarter-deck, when he was pinned through the calf of his right leg by one of the crew with his half-pike, whilst another was going to cut him down, which I prevented, and desired him to be taken to the cockpit . . . Our severe contest with the French admiral lasted more than half an hour, our sides grinding so much against each other that we were obliged to fire the lower-deck guns without running them out.

At length both ships caught fire before the chess trees, and our firemen, with all the coolness and courage so inherent in British seamen, got the engine and played on both ships, and finally extinguished the flames, although two of them were severely wounded in doing so. At length we had the satisfaction of seeing her three lower masts go by the board, ripping the partners up in their fall, as they had been shot through below the deck, and carrying with them all their sharpshooters to look sharper in the next world for as all our boats were shot through we could not save one of them in this. The crew were then ordered with the second lieutenant to board her. They cheered, and in a short time carried her. They found the gallant French Admiral Magon killed at the foot of the poop ladder, and the captain dangerously wounded. Out of eight lieutenants, five were killed with three hundred petty officers and seamen and about one hundred wounded.

By 2.30 p.m. the Allied rear was already effectively destroyed. *Santa-Ana*, *San Juan-Nepomuceno* and *Algeciras* had all struck; within the next hour and a half, Collingwood's column would take five more ships. The battle at the centre had also moved towards its conclusion, with the surrender of first the *Bucentaure* and then the *Redoutable* at around 2.20 p.m.

THE *REDOUTABLE* SURRENDERS: THE REASONS WHY, 2.20 p.m.

Captain Lucas and the officers of the quarter-deck, Redoutable[25]

The *Redoutable* lived up to her name. The report below was written by Lucas and the *Redoutable's* surviving officers whilst in British captivity.

That calamity [the *Redoutable*'s surrender] took place about half-past two p.m., for the following reasons: –

1. Because, out of a crew consisting of six hundred and forty-three men, five hundred and twenty-two were no longer in a situation to continue the fight. Three hundred had been killed, and two hundred and twenty-two were badly wounded. Among the latter were the whole of the Etat Major and ten junior officers.

2. Because the ship was dismasted: the main and mizen masts had gone by the board (dematés au raz du pont). The former fell on the *Téméraire*, and the yards of that ship fell on board the *Redoutable*.

3. Because the tiller and helm and rudder gear and the stern-post itself had been entirely destroyed.

4. Because nearly all our guns were dismounted (la presque totalité de l'artillerie était entièrement démontée) partly in our coming into collision with two three-deckers, partly by their shot, and several of the guns dismounted and in consequence of the bursting of an eighteen-pounder gun on the lower deck, and a thirty-six-pounder carronade on the forecastle.

5. Because the poop had been entirely smashed in (la poupe était entièrement crevée) and the counter timbers and deck beams shattered and wrecked so that the whole of the after part of the ship formed practically a gaping cavity (tellement hachées que toute partie ne formait qu'un large sabord).

6. Because almost all the port lids had been smashed and the ports destroyed by the fire of the *Victory* and *Téméraire*.

7. Because both sides of the ship and the decks were shot through and riddled in such a manner that numbers of the wounded below on the orlop, and as they lay in the cockpit, were being killed helplessly.

8. Because the ship was on fire astern.

9. Because, finally, the ship was leaking in many places, and had several feet of water in the hold, and nearly all the pumps had been destroyed by shot. We had cause to fear that she might go down under our feet.

ONE SHIP'S BATTLE: THE LOG OF HMS *VICTORY*, 21 October 1805

At 4 a.m. wore ship. At 6 observed the Enemy bearing E. by S., distance 10 or 11 miles—bore up to the Eastward—out all reef topsails—set steering-sails and royals. 6 cleared for quarters. At 8 light breezes and cloudy—body of the Enemy's Fleet E. b. S., distance 9 or 10 miles. Still standing for the Enemy's van—the *Royal Sovereign* and her Line of Battle steering for the centre of the Enemy's Line—the Enemy's Line extending about N.N.E. and S.S.W. At 11.40 *Royal Sovereign* commenced firing on the Enemy, they having begun firing at her at 11.30—at 11.50 the Enemy began firing upon us, and 12.4 opened our larboard guns at the Enemy's van. Light airs and cloudy—standing towards the Enemy's van with all sails set. p.m. At 12.4 opened our fire on the Enemy's van. In attempting to pass through their

Line fell on board the tenth and eleventh Ships, when the Action became general. About 1.15 the Right Hon. Lord Nelson, K.B., and Commander-in-Chief, was wounded in the shoulder – at 1.30 the *Redoutable* having struck her colours, we ceased firing our starboard guns, but continued engaged with the *Santisima Trinidada*, and some of the Enemy's Ships on the larboard side – observed the *Téméraire* between the *Redoutable* and another French Ship, both of which had struck. The Action continued general until 3 o'clock, when several of the Enemy's Ships around us had struck – observed the *Royal Sovereign* with the loss of her main and mizen masts, and several of the Enemy's Ships around her dismasted. At 3.30 observed four Sail of the Enemy's van tack, and stand along our Line to windward – fired our larboard guns at those they would reach – at 3.40 made the signal for our Ships to keep their wind, and engaged the Enemy's van coming along our weather line. At 4.15 the Spanish Rear-Admiral to windward struck to some of our Ships which had tacked after them – observed one of the Enemy's Ships blow up, and 14 Sail of the Enemy's Ships standing towards Cadiz, and 3 Sail of the Enemy's Ships standing to the Southward. Partial firing continued until 4.30, when a Victory having been reported to the Right Hon. Lord Viscount Nelson, K.B., and Commander-in-Chief, he died of his wound. At 5 the mizenmast fell about 2 feet above the poop, the lower masts, yards, and bowsprit all crippled, rigging and sails very much cut. The Ships around us very much crippled – several of our Ships pursuing the Enemy to leeward – saw the Vice-Admiral's flag flying on board H. M. Ship *Euryalus*, and some of our Ships taking possession of the Prizes – struck topgallant-masts, got up runners and tackles to secure lower masts – employed clearing the wrecks of the yards and rigging – wore ship and sounded in 32 fathoms sandy bottom – stood to the Southward under the remnants of the foresail and main-topsail – sounded from 19 to 13 fathoms.[26]

THE *SANTISIMA TRINIDAD*: THE SCENE ON DECK, 2.30 p.m.

Anonymous Spanish crewman

Santisima Trinidad (130), the flagship of Rear-Admiral Cisneros, was a four-decker and the largest warship afloat. At the beginning of the battle, she had engaged the *Victory*, before trying to escape northwards. She did not make it.

The scene on board the Santisima Trinidad was simply infernal. All attempts at working the ship had to be abandoned. She could not move. The only thing to be done was to serve the guns as fast as we could and damage the enemy all we could.

The English shot had torn our sails to tatters. It was as if huge invisible talons had been dragging at them. Fragments of spars, splinters of wood, thick hempen cables cut up as corn is cut by the sickle, fallen blocks, shreds of canvas, bits of iron, and hundreds of other things that had been wrenched away by the enemy's fire, were piled along the deck, where it was scarcely possible to move about. . . . Blood ran in streams about the deck, and in spite of the sand, the rolling of the ship carried it hither and thither until it made strange patterns on the planks. The enemy's shot, fired as they were from very short range, caused horrible mutilations. . . . The ship creaked and groaned as she rolled, and through a thousand holes and crevices in her hull the sea spurted in and began to flood the hold.

There was hardly a man to be seen who did not bear marks, more or less severe, of the enemy's iron and lead.

The *Bucentaure*, the French Admiral's ship, surrendered before our very eyes.

When once the leader of the fleet was gone, what hope was there for other ships? The French flag vanished from the gallant vessel's mast and she ceased firing. The *San Agustin* and the *Héros* still struggled on, and the *Rayo* and *Neptuno*, from the van, made an effort to rescue us from the enemy, who were fiercely battering us. Nothing was to be seen of the rest of the line.[27]

After *Santisima Trinidad*'s colours were shot and she lay an unmanageable wreck in the water, the smallest ship on the British side, the *Africa*, coolly sent a boat over to request possession. The Spanish officers politely declined, showed the British party off the quarter-deck and down to their boat, and then recommenced firing. But not for long, and the giant warship sat out the rest of the battle.

It was now that the Combined Fleet tried its one counter-attack of the day.

THE COMBINED FLEET'S LAST THROW— DUMANOIR COUNTER-ATTACKS, 2.30 p.m.

Rear-Admiral Pierre Dumanoir Le Pelley, Formidable[28]

Although Villeneuve had signalled Dumanoir to turn at 1.45 p.m., not until 2.30 p.m. did the Combined Fleet's van do so (with the exception of the disobedient but valourous Infernet in *Intrépide*) and not, until 3.00 p.m. did it enter the battle area. According to Infernet, Lucas of the *Redoutable* and Villemadrin of the French *Swiftsure*, among others, Dumanoir's counter-attack was half-hearted. He barely paused in a flight southwards and was the cause of the Combined's defeat. Here is Dumanoir's version of events, written (in a letter to the London *Times*) when he was a prisoner of war in Devon.

The left column of the English, having Admiral Nelson at its head, bore at first on the French vanguard, which I commanded, but finding it too compact, they exchanged some shots with us, and then struck at the centre of our line, while Vice-Admiral Collingwood attacked our rearguard. Having then no enemy to contend with, I tacked about, the wind being very weak, a movement which I could not risk without the aid of my boats. I was followed by four others, and taking the lead of this division, I bore towards the centre of our fleet, where the fire was hottest. My intention was at the same time to cut off two ships of war of the division of Admiral Nelson, but they gained upon me in swiftness, and in passing ahead of me at the distance of pistol-shot, they did me considerable damage. I had then to combat the enemy's vessels which had broken and passed the centre of our fleet. On my coming up, I found the *Santisima Trinidad* and the *Bucentaure* totally dismasted and taken possession of by the English, as well as a part of the vessels which composed that division.

I continued to bear upon our rearguard, which I found in part surrendered: I engaged successively alongside of twelve vessels, of which four were three-deckers and handled us very severely. There remained then on the field of battle to which I was coming up with my assistance, only thirteen French and Spanish vessels, which had surrendered, and fifteen English vessels (one only dismasted). I was thus cut off from the rest of the Combined Fleet, which was much before the wind. The *Neptune*, a Spanish vessel, which was of the number of those which had tacked about, but which was left very far behind, was surrounded by the enemy, dismasted, and obliged to surrender. My division, consisting of only four disabled ships, was therefore cut off to windward, the rest of the Combined Fleet being at the distance of two long leagues before the wind, and bearing off under all sail. To have rejoined them, I must have fallen in with the English Squadron, which remained entire between those two separated bodies; but this would have been running to certain destruction, without the hope of doing any great damage to the enemy.

HMS *VICTORY*: HARDY VISITS THE DYING NELSON, 2.35 p.m.

Dr William Beatty[29]

On being mortally wounded, Nelson was taken into the cockpit with other wounded, where he was troubled by thirst, heat and the absence of *Victory*'s captain, Hardy. At length, Hardy took a moment from battle to visit the dying admiral.

An hour and ten minutes however, elapsed from the time of his Lordship's being wounded, before Captain Hardy's first subsequent interview with him; the particulars of which are nearly as follow.

They shook hands affectionately, and Lord Nelson said: "Well, Hardy, how goes the battle? How goes the day with us?"

"Very well, my Lord," replied Captain Hardy: "we have got twelve or fourteen of the enemy's ships in our possession; but five of their van have tacked and shew an intention of bearing down upon the *Victory*. I have therefore called two or three of our fresh ships round us, and have no doubt of giving them a drubbing."

"I hope," said his Lordship, "none of *our* ships have struck, Hardy."

"No, my Lord," replied Captain Hardy; "there is no fear of that."

Lord Nelson then said: "I am a dead man, Hardy. I am going fast: it will be all over with me soon. Come nearer to me. Pray let my dear Lady Hamilton have my hair, and all other things belonging to me." Mr Burke was about to withdraw at the commencement of this conversation; but his Lordship, perceiving his intention, desired he would remain.

Captain Hardy observed, that "he hoped Mr Beatty could yet hold out some prospect of life."

"Oh! no," answered his Lordship; "it is impossible. My back is shot through. Beatty will tell you so."

Captain Hardy then returned on deck, and at parting shook hands again with his revered friend and commander.

His Lordship now requested the surgeon, who had been previously absent a short time attending Mr Rivers, to return to the wounded; and give his assistance to such of them as he could be useful to; "for," said he, "you can do nothing for me." The surgeon assured him that the assistant surgeons were doing everything that could be effected for those unfortunate men; but on his Lordship's several times repeating his injunctions to that purpose, he left him surrounded by Dr Scott, Mr Burke, and two of his Lordship's domestics.

After the surgeon had been absent a few minutes attending Lieutenants Peake and Reeves of the marines, who were wounded, he was called by Dr Scott to his Lordship, who said: "Ah, Mr Beatty! I have sent for you to say what I forgot to tell you before, that all power of motion and feeling below my breast are gone; and *you*," continued he, "very well *know* I can live but a short time." The emphatic manner in which he pronounced these last words, left no doubt in the surgeon's mind, that he adverted to the case of a man who had, some months before, received a mortal injury of the spine on board the *Victory*, and had laboured under similar privations of sense and muscular motion. The case had made a great impression on

Lord Nelson: he was anxious to know the cause of such symptoms, which was accordingly explained to him; and he now appeared to apply the situation and fate of this man to himself.

The surgeon answered, "My Lord, you told me so before", but he now examined the extremities, to ascertain the fact; when his Lordship said, "Ah, Beatty! I am too certain of it: Scott and Burke have tried it already. *You know* I am gone."

The surgeon replied: "My Lord, unhappily for our country, nothing can be done for you", and having made this declaration he was so much affected, that he turned round and withdrew a few steps to conceal his emotions.

His Lordship said: "I know it. I feel something rising in my breast," putting his hand on his left side, "which tells me I am gone." Drink was recommended liberally, and Dr Scott and Mr Burke fanned him with paper.

He often exclaimed, "God be praised, I have done my duty", and upon the surgeon's inquiring whether his pain was still very great, he declared, "it continued so very severe, that he wished he was dead. Yet," said he in a lower voice, "one would like to live a little longer, too"; and after a pause of a few minutes, he added in the same tone, "What would become of poor Lady Hamilton, if she knew my situation?"

The surgeon, finding it impossible to render his Lordship any further assistance, left him to attend Lieutenant Bligh, Messrs. Smith and Westphall, midshipmen, and some seamen, recently wounded.

THOMAS MAIN LOSES HIS ARM, HMS *LEVIATHAN*, 3.00 p.m.

Captain Bayntun, HMS Leviathan[30]

Main was one of the 1,241 British wounded at Trafalgar.

We had passed through the line, and had assisted in disabling and silencing the French Admiral's ship, and the four-decker, *Santisima Trinidada*; we were much galled by a distant cannonade from a separated few of the enemy's ships; at last, the Saint Augustin, of 74 guns, bearing the pendant of Commodore

Cagigal, gave us an opportunity of closing with him, which was immediately embraced, and he was soon taken. While this was doing, a shot took off the arm of Thomas Main, when at his gun on the forecastle; his messmates kindly offered to assist him in going to the Surgeon; but he bluntly said, "*I thank you, stay where you are; you will do more good there:*" he then went down by himself to the cockpit. The Surgeon (who respected him) would willingly have attended him, in preference to others, whose wounds were less alarming; but Main would not admit of it, saying, "*Avast, not until it comes to my turn, if you please.*" The Surgeon soon after amputated the shattered part of the arm, near the shoulder; during which, with great composure, smiling, and with a steady clear voice, he sang the whole of "Rule Britannia".

Main later died of gangrene. As did many of the other wounded.

THE DEATH OF NELSON, 3.25–4.30 p.m.

Dr William Beatty[31]

Captain Hardy now came to the cockpit to see his Lordship a second time, which was after an interval of about fifty minutes from the conclusion of his first visit. Before he quitted the deck, he sent Lieutenant Hills to acquaint Admiral Collingwood with the lamentable circumstance of Lord Nelson's being wounded.

Lord Nelson and Captain Hardy shook hands again: and while the captain retained his Lordship's hand, he congratulated him even in the arms of Death on his brilliant victory; "which," he said, "was complete; though he did not know how many of the enemy were captured, as it was impossible to perceive every ship distinctly. He was certain however of fourteen or fifteen having surrendered."

His Lordship answered, "That is well, but I bargained for twenty": and then emphatically exclaimed, "*Anchor*, Hardy, *anchor!*"

To this the captain replied: "I suppose, my Lord, Admiral Collingwood will now take upon himself the direction of affairs."

"Not while I live, I hope, Hardy!" cried the dying chief; and at that moment endeavoured ineffectually to raise himself from the bed.

"No," added he; "do *you* anchor, Hardy."

Captain Hardy then said: "Shall *we* make the signal, Sir?"

"Yes," answered his Lordship; "for if I live, I'll anchor." The energetic manner in which he uttered these his last orders to Captain Hardy, accompanied with his efforts to raise himself, evinced his determination never to resign the command while he retained the exercise of his transcendent faculties, and that he expected Captain Hardy still to carry into effect the suggestions of his exalted mind; a sense of his duty overcoming the pains of death.

He then told Captain Hardy, "he felt that in a few minutes he should be no more", adding in a low tone, "Don't throw me overboard, Hardy."

The captain answered: "Oh! no, certainly not."

"Then," replied his Lordship, "you know what to do: and," continued he, "take care of my dear Lady Hamilton, Hardy; take care of poor Lady Hamilton. Kiss me, Hardy."

The captain now knelt down, and kissed his cheek; when his Lordship said, "Now I am satisfied. Thank God, I have done my duty."

Captain Hardy stood for a minute or two in silent contemplation: he then knelt down again and kissed his Lordship's forehead.

His Lordship said: "Who is that?"

The captain answered: "It is Hardy" to which his Lordship replied, "God bless you, Hardy!"

After this affecting scene Captain Hardy withdrew, and returned to the quarter deck; having spent about eight minutes in this his last interview with his dying friend.

Lord Nelson now desired Mr Chevalier, his steward, to turn him upon his right side; which being effected, his Lordship said: "I wish I had not left the deck, for I shall soon be gone." He afterwards became very low; his breathing was oppressed, and his voice faint.

He said to Dr Scott, "Doctor, I have *not* been a *great* sinner"; and after a short pause, "*Remember*, that I leave Lady Hamilton and my daughter Horatia as a legacy to my country: and," added he, "never forget Horatia."

His thirst now increased; and he called for "Drink, drink", "Fan, fan!" and "Rub, rub!" addressing himself in the last case to Dr Scott, who had been rubbing his Lordship's breast with his hand, from which he found some relief. These words he spoke in a very rapid manner, which rendered his articulation difficult: but he every now and then, with evident increase of pain, made a greater effort with his vocal powers, and pronounced distinctly these last words: "Thank God, I have done my duty"; and this great sentiment he continued to repeat as long as he was able to give it utterance.

His Lordship became speechless in about fifteen minutes after Captain Hardy left him. Dr Scott and Mr Burke, who had all along sustained the bed under his shoulders (which raised him in nearly a semi-recumbent posture, the only one that was supportable to him), forbore to disturb him by speaking to him; and when he had remained speechless about five minutes, his Lordship's steward went to the surgeon, who had been a short time occupied with the wounded in another part of the cockpit, and stated his apprehensions that his Lordship was dying.

The surgeon immediately repaired to him, and found him on the verge of dissolution. He knelt down by his side, and took up his hand; which was cold, and the pulse gone from the wrist.

On the surgeon's feeling his forehead, which was likewise cold, his Lordship opened his eyes, looked up, and shut them again.

The surgeon again left him, and returned to the wounded who required his assistance; but was not absent five minutes before the steward announced to him that "he believed his Lordship had expired." The surgeon returned, and found that the report was but too well founded: his Lordship had breathed his last, at thirty minutes past four o'clock; at which period Dr Scott was in the act of rubbing his Lordship's breast, and Mr Burke supporting the bed under his shoulders.

Alongside Nelson would fall, on the day of battle, 449 of his officers and men.

By the time of the admiral's demise, the conclusion of the battle – as Hardy reported – was certain. The French and Spanish would not quite admit it, and fighting continued for another hour.

THE DEATH OF AN UNPOPULAR MIDSHIPMAN, HMS *REVENGE*, 4.45 p.m.

William Robinson, HMS Revenge[32]

According to *Revenge*'s log, at 4.45 p.m. her "men were firing with all expedition and spirit, having upon us four French ships, and a Spanish three-decker". During this engagement she lost an unpopular midshipman.

. . . We had a midshipman on board our ship of a wickedly mischievous disposition, whose sole delight was to insult the feelings of the seamen, and furnish pretexts to get them punished. His conduct made every man's life miserable that happened to be under his orders. He was a youth not more than twelve or thirteen years of age; but I have often seen him get on the carriage of a gun, call a man to him and kick him about the thighs and body, and with his fist would beat him about the head; and these, although prime seamen, at the same time dared not murmur. It was ordained however, by Providence, that his reign of terror and severity should not last; for during the engagement, he was killed on the quarter-deck by a grape-shot, his body greatly mutilated, his entrails being driven and scattered against the larboard side; nor were there any lamentations for his fate! – No! for when it was known that he was killed, the general exclamation was, "*Thank God, we are rid of the young tyrant!*"

END-PLAY: HMS *PRINCE* SETS *ACHILLE* AFIRE, 4.30 p.m.

Henry Mason, HMS Prince[33]

HMS *Prince* (98) was part of Collingwood's lee column.

We were unfortunately a very dull sailer, and in consequence, being unable to keep our station, were put out of the line, and when at daylight the combined fleet was discovered to leeward, and our fleet bore up in chase, we were astern of the whole fleet, and were totally unable to gain our place, though second to Collingwood on the leeline. It was poor satisfaction that we had a magnificent sight of the battle, but at length we passed through the disabled ships on both sides and perceived a French 90 gunship (the '*Achille*') making all sail for Cadiz, with only her mizen topmast gone. We stood towards her and should have had no chance of coming up with her, but pouring in our broadside brought down her foremast, and she took fire. With the hope of disabling us in masts, she only fired at our rigging, and only having four shots in the hull, we had but six men wounded, and fortunately, although much cut about, not a stick was disabled . . .

END-PLAY: *INTRÉPIDE* STRIKES HER COLOURS, 5.00 p.m.

Lieutenant Marquis Gicquel des Touches, Intrépide[34]

We had soon the honour of drawing on us a number of the enemy:—the *Leviathan*, the *Africa*, the *Agamemnon*, the *Orion*, the *Téméraire* (? the *Britannia*) of 100 guns. They all set on us fiercely, and when, after five in the evening, we had to lower our colours, the only flag on our side that still flew, the *Intrépide* had not a lower mast left standing. She had lost two-thirds of her men and was lying riddled with shot-holes; the port-lids torn away; and with water pouring in below everywhere. Our honour, how-ever, was saved; our work had been done, our duty fulfilled to the uttermost.

I passed the whole time of the battle on the forecastle, where I had charge of the head sails and of the musketry and the boarders. To lead my boarders was throughout my most ardent desire, which unhappily I could not realize. What took much of my attention was to prevent the masts and yards from coming down, and I was able to keep the foremast standing for a considerable time, by means of which we were able to man-œuvre the ship to some extent. While the fighting was very hot, the British *Orion* crossed our bows in order to pour in a raking fire. I got my men ready to board, and pointing out to a midshipman her position and what I wanted to do, I sent him to the captain with a request to have the ship laid on board the Orion. I saw to the rest, and seeing the ardour of my men, I already imagined myself master of the British seventy-four and taking her into Cadiz with her colours under ours! With keen anxiety I waited; but there was no change in the Intrépide's course. Then I dashed off for the quarter-deck myself. On my way I found my midshipman lying flat on the deck, terrified at the sight of the *Téméraire* (? *Britannia*), which ship had come abreast of us within pistol-shot and was thundering into us from her lofty batteries. I treated my emissary as he deserved – I gave him a hearty kick – and then I hurried aft to explain my project personally to the captain. It was then, though, too late. The Orion swept forward across our bows, letting fly a murderous broadside – and no second chance presented itself.

At the moment I reached the poop the brave Infernet was brandishing a small curved sabre which struck off one of the pieces of wooden ornamental work by the rail. The sword-blade went quite close to my face, and I said laughingly, "Do you want to cut my head off, Captain?" "No, certainly not you, my friend," was the reply, "but that's what I mean to do to the first man who speaks to me of surrender." Near by was a gallant colonel of infantry, who had distinguished himself at Marengo. He was terribly perturbed at the broadside from the *Téméraire*. In vain he tried to dodge and shelter behind the stalwart form of the captain, who at length saw what he was doing. "Ah, Colonel," called out the captain, "do you think I am sheathed in metal then?" In spite of the gravity of the moment we could not keep from laughing.

But by now, indeed, the decks had been almost swept clear; our guns were disabled, and the batteries heaped up with dead and dying. It was impossible to keep up a resistance which meant the doom of what remained of our brave ship's company, and ourselves, without the means of striking back and inflicting harm on the enemy. Our flag was hauled down. It had been for some time the last flag to fly in our part of the battle, and I believe after us no other French or Spanish ship maintained resistance.

Des Touches was correct. The Combined Fleet was vanquished and silent save for the moaning of the wounded, the cries of those in the water, and the sound of ships in flames. One of those aflame was the French *Achille*, whose crew were forced to jump overboard at a little after 5.00 p.m., at which British ships nearby lowered boats to rescue them. To the surprise of those aboard HMS *Revenge*, one of the rescued was a Frenchwoman.

RESCUE OF A FRENCH WOMAN SAILOR, 5.15 p.m.

Anonymous officer, HMS Revenge[35]

Towards the conclusion of the battle the French 80-gun ship *Achille*, after surrendering, caught fire on the booms. The poor fellows belonging to her, as the only chance of saving their lives, leaped overboard, having first stripped off their clothes, that they might be the better able to swim to any pieces of floating wreck or to the boats of the ships sent by those nearest at hand to their rescue. As the boats filled, they proceeded to the *Pickle Schooner*, and, after discharging their freight into that vessel, returned for more. The schooner was soon crowded to excess, and, therefore, transferred the poor shivering wretches to any of the large ships near her. The *Revenge*, to which ship I belonged, received nearly a hundred of the number, some of whom had been picked up by our own boats, Many of them were badly wounded, and all naked. No time was lost for providing for the latter want, as the purser was ordered immediately to issue to each man a complete suit of clothes.

On the morning after the action I had charge of the deck, the other officers and crew being at breakfast, when another boat load of these poor prisoners of war came alongside, all of whom, with one exception, were in the costume of Adam. The exception I refer to was apparently a youth, but clothed in an old jacket and trousers, with a dingy handkerchief tied round the head, and exhibiting a face begrimed with smoke and dirt, without shoes, stockings, or shirt, and looking the picture of misery and despair. The appearance of this young person at once attracted my attention, and on asking some questions on the subject, I was answered that the prisoner was a woman. It

was sufficient to know this, and I lost no time in introducing her
to my messmates, as a female requiring their compassionate
attention. The poor creature was almost famishing with hunger,
having tasted nothing for four-and-twenty hours, consequently
she required no persuasion to partake of the breakfast upon the
table. I then gave her up my cabin, for by this time the bulk-
head had been replaced, and made a collection of all the articles
which could be procured to enable her to complete a more
suitable wardrobe. One of the lieutenants gave her a piece of
sprigged blue muslin, which he had obtained from a Spanish
prize, and two new checked shirts were supplied by the purser;
these, with a purser's blanket, and my ditty bag, which contained needles, thread, etc., being placed at her disposal, she, in
a short time, appeared in a very different, and much more
becoming, costume. Being a dressmaker, she had made herself a
sort of a jacket, after the Flemish fashion, and the purser's shirts
she had transformed into an outer petticoat; she had a silk
handkerchief tastily tied over her head, and another thrown
round her shoulders; white stockings and a pair of the chaplain's shoes were on her feet, and, altogether, our guest, which
we unanimously voted her, appeared a very interesting young
woman.

"Jeannette," which was the only name by which I ever knew
her, thus related to me the circumstances. She said she was
stationed during the action in the passage of the fore-magazine,
to assist in handing up the powder, which employment lasted
till the surrender of the ship. When the firing ceased, she
ascended to the lower deck, and endeavoured to get up to
the main deck, to search for her husband, but the ladders
having been all removed, or shot away, she found this impracticable; and just at this time an alarm of fire spread through
the ship, so that she could get no assistance. The fire originated
upon the upper deck, and gradually burnt downwards. Her
feelings upon this occasion cannot be described: but death from
all quarters stared her in the face. The fire, which soon burnt
fiercely, precluded the possibility of her escaping by moving
from where she was, and no friendly counsellor was by with
whom to advise. She remained wandering to and fro upon the
lower deck, among the mangled corses of the dying and the

slain, until the guns from the main deck actually fell through
the burnt planks. Her only refuge, then, was the sea, and the
poor creature scrambled out of the gun-room port, and by the
help of the rudder chains, reached the back of the rudder, where
she remained for some time, praying that the ship might blow
up, and thus put a period to her misery, At length the lead
which lined the rudder-trunk began to melt, and to fall upon
her, and her only means of avoiding this was to leap overboard.
Having, therefore, divested herself of her clothes, she soon found
herself struggling with the waves, and providentially finding a
piece of cork, she was enabled to escape from the burning mass.
A man, shortly afterwards, swam near her, and, observing her
distress, brought her a piece of plank, about six feet in length,
which, being placed under her arms, supported her until a boat
approached to her rescue.

ONE SHIP'S BATTLE: THE LOG OF HMS *POLYPHEMUS*, 21 October 1805

At 5.45 a.m. saw the Enemy's Fleet, consisting of 33 Sail of the
Line, 5 Frigates, and 2 Brigs, formed in a line ahead on the
starboard tack. At 6.30 answered general signal 13 – prepared
for battle – saw the Enemy, in a confused state, forming a line
on the larboard tack – the *Victory* made the general telegraph
signal, "England expects every man will do his duty," which
being told to the Ship's company, was answered with three
cheers, and returned by the *Dreadnought* on our starboard beam
– observed the *Royal Sovereign* break the Enemy's line in the
centre, and placed herself alongside a Spanish three-decker, at
the same time receiving a heavy fire on the starboard quarter
from a French two-decker, and several others at the same time
raking her – when the smoke cleared away a little, observed the
Spanish three-decker and Sovereign had wore on the larboard
tack, still keeping up a heavy fire – the Enemy's centre began a
general firing on the *Tonnant*, *Belleisle*, and *Bellerophon*, who were
standing on also to break the Enemy's line – saw one of their
topmasts shot away – about 20 before 12 observed the *Victory*
fired upon by the Enemy's van, which was returned with a few
of her foremost guns on the starboard side – the Enemy shortly

after shot away her mizenmast, when the *Victory* opened a heavy
fire, which was joined by the *Téméraire*, who was shortly
dismasted – lost sight of the Commander-in-Chief owing to
the smoke. At noon the *Dreadnought* hailed us, and requested we
would permit him to pass, as it was his wish to get alongside a
Spanish three-decker, which was a little on our starboard bow,
yawed to starboard a little, receiving a heavy fire from the
three-decker and the two next Ships astern of her – altered our
course, and stood for the sternmost Ship, which, finding we
could not haul up to, for the Swiftsure being close on our
larboard quarter, and the *Belleisle*, who was totally dismasted,
and receiving a heavy fire from a French two-decker, in the
smoke of which we lost sight of her – the *Dreadnought* exchanged
fire with the Spanish three-decker – the *Swiftsure* ranged up on
our larboard side, and fired athwart our hawse – hailed her, and
requested him not to fire into us – they shot away our ensign
halyards – in about 15 or 20 minutes after, we took in our
steering-sails, and fired two broadsides into the stern of a Ship
next to the Spanish three-decker, who returned it, not having
any other Ship opposing her – hauled up to starboard a little,
and fired on the three-decker who had been raking us, but was
bearing up out of the Line – at 3 commenced firing into the
stern of the French line-of-battle Ship – shortly shot away her
mizenmast and a maintopmast – filled to get on her bow, seeing
she wished to make to join the Enemy's Squadron that were
forming to leeward – shot away her foreyard, and observed her
on fire in the foretop, when she ceased firing, and waved a
Union Jack at her cat-head – hauled out to relieve the *Defence*,
who was engaged by a Spanish two-decker, who, on seeing our
manœuvres, hauled in her colours, which were hanging over
her stern, and waved an English Jack from her traffle – bore up
to prevent two Ships which had struck from joining the Enemy's Squadron – they proved to be the *Berwick* and *Argonauta* –
observed the Prince range alongside the *Achille*, who was on fire,
and fired several broadsides into her, not supposing she had
struck to us, which she returned – sent a party of men and a
petty officer on board the *Berwick*, and a Lieutenant and a party
of men on board the *Argonauta* – saw the *Pickle* and *Guernsey
Schooner* picking up men from the *Achille*. At 4 ceased firing in

the rear. At 6 the van ceased firing. At 7 the *Achille* blew up. Employed repairing damages.[36]

THE END: *ACHILLE* BLOWS UP, 5.45 p.m.

Anonymous officer, HMS Defence[37]

As the sunset, the fire consuming *Achille* reached her magazine and she exploded to bring the battle to an awesome end.

It was a sight the most awful and grand that can be conceived. In a moment the hull burst into a cloud of smoke and fire. A column of vivid flame shot up to an enormous height in the atmosphere and terminated by expanding into an immense globe, representing, for a few seconds, a prodigious tree in flames, speckled with many dark spots, which the pieces of timber and bodies of men occasioned while they were suspended in the clouds.

Four thousand, seven hundred and forty-four men lay dead*, amidst a scene of apocalyptic devastation. Eighteen Combined ships had been taken; eleven had limped into Cadiz (never to take to sea again) and four of Dumanoir's van had fled (only to surrender to Rear Admiral Sir Richard Strachan on 2 November). Nelson had wanted the annihilation of the Combined Fleet. He achieved it.

No British ships, meanwhile, had struck their colours or sunk, although a number were mere floating hulks.

AFTER THE BATTLE: CLEARING THE DECKS OF HMS *REVENGE*, 6.00 p.m.

William Robinson[38]

We were now called to clear the decks, and here might be witnessed an awful and interesting scene, for as each officer and seaman would meet, (oh! what an opportunity for the Christian and man of feeling to meditate on the casualty of fate in this life,) they were inquiring for their messmates. Orders were now given to fetch the dead bodies from the after cock-pit, and throw

* 449 British, 4395 French and Spanish.

them over-board; these were the bodies of men who were taken down to the doctor during the battle, badly wounded, and who by the time the engagement was ended were dead. Some of these, perhaps, could not have recovered, while others might, had timely assistance been rendered, which was impossible; for the rule is, as order is requisite, that every person shall be dressed in rotation as they are brought down wounded, and in many instances some have bled to death.

The next call was, "all hands to splice the main brace," which is the giving out a gill of rum to each man, and indeed they much needed it, for they had not ate or drank from breakfast time: we now had a good night's work before us; all our yards, masts, and sails were sadly cut, indeed the whole of the sails were obliged to be unbent, being rendered completely useless, and by the next morning we were partly jury-rigged: we now began to look for our prizes, as it was coming on to blow hard on the land, and Admiral Collingwood made signals for each ship that was able, to take a prize in tow, to prevent them drifting into their own harbour, as they were complete wrecks and unmanageable.

On boarding the prizes, British seamen were shocked by the carnage wrought by their guns. Midshipman Badcock wrote to his father: "I was on board our prize the *Trinidad* getting the prisoners out of her, she had between 3 and 400 killed and wounded, her Beams were covered with Blood, Brains, and peices [sic] of Flesh, and the after part of her Decks with wounded, some without Legs and some without an Arm; what calamities War brings on and what a number of Lives where [sic] put to an end on the 21st."

As darkness descended over the sea of battle, the wind blew up. Against Nelson's advice, the fleet was not anchored. For those seamen who had survived the calamities of Trafalgar, the perils were not yet over.

Part Four

Aftermath

Part Four

THE BATTLE OF TRAFALGAR: THE COMMANDER REPORTS, 22 October 1805

Vice-Admiral Cuthbert Collingwood[1]

Throughout the 22nd, as the wind freshened, those survivors of the battle not engaged in repair or sailing duties began their first letters and reports home. To the new commander of the British fleet, Admiral Cuthbert Collingwood, fell the burden of epistolary activity.

Euryalus, off Cape Trafalgar, *October 22nd, 1805*

Sir

The ever to be lamented death of Vice-Admiral Lord Viscount Nelson, who, in the late conflict with the Enemy, fell in the hour of victory, leaves to me the duty of informing my Lords Commissioners of the Admiralty, that on the 19th instant it was communicated to the Commander in Chief from the Ships watching the motions of the Enemy in Cadiz, that the Combined Fleet had put to sea. As they sailed with light winds westerly, his Lordship concluded their destination was the Mediterranean, and immediately made all sail for the Streights entrance with the British squadron, consisting of twenty-seven Ships, three of them sixty-fours, where his Lordship was informed by Capt. Blackwood, (whose vigilance in watching, and giving notice of the enemy's movements, has been highly meritorious,) that they had not yet passed the Streights.

On Monday the 21st instant, at daylight, when Cape Trafalgar bore E. by S. about seven leagues, the Enemy was discovered six or seven miles to the eastward, the wind about west, and very light; the Commander in Chief immediately made the signal for the fleet to bear up in two columns, as they are formed in order of sailing; a mode of attack his Lordship had previously directed, to avoid the inconvenience and delay in forming a line of battle in the usual manner. The Enemy's line consisted of thirty-three Ships (of which eighteen were French and fifteen were Spanish), commanded in chief by Admiral Villeneuve; the Spaniards, under the direction of Gravina, wore, with their heads to the northward, and formed their line of battle with great closeness and correctness; but as the mode of attack was unusual, so the structure of their line was new; – it formed a crescent convexing to leeward – so that, in leading down to their centre, I had both their van and rear abaft the beam. Before the fire opened, every alternate Ship was about a cable's length to windward of her second a-head and a-stern, forming a kind of double line, and appeared, when on their beam, to leave a very little interval between them: and this without crowding their Ships. Admiral Villeneuve was in the *Bucentaure* in the centre, and the *Prince of Asturias* bore Gravina's flag in the rear; but the French and Spanish Ships were mixed without any apparent regard to order of National squadron.

As the mode of our attack had been previously determined on, and communicated to the Flag-officers and Captains, few signals were necessary, and none were made except to direct close order as the lines bore down.

The Commander in Chief in the *Victory* led the weather column; and the *Royal Sovereign*, which bore my flag, the lee.

The Action began at twelve o'clock, by the leading Ships of the columns breaking through the Enemy's line, the Commander in Chief about the tenth Ship from the van, the Second in Command about the twelfth from the rear, leaving the van of the Enemy unoccupied; the succeeding Ships breaking through in all parts, a-stern of their leaders, and engaging the Enemy at the muzzles of their guns, the conflict was severe. The Enemy's Ships were fought with a gallantry highly honourable to their Officers, but the attack on them was irresistible; and it pleased the Almighty Disposer of all events to grant His Majesty's arms a complete and glorious victory. About three P.M. many of the Enemy's Ships having struck their colours, their line gave way; Admiral Gravina, with ten Ships, joining their Frigates to leeward, stood towards Cadiz. The five headmost Ships in their van tacked, and standing to the southward to windward of the British line, were engaged, and the sternmost of them taken; the others went off, leaving to His Majesty's squadron nineteen Ships of the line (of which two are first-rates, the *Santisima Trinidad* and the *Santa Anna*.) with three Flag Officers; viz. Admiral Ville-neuve, the Commander in Chief; Don Ignatio Maria d'Alava, Vice-Admiral; and the Spanish Rear-Admiral, Don Baltazar Hidalgo Cisneros.

After such a victory it may appear unnecessary to enter into encomiums on the particular parts taken by the several Commanders; the conclusion says more on the subject than I have language to express; the spirit which animated all was the same: when all exert themselves zealously in their country's service, all deserve that their high merits should stand recorded; and never was high merit more conspicuous than in the battle I have described.

The *Achille* (a French 74), after having surrendered, by some mismanagement of the Frenchmen took fire, and blew up; two hundred of her men were saved by the Tenders.

A circumstance occurred during the Action, which so strongly marks the invincible spirit of British seamen, when engaging the enemies of their country, that I cannot resist the pleasure I have in making it known to their Lordships. The *Téméraire* was boarded by accident, or design, by a French Ship on one side, and a Spaniard on the other: the contest was vigorous; but in the end the Combined ensigns were torn from the poop, and the British hoisted in their places.

Such a Battle could not be fought without sustaining a great loss of men. I have not only to lament, in common with the British Navy and the British Nation, in the fall of the Commander-in-Chief, the loss of a hero whose name will be immortal, and his memory ever dear to his Country; but my heart is rent with the most poignant grief for the death of a friend, to whom, by many years' intimacy, and a perfect knowledge of the virtues of his mind, which inspired ideas superior to the common race of men, I was bound by the strongest ties of affection; a grief to which even the glorious occasion in which he fell, does not bring the consolation which perhaps it ought: his Lordship received a musket ball in his left breast about the middle of the Action, and sent an Officer to me immediately with his last farewell, and soon after expired.

I have also to lament the loss of those excellent Officers, Captains Duff of the *Mars* and Cooke of the *Bellerophon*: I have yet heard of none others.

I fear the numbers that have fallen will be found very great when the returns come to me; but it having blown a gale of wind ever since the Action, I have not yet had it in my power to collect any reports from the Ships.

The *Royal Sovereign* having lost her masts, except the tottering foremast, I called the *Euryalus* to me, while the Action continued, which Ship lying within hail, made my signals, a service Captain Blackwood performed with great attention. After the Action I shifted my flag to her, that I might more easily communicate my orders to, and collect the Ships, and towed the *Royal Sovereign* out to seaward. The whole fleet were now in a very perilous situation; many dismasted; all shattered; in thirteen fathoms water, off the shoals of Trafalgar; and when I made the signal to prepare to anchor, few of the Ships had an anchor to let go, their cables being shot; but the same good Providence which aided us through such a day preserved us in the night, by the wind shifting a few points, and drifting the Ships off the land, except four of the captured dismasted Ships, which are now at anchor off Trafalgar, and I hope will ride safe until those gales are over.

Having thus detailed the proceedings of the fleet on this occasion, I beg to congratulate their Lordships on a victory which, I hope, will add a ray to the glory of His Majesty's crown, and be attended with public benefit to our country.

I am, &c.,

C. COLLINGWOOD

THE ORDER IN WHICH THE SHIPS OF THE BRITISH SQUADRON ATTACKED THE COMBINED FLEETS ON THE 21ST OF OCTOBER, 1805.

VAN	REAR
Victory	Royal Sovereign
Téméraire	Mars
Neptune	Belleisle
Conqueror	Tonnant
Leviathan	Bellerophon
Ajax	Colossus
Orion	Achille
Agamemnon	Polyphemus
Minotaur	Revenge
Spartiate	Swiftsure
Britannia	Defence
Africa	Thunderer

VAN		REAR
Euryalus	Naiad	Defiance
Sirius	Pickle Schooner	Prince
Phœbe	Entreprenante Cutter	Dreadnought

(Signed)　　C. COLLINGWOOD

GENERAL ORDER

TO THE RIGHT HON. REAR-ADMIRAL THE EARL OF NORTHESK,
AND THE RESPECTIVE CAPTAINS AND COMMANDERS.

[From the *London Gazette* of the 6th of November, 1805.]

Euryalus, October 22nd, 1805

The ever-to-be-lamented death of Lord Viscount Nelson, Duke of Bronte, the Commander in Chief, who fell in the Action of the 21st, in the arms of Victory, covered with glory, whose memory will be ever dear to the British Navy, and the British Nation; whose zeal for the honour of his King, and for the interests of his Country, will be ever held up as a shining example for a British Seaman, leaves to me a duty to return my thanks to the Right Hon. Rear-Admiral, the Captains, Officers, Seamen, and detachments of Royal Marines serving on board His Majesty's Squadron now under my command, for their conduct on that day; but where can I find language to express my sentiments of the valour and skill which were displayed by the Officers, the Seamen, and Marines in the Battle with the Enemy, where every individual appeared an Hero, on whom the glory of his Country depended. The attack was irresistible, and the issue of it adds to the page of Naval Annals a brilliant instance of what Britons can do, when their King and their Country need their service.

To the Right Honourable Rear-Admiral the Earl of North-esk, to the Captains, Officers, and Seamen, and to the Officers, Non-commissioned Officers, and Privates of the Royal Marines, I beg to give my sincere and hearty thanks for their highly meritorious conduct, both in the Action, and in their zeal and activity in bringing the captured Ships out from the perilous situation in which they were after their surrender, among the shoals of Trafalgar, in boisterous weather.

And I desire that the respective Captains will be pleased to communicate to the Officers, Seamen, and Royal Marines, this public testimony of my high approbation of their conduct, and my thanks for it.

C. COLLINGWOOD[2]

To The Hon. General Fox, Lieut.-Governor of Gibraltar.
Euryalus, at Sea, *22nd October, 1805*
Sir

Yesterday a Battle was fought by His Majesty's Fleet with the Combined Fleets of Spain and France, which will stand recorded as one of the most decisive and brilliant that ever distinguished the British Navy. The Enemy's Fleet sailed from Cadiz on the 19th in the morning, thirty-three Sail of the Line in number, for the purpose of giving battle to the British Squadron of twenty-seven; and yesterday at 11 a.m. the contest began close in with the shoals off Trafalgar. At 5 p.m. seventeen of the Enemy had surrendered, and one burnt (the *Achille*), amongst which is the *St. Ann*, the Spanish Admiral, Don de Alava, mortally wounded, and the *Santisima Trinidad*. The French Admiral Villeneuve is now a prisoner on board the *Mars*. I believe three Admirals are captured.

Our loss has been great in men; but what is irreparable, and the cause of universal lamentation, is the death of the noble Commander-in-Chief, who died in the arms of Victory. I have not yet had any reports from the Ships, but have heard that Captains Duff and Cooke fell in the Action. – I have to congratulate you upon the great event, and have the honour to be, &c.,

C. COLLINGWOOD[3]

ENGLISH SEAMEN: LETTERS HOME, 22 October 1805

Captain Henry Blackwood, HMS Euryalus[4]

Tuesday 22nd, 1 o'clock at night. The first hour since yesterday morning that I could call my own is now before me, to be devoted to my dearest wife, who, thank God, is not a husband out of pocket. My heart, however, is sad, and penetrated with the deepest anguish. A Victory, such a one as has never been achieved, yesterday took place in the course of five hours; but at such an expense, in the loss of the most gallant of men, and best of friends, as renders it to me a Victory I never wished to have witnessed – at least, on such terms. After performing wonders by his example and coolness, Lord Nelson was wounded by a French Sharpshooter, and died in three hours after, beloved and regretted in a way not to find example. To any other person, my Harriet, but yourself, I could not and would not enter so much into the detail, particularly of what I feel at this moment. But you, who know and enter into all my feelings, I do not, even at the risk of distressing you, hesitate to say that in my life, I never was so shocked or so completely upset as upon my flying to the Victory, even before the Action was over, to find Lord Nelson was then at the gasp of death. His unfortunate decorations of innumerable stars, and his uncommon gallantry, was the cause of his death; and such an Admiral has the Country lost, and every officer and man so kind, so good, so obliging a friend as never was. Thank God, he lived to know that such a Victory, and under circumstances so disadvantageous to the attempt, never was before gained. Almost all seemed as if inspired by the one common sentiment of conquer or die. The Enemy, to do them justice, were not less so. They waited the attack of the British with a coolness I was sorry to witness, and they fought in a way that must do them honour. As a spectator, who saw the faults, or rather mistakes, on both sides, I shall ever do them the justice to say so. They are, however, beat, and I hope and trust it may be the means of hastening a Peace. Buonaparte, I firmly believe, forced them to sea to try his luck, and what it might procure him [in] a pitched battle. They had the flower of the Combined Fleet, and I hope it will convince Europe at large that he has not yet learnt enough to cope with the English at sea. No history can record such a brilliant Victory. At 12 o'clock yesterday it commenced, and ended about 5, leaving in our hands nineteen Sail of the Line, one of whom afterwards blew up (a French Ship, the *Achille*): therefore, except for our prize-money, it is not of so much consequence. They were attacked in a way no other Admiral ever before thought of, and equally surprised them. Lord Nelson (though it was not his station) would lead, supported by Captain Hardy, and Freemantle in *Téméraire*, and *Neptune*. He went into the thickest of it, was successful in his first object, and has left cause for every man who had a heart never to forget him. I closed my last sheet in a great hurry to obey my signal on board the *Victory*, and really I thought that I was sent for to take the command of one of the Ships vacant. It was, however, only to talk to me – explain what he expected from the Frigates in, and after, the action – to thank me (which he did but too lavishly) for my intelligence, and the look-out we kept; and to tell me that if he lived, he should send me home with the despatches. Have I not, therefore, my dearest love, but too much cause to regret such a considerate friend? How completely he has acted up to the letter I send you, which I am sure you will be glad to see and keep, the issue has proved. And how glad I am to possess such a letter I cannot express! I stayed with him till the Enemy commenced their fire on the *Victory*, when he sent me off. He told me, at parting, we should meet no more; he made me witness his Will, and away I came, with a heart very sad. The loss in the *Victory*, and indeed, I believe, in almost all the other Ships, has been sufficient to convince us the Enemy have learnt how to fight better than they ever did; and I hope it is not injustice to the Second in Command, who is now on board the Euryalus, and who fought like a hero, to say that the Fleet under any other, never would have performed what they did under Lord N. But under Lord N. it seemed like inspiration to most of them. To give you an idea of the man, and the sort of heart he had, the last signal he made was such a one as would immortalize any man. He saw the Enemy were determined to see it out, and as if he had not already inspired every one with ardour and determination like himself, he made the following general signal by Sir Home Popham's telegraph, viz., 'England expects every officer and man will do their utmost duty.' This, of course, was conveyed by general signals from his Ship; and the alacrity with which the individual Ships answered it, showed how entirely they entered into his feelings and ideas. Would to God he had lived to see his prizes, and the Admirals he has taken! three in all: amongst them, the French Commander-in-Chief, who, I am sorry to say, is Villeneuve, and not Décres. I fear I shall tire you with all this long account; but so entirely am I depressed with the private loss I have had, that really the *Victory*, and all the prize-money I hope to get (if our prizes arrive safe), appear quite lost by the chasm made by Lord Nelson's death. I am, therefore, persuaded you will not think a tribute like this too much. I can scarcely credit he is no more, and that we have in sight of the Spanish shore obtained so complete, so unheard-of a Victory. Our prizes, I trust, we shall save. Ever since last evening we have had a most dreadful gale of wind, aud it is with difficulty the Ships who tow them keep off the shore. Three, I think, must be lost, and with them, above 800 souls each. What a horrid scourge is war! Would to God that this may pave the way to a general peace, I shall then so [*erased* . . . . . .]. I must, now that I have time, impart my hopes and doubts as to our soon meeting, which I now wish, if possible, more than ever. Hardy (whose despair and grief for the loss of such a friend is touching) told me he should mention it to Admiral Collingwood, Lord Nelson's intention about sending me, and as he must send the account by a fast sailer, as well as a strong Frigate, I hope and think I may be the lucky man to bear Hardy company with such joyful tidings. Admiral Collingwood, who came to hoist his flag here for a week or so, because his own Ship was dismasted, and unfit for him, is a very reserved, though a very pleasing good man; and as he fought like an angel, I take the more to him. As yet he has said nothing on the subject, but I have secret hopes that I shall go, particularly as Lord Nelson's body is to be carried to England, and it will be sent in a safe Ship. The very idea sets me wild; and I assure you I am endeavouring to obtain it, by making my Ship as comfortable as circumstances will admit, and myself as useful in the work he has before him, which, with such a disabled Fleet, and in such weather, is no trifle. I hope, however, that to-morrow we shall have fine weather, and that the Ships and prisoners may be well secured. All will then be well, but at present our situation is an anxious one. This is the first night I shall be undressed since Saturday.

R.F. Roberts, HMS Victory[5]

"*Victory,*" *at Sea*
Off Trafalgar, *22nd Oct.*, 1805.

Dear Parents,

I have just time and opportunity to tell you that we had a desperate engagement with the enemy, and, thank God, I have so far escaped unhurt. The Combined Fleet came out of Cadiz on

Saturday morning with a determination to engage and blow us up (as the prisoners say) out of the water, but they are much – very much – mistaken. I can't tell you how many we have taken and destroyed, they say fifteen, but it is quite uncertain. *I* don't think it is so many; but none of us know at present, but amongst the taken is a fourdecker which struck to the *Neptune*. We engaged her for some time and then she fell astern of us.

I am sorry – very sorry – to tell you that amongst the slain is Lord Nelson, his secretary Mr Scott, and Mr Whipple, Captain Hardy's clerk, whom you know. Out of four marine officers two were wounded and the Captain killed. It was as hard an action, as allowed by all on board this ship, as ever was fought. There were but three left alive on the Quarterdeck, the enemy fired so much grape and small shot from the rigging, there was one ship so close to us that we could not run out our guns their proper length. Only conceive how much we must have smashed her, every gun was trebly shotted for her.

We have a great many killed and wounded – dangerously wounded – 21 amputations. I am happy to say Captain Hardy escaped unhurt, but we have one Lieutenant killed and two wounded, and one midshipman killed and three wounded. We had no less than ten ships on ours.

I forgot to tell you that we engaged them on Monday, we began at 12 o'clock and continued till $\frac{1}{2}$ past 4. The enemy consisted of 35 sail of the Line, 4 frigates, 2 brigs; and our fleet of 27 sail of the line, 4 frigates and a schooner and sloop. Unluckily for us Admiral Lewes had been sent a little time before with 5 sail of the line up the Gut.

This morning the enemy are out of sight and we have the prizes in two, going I believe for Gibraltar. We have several ships fit for the enemy now, and if they should come to attack us we should be able to give them a warm reception, they have most of them had enough of it; there are several lame duck's gone off. The rascals have shot away our mizen mast and we are very much afraid of our main and foremasts. The *Royal Sovereign* has not a stick standing – a total wreck. It was she that began the action in a noble manner, engaging four of them at the same time. Admiral Collingwood had shifted his flag on board of her a few days before. Two of the enemy blew up and one sank. You can have no conception whatsoever what an action between two fleets is; it was a grand but an awful sight indeed; thank God we are all so well over it.

Admiral Nelson was shot early in the action by a musket ball from the enemy's top, which struck him a little below the shoulder, touched the rib and lodged near his heart. He lived about $2\frac{1}{2}$ hours after; then died without a groan. Every ship that struck, our fellows ceased firing and gave three cheers like Noble Britons. The Spaniards fought very well indeed, as did the Frenchmen. Scarcely any prizes have a stick standing. One that we had possession of, and struck to us, had 75 killed in her middle deck, and many more in her lower deck. Capt. Duff (I believe he commands the *Colossus*) is killed, but I have not heard of any more captains being killed. I will give you all the particulars in my next, but you must excuse me now as really we are in such confusion that I can't tell how I have written this. I thought you would be uneasy if you did not hear of me by the first ship, so I have as my duty requires written to you.

Remember me to all that ask for me, and believe me.

Your dutiful son
R. F. Roberts.

P.S. – We have 40 men wounded, 9 officers, and (I think) as many killed. It was a much harder action than the Nile, several in our ship say so. The carpenter whom you saw at Mr Jacob's was there, and has been in several other actions with Lord Nelson, and he says it is the hardest action he was ever in. There were a thousand shot on each deck, and the middle deck in the action was obliged to be supplied with more. One poor fellow lost both his legs in the action, and is since dead of his wounds.

Lord Nelson's last request was that his body might be taken to England. This ship will not be able to come home with him yet, so I suppose he will be sent by some other. We expect to come to England as soon as we can get a jury mast rigged and a little repaired . . .

"UTTER RECKLESSNESS OF LIFE ON OUR PART HAVE FAILED TO AVERT A CALAMITY": A SPANISH ADMIRAL REPORTS, 22 October 1805

Rear-Admiral Don Antonio de Escano[6]

To "The Prince of Peace", Madrid.

Cadiz, *October 22nd, 1805*

Most Excellent Sir,

The unfortunate condition in which Admiral Gravina at present lies, in consequence of his left arm having been shattered by a grapeshot at the close of the late Action, totally incapacitates him from giving your Excellency an account of the sanguinary Engagement of the 21st instant – and although the satisfaction of shedding my own blood in the service of His Majesty has not been denied me, having myself received a similar wound in the leg, yet being less seriously hurt than the worthy and gallant Admiral, to whom His Majesty, in well-founded confidence, has entrusted the command of his Fleet, I am under the painful, but unavoidable necessity of discharging this duty by informing your Excellency that the most strenuous efforts and utter recklessness of life on our part have failed to avert a calamity which would, indeed, be most deplorable, but for the firmest conviction, that everything that could be done, was done, and that, therefore, our honour is intact.

I am aware that by a former dispatch of the 18th instant, Admiral Gravina informed your Excellency, that Admiral Villeneuve had notified to him his determination to sail the next day, inquiring, at the same time, if the Spanish Fleet was in sailing order. Your Excellency also knows that the Admiral's answer was, that his Squadron would promptly and cheerfully act in concert with the French, pursuant to the repeated orders of your Excellency. This being understood, the French Admiral repaired on board his Ship, and immediately made the signal to weigh anchor, and to collect all the smaller craft; signals which were forthwith repeated on board this Ship, the *Principe de Asturias*, and which were followed by the greatest exertions to call in the look-out Vessels, and to get on board the gunners and seamen who, for various causes, were on shore.

On the morning of the 19th, some of the Spanish and French set sail in obedience to the signal made by Admiral Villeneuve; in consequence, however, of the wind shifting to the S.E., we could not all succeed in so doing until the 20th, when the wind got round again to the E.S.E. Scarcely was the Combined Fleet clear of the harbour's mouth, when the wind came to S.S.E. with so much violence and with such threatening appearances, that one of the first signals made by the *Bucentaur,* the Flag-ship of Admiral Villeneuve, was to sail with double-reefed topsails. This change of the wind necessarily caused a considerable dispersion of the Fleet until two o'clock in the afternoon, when, fortunately the wind veered to the S.E., and the horizon being clear and unobscured, signal was made for the forming of five Columns, and afterwards for a junction. An advanced Frigate signalled eighteen Sail of the Enemy in sight, in consequence of which information we cleared for Action, and sailed in fighting order. At three, we all tacked and stood for the Straits, still preserving the same disposition of five Columns in which we had been before the last evolution. After having so done, we descried four of the Enemy's Frigates, to which, by order of Admiral Villeneuve we gave chase; signal being made, at the same time, from our Ship, for the *Achille*, *Algeciras* and *San Juan*, as attached to the Squadron of observation, to reinforce those sent in support, with orders to rejoin the main body of the Fleet before night-fall. At half-past six o'clock a French vessel informed us that they had made out eighteen Enemy's vessels, all in Line of Battle, and shortly afterwards we began to perceive, at no great distance, gleams of light, that could proceed only from the Enemy's Frigates, which were stationed midway between the two Fleets. At nine o'clock, the English Squadron made signals by the firing of guns, and from the interval which elapsed between the flash and the report, they must have been about two miles from us. We informed the French Admiral by signal-lanterns, that it was expedient to lose no time in forming the Line of Battle upon the leeward Ships, upon which an order to that effect was immediately given by the Commander-in-Chief; and, in this position we beheld the dawn of the 21st, with the Enemy in sight, consisting of twenty-eight Ships, eight of which were three-deckers, to windward of us, and in Line of Battle upon the opposite tack.

At three o'clock in the morning, the Enemy stood towards us in different columns, bearing down upon our Centre and Rear, on which account Admiral. Villeneuve ordered the Fleet to tack, the result of which movement was, that the Squadron of observation, under the command of Admiral Gravina, remained in the Rear. The Admiral then signalled that the leading Ship of each Column should haul her wind, as also that all the others should follow in her wake, which obliged the Fleet to work to windward, for the purpose of forming into line. Admiral Gravina gave his Squadron the necessary orders for the due execution of these manœuvres with the celerity and promptitude which the urgency of the case required; and, upon the Enemy's nearing, directed that the distance between each Ship should be lessened, and the line improved.

It wanted eight minutes to noon when an English three-decker broke through the centre of our line, being seconded in this manœuvre by the Vessels which followed in its wake. The other leading Ships of the Enemy's columns did the same; one of them passed down our Rear, a third laid herself between the *Achille* and the *St. Ildefonso*, and from this moment the Action was nothing but so many sanguinary single combats within pistol-shot: the greater part of them being between the whole of the Enemy's Fleet and the half of ours, several boardings necessarily took place. I do not possess the data necessary for giving your Highness a detailed and particular account of these single fights, nor can I speak with certainty of the movements of the Van, which, I am informed, tacked at the commencement of the Battle, in order to support those who were attacked. I can, however, confidently assure you that every Ship, French as well as Spanish, which fought in my sight, performed its duty to the utmost, and that this Ship, after a terrific contest of four hours with three or four of the Enemy's Vessels, its rigging destroyed, its sails shot through and through, its masts and topmasts riddled with balls, and in every respect in a most deplorable condition, was most seasonably relieved by the *San Justo*, a Spanish, and the *Neptune*, a French Ship, which junction drove off the Enemy, and enabled the *Rayo*, the *Montañes*, the *Asis*, and the *San Leandro*, all of which had suffered severely, to unite with the other French Ships, that were in just as bad a plight. As soon as this Vessel found itself free from the

Enemy, it directed the Ships which had joined company to assist such Vessels as were in need of their aid; and at night-fall, the cannonade having ceased on both sides, the Thémis frigate was ordered to tow us towards Cadiz Bay, into which, however, we could not enter that night, in consequence of a severe gale from the S.S.E. accompanied by a heavy rain, which obliged us to ride at anchor, at half-past one o'clock, in the Placer de Rota, with the other Ships above mentioned; and the wind still continuing to freshen, we lost our main and mizen masts, notwithstanding all our efforts to save them: a misfortune which likewise befell the *San Leandro*, also at anchor near us.

It is with the greatest satisfaction that I fulfil the pleasing duty of making known to your Excellency the noble and generous enthusiasm which actuated all the officers and men belonging to my Ship, as well as the zeal with which they performed their respective duties; their cool, gallant, and intrepid bearing was, indeed, beyond all praise. Our loss amounts to 41 killed, amongst whom is the second Lieutenant, Don Luis Perez del Camino, and 107 wounded, all severely, including Don Bernardo Corral, Lieutenant in the Royal Volunteers, and Don Alexandro Rua, Brigadier of the Marines. I have also been informed that Don Francisco Alcedo, Captain and Commander of the Ship *Montañes*, was killed in the Action; and that the Second in Command, Don Antonio Castaños, was severely wounded. The loss on board the Fleet generally, must, there is no doubt, have been very great, many of our Ships having been totally dismasted, a misfortune which always implies a sacrifice of life. A correct list of the killed and wounded, as well as of the Vessels lost, shall be forwarded to your Excellency as soon as they can be ascertained with certainty.

By the late evening of the 22nd, the British fleet and its prizes, heading for Gibraltar, were engulfed by gale-force winds. Ever professional, the British seamen tried to save their prizes and the prisoners aboard them but some enemy ships were so badly holed that there was no possibility of salvation. The first to go was the *Redoutable*, who was towed by *Swiftsure*. The loss of life was appalling.

INTRÉPIDE FOUNDERS IN THE GALE, 10.14 p.m., 22 October 1805

Midshipman G. A. Barker, HMS Swiftsure[7]

On the 22nd it came on a most Violent gale of wind, the Prize in Tow seem'd to weather it out tolerable well not withstanding her shattered state until about three in the afternoon, when from her rolling so violently in a heavy sea she carried away her fore Mast, the only mast she had standing. Towards the evening she repeatedly made signals of distress to us: we now hoisted out our Boats, and sent them on board of her although there was a very high Sea and we were afraid the boats would be swampt alongside the Prize, but they happily succeeded in saving a great number, including our Lieut, and part of the Seamen we sent on board, likewise a Lieut, two Midshipmen with some Seamen belonging to the *Téméraire*. If our situation was disagreeable from the fatigue and inclemency of the weather what must the unfortunate Prisoners have suffered on board with upwards of 8,000 men, nearly 500 were killed, and wounded in the engagement, and more than one half of the remainder were drowned. What added to the horrors of the night was the inability of our saving them all, as we could no longer endanger the lives of our people in open boats, at the mercy of a heavy sea and most violent Gale of Wind; at about 10.p.m. the *Redoutable* sunk, and the Hawser, by which we still kept her in Tow, (in order if the weather should moderate and the Prize be able to weather the tempestous night) was carried away with the violent shock; this was the most dreadful scene that can be imagined as we could distinctly hear the cries of the unhappy people we could no longer assist. Towards the morning the weather moderated and we had the good fortune, to save many that were floating past on rafts – at 9 a.m. discovered a large raft ahead and shortly after another, many of the unfortunate people were seen clinging to the wreck, the merciless sea threatening almost instant destruction to them, the Boats were immediately lowered down, and we happily saved thirty-six people from the Fury of the Waves. When the Boats came alongside, many of these unfortunate men were unable to get up the Ship's side, as most of them were not only fainting from fatigue, but were wounded in the most shocking manner, some expired in the Boats before they could get on board, completely exhausted and worn out with struggling to preserve their lives, having been the whole of a Tempestous Night, upon a few crazy planks exposed to every inclemency of the weather. If our Seamen had conducted themselves as brave men during the Action, now it was they evinced themselves as human, and generous, as they were Brave. When these unfortunate people came on board you might have seen them cloathing them as well as a scanty stock would admit of, though scanty yet hard earn'd, and that in the Defence of His King, his Family, and Country at large.

The *Intrépide* also sank. Meanwhile, *Bucentaure* and *Fougueux* ran ashore. When the almost unmanageable *Algeciras* threatened to join them, its British prize crew allowed the 600 French prisoners aboard to be brought up – at which the prisoners seized the ship, and with considerable difficulty made their way to Cadiz (where they honourably released the British prize crew and provided them with a frigate for their return).

It was at this juncture, that the Combined Fleet's Commodore Cosmao-Kerjulien emerged from Cadiz with five ships of the line and five frigates to reseize some of the prizes. It was a rash venture. Although Cosmao-Kerjulien managed to repossess *Neptuno* and *Santa-Ana* on the 23rd, two of his ships grounded in the gale and another was captured.

Nor had the elements yet finished with the sailors of Trafalgar. Another of the lost prizes was the *Monarca*, whose prize crew struggled for three days to save her.

A MIDSHIPMAN'S NIGHT IN THE *MONARCA*, 23 October 1805

Anonymous British Midshipman[8]

Our second Lieutenant, myself, and eight men, formed the party that took possession of the Monarca: we remained until the morning without further assistance, or we should most probably have saved her, though she had suffered much more than ourselves. We kept possession of her, however, for four days, in the most dreadful weather, when, having rolled away all our masts, and being in danger of immediately sinking or running on shore, we were fortunately saved by the Leviathan, with all but about 150 prisoners, who were afraid of getting into the boats. I can assure you I felt not the least fear of death during the action, which I attribute to the general confidence of victory which I saw all around me; but in the prize, when I was in danger of, and had time to reflect upon the approach of death, either from the rising of the Spaniards upon so small a number as we were composed of, or what latterly appeared inevitable, from the violence of the storm, I was most certainly afraid, and at one time, when the ship made three feet of water in ten minutes, when our people were almost all lying drunk upon deck, when the Spaniards, completely worn out with fatigue, would no longer work at the only chain pump left serviceable, when I saw the fear of death so strongly depicted on the countenances of all around me, I wrapped myself up in a Union Jack, and lay down upon deck for a short time, quietly awaiting the approach of death; but the love of life soon after again roused me, and after great exertions on the part of the British and Spanish officers, who had joined together for the mutual preservation of their lives, we got the ship before the wind, determined to run her on shore: this was at midnight, but at daylight in the morning, the weather being more moderate, and having again gained upon the water, we hauled our wind.

THE SCUTTLING OF *SANTISIMA TRINIDAD*, 23 October 1805

Mistakenly concluding that Cosmao-Kerjulien's foray meant that there were enough seaworthy Combined vessels to threaten the British prizes, Collingwood ordered the prizes nearest the Spanish coast to be scuttled. Among them was *Santisima Trinidad*, the biggest warship in the world.

Lieutenant John Edwards, HMS Prince[9]

All the necessary signals were made to leave the prizes, and we, being effective, took the *Trinidad*, the largest ship in the world, in tow; all the other ships that could render assistance to the disabled doing the same. Before four in the morn it blew so strong that we broke the hawsers twice, and from two such immense bodies as we were, found it difficult to secure her again; however, every exertion was made, and we got her again. By eight in the morning it blew a hurricane on the shore, and so close in that we could not weather the land either way. 'Tis impossible to describe the horrors the morning presented, nothing but signals of distress flying in every direction, guns firing, and so many large ships driving on shore without being able to render them the least assistance. After driving about four days without any prospect of saving the ship or the gale abating, the signal was made to destroy the prizes. We had no time before to remove the prisoners, and it now became a most dangerous task; no boats could lie alongside, we got under her stern, and the men dropped in by ropes; but what a sight when we came to remove the wounded, which there were between three and four hundred. We had to tie the poor mangled wretches round their waists, or where we could, and lower them down into a tumbling boat, some without arms, others no legs, and lacerated all over in the most dreadful manner. About ten o'clock we had got all out, to about thirty-three or four, which I believe it was impossible to remove without instant death. The water was now at the pilot deck, the weather dark and boisterous, and taking in tons at every roll, when we quitted her, and supposed this superb ship could not remain afloat longer than ten minutes. Perhaps she sunk in less time, with the above unfortunate victims, never to rise again.

William Robinson, HMS Revenge[10]

On quitting the ship our boats were so overloaded in endeavouring to save all the lives we could, that it is a miracle they were not upset. A father and his son came down the ship's side to get on board one of our boats; the father had seated himself, but the men in the boat, thinking from the load and the boisterous weather that all their lives would be in peril, could not think of taking the boy. As the boat put off the lad, as though determined not to quit his father, sprang from the ship into the sea and caught hold of the gunwale of the boat, but his attempt was resisted, as it risked all their lives; and some of the men resorted to their cutlasses to cut his fingers off in order to disentangle the boat from his grasp. At the same time the feelings of the father were so worked upon that he was about to leap overboard and perish with his son. Britons could face an enemy but could not witness such a scene of self-devotion: as it were a simultaneous thought burst forth from the crew, which said, "Let us save both father and son or die in the attempt!" The Almighty aided their design, they succeeded and brought both father and son safe on board our ship . . . On the last boat's load leaving the ship, the Spaniards who were left on board appeared on the gangway and ship's side, displaying their bags of dollars and doubloons and eagerly offering them as a reward for saving them from the expected and unavoidable wreck; but however well inclined we were, it was not in our power to rescue them, or it would have been effected without the proffered bribe.

When Nature and Collingwood had finished their business, only four prizes remained out of the rich catch of 21 October.

"A CONTINUED SERIES OF MISFORTUNES": THE BRITISH FLEET 22 October–4 November 1805

Vice-Admiral Cuthbert Collingwood

To James Gambier, esq, Consul-General, Lisbon
[Autograph in the possession of Captain Gambier, R.N.]

Euryalus, off Cadiz, *October 24th, 1805*

Sir,

I congratulate you on the most complete Victory that ever was obtained over an Enemy. The Battle commenced exactly at noon on the 21st, off Cape Trafalgar. The Combined Fleet under Villeneuve consisted of thirty-three or thirty-four Ships; His Majesty's of twenty-seven. At three o'clock they were defeated. Gravina went off with nine or ten to Cadiz: four French Ships went to the Southward, I suppose for the Mediterranean, leaving us twenty Sail of the Line captures. Villeneuve, the Commander in Chief; Don D'Alava, Vice-Admiral; Cisneros, Rear-Admiral, are captive, and I believe Rear-Admiral Magon. But the gale of wind that immediately succeeded has thrown us into a confusion which the Battle did not.

The captures are dispersed, and some gone on shore, others sunk, two burnt. The *Santisima Trinidad* sunk, the *Rayo* ashore, and the *Santa Ana* is missing from us, ashore also I hope. In short, the Victory is complete; and had the Battle been fought on the Ocean, the probability is, that not a Ship would have escaped. The Combined Fleet is destroyed, but I do not know that we shall have one Ship of them which we can get into *Port*.

In this Conflict we have to lament the loss of many brave Officers. The Commander-in Chief, whose name will be immortal in Naval History, fell during the Action; and England may mourn, for there is nothing left like him. Captains Duff and Cooke also fell; and some other Captains, as Morris, Durham, and Tyler, wounded, but I hope not severely. I have the honour to be, Sir, your most obedient humble servant,

CUTHBERT COLLINGWOOD[11]

GENERAL ORDER
To The Respective Captains And Commanders

Euryalus, off Cadiz, *October 24th, 1805*

Sir,

The Almighty God, whose arm is strength, having of his great mercy been pleased to crown the exertion of His Majesty's Fleet with success, in giving them a complete victory over their Enemies, on the 21st of this month; and that all praise and thanksgiving may be offered up to the Throne of Grace for the great benefits to our Country and to Mankind.

I have thought proper that a day should be appointed of general humiliation before God, and thanksgiving for this his merciful goodness, imploring forgiveness of sins, a continuation of his divine mercy, and his constant aid to us, in the defence of our Country's liberties and laws, without which the utmost efforts of man are nought; and direct therefore that be appointed for this holy purpose.

Given on board the *Euryalus*, off Cape Trafalgar, 22nd October, 1805.

C. COLLINGWOOD[12]

N.B.—The Fleet having been dispersed by a gale of wind, no day has yet been able to be appointed for the above purpose.

To William Marsden, Esq., Admiralty

Euryalus, October 24th, 1805

Sir,

In my letter of the 22nd, I detailed to you, for the information of my Lords Commissioners of the Admiralty, the proceedings of His Majesty's Squadron on the day of the Action, and that preceding it, since which I have had a continued series of misfortunes, but they are of a kind that human prudence could not possibly provide against, or my skill prevent.

On the 22nd, in the morning, a strong Southerly wind blew, with squally weather, which however did not prevent the activity of the Officers and Seamen of such Ships as were manageable from getting hold of many of the Prizes (thirteen or fourteen), and towing them off to the Westward, where I ordered them to rendezvous round the *Royal Sovereign*, in tow by the *Neptune*; but on the 23rd the gale increased, and the sea ran so high, that many of them broke the tow rope, and drifted far to leeward before they were got hold of again; and some of them, taking advantage of the dark and boisterous night, got before the wind, and have perhaps drifted upon the shore and sunk. On the afternoon of that day the remnant of the Combined Fleet, ten sail of Ships, who had not been much engaged, stood up to leeward of my shattered and straggled charge, as if meaning to attack them, which obliged me to collect a force out of the least injured Ships, and form to leeward for their defence. All this retarded the progress of the Hulks, and the bad weather continuing, determined me to destroy all the leewardmost that could be cleared of the men, considering that keeping possession of the Ships was a matter of little consequence compared with the chance of their falling again into the hands of the Enemy: but even this was an arduous task in the high sea which was running. I hope, however, it has been accomplished to a considerable extent. I entrusted it to skilful Officers, who would spare no pains to execute what was possible. The Captains of the *Prince* and *Neptune* cleared the *Trinidad* and sunk her. Captains Hope, Bayntun, and Malcolm, who joined the Fleet this moment from Gibraltar, had the charge of destroying four others. The *Redoutable* sunk astern of the *Swiftsure* while in tow. The *Santa Anna*, I have no doubt, is sunk, as her side was almost entirely beat in; and such is the shattered condition of the whole of them, that unless the weather moderates, I doubt whether I shall be able to carry a Ship of them into Port. I hope their Lordships will approve of what I (having only in consideration the destruction of the Enemy's Fleet) have thought a measure of absolute necessity.

I have taken Admiral Villeneuve into this Ship; Vice-Admiral Don Alava is dead. Whenever the temper of the weather will permit, and I can spare a Frigate, (for there were only four in the action with the Fleet, *Euryalus*, *Sirius*, *Phœbe*, and *Naiad*; the *Melpomene* joined the 22nd, and the *Eurydice* and *Scout* the 23rd), I shall collect the other Flag Officers, and send them to England with their Flags, (if they do not all go to the bottom), to be laid at His Majesty's feet.

There were four thousand Troops embarked, under the command of General Contamin, who was taken with Admiral Villeneuve in the *Bucentaure*.   I am, Sir, &c.,

C. COLLINGWOOD[13]

To William Marsden, ESQ., Admiralty:
[From the London Gazette of the 16th of November, 1805.]

Euryalus, off Cadiz, *28th October, 1805*
Sir,

Since my letter to you of the 24th, stating the proceedings of His Majesty's Squadron, our situation has been the most critical, and our employment the most arduous, that ever a Fleet was engaged in. On the 24th and 25th it blew a most violent gale of wind, which completely dispersed the Ships, and drove the captured Hulls in all directions.

I have since been employed in collecting and destroying them, where they are at anchor upon the coast between Cadiz and six leagues Westward of San Lucar, without the prospect of saving one to bring into Port. I mentioned in my former letter the joining of the Donegal and Melpomene, after the Action; I cannot sufficiently praise the activity of their Commanders, in giving assistance to the Squadron in destroying the Enemy's Ships. The *Defiance*, after having stuck to the *Aigle* as long as it was possible, in hope of saving her from wreck, which separated

her for some time from the Squadron, was obliged to abandon
her to her fate, and she went on shore. Captain Durham's
exertions have been very great. I hope I shall get them all
destroyed by to-morrow, if the weather keeps moderate. In the
gale the *Royal Sovereign* and *Mars* lost their foremasts, and are
now rigging anew, where the body of the Squadron is at anchor
to the N.W. of San Lucar.

I find that on the return of Gravina to Cadiz he was
immediately ordered to sea again, and came out, which made
it necessary for me to form a line, to cover the disabled Hulls:
that night it blew hard, and his Ship, the *Prince of Asturias*, was
dismasted, and returned into Port; the *Rayo* was also dismasted,
and fell into our hands; Don Enrigue M'Donel had his broad
pendant in the *Rayo*, and from him I find the *Santa Ana* was
driven near Cadiz, and towed in by a Frigate. – I am, Sir, &c.,

C. COLLINGWOOD[14]

To The Respective Captains of His Majesty's Ships General Memorandum.

[Original.]

Queen, off Cape Trafalgar, *2nd November, 1805*

Vice-Admiral Collingwood, in attending to the wishes and
feeling in common with all lately serving under the orders of
Vice-Admiral Lord Nelson, those sentiments of attachment and
affection due to so exalted a character, submits to the Admiral,
Captains, Officers, Seamen, and Marines, his compliance with
the request made him of assenting to the erecting, at the general
expense of the Squadron, on Post Down Hill, a lasting Monument to their late Chief's memory and great name: he does, in
consequence, request the Captains of the respective Ships will
make the same known to their crews, that if approved it may be
adopted; and in order to procure a fund for so laudable a
purpose, that the sum of 2000*l.* shall be deducted and paid by
the Agents for that object, out of the prize-money arising from
the Action off Cape Trafalgar the 21st ultimo, subject to the
disposal of Commissioners to be named by the Commander-in-
Chief.

The Commander-in-Chief invites Rear-Admiral Louis, with those of the Squadron under his orders at that time, to unite with him, in the way he thinks most advisable, for the accomplishment of this National object.

Should this meet your concurrence, as well as those on board the Ship you command, you will be pleased to note it in your Log Book, and report to me in writing, signed by yourself, First Lieutenant, and signing Officers.

CUTHT. COLLINGWOOD[15]

To William Marsden, Esq. Admiralty
[From the *London Gazette* of the 27th of November, 1805.
This Letter was brought to the Admiralty in the night
of the 26th of November, by Captain the Honourable
Henry Blackwood, of the Euryalus.]

His Majesty's Ship the *Queen*, off Cape Trafalgar,
November 4th, 1805

Sir,

On the 28th ultimo, I informed you of the proceedings of the Squadron to that time. The weather continuing very bad, the wind blowing from the S.W., the Squadron not in a situation of safety, and seeing little prospect of getting the captured Ships off the land, and great risk of some of them getting into Port, I determined no longer to delay the destroying them, and to get the Squadron out of the deep bay.

The extraordinary exertion of Captain Capel, however, saved the French *Swiftsure*; and his Ship the *Phœbe*, together with the *Donegal*, Captain Malcolm, afterwards brought out the *Bahama*. Indeed, nothing can exceed the perseverance of all the Officers employed in this service. Captain Hope rigged and succeeded in bringing out the *Ildefonso*; all of which will, I hope, have arrived safe at Gibraltar. For the rest, Sir, I enclose you a list of all the Enemy's Fleet which were in the Action, and how they are disposed of, which, I believe, is perfectly correct.

I informed you, in my letter of the 28th, that the remnant of the Enemy's Fleet came out a second time to endeavour, in the bad weather, to cut off some of the Hulks, when the *Rayo* was dismasted, and fell into our hands; she afterwards parted her cable, went on shore, and was wrecked. The *Indomptable*, one of the same Squadron, was also driven on shore, wrecked, and her crew perished.

The *Santa Ana* and *Algeciras* being driven near the shore of Cadiz, got such assistance as has enabled them to get in; but the ruin of their Fleet is as complete as could be expected, under the circumstances of fighting them close to their own shore. Had the Battle been in the Ocean, still fewer would have escaped. Twenty Sail of the Line are taken or destroyed; and of those which got in, not more than three are in a repairable state for a length of time.

Rear-Admiral Louis in the *Canopus*, who had been detached with the *Queen*, *Spencer*, and *Tigre*, to complete the water, &c. of these Ships, and to see the Convoy in safety a certain distance up the Mediterranean, joined me on the 30th.

In clearing the captured Ships of prisoners, I found so many wounded men, that to alleviate human misery as much as was in my power, I sent to the Marquis de Solana, Governor-General of Andalusia, to offer him the wounded to the care of their Country, on receipts being given; – a proposal which was received with the greatest thankfulness, not only by the Governor, but the whole Country resounds with expressions of gratitude. Two French Frigates were sent out to receive them, with a proper Officer to give receipts, bringing with them all the English who had been wrecked in several of the Ships, and an offer from the Marquis de Solana of the use of their hospitals for our wounded, pledging the honour of Spain for their being carefully attended.

I have ordered most of the Spanish prisoners to be released; the Officers on parole; the men for receipts given, and a condition that they do not serve in war, by sea or land, until exchanged.

By my correspondence with the Marquis, I found that Vice-Admiral d'Alava was not dead, but dangerously wounded; and I wrote to him a letter, claiming him as a prisoner of war, a copy of which I enclose, together with a State of the Flag Officers of the Combined Fleet.   I, am, &c.,

                                        C. COLLINGWOOD

A LIST OF THE COMBINED FLEETS OF FRANCE AND SPAIN IN THE ACTION OF 21ST OCTOBER, 1805, OFF CAPE TRAFALGAR, SHOWING HOW THEY ARE DISPOSED OF.

1. Spanish Ship *San Ildefonso*, of 74 guns, Brigadier Don Joseph de Vargas; sent to Gibraltar.

2. Spanish Ship *San Juan Nepomuceno*, of 74 guns, Brigadier Don Cosme Churruca; sent to Gibraltar.

3. Spanish Ship *Bahama*, of 74 guns, Brigadier Don A. D. Galiano; sent to Gibraltar.

4. French Ship *Swiftsure*, of 74 guns, Monsieur Villemadrin; sent to Gibraltar.

5. Spanish Ship *Monarca*, of 74 guns, Don Teodoro Argumosa; wrecked off San Lucar.

6. French Ship *Fougueux*, of 74 guns, Monsieur Beaudouin; wrecked off Trafalgar, all perished, and thirty of the *Téméraire*'s men.

7. French Ship *Indomptable*, of 84 guns, Monsieur Hubert; wrecked off Rota, all perished.

8. French Ship *Bucentaur*, of 80 guns, Admiral Villeneuve, Commander-in-Chief; Captains Prigny and Magendie; wrecked on the Porques, some of the crew saved.

9. Spanish Ship *San Francisco de Asis*, of 74 guns, Don Luis de Flores; wrecked near Rota.

10. Spanish Ship *El Rayo*, of 100 guns, Brigadier Don Henrique Macdonel; wrecked near San Lucar.

11. Spanish Ship *Neptuno*, of 84 guns, Brigadier Don Cayetano Valdes; wrecked between Rota and Catolina.

12. French Ship *Argonaute*, of 74 guns, Monsieur Epron; on shore in the Port of Cadiz.

13. French Ship *Berwick*, of 74 guns, Monsieur Camas; wrecked to the Northward of San Lucar.

14. French Ship *Aigle*, of 74 guns, Monsieur Courrege; wrecked near Rota.

15. French Ship *Achille*, of 74 guns, Monsieur d'Nieuport; burnt during the Action.

16. French Ship *Intrépidé*, of 74 guns, Monsieur Infornet; burnt by the *Britannia*.

17. Spanish Ship *San Agustin*, of 74 guns, Brigadier Don Felipe X. Cagigal; burnt by the *Leviathan*.

18. Spanish Ship *Santisima Trinidad*, of 140 guns, Rear-Admiral Don Baltazar H. Cisneros; Brigadier Don F. Uriarte; sunk by the *Prince*, *Neptune*, &c.

19. French Ship *Redoutable*, of 74 guns, Monsieur Lucas; sunk astern of the *Swiftsure*; *Téméraire* lost thirteen, and *Swiftsure* five men.

20. Spanish Ship *Argonauta*, of 80 guns, Don Antonio Parejo; sunk by the *Ajax*.

21. Spanish Ship *Santa Ana*, of 112 guns, Vice-Admiral Don Ignacio D'Alava; Captain Don Joseph de Gardoqui; taken, but got into Cadiz in the gale; dismasted.

22. French Ship *Algeciras*, of 74 guns, Rear-Admiral Magon (killed); Captain Monsieur Bruaro; taken, but got into Cadiz in the gale, dismasted.

23. French Ship *Pluton*, of 74 guns, Monsieur Cosmao; returned to Cadiz in a sinking state.

24. Spanish Ship *San Juste*, of 74 guns, Don Miguel Gaston; returned to Cadiz; has a foremast only.

25. Spanish Ship *San Leandro*, of 64 guns, Don Joseph de Quevedo; returned to Cadiz dismasted.

26. French Ship *Neptune*, of 84 guns, Monsieur Maistral; returned to Cadiz, and perfect.

27. French Ship *Heros*, of 74 guns, Monsieur Poulain; returned to Cadiz, lower masts in, and Admiral Rossilly's Flag on board.

28. Spanish Ship *Principe de Asturias*, of 112 guns, Admiral Don F. Gravina; Don Antonio Escano, &c.; returned to Cadiz dismasted.

29. Spanish Ship *Montanez*, of 74 guns, Don Francisco Alcedo; returned to Cadiz.

30. French Ship *Formidable*, of 80 guns, Rear-Admiral Dumanoir; hauled to the southward, and escaped.

31. French Ship *Mont-Blanc*, of 74 guns, Monsieur Le Villegries; hauled to the southward, and escaped.

32. French Ship *Scipion*, of 74 guns, Monsieur Berenger; hauled to the southward, and escaped.

33. French Ship *Duguay-Trouin*, of 74 guns, Monsieur Touffet; hauled to the southward, and escaped.

N.B.—These four Ships were captured by Sir Richard Strachan on the 4th instant.

ABSTRACT.

At Gibraltar	4
Destroyed.	16
In Cadiz, wrecks . . . . 6⎱	
In Cadiz, serviceable . . . . 3⎰	9
Escaped to the southward. . . .	4

Total 33

A LIST OF THE NAMES AND RANK OF THE FLAG-OFFICERS OF THE
COMBINED FLEET OF FRANCE AND SPAIN IN THE ACTION OF THE 21ST OF
OCTOBER, 1805.

Admiral Villeneuve, Commander-in-Chief; *Bucentaur* –
Taken.

Admiral Don Frederico Gravina; *Principe de Asturias* – Escaped, in Cadiz, wounded in the arm.

Vice-Admiral Don Ignatio Maria D'Alava; *Santa Ana* –
Wounded severely in the head, taken, but was driven back
into Cadiz in the *Santa Ana*.

Rear-Admiral Don Baltazar Hidalgo Cisneros; *Santisima
Trinidad* – Taken.

Rear-Admiral Magon; *Algeciras* – Killed.

Rear-Admiral Dumanoir; *Formidable* – Escaped.

AN ABSTRACT OF THE KILLED AND WOUNDED ON BOARD THE RE-
SPECTIVE SHIPS COMPOSING THE BRITISH SQUADRON UNDER THE
COMMAND OF THE RIGHT HONOURABLE VICE-ADMIRAL LORD VISCOUNT
NELSON, IN THE ACTION OF THE 21ST OF OCTOBER, 1805, OFF CAPE
TRAFALGAR, WITH THE COMBINED FLEETS OF FRANCE AND SPAIN.

* [From the *London Gazette* of the 27th of November and 3rd of December, 1805.]

Victory: 4 Officers, 3 Petty Officers, 32 Seamen, and 18
Marines, killed; 4 Officers, 3 Petty Officers, 59 Seamen, and 9
Marines, wounded. Total 132. *Royal Sovereign:* 3 Officers, 2 Petty
Officers, 29 Seamen, and 13 Marines, killed; 3 Officers, 5 Petty
Officers, 70 Seamen, and 16 Marines, wounded. Total, 141.
Britannia: 1 Officer, 8 Seamen, and 1 Marine, killed; 1 Officer, 1

Petty Officer, 33 Seamen, and 7 Marines, wounded. Total, 52.
Téméraire: 3 Officers, 1 Petty Officer, 35 Seamen, and 8 Marines,
killed; 3 Officers, 2 Petty Officers, 59 Seamen, and 12 Marines,
wounded. Total, 123. *Prince:* none. *Neptune:* 10 Seamen, killed; 1
Petty Officer, 30 Seamen, and 3 Marines, wounded. Total, 44.
Dreadnought: 6 Seamen and 1 Marine, killed; 1 Officer, 2 Petty
Officers, 19 Seamen, and 4 Marines, wounded. Total, 33.
Tonnant: 1 Petty Officer, 16 Seamen, and 9 Marines, killed; 2
Officers, 2 Petty Officers, 30 Seamen, and 16 Marines, wounded.
Total, 76. *Mars:* 1 Officer, 3 Petty Officers, 17 Seamen, and 8
Marines, killed; 4 Officers, 5 Petty Officers, 44 Seamen, and 16
Marines, wounded. Total, 98. *Bellerophon:* 2 Officers, 1 Petty
Officer, 20 Seamen, and 4 Marines, killed; 2 Officers, 4 Petty
Officers, 97 Seamen, and 20 Marines, wounded. Total, 150.
Minotaur: 3 Seamen killed; 1 Officer, 1 Petty Officer, 17 Seamen,
and 3 Marines, wounded. Total 25. *Revenge:* 2 Petty Officers, 18
Seamen, and 8 Marines, killed; 4 Officers, 38 Seamen, and 9
Marines, wounded. Total, 79. *Conqueror:* 2 Officers, 1 Seaman,
killed; 2 Officers, 7 Seamen, wounded. Total, 12. *Leviathan:* 2
Seamen, and 2 Marines, killed; 1 Petty Officer, 17 Seamen, and 4
Marines, wounded. Total, 26. *Ajax:* 2 Seamen, killed; 9 Seamen,
wounded. Total, 11. *Orion:* 1 Seaman, killed; 2 Petty Officers, 17
Seamen, and 4 Marines, wounded. Total 24. *Agamemnon:* 2
Seamen, killed; 7 Seamen, wounded. Total, 9. *Spartiate:* 3 Sea-
men killed; 1 Officer, 2 Petty Officers, 16 Seamen, and 1 Marine,
wounded. Total, 23. *Africa:* 12 Seamen, and 6 Marines, killed; 2
Officers, 5 Petty Officers, 30 Seamen, and 7 Marines, wounded.
Total, 62. *Belleisle:* 2 Officers, 1 Petty Officer, 22 Seamen, and 8
Marines, killed; 3 Officers, 3 Petty Officers, 68 Seamen, and 19
Marines, wounded. Total 126. *Colossus:* 1 Officer, 31 Seamen,
and 8 Marines, killed; 5 Officers, 9 Petty Officers, 115 Seamen,
and 31 Marines, wounded. Total, 200. *Achille*: 1 Petty Officer, 6
Seamen, and 6 Marines, killed; 4 Officers, 4 Petty Officers, 37
Seamen, and 14 Marines, wounded. Total, 72. *Polyphemus:* 2
Seamen, killed; 4 Seamen, wounded. Total 6. *Swiftsure:* 7 Sea-
men, and 2 Marines, killed; 1 Petty Officer, 6 Seamen, and 1
Marine, wounded. Total, 17. *Defence:* 4 Seamen, and 3 Marines,
killed; 23 Seamen, and 6 Marines, wounded. Total, 36. *Thunderer:* 2 Seamen, and 2 Marines, killed; 2 Petty Officers, 9

Seamen, and 1 Marine, wounded. Total, 16. *Defiance:* 2 Officers, 1 Petty Officer, 8 Seamen, and 6 Marines, killed; 1 Officer, 4 Petty Officers, 39 Seamen, and 9 Marines, wounded. Total, 70.

Total. – 21 Officers, 16 Petty Officers, 299 Seamen, and 113 Marines, killed; 43 Officers, 59 Petty Officers, 900 Seamen, and 212 Marines, wounded. Total, 1663.

C. COLLINGWOOD

RETURN OF THE NAMES OF THE OFFICERS AND PETTY OFFICERS KILLED AND WOUNDED ON BOARD THE SHIPS OF THE BRITISH SQUADRON IN THE ACTION WITH THE COMBINED FLEETS OF FRANCE AND SPAIN OFF CAPE TRAFALGAR, ON THE 21ST OCTOBER, 1805.

KILLED.

Victory: The Right Hon. Lord Viscount Nelson, K.B., Vice-Admiral of the White, Commander in Chief, &c. &c. &c.; John Scott, Esq., Secretary; Charles W. Adair, Captain Royal Marines; William Ram, Lieutenant; Robert Smith and Alexander Palmer, Midshipmen; Thomas Whipple, Captain's Clerk. – *Royal Sovereign:* Brice Gilliland, Lieutenant; William Chalmers, Master; Robert Green, Second Lieutenant of Royal Marines; John Aikenhead and Thomas Braund, Midshipmen. – *Britannia:* Francis Roskruge, Lieutenant. – *Téméraire:* Simeon Busigny, Captain of Royal Marines; John Kingston, Lieutenant of Royal Marines; Lewis Oades, Carpenter; William Pitts, Midshipman. – *Prince:* none. – *Neptune:* none. – *Dreadnought:* none. – *Tonnant:* William Brown, Midshipman. – *Mars:* George Duff, Captain; Alexander Duff, Master's Mate; Edmund Corlyn and Henry Morgan, Midshipmen. – *Bellerophon:* John Cooke (1st) Captain; Edward Overton, Master; John Simmons, Midshipman. – *Minotaur:* none. – *Revenge:* Thomas Grier and Edward F. Brooks, Midshipmen. – *Conqueror:* Robert Lloyd and William M. St. George, Lieutenants. – *Leviathan:* none. – *Ajax:* none. – *Orion:* none. – *Agamemnon:* none. – *Spartiate:* none. – *Africa:* none. – *Belleisle:* Ebenezer Geall, and John Woodin, Lieutenants; George Nind, Midshipman. – *Colossus:* Thomas Scriven, Master. – *Achille:* Francis John Mugg, Midshipman. – *Polyphemus:* none. – *Swiftsure:* none. – *Defence:* none. – *Thunderer:* none. – *Defiance:* Thomas Simens, Lieutenant; William Forster, Boatswain; James Williamson, Midshipman.

WOUNDED.

Victory. John Pasco, and G. Miller Bligh, Lieutenants; Lewis B. Reeves, and J.G. Peake, Lieutenants Royal Marines; William Rivers (slightly), G. A. Westphal, and Richard Bulkeley, Midshipmen; John Geoghehan, Agent Victualler's Clerk. – *Royal Sovereign:* John Clayell, and James Bashford, Lieutenants; James le Vesconte, Second Lieutenant Royal Marines; William Watson, Master's Mate; Gilbert Kennicott, Grenville Thompson, John Campbell, and John Farrant, Midshipmen; Isaac Wilkinson, Boatswain. – *Britannia:* Stephen Trounce, Master; William Grint, Midshipman. – *Téméraire:* James Mould, Lieutenant; Samuel J. Payne, Lieutenant Royal Marines; John Brooks Boatswain; T. S. Price, Master's Mate; John Eastman, Midshipman. – *Prince:* none. – *Neptune:* —— Hurrell, Captain's Clerk. – *Dreadnought:* James L. Lloyd (slightly), Lieutenant; Andrew M'Cullock, and James Saffin, Midshipmen. – *Tonnant:* Charles Tyler, Captain; Richard Little, Boatswain; William Allen, Clerk; Henry Ready, Master's Mate; the three last slightly. – *Mars:* Edward Garratt, and James Black, Lieutenants; Thomas Cook, Master; Thomas Norman, Second Captain of Royal Marines; John Yonge, George Guiren, William John Cooke, John Jenkins, and Alfred Luckraft, Midshipmen. – *Bellerophon:* James Wemyss, Captain of Royal Marines; Thomas Robinson, Boatswain; Edward Hartley, Master's Mate; William N. Jewell, James Stone, Thomas Bant, and George Pearson, Midshipmen. – *Minotavr:* James Robinson, Boatswain; John Samuel Smith, Midshipman. – *Revenge:* Robert Moorsom, Captain (slightly); Luke Brokenshaw, Master; John Berry, Lieutenant; Peter Lily (slightly), Captain of Royal Marines. – *Conqueror:* Thomas Wearing, Lieutenant of Royal Marines; Philip Mendel, Lieutenant of His Imperial Majesty's Navy (both slightly). – *Leviathan:* J. W. Watson, Midshipman (slightly). – *Ajax:* none. – *Orion:* ——Sause, C. P. Cable, Midshipmen, (both slightly). – *Agamemnon:* none. – *Spartiate:* John Clarke, Boatswain; —Bellaires and ——Knapman, Midshipmen. *Africa:* Matthew Hay, acting Lieutenant; James Fynmore, Captain of Royal Marines; Henry West, and Abraham Turner, Master's Mates; Frederick White, (slightly), Philip J. Elmhurst, and John P. Bailey, Midshipmen. – *Belleisle:* William Terrie, Lieutenant; John Owen, First Lieutenant of Royal Marines; Andrew Gibson, Boatswain; William Henry Pearson, and

William Culfield, Master's Mates; Samuel Jago, Midshipman; J. T. Hodge, Volunteer, first class. – *Colossus:* James N. Morris, Captain; George Bully, Lieutenant; William Forster, acting Lieutenant; John Benson, Lieutenant of Royal Marines; Henry Milbanke, Master's Mate; William Herringham, Frederick Thistlewayte (slightly), Thomas G. Reece, Henry Snellgrove, Rawden Maclean, George Wharrie, Tim. Renou, and George Denton, Midshipmen; William Adamson, Boatswain. – *Achille:* Parkins Prynn (slightly), and Josias Bray, Lieutenants; Pralms Westroppe, Captain of Royal Marines; William Leddon, Lieutenant of Royal Marines; George Pegge, Master's Mate; William H. Staines, and W. J. Snow, Midshipmen; W. Smith Warren, Volunteer, first class. – *Polyphemus:* none. – *Swiftsure:* Alexander Bell Handcock, Midshipman. – *Defence:* none. – *Thunderer:* John Snell, Master's Mate; Alexander Galloway, Midshipman. – *Defiance:* P. C. Durham (slightly), Captain; James Spratt and Robert Browne, Master's Mates; John Hodge and Edmund Andrew Chapman, Midshipmen.

C. COLLINGWOOD[16]

While Collingwood remained on station off Cadiz, intelligence of the Battle of Trafalgar was brought to England with the schooner *Pickle*. Collingwood's dispatch (pp. 209–212) reached the Admiralty at 1.00 p.m. on the morning of 6 November, and was immediately printed in an extraordinary edition of *the London Gazette*. England rejoiced for her victory – and cried for her fallen victor. In this, the response of the Prime Minister, Pitt, as recorded by Lord Malmesbury, was typical.

On the receipt of the news of the memorable Battle of Trafalgar (some day in November, 1805), I happened to dine with Pitt, and it was naturally the engrossing subject of our conversation. I shall never forget the eloquent manner in which he described his conflicting feelings when roused in the night to read Collingwood's dispatches. Pitt observed, that he had been called up at various hours in his eventful life by the arrival of news of various hues, but that whether good or bad, he could always lay his head on his pillow and sink into sound sleep again. On this occasion, however, the great event announced brought with it so much to weep over, as well as to rejoice at, that he could not calm his thoughts, but at length got up, though it was three in the morning.[17]

"When Nelson died," wrote Samuel Taylor Coleridge, who was in Naples in late October,

> it seemed as if no man was a stranger to another: for all were made acquaintances in the rights of a common anguish. Never can I forget the sorrow and consternation that lay on every countenance . . . Numbers stopped and shook hands with me, because they had seen tears on my cheek, and conjectured I was an Englishman; and some, as they held my hand, burst themselves into tears.[18]

There were vast outpourings of public grief. And private grief too. Lady Emma Hamilton was told of Nelson's death personally, before it appeared in the papers. She was in bed at Merton when the messenger, Captain Whitby arrived. "I sent to enquire who was arrived," recorded Lady Hamilton.

> They brought me word, Mr Whitby from the Admiralty. "Show him in directly," I said. He came in, and with a pale countenance and faint voice said, "We have gained a great Victory." – "Never mind your Victory," I said. "My letters – give me my letters" – Captain Whitby was unable to speak – tears in his eyes and a deathly paleness over his face made me comprehend him. I believe I gave a scream and fell back, and for ten hours I could neither speak nor shed a tear.[19]

Meanwhile, the body of Nelson had not been thrown overboard (the usual fate of dead sailors), but brought back to England, preserved in a tub of brandy. At Spithead, there was a post-mortem on his body.

NELSON: THE POST-MORTEM, 11 December 1805

Dr William Beatty[20]

The report on Nelson's wound and death:

> His Majesty's Ship *Victory*, at Sea,
> *11th December, 1805.*
> About the middle of the Action with the Combined Fleets on

the 21st of October last, the late illustrious Commander-in-Chief Lord Nelson was mortally wounded in the left breast by a musket-ball, supposed to be fired from the mizen-top of *La Redoutable*, French Ship of the Line, which the Victory fell on board of early in the battle. His Lordship was in the act of turning on the quarter-deck with his face towards the Enemy, when he received his wound: he instantly fell; and was carried to the cockpit, where he lived about two hours. On being brought below, he complained of acute pain about the sixth or seventh dorsal vertebra, and of privation of sense and motion of the body and inferior extremities. His respiration was short and difficult; pulse weak, small, and irregular. He frequently declared his back was shot through, that he felt every instant a gush of blood within his breast, and that he had sensations which indicated to him the approach of death. In the course of an hour his pulse became indistinct, and was gradually lost in the arm. His extremities and forehead became soon afterwards cold. He retained his wonted energy of mind, and exercise of his faculties, till the last moment of his existence; and when the victory as signal as decisive was announced to him, he expressed his pious acknowledgments, and heartfelt satisfaction at the glorious event, in the most emphatic language. He then delivered his last orders with his usual precision, and in a few minutes afterwards expired without a struggle.

Course and site of the Ball, as ascertained since death

The ball struck the fore part of his Lordship's epaulette; and entered the left shoulder immediately before the processus acromoni scapulæ, which it slightly fractured. It then descended obliquely into the thorax, fracturing the second and third ribs: and after penetrating the left lobe of the lungs, and dividing in its passage a large branch of the pulmonary artery, it entered the left side of the spine between the sixth and seventh dorsal vertebræ, fractured the left transverse process of the sixth dorsal vertebra, wounded the medulla spinalis, and fracturing the right transverse process of the seventh vertebra, made its way from the right side of the spine, directing its course through the muscles of the back; and lodged therein, about two inches below the inferior angle of the right scapula. On removing the ball, a portion of the gold-lace and pad of the epaulette, together with a small piece of his Lordship's coat, was found firmly attached to it.

W. Beatty

Dr Beatty then relates the embalming of Nelson's corpse.

The remains were wrapped in cotton vestments, and rolled from head to foot with bandages of the same material, in the ancient mode of embalming. The body was then put into a leaden coffin, filled with brandy holding in solution camphor and myrrh. This coffin was inclosed in a wooden one, and placed in the after-part of his Lordship's cabin; where it remained till the 21st of December, when an order was received from the Admiralty for the removal of the body. The coffin that had been made from the mainmast of the French Commander's Ship *l'Orient*, and presented to his Lordship by his friend Captain Hallowell, after the battle of the Nile, being then received on board, the leaden coffin was opened, and the body taken out; when it was found still in most excellent condition, and completely plastic. The features were somewhat tumid, from absorption of the spirit; but on using friction with a napkin, they resumed in a great degree their natural character. All the Officers of the Ship, and several of his Lordship's friends, as well as some of Captain Hardy's, who had come on board the *Victory* that day from the shore, were present at the time of the body's being removed from the leaden coffin; and witnessed its undecayed state after a lapse of two months since death, which excited the surprise of all who beheld it. This was the last time the mortal part of the lamented Hero was seen by human eyes; as the body, after being dressed in a shirt, stockings, uniform small-clothes and waistcoat, neckcloth, and night-cap, was then placed in the shell made from *l'Orient*'s mast, and covered with the shrouding. This was inclosed in a leaden coffin; which was soldered up immediately, and put into another wooden shell: in which manner it was sent out of the Victory into Commissioner Grey's yacht, which was hauled alongside for that purpose. In this vessel the revered remains were conveyed to Greenwich Hospital; attended by the Reverend Doctor Scott. and Messrs. Tyson and Whitby.

Lord Nelson had often talked with Captain Hardy on the subject of his being killed in battle, which appeared indeed to be a favourite topic of conversation with him. He was always prepared to lay down his life in the service of his Country; and whenever it should please Providence to remove him from this world, it was the most ambitious wish to his soul to die in the fight, and in the very hour of a great and signal victory. In this he was gratified: his end was glorious; and he died as he had lived, one of the greatest among men.

Nelson's body had been returned to England on his flagship, the *Victory*. Among the crew was seaman James Bagley, who took the opportunity to pen a few lines to his sister.

"SO NEVER THINK IT A DISGRACE TO HAVE BROTHERS IN THE SERVICE": SEAMAN BAGLEY WRITES HOME ON HIS ARRIVAL IN ENGLAND, 5 December 1805

James Bagley, HMS Victory[21]

Victory, Spithead
Dec. 5, 1805

Dear Sister,

Comes with my kind love to you are in good health so thank God I am; for I am very certain that it is by his mercy that me and my country is, and you and your religion is kept up; for it has pleased the Almighty God for to give us a complete victory of the combined fleets of France and Spain; for there was a signal for them being out of Cadiz the 19th of October, but we did not see them till the 21st, in the morning, and about 12 o'clock we gave three cheers, and then the engagement began very hot on both sides, but about five o'clock the victory was ours, and twenty sail-of-the-line struck to us. They had 34 sail-of-the-line and we had 27 of the line, but the worst of it was, the flower of the country, Lord Nelson, got wounded at twelve minutes past one o'clock, and closed his eyes in the midst of victory. Dear Sister, it pleased the Lord to spare my life, and my brother Thomas his, for he was with the same gentleman.

It was very sharp for us, I assure you, for we had not a moment's time till it was over, and the 23rd of the same instant we got a most shocking gale of wind, and we expected to go to the bottom, but, thanks be to God, He had mercy on us, every ship of ours got safe into harbour, and all the French but four got knocked to pieces on the rocks. . . . We had 125 killed and wounded, and 1500 in the English fleet killed and wounded and the enemy 12,000; so I shall leave you to judge how your country fight for the religion you enjoy, the laws you possess, and on the other hand how Bounaparte has trampt them causes down in the places he has had concern with, for nothing but torment is going forward. So never think it a disgrace to having brothers in service. . . . My dear, I shall just give you a description of Lord Nelson. He is a man about five feet seven, very slender, of an affable temper; but a rare man for his country, and has been in 123 actions and skrimmages, and got wounded with a small ball, but it was mortal. It was his last words, that it was his lot for me to go, but I am going to heaven, but never haul down your colours to France, for your men will stick to you. These words was to Captain Hardy, and so we did, for we came off victorious, and they have behaved well to us, for they wanted to take Lord Nelson from us, but we told Captain as we brought him out we would bring him home; so it was so, and he was put into a cask of spirits. So I must conclude. Your loving brother,

James Bagley

After the post-mortem, Nelson's corpse was brought – this time inside a lead coffin—to Greenwich where it lay in state for three days. So large were the crowds of mourners and sightseers that the Governor of the Royal Hospital at Greenwich considered it advisable to inform the Home Secretary.

The Mob assembled here is so very numerous & tumultuous that it is absolutely necessary that your Lordship should apply for a very *strong* party of Cavalry to line the street on each side from Deptford Bridge to the entrance of the Hospital & to attend the other Gates early on Wednesday morning or it will not be possible for the procession to move from here – The mob consisted yesterday of upwards of 30,000 & equally so today and more outrageous. Townsend & the other peace officers from Bow Street say they never saw anything like it before.[22]

From Greenwich, the coffin of Horatio Nelson was taken to London for a state funeral.

THE FUNERAL OF VISCOUNT NELSON, VICE-ADMIRAL OF THE WHITE SQUADRON, RN, 8–9 January 1806

The London Gazette

On Wednesday, the 8th instant, the remains of the late Right Honourable Horatio Viscount and Baron Nelson, K.B., Vice-Admiral of the White Squadron of His Majesty's Fleet, were conveyed from the Royal Hospital of Greenwich, where they had lain in state in the Painted Hall, on the three preceding days, to the Admiralty.

Soon after ten o'clock in the morning, the several persons appointed to attend the remains from Greenwich, assembled at the Governor's House within the Royal Hospital; and, at about one o'clock, proceeded in the Barges according to the following order, viz.: –

FIRST BARGE, covered with black cloth.

Drums – two trumpets, with their banners in the steerage.

The Standard, at the head, borne by Captains Sir Francis Laforey, Bart., of the Spartiate, supported by Lieutenants William Collins Barker and George Antram, of the Royal Navy.

The Guidon, at the door-place, borne by Captain Henry William Bayntun, of the Leviathan, (in the absence, by indisposition, of Captain Durham,) supported by two Lieutenants of the Royal Navy, all in their full uniform coats, with black waistcoats, breeches, and stockings, and crape round their arms and hats.

Rouge Croix and Blue Mantle, Pursuivants of Arms, in close mourning, with their tabards over their cloaks, and hatbands and scarves.

SECOND BARGE, covered with black cloth.
Four trumpets in the steerage.

Heralds of Arms, habited as those in the first Barge, bearing the
Surcoat, Target, and Sword, Helm and Crest, and the
Gauntlet and Spurs, of the Deceased.

The Banner of the Deceased as a Knight of the Bath, at the
head, borne by Captain Edward Rotherham, of the Royal
Sovereign, supported by two Lieutenants of the Royal Navy.

The Great Banner, with the augmentations, at the door-place,
borne by Captain Robert Moorsom, of the *Revenge*, supported
by Lieutenants David Keys and Nicholas Tucker, of the
Nassau, all habited as those in the first Barge.

THIRD BARGE,

Covered with black velvet, the top adorned with plumes of
black feathers; and in the centre, upon four shields of the
Arms of the Deceased joining in point, a Viscount's
coronet. Three bannerolls of the family lineage of the
Deceased, on each side, affixed to the external parts of
the Barge.

Six trumpets with the banners as before, in the steerage.

Six Officers of the Royal Navy, habited as those in the other
Barges; one to each banneroll, viz.: –

Lieutenant (now Captain) John Pasco.
Lieutenant (now Captain) John Yule.
Thomas Atkinson, Master of the *Victory*.
Lieutenant (now Captain)——Williams.
Lieutenant George Browne.
Lieutenant James Uzuld Purches.
The Body,

Covered with a large sheet, and a pall of velvet adorned
with six escutcheons.

Norroy King of Arms, (in the absence by indisposition, of
Clarenceux,) habited as the other Officers of Arms, and
bearing, at the head of the Body, a Viscount's coronet upon
a black velvet cushion.

Six Trumpets.

Norroy King of Arms, in the absence of Clarenceux,
bearing the Coronet on a black velvet cushion.

Three Bannerolls of {Two Supporters of the Pall} The Body, {Two Supporters of the Pall} Three Bannerolls the Family lineage Covered with a of the Family line-of the Deceased, black velvet Pall, age of the De-borne as before adorned with ceased, borne as mentioned. Escutcheons, under before mentioned. a Canopy supported by six Admirals.

Garter Principal King of Arms (absent, by indisposition).

Supporter, {THE CHIEF MOURNER, Sir Peter Parker, Bart., Admiral of the Fleet, Train-Bearer} Supporter,
Adm. Lord Radstock. Adm. Viscount Hood.

Captain the Honourable Henry Blackwood.
The Six Admirals before named, Assistant Mourners.
Windsor Herald, acting for Norroy King of Arms.
The Banner of Emblems, borne and supported as in the Barge.
Attendants on the Body while at Greenwich.

Upon arrival at the Admiralty, the BODY was there deposited, privately, till the following day, and the persons who were in the Procession retired.

Early in the morning of Thursday the 9th instant, His Royal Highness the Prince of Wales, their Royal Highnesses the Dukes of the Blood Royal, with several of the great Officers, and the Nobility and Gentry, in their carriages; the relations of the Deceased, with the Officers and others of his household, the Officers of Arms, and a number of Naval Officers, in mourning coaches, assembled in Hyde Park; having been admitted at Cumberland and Grosvenor Gates upon producing tickets issued from the College of Arms; and, having there been marshalled within the rails, proceeded, one by one, across Piccadilly, into St. James's Park, by the gate at the top of Constitution Hill, and onwards, through the Horse Guards, to the Admiralty, in the order in which they were to move in the Procession. The Chief Mourner, with his Supporters and Train-bearer, and the several Naval Officers to whom duties were assigned in the solemnity, assembled at the Admiralty: the Seamen and Marines of the Victory, the Pensioners from Greenwich Hospital, the Watermen of the Deceased, the six Conductors, the Messenger of the College of Arms, and the Marshal's-Men, with the trumpets and drums, were stationed in the Admiralty Yard. Those persons in the Procession who were not to wear mourning cloaks, official gowns, or habits, appeared in mourning, without weepers and with mourning swords; Knights of the several Orders wore their Collars; Naval and Military Officers were in their full uniforms, with crape around their arms and in their hats; the Naval Officers, to whom particular duties were assigned, had black cloth waist-coats and breeches, and black stockings; and the Clergy were in their clerical habits. Servants not in mourning, attending the carriages, were admitted with silk or crape hatbands and gloves. The Troops, ordered by His Majesty to attend at the Funeral, under the command of General Sir David Dundas, K.B., were assembled and formed by the several General Officers under whose command they respectively were, on the Parade in St. James's Park, before the Horse Guards, at half-past eight o'clock in the morning. The whole fronted towards the Horse Guards, and were formed as follows (the Infantry being three deep), viz., four Companies of Grenadiers, with their right near to the angle of the Treasury building; four Companies of Light Infantry, in a line with the Grenadiers, and their right to the road leading through the Horse Guards; the second Brigade of Infantry, about sixty yards behind the Grenadiers, and their right to the Treasury Wall; the first Brigade of Infantry, about sixty years behind the second, and parallel to it. The Cavalry formed in one line behind the Infantry; their right to sluice cover on the parade and extending towards the end of the Mall, being parallel to the rows of trees, which were close in the rear. The Artillery assembled, and formed fronting to the Treasury, with their right at the parade gun. This disposition being made, the march began at twelve o'clock in the following order; the General Officers and their Staff at the head of their respective Brigades.

General Sir David Dundas, K.B.,
Lieutenant-General Harry Burrard.

A Detachment of Light Dragoons.

Four Companies of Light Infantry.

The 92nd Regiment ⎫ Commanded by the Honourable
The 79th Regiment ⎬ Major-General Charles Hope.

The 31st Regiment ⎫ Commanded by the Honourable
The 21st Regiment ⎬ Brigadier-General Robert Meade.

The 14th – 2 Squadrons ⎫ Commanded by Major-General
The 10th – 2 Squadrons ⎬ William St. Leger.
The 2nd – 2 Squadrons ⎭

The Royal Artillery, with eleven pieces of cannon.

Four Companies of Grenadiers.

Each corps marched off, and followed in succession from its left. The Infantry marched in sections of six or seven files: the Cavalry four men in front: the Artillery and its carriages two a-breast: Officers of Infantry in front of the divisions, and not on the flanks.

As soon as the Troops had passed the Admiralty, the Procession moved in the following order:

Marshal's-Men, on foot, to clear the way.

Messenger of the College of Arms, in a mourning cloak with a Badge of the College on his shoulder, his Staff tipped with silver and furled with sarsnet.

Six Conductors, in mourning cloaks, with black staves headed with Viscounts' coronets.

Forty-eight Pensioners from Greenwich Hospital, two and two, in mourning cloaks, with badges of the Crest of the Deceased on the shoulders, and black staves in their hands.

Forty-eight Seamen and Marines of His Majesty's Ship the *Victory*, two and two, in their ordinary dress, with black neck handkerchiefs and stockings, and crape in their hats.

Watermen of the Deceased, in black coats, with their Badges.

Drums and Fifes.

Drum-Major.

Trumpets.

Serjeant Trumpeter.

Rouge Croix, Pursuivant of Arms (alone in a mourning coach),
in close mourning, with his Tabard over his cloak.

The Standard, borne in front of a mourning coach, in which
were Captain Sir Francis Laforey, Bart., and his two
Supporters, Lieutenants William Collins Barker and
George Antram, of the Royal Navy.

Trumpets.

Blue Mantle, Pursuivant of Arms (alone in a mourning coach),
habited as Rouge Croix.

The Guidon, borne in front of a mourning coach, in which were
Captain Edward Rotherham, of the *Royal Sovereign*, sup-
ported by Lieutenants James Bradshaw and Thomas
Errington, of the Royal Navy.

Servants of the Deceased, in mourning, in a mourning coach.

Officers of His Majesty's Wardrobe, in mourning coaches.

Gentlemen.

Esquires.

Deputations from the Great Commercial Companies
of London.

Physicians of the Deceased, in a mourning coach.

Divines, in clerical habits.

Chaplains of the Deceased, in clerical habits, and Secretary of
the Deceased, in a mourning coach.

Trumpets.

Rouge Dragon and Portcullis, Pursuivant of Arms (in a mourning coach), habited as before.

The Banner of the Deceased, as a Knight of the Bath, borne in
front of a mourning coach, in which were Captain Philip
Charles Durham, of the *Defiance*, supported by Lieutenants
James Usuld Purches and James Poate, of the Royal Navy.

Attendants on the Body while it lay in State at Greenwich; viz.,
Reverend Alexander John Scott (Chaplain to His Royal
Highness the Prince of Wales), Joseph Whidbey, Esquire,
and John Tyson, Esquire, in a mourning coach.

Knights Bachelors.

Sergeants at Law.

Deputy to the Knight Marshal on horseback.

Knights of the Bath; viz.,

Sir Samuel Hood and Sir Thomas Trigge.
Baronets.
A Gentleman Usher (in a mourning coach) carrying a carpet and black velvet cushion, whereon the Trophies were to be deposited in the Church.
William Haslewood, Esq.; Alexander Davison, Esq.; and William Marsh, Esq.; as Comptroller, Treasurer, and Steward of the Household of the Deceased (in a mourning coach), in mourning cloaks, bearing white Staves.
Younger Sons of Barons, viz.,
Honourable Augustus Cavendish Bradshaw.
Honourable Richard Ryder, M.P. Honourable Charles James Fox, M.P.
Privy Counsellors, not Peers, viz.,
Right Honourable Sir Evan Nepean, Baronet, M.P., and a Lord of the Admiralty.
Right Honourable George Tierney, M.P.
Right Honourable Sir William Scott, Knt., M.P., Judge of the Admiralty.
Right Honourable William Windham, M.P.
Younger Sons of Earls, viz.,
Honourable Thomas William Fermor.
Honourable – Bennet. Honourable Alexander Murray.
Eldest Sons of Viscounts, viz.,
Honourable Thomas Newcomen. Honourable Henry Hood.
Honourable Thomas Knox.
Barons, viz.,
Lord Hutchinson, K.B.   Lord Donalley.
Lord de Blaquiere, K.B.   Lord Holland.
Lord Aston.
Lord Mulgrave, one of His   Lord Hawkesbury, one of
Majesty's Principal Secretaries   His Majesty's Principal
of State.   Secretaries of State.
Lord Bishop of Exeter.
Younger Sons of Marquisses, viz.,
Lord Henry Moore.   Lord Henry Petty.
Eldest Sons of Earls, viz.,
Viscount Castlereagh, Viscount Duncannon.
One of His Majesty's Principal Secretaries of State.

Lord Delvin.

Viscount Fitzharris.   Lord Hervey.

Lord Ossulston.

Viscount Kirkwall.   Lord Fincastle.

Viscounts,

Viscount Sidmouth.

Viscount Hawarden.   Viscount Gosford.

Viscount Chetwynd,   Viscount Ranelagh.

Younger son of a Duke,

Lord Archibald Hamilton.

Eldest Son of a Marquis,

Earl of Altamont.

Earls,

Earl of Clancarty.   Earl of Moira.

Earl of Fife.   Earl of Bessborough.

Earl of Darnley.   Earl of Westmeath.

Earl of Leicester.   Earl of Buckinghamshire.

Earl of Portsmouth.   Earl Cowper.

Earl of Bristol.   Earl of Scarborough.

Earl of Winchelsea, K.G.   Earl of Suffolk.

Earl of Dartmouth, K.G., Lord Chamberlain of His Majesty's
Household.

Eldest Sons of Dukes,

Marquis of Douglas.

Marquis of Blandford.   Marquis of Hartington.

Dukes,

Duke of Montrose, K.T.

Duke of Devonshire, K.G.   Duke of St. Albans.

Duke of Norfolk, Earl Marshal.

Earl Camden, K.G., Lord President of the Council.

Archbishop of Canterbury.

Dukes of the Blood Royal.

His Royal Highness the Duke of Cambridge.

His Royal Highness the Duke of Sussex.

His Royal Highness the Duke of Cumberland.

His Royal Highness the Duke of Kent.

His Royal Highness the Duke of Clarence.

His Royal Highness the Duke of York, Commander-in-Chief.

His Royal Highness the Prince of Wales.

Richmond Herald (alone in a mourning coach), habited as the
other Officers of Arms.

The Great Banner, borne in front of a mourning coach, in
which were Captain Robert Moorsom, and his Supporters,
Lieutenants David Keys and Nicholas Tucker, of the Royal
Navy.

Gauntlet and Spurs, ⎫ In front of four mourning coaches,
Helm and Crest, Target ⎬ in which were York, Somerset,
and Sword, Surcoat, ⎭ Lancaster, and Chester Heralds,
habited as before.

A mourning coach, in which were the Coronet of the Deceased,
on a black velvet cushion, was borne by Norroy King of Arms,
in the absence of Clarenceux, habited as before, and attended
by two Gentlemen Ushers.

The six Lieutenants of the Royal Navy, habited as before, who
were to bear the Bannerolls, in two mourning coaches.

The six Admirals, in like habits, who were to bear the Canopy,
in two mourning coaches.

The four Admirals, in like habits, who were to support the Pall
in a mourning coach.

The Body

Placed on a Funeral Car, or open Hearse, decorated with
a carved imitation of the Head and Stern of His Majesty's
Ship the *Victory*, surrounded with escutcheons of the Arms
of the Deceased, and adorned with appropriate Mottoes
and emblematical Devices; under an elevated Canopy, in
the form of the upper part of an ancient Sarcophagus,
with six sable Plumes, and the Coronet of a Viscount in
the centre, supported by four columns, representing palm
trees, with wreaths of natural laurel and cypress entwining
the shafts; the whole upon a fourwheeled carriage, drawn
by six led horses, the caparisons adorned with armorial
escutcheons.

N.B.—*The black velvet Pall, adorned with six Escutcheons of the
Arms of the Deceased, and the six Bannerolls of the Family Lineage, were
removed from the Hearse, in order to afford an unobstructed view of the
Coffin containing the Remains of the gallant Admiral.*

Garter Principal King of Arms, in his official habit, with his
   Sceptre (in his carriage, his servants being in full mourning),
   attended by two Gentlemen Ushers.

THE CHIEF MOURNER,
In a mourning coach, with his two Supporters, and his Train-
              bearer, all in mourning cloaks.
Six assistant Mourners (in two mourning coaches), in mourning
cloaks as before. Windsor Herald, acting for Norroy King of
Arms, in a mourning coach, habited as the other Officers of
   Arms, and attended by two Gentlemen Ushers.
The Banner of Emblems in front of a mourning coach, in which
    were Captains Thomas Masterman Hardy and Henry
 William Bayntun, supported by Lieutenants Andrew King
and George Miller Bligh, of the Royal Navy. Relations of
       the Deceased, in mourning coaches.
Officers of the Navy and Army, according to their respective
     ranks, the seniors nearest the Body.

    Within Temple Bar the Procession was received by the Right
Honourable the Lord Mayor of London, attended by the
Aldermen and Sheriffs and the Deputation from the Common
Council. The six carriages of the Deputation from the Common
Council fell into the Procession between the Deputation of the
Great Commercial Companies of London and the Physicians of
the Deceased, a Conductor on horseback being appointed to
indicate the station. The carriages of the Aldermen and Sheriffs
fell into the Procession between the Knights Bachelors and the
Sergeants at Law; a Conductor on horseback being also there
stationed for the purpose, as before. The Right Honourable the
Lord Mayor, on horseback, bearing the City Sword, was
marshalled and placed in the Procession between His Royal
Highness the Prince of Wales and the Herald of Arms, who
preceded the Great Banner, in obedience to a warrant under
His Majesty's Royal Signet and Sign Manual, bearing date 6th
instant, directing Garter Principal King of Arms to marshal
and place the Lord Mayor of London, on the present occasion,
in the same station wherein his Lordship would have been
placed if His Majesty had been present. When the head of the

troops arrived at St. Paul's, the light companies entered within the railing, drew up, and remained. The rest of the column proceeded round St. Paul's, down Cheapside, along the Old Jewry and Coleman-street, to Moorfields, round which they were formed and posted. The Grenadiers quitted the column at St. Paul's, and entered within the railing. The Light Infantry lined each side of the space from the gate of the Church-yard to the door of the Church. The Grenadiers lined the great nave of the Church on each side, from the outer door to the place where the Body was deposited, and from thence to the door of the Choir. The two Corps (who had their arms reversed during the time of their remaining at St. Paul's) formed two deep for that purpose; and the 2nd Dragoons, in passing St. Paul's, left an Officer and twenty men, who formed up, and remained within the outer gate of the iron railing, Upon arrival of the Procession at St. Paul's Cathedral, the six Conductors, forty-eight Pensioners from Greenwich Hospital, and forty-eight Seamen and Marines of the Victory, ascended the steps, divided and ranged on each side, without the great west door; and the rest of the Procession having alighted at the west gate of the Church-yard, entered the Church, and divided on either side, according to their ranks; those who had proceeded first remaining nearest the door. The Officers of Arms and the Bearers of the Banners, with their Supporters, entered the Choir, and stood within, near the door; and all above and including the rank of Knights Bachelors, as well as the Staff Officers, and the Naval Officers who attended the Procession, had seats assigned to them in the Choir. The Lord Mayor, with the Aldermen and Sheriffs, City Officers, and Deputation from the Common Council, occupied their seats on the north side of the Choir. Near the entrance of the Church, the Dean and Prebendaries, attended by the Choir, fell into the Procession immediately after the Great Banner, and before the Heralds who bore the Trophies; the Choir singing the Sentence in the Office for Burial, "I am the Resurrection and the Life," &c. with the two following Sentences, and continuing to sing until the Body was placed in the Choir. The Body, having been taken from the Funeral Car, was borne into the Church and Choir according to the following order: –

Richmond Herald.

Supporter,	THE GREAT BANNER,	Supporter,
Lieut. Nicholas Tucker.	borne by Capt. Robert Moorsom.	Lieut. David Keys.

The Gauntlet and Spurs, borne by York Herald.

The Helm and Crest, borne by Somerset Herald.

The Target and Sword, borne by Lancaster Herald.

The Surcoat, borne by Chester Herald.

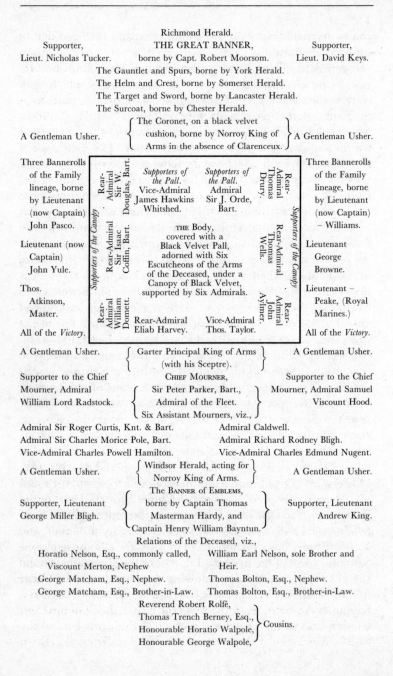

A Gentleman Usher. { The Coronet, on a black velvet cushion, borne by Norroy King of Arms in the absence of Clarenceux. } A Gentleman Usher.

Three Bannerolls of the Family lineage, borne by Lieutenant (now Captain) John Pasco.

Rear-Admiral Sir W. Douglas, Bart.

Supporters of the Pall.
Vice-Admiral James Hawkins Whitshed.

Supporters of the Pall.
Admiral Sir J. Orde, Bart.

Rear-Admiral Thomas Drury.

Three Bannerolls of the Family lineage, borne by Lieutenant (now Captain) – Williams.

Supporters of the Canopy.

Rear-Admiral Sir Isaac Coffin, Bart.

THE Body, covered with a Black Velvet Pall, adorned with Six Escutcheons of the Arms of the Deceased, under a Canopy of Black Velvet, supported by Six Admirals.

Supporters of the Canopy.

Rear-Admiral Thomas Wells.

Lieutenant (now Captain) John Yule.

Lieutenant George Browne.

Thos. Atkinson, Master.

Rear-Admiral William Domett.

Rear-Admiral Eliab Harvey.

Vice-Admiral Thos. Taylor.

Rear-Admiral John Aylmer.

Lieutenant – Peake, (Royal Marines.)

All of the *Victory*.

All of the *Victory*.

A Gentleman Usher. { Garter Principal King of Arms (with his Sceptre). } A Gentleman Usher.

Supporter to the Chief Mourner, Admiral William Lord Radstock. { CHIEF MOURNER, Sir Peter Parker, Bart., Admiral of the Fleet. Six Assistant Mourners, viz., } Supporter to the Chief Mourner, Admiral Samuel Viscount Hood.

Admiral Sir Roger Curtis, Knt. & Bart.	Admiral Caldwell.
Admiral Sir Charles Morice Pole, Bart.	Admiral Richard Rodney Bligh.
Vice-Admiral Charles Powell Hamilton.	Vice-Admiral Charles Edmund Nugent.

A Gentleman Usher. { Windsor Herald, acting for Norroy King of Arms. } A Gentleman Usher.

Supporter, Lieutenant George Miller Bligh. { The BANNER of EMBLEMS, borne by Captain Thomas Masterman Hardy, and Captain Henry William Bayntun. } Supporter, Lieutenant Andrew King.

Relations of the Deceased, viz.,

Horatio Nelson, Esq., commonly called, Viscount Merton, Nephew	William Earl Nelson, sole Brother and Heir.
George Matcham, Esq., Nephew.	Thomas Bolton, Esq., Nephew.
George Matcham, Esq., Brother-in-Law.	Thomas Bolton, Esq., Brother-in-Law.

{ Reverend Robert Rolfé, Thomas Trench Berney, Esq., Honourable Horatio Walpole, Honourable George Walpole, } Cousins.

The Remainder of the Procession followed in the order as before marshalled.

The CHIEF MOURNER, his two Supporters and Train-bearer, were seated on chairs near the Body, on the opposite side nearest the Altar; and the six assistant Mourners, four Supporters of the Pall, and six supporters of the Canopy, on stools on each side. The Relations also near them in the Choir, and Garter was seated near the Chief Mourner. The Body, when placed in the Choir, was not covered with the Pall, nor the Canopy borne over it; the rule in that respect being dispensed with, for the reason before mentioned. The Bannerolls were borne on each side the Body. The Officers of the Navy, and the Staff Officers commanding the Troops, were seated near the Altar. The carpet and cushion (on which the Trophies were afterwards to be deposited) were laid, by the Gentleman Usher who carried them, on a table placed near the grave, which was under the centre of the dome, and behind the place which was to be there occupied by the Chief Mourner. The Coronet and Cushion borne by Norroy King of Arms, in the absence of Clarenceux, was laid on the Body. During the service in the Choir, an anthem suitable to the occasion was sung; and, at the conclusion, a Procession was made from thence to the grave, with the Banners and Bannerolls as before; the Officers of Arms preceding with the Trophies; the Body borne and attended as before; the Choir singing, "Man that is born of a Woman," &c., and the three following sentences. The Chief Mourner, with his Supporters, and, near them, Garter, had seats at the east end of the grave; the Train-bearer stood behind the Chief Mourner, and near him the Relations of the Deceased. At the opposite end sat the Right Reverend the Lord Bishop of Lincoln, Dean of the Cathedral, attended by three Canons Residentiaries. A Supporter of the Pall stood at each angle. The Assistant Mourners, Supporters of the Canopy, and Bearers of the Bannerolls, on either side. On the right of the Dean were the Chaplains; on the left, the Officers of the Household of the Deceased. The Great Banner was borne on the north, the Banner of the Deceased as a Knight of the Bath, on the south of the grave; the Standard and Guidon behind the Dean; the Banner of Emblems behind the Chief Mourner; the Trophies in the angles. Then the Dean read, "Forasmuch as it hath pleased Almighty God," &c.; then the Choir sung part of an anthem, "His Body is buried in peace; but his Name liveth evermore." The service at the interment being over, Garter proclaimed the style; and the Comptroller, Treasurer, and Steward of the Deceased, breaking their staves, delivered the pieces to Garter, who threw them into the grave. Upon a signal given from St. Paul's that the Body was deposited, the Troops being drawn up in Moorfields, the Artillery fired their guns, and the Infantry gave vollies, by corps, three times repeated. The interment ended, the Standard, Banners, Bannerolls, and Trophies, were deposited on the table behind the Chief Mourner; and all persons in the Procession retired. During the whole of this solemn ceremony, the greatest order prevailed throughout the metropolis; and as the Remains of the much-lamented Hero proceeded along, every possible testimony of sorrow and of respect was manifested by an immense concourse of spectators of all ranks. From the Admiralty to the Cathedral, the streets were lined with the several Volunteer Corps of London and Westminster, the Militis, and many other military bodies, both Cavalry and Infantry.

The Naval Chronicle gives the following list of Officers who attended the Funeral, with some additional particulars:—

Admiral Sir Peter Parker, Bart.
—Charles Chamberlayne
—Murray
—Sir John Orde
—Viscount Hood
—Sir Charles M. Pole
Vice-Admiral Taylor
—Stanhope
—Savage
—C. P. Hamilton
—Nugent
Rear-Adm. Sir Edmund Nagle, Knt.
—Bertie
—Sir Isaac Coffin
—Wells
—T. Drury
—Eliab Harvey
—Aylmer

Admiral Bligh
—Lord Radstock
—Caldwell
—Sir Roger Curtis, Bart.
Vice-Admiral Ed. Edwards
—Whitshed
Captain Alexander Skene
—John Broughton
—John Smith
—William Richardson
—Richard Williams
—Thomas Surridge
—Walter Tremenheere
—William Price Curnby
—Richard Carruthers
—Alexander
—Archibald Duff
—Charles Dikes

—Domett
—Waymouth
—Peacock
—Thomas West
—John Markhan
—Edmund Bowater
—Wells
Hon. Captain Gardner
—Captain H. Blackwood,
   Euryalus
Captain Sir Samuel Hood, K.B.
—Fred. Belton
—Burlton
—John Hayes
—Lumley
—Whyte
—S. Scudamore Heming
—John Tower
—Watkins
—Edward Williams
—Thomas Wholley
—Thomas Cooke
—J. Walton
—H. Stacpole
—J. W. Trotter
—Dalling
—D. Scott, (Bellerophon)
—Sir Rupert George
—George Pearson
—William Kent
—Thomas Surcombe
—Richard Lee
—James Green
—Galway
—Towry
—William Browne
—Toker
—H.E. R. Baker
—Andrews
—Edward O'Bryan
—William Waller
—William Mounsey
—Edward Lloyd Graham
—Abdy
—Hon. Henry Bennett
—H. Tarnall

—Isaac Smith
—John Hatley
—A. S. Burrows
—Sir Francis Laforey
—James Nicolson
—Kennedy
—Humphries
—John Boyle
—Richbell
—E. Rotherham, Royal Sovereign
—Samuel Sutton
—Hardy, Victory
—Robert Lambert
—James Oswald
—Henry Samuel Butt
—Henry Stuart
—John Temple
—T. O. G. Skinner
—A. Tinling
—James Dunbar
—Courtnay Boyle
—Richards
—Vincent
—Cotterell
—Guyot
—Alexander Mackenzie
—Durham, Defiance
—Hallard
—Haywood
—D. Miller
—John Tower
—Moorsom, Revenge
—Ballar
—Farquhar
—Cartier
—Yeo
—Thomas Staines
—W. Pierrepoint
—William Green
—William Roberts
—William Hotham
—J. K. Shepherd
—William Ponsonby
—Cunningham
—Robert Jackson
—Sir W. H. Douglas

—Sir Edward Hamilton

—Thomas Boys

Lieut.-Col. Berkeley ⎤

Captain Henry Cox. ⎥

—Burn ⎥

—Lodington ⎥

—T. Sherman ⎥

—Thompson ⎥

—Tremenhee ⎥

—Percival ⎥

Lieutenant Lawson ⎬ Royal Marines.

—Crofton ⎥

—Morgan ⎥

—Cowperthwaite ⎥

—Bate ⎥

—Goltwaltz ⎥

—Campbell ⎥

—Joseph Coome ⎥

—Seele ⎥

—James Tithall ⎦

—James Wallace

—Purchase, of the Defence

—L. B. Reeves ⎤

—J. G. Peake ⎬ Victory.

—King ⎥

—Bligh ⎦

—Richard Crawford

—Henry Hargrave

—G. Murray

—Maxwell

Lieutenant James Milne

—William Colliers Barker

—Fisher

—John Murray Wegg

—Geo. Antrim

—Charles Jones

—William Field

—John Read

—William Somerville

—Jones

—Thomas Wing

—Janverin, Defence

—Henry Thomas Hardacre

—John Bowen

—Thomas Wilkins

—Robert Dunham

—Williams

—Yule

—Pasco

—Browne

—Hills

—Thomas Hughes

—Edmund Hanning Thomas

—J. W. Bazelgette

—Ballard

So early as three and four o'clock on the morning of Thursday, thousands of people were in motion, lest they should not reach the places whence they intended to witness, what may almost be termed the apotheosis of Lord Nelson. An hour before daylight, the drums of the respective volunteer corps, in every part of the metropolis, beat to arms. The summons was quickly obeyed; and, soon after, the troops lined the streets, from the Admiralty to St. Paul's, agreeably to the orders which had been issued. By day-break the Life Guards also were mounted at their post in Hyde Park; and in St. James's Park were drawn up all the regiments of cavalry and infantry quartered within a hundred miles of London, who had served in the glorious campaigns in Egypt, after the ever-memorable Victory of the Nile. There was also a detachment of flying artillery, with twelve field-pieces and their ammunition tumbrils. Between eight and nine o'clock, eight mourning coaches and four brought the Heralds and Pursuivants of Arms from their college to the Admiralty. No carriages, but those which were connected with the Procession, (the carriages of Foreign Ambassadors excepted,) were permitted to pass through the Strand, Fleet Street, or Ludgate Hill. The remainder of the Procession followed, as nearly as might be, in the order which had been presented. The chief deviation was, that, to afford the spectators a more complete view of the Coffin, it appeared on the Car, stripped of its pall, on a platform covered with black cloth, festooned with velvet richly fringed, and decorated with escutcheons on each side, between which were inscribed the words "*Trinidad*" and "*Bucentaur*". The Car stopped for some moments, immediately opposite to the statue of King Charles, at Charing Cross. Every hat was off, every sound was hushed, and the most awful silence prevailed. The whole moved on in solemn pace, through the Strand to Temple Bar Gate, where the Lord Mayor of London, attended by the Aldermen and Sheriffs and the Deputation from the Common Council, were waiting to receive them. As the Procession advanced within the City, the six carriages of the Deputation from the Common Council fell in between the Deputation of the great Commercial Companies of London and the Physicians of the Deceased, who were in a mourning coach; a conductor on horseback having been appointed to indicate the station. The carriages of the Aldermen and Sheriffs fell in between the Knights Bachelors, and the Masters in Chancery. The Lord Mayor rode from Temple Bar to St. Paul's on horseback, uncovered, and carrying in his hand the City sword. His Royal Highness the Duke of York and his Staff, with the Colonels of Volunteers, followed the Funeral Car on horseback. On the arrival of the Procession at St. Paul's, the cavalry marched off to their barracks: the Scotch regiments drew up in the area fronting the Church, and marched into the western gate, and so remained. The forty-eight Greenwich Pensioners, with forty-eight Seamen and twelve Marines from the Victory, entered the western gate, ascended the steps, and divided in a line on each side under the great western portico, and the remainder of the Procession

entered the Church, dividing on each side, and taking the rank
and stations assigned them. When the Funeral Car reached the
great entrance, it was drawn up without the western gate. The
Body was taken from the Car, covered with the pall, and borne
by twelve Seamen from the Victory, and was received within
the gate by the Supporters and Pall-bearers, who had previously alighted for its reception. The Procession entered at the
great western gate. The noble Cathedral of St. Paul had been
thrown open for the reception of visitors, at the early hour of
seven in the morning. Such, however, was the anxiety of the
public to witness the solemnities of the day, that many suffered
from the pressure before the opportunity for admission was
afforded. A very short time elapsed after the doors were opened,
before the principal part of the seats were occupied; and the
interest was so deep, that no uneasiness whatever appeared to
be produced by the time which it became necessary to wait,
exposed to a great severity of cold. From seven o'clock till one,
the company sat still, and not a symptom of impatience was
discoverable. A few minutes after one o'clock the approach of
the Procession was announced, and the great western door was
thrown open. At half-past one General Sir David Dundas
marched in at the head of the Grenadier companies of the
21st and 31st Foot, and the 79th and 92nd Highland regiments,
amounting altogether to about 300 men. These Troops moved
in slow time by single files, and formed lines on each side of the
way assigned for the Procession from the western gate, along the
aisle, the dome, and on to the gate of the choir. Having turned
to the front, they, after some preliminary manœuvres, were
ordered to rest on their arms reversed; and in this position they
remained until the whole ceremony was concluded. The appearance of this fine body of men considerably augmented the
interest of the scene. Upon any other occasion, the manly,
soldier-like figures, which the Highland grenadiers presented,
would have been deservedly the objects of particular notice and
admiration. The 92nd were placed at the eastward of the aisle;
the 79th under the dome, and the other companies took the
western extremity. Previously to the introduction of these
companies, a great part of 200 men belonging to the West
London Regiment of Militia were employed in the body of the

Church to guard particular seats, and to prevent any part of the crowd from getting into those places which were set apart for the accommodation of those nobility, &c., who were expected in the Procession. The whole of the Militia were placed under the command of the Dean, who had parties of them stationed at the several doors of the Church, in order to prevent pressure or riot. Some time had elapsed before the regiments to which the flank companies belonged had filed off to make way for the Procession. The part of it which entered the Church did not appear until two o'clock. It was preceded by some Marshal's men to clear the way. They were followed by two Naval Captains, the first bearing the Standard, the other the Guidon. These Captains were Bayntun and Laforey. Each was supported by two Lieutenants. Of the different degrees of rank, the Gentlemen and Esquires led the way; and among them were several of the most respectable men belonging to the Commercial community. The Aldermen of London went in on the north side of the Procession, and took their station opposite to the box assigned for their accommodation. His Royal Highness the Prince of Wales, accompanied by the Dukes of Clarence and Cumberland, and conducted by the Dean, walked through the Church to the choir, where they remained for a short time, and then returned to join the Procession. His Royal Highness the Prince of Wales took his place in the Procession immediately after the Lord President of the Council (Earl Camden), and was followed by the Dukes of York, Clarence, Kent, Cumberland, Sussex, and Cambridge. The Lord Mayor and his suite were next to the Royal Dukes. His Lordship wore a large black silk gown, provided for the occasion, highly fringed with gold lace, several rows of which were on the arms and round the collar. The most interesting part of the cavalcade – that which was certainly best calculated to make a strong impression upon the minds of the spectators, was the exhibition made by the brave Seamen of the Victory, who bore two Union Jacks, and the St. George's Eusign, belonging to that Ship. These colours were perforated in various places by the effects of the shot of the Enemy. Several parts of the Ensign were, literally, shattered. These parts were particularly exposed to view, and the effect which such a display was calculated to produce may be more easily conceived than described. Immediately on the van of the Procession entering the great western door, the organ commenced. The Minor Canons, Vicars Choral of the Cathedral, assisted by the Choristers from the Chapel Royal, and the Minor Canons and Vicars Choral belonging to the Church of St. Peter, Westminster; together with some Gentlemen from Windsor, amounting together to upwards of 100, sung as the Procession moved from the west door to the choir the following Anthems, which were set to music by Dr. Croft: –

"I am the resurrection and the life, saith the Lord: he that believeth in me, though he were dead, yet shall he live. And whosoever liveth and believeth in me, shall never die." St. John, xi. 25, 26.

"I know that my Redeemer liveth, and that he shall stand at the latter day upon the earth. And though after my skin, worms destroy this body; yet in my flesh shall I see God: whom I shall see for myself, and my eyes shall behold, and not another." Job, xix. 25, 26, 27.

"We brought nothing into this world, and it is certain we can carry nothing out. The Lord gave, and the Lord hath taken away; blessed be the name of the Lord." I Tim. vi. 7. Job, i. 21.

The Procession passed through the inclosed place in the centre of the dome, and of course over the grave, on its way to the choir. Although the first part entered the Church about two o'clock, the whole did not reach the choir till four. It remained in the choir during the performance of evening service, in the course of which the following Anthems, &c., were sung: –

Dixi Custodiam, Psalm xxxix; Domine, refugium, Psalm xc; Magnificat, Luke, i. 46.

During the performance of the service in the choir, the evening approached, and lights became necessary. Arrangements had been made for the purpose, and, as soon as it was found requisite, a number of torches were lighted up in the choir, both below and in the galleries. At the same time, the vast space under the dome was illuminated; (for the first time since its construction,) to a sufficient degree for the solemn purposes of the occasion, by a temporary lanthorn, consisting of an octagonal framing of wood, boarded on the outside, and finished at top by eight angles, and at bottom by a smaller octagon. This was painted black, and upon it were disposed about 130 patent lamps. It was suspended by a rope from the centre of the lanthorn; and, when drawn up, it gave as much light as was wanted in the church. There were some other lights placed in the aisles, but these were of no great consequence. The grand central light, though inferior to the celebrated annual illuminated crucifix of St. Peter's, had a most impressive and grand effect, and contributed greatly to the grandeur of a spectacle in which the burial of one of the first of Warriors and of Heroes was graced by the appearance of all the Princes of the Blood, of many of the first Nobility of the land, and of an unexampled number of the Subjects of His Majesty in general. A Bier, covered with black velvet, and ornamented with gold fringe and tassels, was placed in the choir, for the reception of the Coffin, during the service which was performed there. About five o'clock, the Procession returned from the choir to the grave in an inverted order, the rear, in proceeding to the choir, forming the van on its return. On reaching the dome, the Dukes of York, Kent, Sussex, and Cambridge, filed off to the Royal box, where, however, they remained but a short time before they proceeded to the inclosure which surrounded the grave. The Lord Mayor and Aldermen repaired to their box, where they remained till the ceremony of interment was over. The Officers of the Navy and Army, who assisted in the Procession, continued in the body of the Church. The Dean (Bishop of Lincoln) and the Residentiary (Bishop of Chester); with two Prebends, ascended a desk which had been constructed for the solemn occasion. On the return of the Coffin from the choir, a grand Funeral Canopy of State was borne over it by six Admirals. It was composed of black velvet, supported by six small pillars covered with the same material, and crowned by six plumes of black ostrich feathers; the valance were fringed with black, and decorated with devices of festoons and symbols of his Lordship's victories, and his arms, crest, and coronet in gold. When the Coffin was brought to the centre of the dome, it was placed on a platform sufficiently elevated to be visible from every part of the Church. The state canopy was then withdrawn, and the pall taken off. The carpet and cushion on which the trophies were deposited, were laid, by the Gentleman Usher who carried them, on a table placed near the grave, and behind the place which was occupied by the Chief Mourner. The coronet and cushion, borne by Clarenceux, King of Arms, was laid on the body. The Chief Mourner and his Supporters placed themselves at the head of the grave, and the Assistant Mourners, with the Relations of the Deceased, near to them. During the return of the Corpse from the choir to the place of interment, a solemn dirge was performed on the organ; after which was sung the following Anthem, &c. Then the officiating Minister said, "Forasmuch as it hath pleased Almighty God, of his great mercy, to take unto himself the soul of our dear brother here departed, we therefore commit his body to the ground; earth to earth, ashes to ashes, dust to dust; in sure and certain hope of the resurrection to eternal life, through our Lord Jesus Christ, who shall change our vile body, that it may be like unto his glorious body, according to the mighty working, whereby he is able to subdue all things to himself." After which was sung by the whole choir, "I heard a voice from heaven saying unto me, Write, from henceforth blessed are the dead, which die in the Lord: even so saith the spirit; for they rest from their labours." – Rev. xiv. 13. Concluding Anthem. Verse. – "His body is buried in peace." Chorus. – "But his name liveth evermore."

Precisely at thirty-three minutes and a half past five o'clock, the Coffin was lowered into the grave, by balance weight, secret machinery having been constructed expressly for the purpose. The funeral service having been concluded in the most solemn and impressive manner, Sir Isaac Heard, Garter King at Arms, proclaimed the Style and Titles of the deceased Lord, in nearly the following words: – "Thus it hath pleased Almighty God to take out of this transitory life, unto his divine mercy, the Most Noble Lord Horatio Nelson, Viscount and Baron Nelson of the Nile, and of Burnham Thorpe, in the County of Norfolk, Baron Nelson of the Nile, and of Hilborough, in the same County; Knight of the Most Honourable Order of the Bath; Vice-Admiral of the White Squadron of the Fleet, and Commander-in-Chief of His Majesty's Ships and Vessels in the Mediterranean: also Duke of Bronte in Sicily;

Knight Grand Cross of the Sicilian Order of St. Ferdinand and of Merit; Member of the Ottoman Order of the Crescent; Knight Grand Commander of the Order of St. Joachim; and the Hero who, in the moment of Victory, fell covered with immortal glory! – Let us humbly trust, that he is now raised to bliss ineffable, and to a glorious immortality." The Comptroller, Treasurer, and Steward of his Lordship's household then broke their staves, and gave the pieces to Garter, who threw them into the grave, in which also the flags of the *Victory*, furled up by the sailors, were deposited. – These brave fellows, however, desirous of retaining some memorials of their great and favourite Commander, had torn off a considerable part of the largest flag, of which most of them obtained a portion. The ceremony was finally concluded a little before six o'clock, but the Church was not entirely vacated till past nine. The Procession left the Church in nearly its original order, but gradually separated, according as its respective members retired after the fatigues of the day. Thus terminated one of the most impressive and most splendid solemnities that ever took place in this Country, or perhaps in Europe. The Funeral Car, which attracted so much notice in the Procession, was designed by, and executed under the direction of the Rev. Mr. M'Quin, a particular friend of Sir Isaac Heard. It was modelled, at the ends, in imitation of the hull of the *Victory*. Its head, towards the horses, was ornamented with a figure of Fame. The stern, carved and painted in the Naval style, with the word "*Victory*," in yellow raised letters on the lanthorn over the poop. The sides were decorated with escutcheons, three on each. Between them, two on each side, were represented four scrolls, surrounded by branches and wreaths of palm and laurel, and bearing the names of the four principal French and Spanish men-of-war which had been taken or destroyed by the deceased Hero, viz., the *San Josef*, *l'Orient*, *Trinidad*, and *Bucentaure*. The body of the Car consisted of three platforms, each elevated above the other. On the third was the Coffin, placed, as on the quarter-deck, with its head towards the stern, with an English Jack [? Ensign] pendant over the poop, and lowered half staff. There was an awning over the whole, consisting of an elegant canopy, supported by four pillars, in the form of palm-trees, and partly covered with black velvet. The corners and sides were decorated with black ostrich feathers, and festooned with black velvet, richly fringed. It was at first intended that the fringe should be gold; but it was afterwards considered that it would give too gaudy an appearance to the solemn vehicle, and therefore black fringe was adopted everywhere instead of it. Immediately above the festoons, in the front, was inscribed, in gold, the word NILE, at one end: on one side, the following motto, – "Hoste devicto, requievit:" behind, the word TRA-FALGAR; and, on the other side, the motto – "Palman qui meruit ferat." The carriage was drawn by six led horses, in elegant furniture. It is a curious circumstance that, after the construction of the Car, necessity required it to be twice altered. In the first instance, it was discovered to be too high to pass under the arch at Temple Bar; and after this had been remedied, it was found to be too wide to enter the gates of the Admiralty. During the Friday and Saturday after the Procession, the Car was exhibited to the populace, in the King's Mews, Charing Cross. The preservation of this truly magnificent carriage, in the construction and embellishment of which the sum of 700l is said to have been expended, being desirable, the following letter was dispatched from the Admiralty to Greenwich Hospital: –

"Sir,   "Admiralty Office, Jan. 11.
    "My Lords Commissioners of the Admiralty being desirous that the Funeral Car, which yesterday conveyed the remains of the late Vice-Admiral Lord Viscount Nelson, K.B., from hence to St. Paul's Cathedral for interment, should be deposited in the Royal Hospital for Seamen at Greenwich, to perpetuate the memory of the Deceased, I have their Lordships' commands to desire that you will acquaint the Directors therewith, and request their acceptance of the said Car, for the purpose above mentioned, directions having been given for its being conveyed to the Hospital to-morrow, and delivered into the charge of such person as may be appointed to receive it. – I am, Sir, your very humble servant,

"WILLIAM MARSDEN."

In consequence of the above, the Car was, on Sunday morning, conveyed to Greenwich Hospital, drawn by six of the King's black horses, with three postillions in the royal liveries, attended by a coachman on horseback, and escorted by a strong detachment of the Royal Westminster Volunteers, accompanied by a part of the band of that corps. "It arrived on the Green, where it was received by Lord Hood, about noon; and, at one o'clock, it was deposited in the Painted Chamber." The Car has only lately been broken up.

APPENDIX I

The Battle of Trafalgar: A History
*Sir Nicholas Harris Nicolas**

Compiled by Nicolas from William James' standard work, *The Naval History of Great Britain* (1837), William Beatty's *The Death of Lord Nelson* and other sources, to make a blow-by-blow account of 21 October 1805.

* Reprinted from *The Dispatches and Letters of Lord Nelson*, Vol VII, Henry Coburn, 1846

The following is a List of the BRITISH and COMBINED FLEETS, their force, and the names of their Commanders;—

BRITISH FLEET

Gun-ship.

100	Victory	Vice-Admiral (w) Lord Nelson, K.B.	
		Captain Thomas Masterman Hardy.	
	Royal Sovereign	Vice-Admiral (b) Cuthbert Collingwood.	
		Captain Edward Rotheram.	
	Britannia	Rear-Admiral (w) the Earl of Northesk.	
		Captain Charles Bullen.	
98	Téméraire	″	Eliab Harvey.
	Prince	″	Richard Grindall.
	Neptune	″	Thomas Francis Fremantle.
	Dreadnought	″	John Conn.
80	Tonnant	″	Charles Tyler.
74	Belleisle	″	William Hargood.
	Revenge	″	Robert Moorsom.
	Mars	″	George Duff.
	Spartiate	″	Sir Francis Laforey, Bart.
	Defiance	″	Philip Charles Durham.
	Conqueror	″	Israel Pellew.
	Defence	″	George Hope.
	Colossus	″	James Nicoll Morris.
	Leviathan	″	Henry William Bayntun.
	Achille	″	Richard King.
	Bellerophon	″	John Cooke.
	Minotaur	″	Charles John Moore Mansfield.
	Orion	″	Edward Codrington.
	Swiftsure	″	William George Rutherford.
	Ajax	Lieutenant John Pilford,	Acting*
	Thunderer	″ John Stockham,	
64	Polyphemus	″	Robert Redmill.
	Africa	″	Henry Digby.
	Agamemnon	″	Sir Edward Berry.

Frigates: *Euryalus, Naïad, Phœbe,* and *Sirius*; Captains the Hon. Henry Blackwood, Thomas Dundas, the Hon. Thomas Biaden Capel, and William Prowse.

Schooner: *Pickle*, Lieutenant John Richard Lapenotiere; and Cutter: *Entreprenante*, Lieutenant Robert Benjamin Young.

* For Captains William Brown and William Lechmere, gone to England to attend as witnesses on Sir Robert Calder's court-martial.

ENEMIES' FLEET

Gun-ship.		FRENCH.	
	Bucentaure	Vice-Ad. P. Ch. J. B. S. Villeneuve.	
		Captain Jean Jacques Magendie.	
80	Formidable	Rear-Ad. P. R. M. E. Dumanoir le Pelley.	
		Captain Jean Marie Letellier.	
	Neptune	Commodore Esprit Tranquille Maistral.	
	Indomptable	"	Jean Joseph Hubert.
	Algeciras	Rear-Ad. Charles Magon.	
		Captain Gabriel Auguste Brouard.	
	Pluton	Commodore Julian Marie Cosmao Kerjulien.	
	Mont-Blanc	"	Guill. Jean Noël La Villegris.
	Intrépide	"	Louis Antoine Cyprien Infernet.
	Swiftsure	Captain C. E. L'Hospitalier Villemadrin.	
	Aigle	"	Pierre Paul Gourrège.
74	Scipion	"	Charles Berenger.
	Duguay-Trouin	"	Claude Touffet.
	Berwick	"	Jean Gilles Filhol Camas.
	Argonaute	"	Jacques Epron.
	Achille	"	Gabriel Denieport.
	Redoutable	"	Jean Jacques Etienne Lucas.
	Fougueux	"	Louis Alexis Beaudouin.
	Héros	"	Jean Bap. Jos. Remi Poulain.

Gun-ship.		SPANISH.	
130	Santisima Trinidad	Rear-Ad. don B. Hidalgo Cisneros	
		Commod. don Francisco de Uriarte.	
	Principe de Asturias	Admiral don Frederico Gravina.	
112		Rear-Ad. don Antonio Escano.	
	Santa Ana	Vice-Ad. don Ign. Maria de Alava.	
		Captain don Josef Gardoqui.	
100	Rayo	Commod. don Enrique Macdonel.	
80	Neptuno	"	don Cayetano Valdés.
	Argonauta	"	don Antonio Parejas.
	Bahama	Captain don Dionisio Galiano.	
	Montanes	"	don Josef Salzedo.
	San Augustin	"	don Felipe Xado Cagigal.
74	San Ildefonso	"	don Josef Bargas.
	S. Juan Nepomuceno	"	don Cosme Churruca.
	Monarca	"	don Teodoro Argumosa.
	S. Francisco de Asis	"	don Luis de Flores.
	San Justo	"	don Miguel Gaston.
64	San Leandro	"	don Josef Quevedo.

Frigates: (all French): *Cornélie, Hermione, Hortense, Rhin, Thémis*;
Brigs:, *Argus* and *Furet*.

[21 October 1805] The near approach of the British Fleet rendering an Action unavoidable, the French admiral, at 8h. 30m. a.m., made the signal for his Ships to wear together, and form the Line in close order upon the larboard tack; and thereby to bring Cadiz on his lee bow, and facilitate, if necessary, his ecape to that Port. It was near 10 a.m. before the manoeuvre was completed; and then, owing to the lightness of the wind, the partial flaws from off the land, the heavy ground swell, and the incapacity or inexperience of some of the Captains, the Franco-Spanish line was very irregularly formed; so much so that, instead of being straight, it was curved or crescent-like; and, instead of the Ships being in line ahead, some were to leeward, others to windward, of their proper stations. For the most part, indeed, the Ships were two, and in a few cases three, deep; thus accidentally presenting more obstacles to the success of the plan of attack decided upon by the British Admiral, than if each French and Spanish Ship had been in the wake of her leader. The Ships, generally, were under topsails and topgallantsails, with the main topsail shivering, and lay a point, or rather more, off the wind. Owing to the lightness of the breeze, the British Fleet, after bearing up, made very slow progress, scarcely going, with studding-sails set, three knots an hour.

As the Victory drew near to the Enemy, (says Dr. Beatty), his Lordship, accompanied by Captain Hardy, and the Captains of the four Frigates, who had been called on board by signal to receive instructions, visited the different decks of the Ship. He addressed the crew at their several quarters, admonished them against firing a single shot without being sure of their object; and expressed himself to the Officers highly satisfied with the arrangements made at their respective stations. It was now plainly perceived by all on board the *Victory*, that from the very compact line which the Enemy had formed, they were determined to make one great effort to recover in some measure their long-lost Naval reputation. They wore in succession about twenty minutes past seven o'clock; and stood on the larboard tack, with their heads towards Cadiz. They kept a good deal of sail set, steering about two points from the wind, with topsails shivering. Their Van was particularly closed, having the *Santisima Trinidada*, and the *Bucentaur* the ninth and tenth Ships, the latter the Flag-Ship of Admiral Villeneuve; but as the Admirals of the Combined Fleets declined showing their flags till the heat of the Battle was over, the former of these Ships was only distinguished from the rest by her having four decks, and Lord Nelson ordered the Victory to be steered for her bow. Several Officers of the Ship now communicated to each other their sentiments of anxiety for his Lordship's personal safety, to which every other consideration seemed to give way. Indeed, all were confident of gaining a glorious Victory, but the apprehensions for his Lordship were great and general; and the Surgeon made known to Doctor Scott his fears that his Lordship would be made the object of the Enemy's marksmen, and his desire that he might be entreated by somebody to cover the stars on his coat with a handkerchief. Doctor Scott and Mr. Scott (Public Secretary) both observed, however, that such request would have no effect, as they knew his Lordship's sentiments on the subject so well, that they were sure he would be highly displeased with whoever should take the liberty of recommending any change in his dress on this account; and when the Surgeon declared to Mr. Scott, that he would avail himself of the opportunity of making his sick-report for the day, to submit his sentiments to the Admiral, Mr. Scott replied, "Take care, Doctor, what you are about: I would not be the man to mention such a matter to him." The Surgeon, notwithstanding, persisted in his design, and remained on deck to find a proper opportunity for addressing his Lordship, but this never occurred, as his Lordship continued occupied with the Captains of the Frigates, (to whom he was explaining his intentions respecting the services they were to perform during the Battle,) till a short time before the Enemy opened their fire on the *Royal Sovereign*, when Lord Nelson ordered all persons not stationed on the quarter-deck or poop, to repair to their proper quarters; and the Surgeon, much concerned at this disappointment, retired from the deck with several other Officers. The boats on the quarters of the Ship, being found in the way of the guns, were now lowered down and towed astern. Captain Blackwood of the *Euryalus*, remained on board the *Victory* till a few minutes

No. Signal.	Telegraph, Admiralty, or accompanying telegraph, or pendants.	Purport.	By whom made.	To whom made.	At what time made.	Remarks.
					a.m.	
13	Admiralty	Prepare for battle	Commander-in-Chief	General	6h 40m	Answered by the Fleet immediately, which was complied with
76	Admiralty	Bear up, sail large on the course steered by Admiral, or that pointed out by Compass Signal	*Victory*	General	6.50	Answered and complied with immediately
	Naiad's pendant	Signal for Captain Dundas	*Victory*		7.50	Ditto
76	Admiralty and *Prince*'s pendant	Bear up, sail large on the course steered by Admiral, or that pointed out by Compass Signal	*Victory*	*Prince*	8.40	Answered by the *Prince* immediately
92	Admiralty, and S. pendant.	Shorten sail, and carry as little sail as possible	*Victory*	General	10.0	Answered and complied with immediately

No.	Signal		From	To	Time	Remarks
420	Admiralty and R. Sovereign's pendant.	[The Enemy are coming out of Port, or getting under weigh.] Added by the Editor—no purport stated in the log	*Victory*	*R. Sovereign*	10.50	Ditto
642	Admiralty	The chase, or strange sail, is a Vessel of War	*Victory*	*R. Sovereign*	10.50	Ditto
307	Admiralty and S. pendant, red with white fly, over yellow	Make all sail possible with safety to the Masts	*Victory*	Not known, supposed *Thunderer**	11.5	Repeated the Signal to the Thunderer, with her No. immediately
	Telegraph	England expects that every man will do his duty	*Victory*	General	11.35	Repeated by the *Naiad* immediately
63	Admiralty, preparative	Prepare to anchor	*Victory*	General	12.0	Repeated by the *Naiad* immediately, and complied with
8		The above Signal to take place immediately after the close of day				

* The Pendants show that this signal was made to the *Africa*.

before the Enemy began the fire upon her. He represented to his Lordship that his Flag-Ship would be singled out, and much pressed by the Enemy; and suggested the propriety therefore of permitting one or two Ships of his Line to go ahead of the *Victory*, and lead her into Action, which might be the means of drawing in some measure the Enemy's attention from her. To this Lord Nelson assented, and at half-nine o'clock, he ordered the *Téméraire* and *Leviathan* by signal (the former of which Ships, being close to the *Victory*, was hailed by his Lordship,) to go a-head for that purpose; but from the light breeze that prevailed, they were unable, notwithstanding their utmost efforts, to attain their intended stations. Captain Blackwood foresaw that this would be the case, and as the *Victory* still continued to carry all her sail, he wished Captain Hardy to acquaint his Lordship, that unless her sail was in some degree shortened, the two Ships just mentioned could not succeed in getting a-head previously to the Enemy's Line being forced. This, however, Captain Hardy declined doing, as he conceived his Lordship's ardour to get into battle would on no account suffer such a measure.

Mr. James relates this circumstance rather differently: –

"Captain Blackwood undertook the delicate task of broaching the matter to the Admiral. He did so; and Lord Nelson, smiling significantly at Captain Hardy, replied, 'Oh yes, let her go a-head;' meaning, if she could. At about 9h. 40m. A.M. the *Téméraire* was accordingly hailed, to take her station ahead of the *Victory*. At about the same time Lieutenant John Yule, who then commanded upon the forecastle, observing that the lee or starboard lower studding-sail was improperly set, caused it to be taken in for the purpose of setting it afresh. The instant this was done, Lord Nelson ran forward, and rated the Lieutenant severely for having, as he supposed, begun to shorten sail without the Captain's orders. The studding-sail was quickly replaced; and the *Victory*, as the gallant Chief intended, continued to lead the column."

But Captain Blackwood's own statement differs from both these accounts: –

"About ten o'clock, Lord Nelson's anxiety to close with the Enemy became very apparent: he frequently remarked that they put a good face upon it; but always quickly added, 'I'll give them such a dressing as they never had before,' regretting at the same time the vicinity of the land. At that critical moment I ventured to represent to his Lordship, the value of such a life as his, and particularly in the present battle; and I proposed hoisting his Flag in the Euryalus, whence he could better see what was going on, as well as what to order in case of necessity. But he would not hear of it, and gave as his reason the force of example; and probably he was right. My next object, therefore, was to endeavour to induce his Lordship to allow the *Téméraire*, *Neptune*, and *Leviathan* to lead into Action before the *Victory*, which was then the headmost. After much conversation, in which I ventured to give it as the joint opinion of Captain Hardy and myself, how advantageous it would be to the Fleet for his Lordship to keep as long as possible out of the Battle, he at length consented to allow the *Téméraire* which was then sailing abreast of the *Victory*, to go a-head, and hailed Captain Harvey to say such were his intentions, if the *Téméraire* could pass the *Victory*. Captain Harvey being rather out of hail, his Lordship sent me to communicate his wishes, which I did; when, on returning to the *Victory*, I found him doing all he could to increase rather than diminish sail, so that the Téméraire could not pass the *Victory*: consequently when they came within gun-shot of the Enemy, Captain Harvey, finding his efforts ineffectual, was obliged to take his station astern of the Admiral."

To these statements it may for the first time be added, that at fifteen minutes after Noon, the *Téméraire* was expressly ordered by signal to take her station astern of the *Victory*.

Mr. James proceeds: "The direction in which the Combined Fleet now lay, with a home-port scarcely seven leagues off on the lee bow, and the evident forging ahead of the Ships, whereby that distance was every minute diminishing, induced Lord Nelson to steer a trifle more to the northward, and to telegraph his Second in Command, 'I intend to pass through the Van of the Enemy's Line, to prevent him from getting into Cadiz.' The reserved order of that Line, in the prevailing state of the wind, had produced another danger to be guarded against: it had brought the shoals of San-Pedro and Trafalgar under the lee of both Fleets. Accordingly, at 11h. 30m. a.m., the *Victory* made the signal (No. 63, with the preparative) for the British Fleet to prepare to anchor at the close of day."

"During the five hours and a half," says Captain Blackwood, "that I remained on board the *Victory*, in which I was not ten times from his side, he frequently asked me, what I should consider as a victory? The certainty of which he never for an instant seemed to doubt, although from the situation of the land he questioned the possibility of the subsequent preservation of the Prizes. My answer was, 'That considering the handsome way in which the Battle was offered by the Enemy, their apparent determination for a fair trial of strength, and the proximity of the land, I thought if fourteen Ships were captured, it would be a glorious result;' to which he always replied, 'I shall not, Blackwood, be satisfied with anything short of twenty.'"

At thirty-five minutes past eleven, Lord Nelson ordered that Signal to be made to his Fleet, which will ever form the watchword of Englishmen, and be coexistent with the English language and the British Empire: – ENGLAND EXPECTS THAT EVERY MAN WILL DO HIS DUTY. There are several relations of the circumstances connected with this memorable Signal. Captain Blackwood says,

"I was walking with him, on the poop, when he said, 'I'll now amuse the Fleet with a signal;' and he asked me, 'if I did not think there was one yet wanting?' I answered, that I thought the whole of the Fleet seemed very clearly to understand what they were about, and to vie with each other who should first get nearest to the *Victory* or *Royal Sovereign*. These words were scarcely uttered, when his last well-known. Signal was made, ENGLAND EXPECTS EVERY MAN WILL DO HIS DUTY. The shout with which it was received throughout the Fleet was truly sublime. 'Now,' said Lord Nelson, 'I can do no more. We must trust to the great Disposer of all events, and the justice of our cause. I thank God for this great opportunity of doing my duty.'"

Mr. James, after mentioning that the signal to prepare to anchor had been made at 11h. 30m., says, –

"This done, no other signal seemed wanting, when Lord Nelson remarked, that he must give the Fleet something by way of a fillip. After musing awhile, he said, 'Suppose we telegraph that "Nelson expects every man to do his duty?"' The Officer, whom he was then addressing, suggested whether it would not be better, 'England expects,' &c. Lord Nelson rapturously exclaimed, 'Certainly, certainly;' and, at 11h. 40m. A.M., up went to the *Victory*'s mizen topgallantmast-head, the first flag of the celebrated telegraphic message, 'ENGLAND EXPECTS THAT EVERY MAN WILL DO HIS DUTY;' a signal which, the instant its signification became fully known, was greeted with three cheers on board of every Ship in the Fleet, and excited among both Officers and Men the most lively enthusiasm."

The following are, however, the real facts as they have been related by Captain John Pasco, who acted as Flag Lieutenant of the *Victory*, and who has been so good as to testify to their accuracy in a letter to the Editor: –

"His Lordship came to me on the poop, and after ordering certain signals to be made, about a quarter to noon, he said, 'Mr. Pasco, I wish to say to the Fleet, ENGLAND CONFIDES THAT EVERY MAN WILL DO HIS DUTY;' and he added, 'you must be quick, for I have one more to make, which is for Close Action.' I replied, 'If your Lordship will permit me to substitute the *expects* for *confides* the signal will soon be completed, because the word *expects* is in the vocabulary, and *confides* must be spelt.' His Lordship replied, in haste, and with seeming satisfaction, 'That will do, Pasco, make it directly.' When it had been answered by a few Ships in the Van, he ordered me to make the signal for Close Action, and to *keep it up:* accordingly, I hoisted No. 16 at the top-gallant mast-head, and there it remained until shot away."

Captain Blackwood says, "When Lord Nelson found the shot pass over the *Victory*, he desired Captain Prowse of the Sirius and myself, to go on board our Ships, and in our way to tell all the Captains of Line-of-Battle Ships, that he depended on their exertions; and that if, by the mode of attack prescribed, they found it impracticable to get into Action immediately, they might adopt whatever they thought best, provided it led them quickly and closely alongside an Enemy. He then again desired me to go away; and as we were standing on the front of the poop, I took his hand, and said, 'I trust, my Lord, that on my return to the *Victory*, which will be as soon as possible, I shall find your Lordship well, and in possession of twenty Prizes.' On which he made this reply, 'God bless you, Blackwood, I shall never speak to you again.'"

The position of the two Fleets, shortly before the Battle commenced, is shown, with all attainable accuracy. The Enemy were lying-to, with their heads to the Northward, and did not, as is generally supposed, form one line, converging slightly to leeward, but in many cases their Ships were doubled on each other, so as to form two irregular lines, extending from about N.N.E. to S.S.W.: the Spaniards and French being mixed together without any regard to the Nation to which they belonged. The British Fleet approached the Enemy in two columns, the weather led by Lord Nelson in the *Victory*, followed by the *Téméraire*, *Neptune*, *Conqueror*, *Leviathan*, *Ajax*, *Orion*, *Agamemnon*, *Minotaur*, *Spartiate*, and *Britannia*; and the *Africa*, which had been sent to look out, approaching from the North-ward. The lee column was led by Vice-Admiral Collingwood in the *Royal Sovereign*, followed by the *Belleisle*, *Mars*, *Tonnant*, *Bellerophon*, *Colossus*, *Achille*, *Polyphemus*, *Revenge*, *Swiftsure*, *Defence*, *Thunderer*, *Defiance*, *Prince*, and *Dreadnought*. The wind was very light from the N.W., with a heavy ground swell from the Westward, and though all possible sail was set, our Ships did not advance at a greater rate than a mile and a half an hour. Cape Trafalgar at noon bore from the *Victory* about E. b. S. eighteen or twenty miles.

Mr. James says, "The Commander-in-chief in the *Bucentaure*, with the *Santisima Trinidad* as his second ahead, was directly in front of the *Victory*, the leader of the weather column; and the *Santa Ana*, the flag-ship of Vice-Admiral Alava, was in the same direction from the *Royal Sovereign*, the leader of the lee column. The Spanish Commander-in-chief, Admiral Gravina, in the *Principe-de-Asturias*, was the rearmost ship of the Fleet. Of the Frigates it may suffice to state, that they were ranged in an inner line considerably to leeward of the fighting line. One, however, in the centre, believed to have been the *Rhin*, was so near as to be seen by the *Royal Sovereign* repeating signals; a circumstance that induced Vice-Admiral Collingwood, a few minutes before the action commenced, to telegraph Lord Nelson, that the Enemy's Commander-in-chief was on board a frigate.

"According to the average time noted down on board the different ships of the British Fleet, it was just at noon, the wind very light, the sea smooth with a great ground swell setting from the westward, and the sun shining, in a beautiful manner, upon the fresh painted sides of the long Line of French and Spanish ships, that the *Fougueux*, the second astern of the *Santa Ana*, whose station was a little abaft the centre of the combined Line, opened by signal a fire upon the *Royal Sovereign*, then bearing on the French ship's larboard bow, and considerably within gun-shot; also bearing from the *Victory* south-east, distant about two miles, and from her own second astern, the *Belleisle*, about west by south three quarters of a mile. Immediately the three British Admirals hoisted their respective flags, and the ships of both divisions of the Fleet, the white or St. George's ensign; a measure adopted to prevent any confusion in the heat of battle, from a variety of National flags. As an additional mark of distinction, each British ship carried, or was ordered to carry, a Union-jack at her main topmast-stay, and another at her fore topgallant-stay. At the *Victory*'s main topgallantmast-head, also, was fast belayed Lord Nelson's customary signal on going into action, No. 16, 'Engage the Enemy more closely;' consist-ing of two flags, quarter red and white over blue, white, and red, or the Dutch republican ensign reversed. At about the same time that the firing commenced, the ships of the Combined Fleet hoisted their ensigns, and the Admirals (with the excep-tion, to which we shall presently advert, of the French Com-mander-in-chief), their flags. In addition to her ensign, every Spanish ship also hung to the end of the spanker-boom a large wooden cross."

"At about 10 minutes past noon, having reached a position close astern of the *Santa Ana*, the *Royal Sovereign* fired into her, with guns double-shotted; and with such precision as, by the subsequent acknowledgment of the Spanish Officers, to kill or wound (incredible as it may appear) nearly 400 of her crew, and to disable fourteen of her guns. With her starboard broadside, similarly charged, the *Royal Sovereign* raked the *Fougueux*, but, owing to the distance and the smoke, with little if any effect. It was just as the *Royal Sovereign* was passing between these two Enemy's ships, that Vice-Admiral Collingwood called out to his Captain: 'Rotheram, what would Nelson give to be here!' And, by a similar coincidence, Lord Nelson, the moment he saw his friend in his enviable position, exclaimed, 'See how that noble fellow Collingwood carries his ship into action.'"

"Having, in the most gallant manner, passed under the stern of and saluted the *Santa Ana* in the way already mentioned, the *Royal Sovereign* put her helm a-starboard, and, without any difficulty, ranged close alongside of her; so close that the guns were nearly muzzle to muzzle. Between the two three-deckers a tremendous cannonade ensued. But the *Royal Sovereign* soon found that she had more than one opponent to contend with. The *Fougueux*, having bore up, raked her astern; and ahead of the English ship, at the distance of about 400 yards, lay the *San Leandro*, who, wearing, raked her in that direction; while, upon the *Royal Sovereign*'s starboard bow and quarter, within less than 300 yards, were the *San Justo* and *Indomptable*.

"So incessant was the fire kept up by all these ships, that the people of the *Royal Sovereign* frequently saw the shots come in contact with each other. Aware, at length, of the injury which they were thus sustaining by their own cross fire, and observing that three or four British ships were fast approaching to the support of their gallant leader, the four two-deckers, one by one, drew off from the *Royal Sovereign*, and left her to combat solely with the *Santa Ana*; who, although in force rather more than a match for her antagonist, began already to exhibit proofs that, in practical gunnery, she was decidedly her inferior.

"For upwards of 15 minutes the *Royal Sovereign* was the only British ship in close Action. At the end of that time, when the former had taken a position upon her opponent's lee bow, and was making the best possible use of it, the *Belleisle*, hauling up, fired a broadside into the lee quarter of the *Santa Ana*, and then bore away towards the *Indomptable*. Owing to some of the ships astern of the *Fougueux* pressing forward to support the centre, while others remained with their sails aback or shivering, the Franco-Spanish line (if line we must call it) was becoming even more irregular than it had been. The slanting direction in which, on account of this movement, the British lee column was obliged to advance, enabled the ships to discharge their starboard guns at the Enemy's rear; and an interchange of animated firing ensued, the smoke from which, for the want of a breeze to carry it off, spread its murky mantle over the combatants, and increased the confusion into which the rear of the combined Fleet had already been thrown by the crash at its centre.

"Lord Nelson had already, in a two-decker, evinced how little he dreaded coming in contact with a Spanish first-rate; and even the towering and formidable-looking four-decker at present in front of him had, on that very occasion, been driven from her purpose by his well-known prowess. But, although he directed the *Victory* to be steered towards the bow of his old opponent, it was not with the intention of attacking her: a Spanish Rear-Admiral, whatever the force of his ship, was considered an unworthy object while a French Vice-Admiral commanded the Fleet. Lord Nelson did not feel a doubt, and the sequel proved he was correct, that M. Villeneuve was in one of the two or three ships next astern of the four-decker; and, knowing that, to fetch a ship laying to at a distance ahead, he must keep her on his lee bow, he ordered the *Victory* to be steered in the manner just related.

"Although every glass on board the *Victory* was put in requisition to discover the Flag of the French Commander-in-chief, all the answers to the repeated questions of Lord Nelson on the subject ended in disappointment. The four-decker's Flag at the mizen could be made out, and some signals were occasionally seen at the main of two or three of the ships, but no French Flag at the fore. Often did the little man himself, with his remaining eye, cast an anxious glance towards the Franco-Spanish line in search of the ship which he meant the *Victory* first to grapple with; and so lightly did Lord Nelson value personal risk, that, although urged more than once on the subject, he would not suffer those barriers from the Enemy's grape and musketry, the hammocks, to be placed one inch higher than, to facilitate his view of objects around him, they were accustomed to be stowed. The *Victory*, meanwhile, was slowly advancing to a gun-shot distance from the Enemy's Line.

"At 20 minutes past noon, which was about 20 minutes after the *Fougueux* had opened her fire upon the *Royal Sovereign*, and about 10 after the latter had passed under the stern of the *Santa Ana*, the *Bucentaure* fired a shot at the *Victory*, then, with studding-sails set on both sides, steering about east and going scarcely a knot and a half through the water. The shot fell short. Two or three minutes elapsed, and a second shot was fired; which, the *Victory* then about a mile and a quarter distant, fell alongside. A third shot almost immediately followed, and that went over the ship. One or two others did the same, until, at length, a shot went through the *Victory*'s main top-gallantsail; affording to the Enemy the first visible proof that his shot would reach. A minute or two of awful silence ensued; and then, as if by signal from the French Admiral, the whole van, or at least seven or eight of the weather-most ships, opened a fire upon the *Victory*, such a fire as had scarcely before been directed at a single ship. In a few minutes a round shot killed Mr. John Scott, Lord Nelson's public secretary, while he was conversing with Captain Hardy.

"Since the commencement of the firing the wind had gradually died away to a mere breath. Still the *Victory*, driven onward by the swell and the remains of her previous impetus, was going slowly ahead, in the direction, now, of the interval between the *Santisima Trinidad* and *Bucentaure*: both of which ships, aided occasionally by the *Redoutable* astern of the latter, continued upon her a very heavy and destructive fire. To this heavy and unremitting cannonade the *Victory* neither did, nor from her position could, bestow any return. In a very few minutes, however, after the firing had opened upon her, one of the foremost guns on the starboard side went off by accident. In a private ship this would scarcely have been noticed; but, as happening on board the ship of the Commander-in-Chief, it excited the attention of the Fleet, and was minuted down in the log of one ship, the *Polyphemus*, as a real commencement of the Action by the *Victory*.

"Seeing, by the direction of her course, that the *Victory* was about to follow the example of the *Royal Sovereign*, the French and Spanish ships ahead of the British weather column closed like a forest. This movement, headed by the stoppage in the headway of the *Santa Ana*, and by the bearing up of the two Spanish ships ahead of her in the manner already related, divided the Combined Line nearly in the centre, leaving, including the *Redoutable* from her station astern of the *San Leandro*, 14 ships in the van, and 19 in the rear, with an interval between them of at least three quarters of a mile.

"Just as she had got within about 500 yards of the larboard beam of the *Bucentaure* the *Victory*'s mizen topmast was shot away about two thirds up. A shot also struck and knocked to pieces the wheel; and the ship was obliged to be steered in the gun-room, the first Lieutenant (John Quilliam) and Master (Thomas Atkinson) relieving each other at this duty. Scarcely had two minutes elapsed before a double-headed shot killed eight Marines on the poop, and wounded several others: on which the Admiral ordered Captain Adair to disperse his men round the ship, that they might not suffer so much from being together. Presently a shot, that had come through a thickness of four hammocks near the larboard chess-tree, and had carried away a part of the laboard quarter of the launch as she lay on the booms, struck the fore-brace bits on the quarterdeck, and passed between Lord Nelson and Captain Hardy; a splinter from the bits bruising the left foot of the latter, and tearing the buckle from his shoe. 'They both,' says Doctor Beatty, 'instantly stopped, and were observed by the Officers on deck to survey each other with inquiring looks, each supposing the other to be wounded. His Lordship then smiled and said, 'This is too warm work, Hardy, to last long;' and declared that, through all the battles he had been in, he had never witnessed more cool courage than was displayed by the *Victory*'s crew on this occasion.

"In a few seconds afterwards, as the *Bucentaure* slowly forged ahead, a large French ship was seen on her lee quarter, and another ship astern of the former, in the act of ranging up, as if with the intention of completely closing the interval. Now it was that Captain Hardy represented to Lord Nelson the impracticability of passing through the Line without running on board one of the ships. His Lordship quickly replied, 'I cannot help it:

it does not signify which we run on board of. Go on board which you please: take your choice.' At this moment, such had been the effect of the heavy and unremitting fire to which she had so long been exposed, the loss on board the *Victory* amounted to 20 Officers and Men killed, and 30 wounded; a loss that would have been still more severe, had not the Enemy's guns been pointed at the rigging and sails, rather than at the hull of the ship. In consequence of this, every studding-sail boom on the foremast (the *Victory*, unlike other ships, had no booms rigged out upon her mainmast) had been shot off close to the yard-arm, and every sail, especially on the foremast, was like a riddle: her almost new foresail, indeed, had from 80 to 100 yards of it stripped from the yard. This clearly shows what an advantage the centre and rear had lost in not having opened an earlier fire upon the *Royal Sovereign*. 'Quel but avantageux,' says a French writer, 'offraient aux canonniers ces deux groupes de vaisseaux, dont chacun présentait une quantité de mâts et de vergues et une masse de cordages et de voiles, où pas un boulet ne devait être perdu.'

"At 1 p.m. the 68-pounder carronade on the larboard side of the Victory's forecastle, containing its customary charge of one round shot and a keg filled with 500 musket balls, was fired right into the cabin windows of the *Bucentaure*. As the *Victory* slowly moved a-head, every gun of the remaining 50 upon her broadside, all double, and some of them treble shotted, was deliberately discharged in the same raking manner. So close were the ships, that the larboard main yard-arm of the British three-decker, as she rolled, touched the vangs of her opponent's gaff: so close indeed, that had there been wind enough to blow it out, the large French ensign trailing at the Bucentaure's peak might, even at this early period of the action, have been a trophy in the hands of the *Victory*'s crew. While listening, with characteristic avidity, to the deafening crash made by their shot in the French ship's hull, the British crew were nearly suffocated with clouds of the black smoke that entered the *Victory*'s port holes; and Lord Nelson, Captain Hardy, and others that were walking the quarterdeck, had their clothes covered with the dust which issued from the crumbled wood-work of the *Bucentaure*'s stern.

"Although the work of scarcely two minutes, and although not a mast or yard of the *Bucentaure* was seen to come down, the effects of the British three-decker's broadside upon the *personnel* of the French ship, as acknowledged a day or two afterwards by Vice-Admiral Villeneuve, and long subsequently by his Flag-Captain, M. Magendie, was of the same destructive character as the broadside poured by the *Royal Sovereign* into the stern of the *Santa Ana*. The amount which the *Bucentaure*'s Officers gave, as the extent of their loss in killed and wounded by the *Victory*'s fire, was 'nearly 400 men.' They represented, also, that twenty of their guns were dismounted by it, and that the *Bucentaure* was reduced to a comparatively defenceless state.

"Prevented by position, even had she not been incapacitated by loss, from returning the *Victory*'s tremendous salute, the *Bucentaure* found an able second in the *Neptune*. This fine French 80, the moment the *Victory*'s bows opened clear of the *Bucentaure*'s stern, poured into them a most destructive fire. Among other damages occasioned by it, the flying jib-boom and spirit and sprit topsailyards were cut away; also the starboard cathead was shot completely off, notwithstanding its immense stoutness. The bower anchor, and a sheet anchor stowed near it, were also quite disabled: and a third anchor on that side was much injured. Several shot also entered the *Victory*'s bows between wind and water, and the foremast and bowsprit were badly wounded.

"The *Neptune*, fearing, as the *Victory* advanced, that she intended to run on board of her, set her jib, and keeping away a little, ranged ahead; but, Captain Hardy having decided to run on board the ship on his starboard hand, and into which a broadside had been poured the instant it would bear with effect, the *Victory* put her helm hard a-port. This quickly brought her head in the direction of the *Redoutable*; who, with her foremost guns continued to aid the *Neptune* in raking the *Victory*, and with her aftermost ones fired occasionally at the *Téméraire*, as the latter drew out from the wake of her leader. Just, however, as the *Victory* was coming in contact with her, the *Redoutable* shut most of her lowerdeck ports, and fired from them no more. In about a minute after she had shifted her helm, the *Victory* ran foul of the *Redoutable*; the sheet anchor of the one striking the spare anchor of the other.

"Very soon afterwards, or at about 1 h. 10m. p.m., the two ships dropped alongside of each other. This account corresponds with that given by the French. 'Nelson,' says M. Parisot, 'voyant qu'il (the *Redoutable*'s Captain) n'était pas disposé à plier, fit venir le *Victory* au vent tout d'un coup, et le laissant tomber en travers, il aborda de long en long le *Redoutable*' Owing to the slight impetus in the *Victory*, caused by the want of wind, the concussion of the firing would probably have separated her from the *Redoutable*, had not the *Victory*'s starboard fore topmast studding-sail boom-iron, as the ships were in the act of rebounding off, hooked into the leech of the *Redoutable*'s fore topsail. This held the ships together; and with the lowerdeck guns of the *Victory* touching the side of the *Redoutable*, and the latter's mainmast in a line about midway between the former's fore and main masts, the two ships fell off a few points from the wind.

"Almost immediately after the *Victory* had got hooked alongside the *Redoutable*, Mr. William Willmet, the boatswain of the former, found a ready means of clearing the French ship's gangways by firing the starboard 68-pounder carronade, loaded as the larboard one had been, right upon the *Redoutable*'s decks. The guns of the middle and lower decks were also occasionally fired into the *Redoutable*, but very few of the 12-pounders, on account chiefly of the heavy loss among those who had been stationed at them. The *Redoutable*, on her part, fired her maindeck guns into the *Victory*, and used musketry, as well through her ports into those of the *Victory*, as from her three tops down upon the latter's deck. In her fore and main tops, also, the *Redoutable* had some brass cohorns, which, loaded with langridge, were frequently fired with destructive effect upon the *Victory*'s forecastle. The larboard guns of the *Victory* were fired occasionally at the *Bucentaure*; but it was with little or no effect, the latter ship continuing to move to the northward, while the *Victory* and *Redoutable* kept inclining their heads to the eastward. The *Santisima Trinidad* also received into her starboard or lee quarter and stern a portion of the *Victory*'s fire.

"Never allowing mere personal comfort to interfere with, what he considered to be, the good of the service, Lord Nelson, when the *Victory* was fitting to receive his Flag, ordered the large sky-light over his cabin to be removed, and the space planked up, so as to afford him a walk amidships, clear of the guns and ropes. Here, along an extent of deck of about 21 feet in length, bounded abaft by the stancheon of the wheel and forward by the combings of the cabin ladder-way, were the Admiral and Captain Hardy, during the whole of the operations we have just detailed, taking their customary promenade. At about 1 h. 25 m. p.m., just as the two had arrived within one pace of the regular turning spot at the cabin ladder-way, Lord Nelson, who, regardless of quarterdeck etiquette, was walking on the larboard side, suddenly faced left about. Captain Hardy, as soon as he had taken the other step, turned also, and saw the Admiral in the act of falling. He was then on his knees with his left hand just touching the deck. The arm giving way, Lord Nelson fell on his left side, exactly upon the spot where his Secretary, Mr. Scott, had breathed his last, and with whose blood his Lordship's clothes were soiled.

"On Captain Hardy's expressing a hope that he was not severely wounded, Lord Nelson replied: 'They have done for me at last, Hardy.' 'I hope not,' answered Captain Hardy. 'Yes,' replied his Lordship, 'my backbone is shot through' The wound was by a musket-ball, which had entered the left shoulder through the fore part of the epaulet, and, descending, had lodged in the spine. That the wound had been given by some one stationed in the *Redoutable*'s mizen top was rendered certain, not only from the nearness (about 15 yards) and situation of the mizen top in reference to the course of the ball, but from the circumstance that the French ship's maintop was screened by a portion of the *Victory*'s mainsail as it hung when clewed up. That the ball was intended for Lord Nelson is doubtful, because, when the aim must have been taken, he was walking on the outer side, concealed in a great measure from view by a much taller and stouter man. Admitting, also (which is very doubtful), that the French seaman or marine, whose shot had proved so fatal, had selected for his object, as the British Commander-in-chief, the best dressed officer of the two, he would most probably have fixed upon Captain Hardy, or, indeed, such, in spite of Dr. Beatty's print, was Lord Nelson's habitual carelessness, upon any one of the *Victory*'s Lieutenants who might have been walking by the side of him. Serjeant Secker of the marines, and two seamen, who had come up on seeing the Admiral fall, now, by Captain Hardy's direction, bore their revered and much lamented Chief to the cockpit.

"Previously to our entering upon the account of each ship's proceedings, we will endeavour to present a general view of the engagement, and of its immediate result. Soon after the first four ships of the British lee division had cut through between the centre and rear of the Franco-Spanish line, the remainder, successively as they came up, pierced the mass (for it could no longer be called line) of Enemy's ships, in various directions, and found opponents as they could. Meanwhile the leading ships of the weather division had begun to engage in a similar manner, a little ahead of the centre. The Action, which had commenced, as we have elsewhere shown, at noon, arrived at its height about 1 h. 30 m. p.m. At 3 p.m. the firing began to slacken, and, at about 5 p.m., wholly ceased. Of the 14 van-ships of the Combined Line, reckoning to the *Redoutable* inclusive, three only were captured in their places. The remaining 11 wore out of the line. Of these 11, three were captured, and eight escaped; four, by hauling to windward, and four by running into Cadiz. Of the 19 rear-ships, 12, including one burnt, were taken, and seven escaped into Cadiz; making, as the result of the first day's proceedings, nine French (including one burnt), and nine Spanish, sail of the Line captured, total 18, and nine French, and six Spanish, sail of the Line escaped, total 15: of which latter number four French ships got away to the southward, and 11, five of them French and six Spanish, and most of the ships much shattered, with all the frigates and brigs, reached the bay of Cadiz.

"So far as to the collective operations of the two fleets in the Trafalgar Battle. Our attention is now due to the individual exertions of the ships on each side; and we shall proceed to give the most accurate account that our researches, far and near, have enabled us obtain, taking the British ships of each division, in the order in which, according to the best judgment to be formed from the variety of times noted down in their logs, they successfully got into action.

"The *Royal Sovereign* we left just as, after 15 minutes of close action with three or four ships, the *Belleisle* had come to her relief. The latter, passing on to the eastward, left the *Royal Sovereign* upon the *Santa Ana*'s starboard bow. In a short time the Spanish three-decker lost her mizen topmast; and, at the end of about an hour and a quarter from the commencement of the combat, her three masts fell over the side. At about 2 h. 15 m. p.m., after a hot, and with the exception of the *Belleisle*'s broadside, an uninterrupted, engagement between the two ships from 10 minutes past noon, the *Santa Ana* struck to the *Royal Sovereign*.

"This occurrence took place just as the mizenmast of the *Royal Sovereign* came down, and when her fore and main masts, from their shattered condition, were ready to follow it. No sooner, indeed, did the *Royal Sovereign* in order to put herself a little to rights, move a short distance ahead of her prize, then her mainmast fell over on the starboard side, tearing off two of the lowerdeck ports. The foremast, having been shot through in several places, and stripped of nearly the whole of its rigging, was left in a tottering state. Hence the English three-decker was reduced to almost, if not quite, as unmanageable a state as the Spanish three-decker, which she had so gallantly fought and captured.

"The French accounts say: 'Le vaisseau la *Santa Ana*, vaillamment attaqué par l'Amiral Collingwood, fut non moins vaillamment défendu par le Vice-amiral Alava; mais, accablé par le nombre, il dut céder;' and yet out of the 26 remaining British ships, no ship except the *Belleisle*, and that with merely a broadside in passing, asserts that she fired into the *Santa Ana*. Here is the proper place to notice the modesty with which Vice-Admiral Collingwood, in his official dispatch, refers to the part taken by his own ship. 'The Commander-in-chief in the *Victory*,' he says, 'led the weather column, and the *Royal Sovereign*, which bore my flag, the lee. The action began at 12 o'clock by the leading ships of the columns breaking through the Enemy's Line, the Commander-in-chief about the tenth ship from the van, the second in command about the twelfth from the rear, &c.' The *Royal Sovereign* is not again mentioned, except in reference to matters that occurred subsequently to the battle.

"The loss sustained by the *Royal Sovereign* was tolerably

severe: she had one lieutenant (Brice Gilliland), her master
(William Chalmers), one lieutenant of marines (Robert Green),
two midshipmen (John Aikenhead and Thomas Braund), 29
seamen, and 13 marines killed; two lieutenants (John Clavell
and James Bashford), one lieutenant of marines (James le
Vesconte), one Master's Mate (William Watson), four midshipmen (Gilbert Kennicott, Granville Thompson, John Farrant,
and John Campbell), her boatswain (Isaac Wilkinson), 69
seamen, and 16 marines wounded.

"Respecting the *Santa Ana*'s loss in killed and wounded,
nothing is known beyond the amount already specified as
the alleged effect of her opponent's raking fire. That the Spanish
ship's loss must have been uncommonly severe may be inferred,
as well from the length and closeness of the action, as from the
fact, that her starboard side was nearly beaten in by the *Royal
Sovereign*'s shot. Among the Santa Ana's dangerously, if not
mortally wounded, was Vice-Admiral Alava; and it was understood that her killed and wounded comprised a great proportion of officers.

"After having, for the space of 20 minutes, sustained the
tremendons fire opened by the rear of the Combined Line, and
after having suffered, in consequence, a loss of between 50 and
60 men in killed and wounded, the *Belleisle*, at about a quarter
past noon, exchanged a few shot with the *Monarca*, and passed
through the Line abreast of the *Fougueux*; then distantly raking
the *Royal Sovereign*. In hauling up on the larboard tack, the
Belleisle was enabled, owing to the advanced position of the
latter, to pour a full broadside into the lee quarter of the *Santa
Ana*. Bearing away a little, the *Belleisle* then passed close astern
of the *Indomptable*; who, quickly wearing, exchanged a few
broadsides with her, and then bore up to the south-east. In
the mean time the *Belleisle* was engaged with a Spanish Ship,
the *San Juan Nepomuceno*, at some distance on her starboard
beam. At about 45 minutes past noon the *Belleisle*'s main
topmast was shot away; and, as the Enemy's rear Ships were
now pressing forward to support the centre, her situation
become extremely critical.

"At 1 p.m. the *Fougueux* ranged up in the smoke on the
Belleisle's starboard beam, and struck her at the gangway with

her larboard bow, rolling at the same time with her fore yard over the British ship's quarterdeck. The *Fougueux* immediately began engaging the *Belleisle*, and in 10 minutes shot away her mizenmast about six feet above the deck, the wreck falling over the larboard quarter. In about 10 minutes more, on the *Mars* beginning to engage her, the *Fougueux*, who had received a smart fire from the *Belleisle*'s aftermost guns, dropped astern and hauled to the northward. At 1 h. 30 m. p.m. the French *Achille* came ranging past the stern of the *Belleisle*'s, then with her head a little to the southward of east, and stationed herself on the latter's larboard quarter. In this position, the *Achille* kept up a steady fire, with comparative impunity; on account of the wreck of the *Belleisle*'s mizenmast masking her aftermost guns. Meanwhile the *Aigle*, having replaced the *San Juan*, was distantly cannonading the British ship on the starboard side; and the *San Justo* and *San Leandro*, as they stood athwart the bows of the *Belleisle* to join Admiral Gravina in the rear, opened a passing fire.

"Thus in a manner surrounded, the *Belleisle* soon had her rigging and sails cut to pieces, and at 2 h. 10 m. p.m. lost her mainmast about four feet above the deck; the wreck of which fell upon the break of the poop, while the topmast, with the yards, sails, and shrouds, hung over upon the larboard side, where already lay the wreck of the mizenmast. Her larboard guns thus completely covered by wreck, the *Belleisle* was prevented from returning by a single shot the *Achille*'s animated and destructive fire. At 2 h. 30 m. p.m., driven from her capital station upon the bows of the *Victory* and *Téméraire*, by the approach of the *Leviathan*, the French *Neptune* placed herself across the starboard bow of the *Belleisle*; and at 2 h. 45 m. the foremast and bowsprit of the latter, still engaged by two other ships, were shot away by the board.

"At 3 h. 15 m. p.m. the *Polyphemus* interposed herself between the *Belleisle* and *Neptune*. In five minutes more the *Defiance* took off the fire of the *Aigle*; and at 3 h. 45 m. p.m. the *Swiftsure*, passing astern of the *Belleisle*, commenced engaging the *Achille*, who about this time lost her main and mizen topmasts. As the *Swiftsure* passed close under the *Belleisle*'s stern the two ships cheered each other; and to signify that, notwithstanding her dismasted and shattered state, the *Belleisle* still remained un-conquered, a Union-jack was suspended at the end of a pike and held up to view, while an ensign was being made fast to the stump of her mizenmast. Thus, by the timely arrival of her friends, saved from being crushed by the overwhelming force around her, the *Belleisle* ceased firing. Observing soon after-wards on his larboard beam a Spanish two-decker that had already surrendered, Captain Hargood sent the master, Mr. William Hudson, and Lieutenant Owen of the marines (who volunteered although wounded) in the only remaining boat, the pinnace, and took possession of the 80-gun ship *Argonauta*.

"The *Belleisle*'s hull was knocked almost to pieces: both sides of it were about equally damaged. Ports, port-timbers, chan-nels, chain-plates, all exhibited unequivocal marks of the ter-rible mauling she had received. Her three masts and bowsprit, as we have seen, were shot away, and so was her figure-head. Her boats and anchors shared the same fate. If the *Belleisle*'s damages were severe, her loss of men was not less so: she had two lieutenants (Ebenezer Geall and John Woodin), one mid-shipman (George Nind), 22 seamen, and eight marines killed; one lieutenant (William Ferrie), one lieutenant of marines (John Owen), her boatswain (Andrew Gibson), two Master's Mates (William Henry Pearson and William Cutfield), one midshipman (Samuel Jago), one first-class volunteer (J. T. Hodge), 67 seamen, and 19 marines wounded.

"In her way down astern of the *Belleisle*, the *Mars* suffered severely from the heavy raking fire of the ships ahead of her, the *San Juan Nepomuceno*, *Pluton*, *Monarca*, and *Algeciras*. As the *Mars* was directing her course to cut the line between the first two of these Ships, the *Pluton*, who was to windward of the *San Juan*, ranged ahead: whereupon, to avoid being raked by so close an opponent, the *Mars* hauled up, with the intention to pass on and cut the Line ahead of the *San Juan*. In attempting this manœuvre, the *Mars* was followed and engaged by the *Pluton*. Having by that time had her rigging and sails greatly damaged, the *Mars* was obliged to come head to wind in order to avoid running on board the *Santa Ana*; whereby the *Mars* lay with her stern exposed to the *Monarca* and *Algeciras*. At this moment, however, the *Tonnant* came up, and soon found full employment for both of those ships. Meanwhile, as she paid off in her completely unmanageable state, the *Mars* became also exposed to a heavy fire from the *Fougueux*, then with her larboard guns engaging the *Belleisle*, and presently received into her stern a most destructive fire from the *Pluton*; a fire that almost cleared the poop and quarterdeck of both Officers and men. It was at about 1 h. 15m. p.m., while Captain Duff was standing at the break of the quarterdeck looking over the side, that a cannon-shot from the *Pluton* struck him on the breast, knocked off his head, and cast his body on the gangway. The same shot killed two Seamen, who were standing close behind their Captain. The command now devolved upon Lieutenant William Hennah. By this time succour was at hand; and, while the *Fougueux* made off to the northward in the direction of the *Téméraire*, the *Pluton* stood away to the south-east to join Admiral Gravina.

"The *Mars* had her main topmast and spankerboom shot away, and her three lower masts, fore and main yards, and fore topmast, very badly wounded: her foremast, indeed was left in so shattered a state that it subsequently fell overboard. The main piece of her rudder was badly wounded, her stern and quarter much cut, and nine of the poop-beams, besides sundry knees, &c., shot to pieces. The Ship had also some guns disabled, and had received several shot between wind and water. The loss on board the *Mars* was proportionably severe: she had her captain, one master's mate (Alexander Duff), two midshipmen (Edward Corbyn and Henry Morgan), 17 seamen, and eight marines killed, and two lieutenants (Edward William Garrett and James Black), her master (Thomas Cook), one captain of marines (Thomas Norman), five midshipmen (John Young, George Guiren, William John Cook, John Jenkins, and Alfred Luckraft), 44 seamen, and 16 marines wounded.

"With respect to the injuries sustained by the *Pluton*, the ship is represented to have been unable, after the Action, to muster more than 400 effective men out of a complement of about 700: consequently, her loss must have been severe. It appears, also, that the *Pluton* made three feet water an hour from the shot she had received in the hull.

"Having, as already stated, fired at the ships that were pressing upon the *Mars*, the *Tonnant* steered straight for the larboard bow of the *Algeciras*, then moving slowly onwards the same as her companions in the line, and very near to her present leader, the *Monarca*. As the *Tonnant* advanced, the *Algeciras*, having already her main topsail to the topmast, backed her mizen topsail, and thus enabled the former, at about 45 minutes past noon, to run close under the Spanish ship's stern. Pouring in a raking fire, the *Tonnant* hauled up, and engaged the *Monarca* alongside: but, dreading to encounter so large and powerful a ship, the latter fired a few ineffective shot, dropped astern, and struck her colours, although she afterwards re-hoisted them. The *Tonnant*'s people believed, although they were not certain, that the *Monarca* struck; but the *Spartiate* who, not being engaged until late, had leisure for observation, saw the flag hauled down, and in her log says accordingly: 'At 1 h. 7 m. a Spanish two-decker struck to the *Tonnant*.'

"Filling her main and mizen topsails, the *Algeciras* now evinced an intention to cross the stern of the *Tonnant*, who, by this time, had had her fore topmast and main-yard shot away; but the *Tonnant*, putting her helm hard-a-port, ran the *Algeciras* on board, and defeated the manœuvre. The bowsprit and anchors of the *Algeciras* getting entangled with the main rigging of the *Tonnant*, the two ships were held fast together, greatly, on account of their relative positions, to the advantage of the *Tonnant*. It was, doubtless, while the *Tonnant*'s attention was thus occupied, that the *Monarca*, being left to herself, and having suffered comparatively little in the action, rehoisted her colours.

"While thus fast to the *Algeciras* on her starboard side, the *Tonnant* fired her larboard aftermost guns athwart the hawse of the *Mars* at the *Pluton* lying upon the latter's larboard bow, and her larboard foremost guns at the *San Juan Nepomuceno* lying upon her own bow. Meanwhile the *Mars*, until she and the *Pluton* dropped astern, fired several well-directed shot into the larboard quarter of the *Algeciras*.

"At about 1 h. 40 m. p.m. Captain Tyler received a severe wound, and was obliged to be taken below. The command of the *Tonnant* thereupon devolved upon Lieutenant John Bedford. In the mean time an animated cannonade was kept up between the two Ships; by which the *Algeciras* soon lost her foremast, and the *Tonnant* her main and mizen topmasts. The *Algeciras* made a serious attempt to board; but the Marines of the *Tonnant* maintained so steady and well-directed a fire, that the French crew did not succeed, except in the case of one man, who contrived to enter one of the *Tonnant*'s main-deck ports, and whose life, to the credit of those who took him, was spared. At about 2h. 15m. p.m., just as her main and mizen masts were about to share the fate of her foremast, the *Algeciras*, after a very gallant defence, struck her colours; and Lieutenant Charles Bennett, with Lieutenant of Marines Arthur Ball, and about 48 men, stepped on board and took possession of her. In another quarter of an hour the *San Juan* hailed that she surrendered; and Lieutenant Benjamin Clement was sent in the jollyboat, with two hands, to take possession. The boat being damaged by shot, swamped, before she reached a quarter of the way. The two men could swim, but not the Lieutenant. While the latter was clinging to the boat, a shot struck her and knocked off her quarter. The boat then turned bottom upwards; and Lieutenant Clement held fast by the boat's fall until one of his two companions, a black man, Macnamara by name, swam to the *Tonnant*, and returned with a rope that led out of the ship's stern port. By this means a brave young Officer, who had been in two or three general actions of the preceding war, was saved to his country.

"Among the damages sustained by the *Tonnant* in the hull, was a bad wound in the rudder, a portion of the head of which was shot away; and a great part of her starboard quarter-piece, with the rails and gallery, was carried away by the *Algeciras* when the vessels got foul. The loss on board the *Tonnant* amounted to one midshipman (William Brown), 16 seamen, and nine marines killed; her captain (severely), boatswain (Richard Little), the captain's clerk (William Allen), one master's mate (Henry Ready), 30 seamen, and 16 marines wounded. The *Algeciras* had upwards of 200 men killed and wounded, including several officers; and among the mortally wounded, the brave and highly-respected Rear-Admiral Magon, who had previously been wounded in two places, but would not quit the deck.

"After having captured the *Algeciras* and disengaged herself

from her prize, the *Tonnant* fired several shot at the squadron of
M. Dumanoir passing to windward; but, having no boat left,
could not send again to take possession of the *San Juan*. That
Spanish ship, however, was shortly afterwards engaged and
secured by the *Dreadnought*.

"In consequence of the novel mode of attack adopted by the
Commander-in-Chief, each British ship, as she bore up in line
ahead, was obliged to follow in the wake of her leader until close
upon the enemy's line: her commander, then, acting up to Lord
Nelson's instructions, as contained in the Memorandum, that
no captain could do very wrong who placed his ship alongside
that of an enemy, attached himself to the first Frenchman or
Spaniard that crossed his path. Most of the captains had also
received, on the morning of the action, Lord Nelson's verbal
directions, transmitted through the captains of the frigates, that
they were to break the enemy's line wherever they conveniently
could. This, in effect, discretionary power was particularly
beneficial towards the height of the battle, when the enemy's
ships, by an irregular movement from the rear to the centre,
and in some instances, from the centre and van to the rear, were
every instant shifting their positions, and giving to their line, if
line it could be called, a new face.

"It was not until full 15 minutes after the *Tonnant* had cut the
Line, that her second astern, the *Bellerophon*, owing to her
distance from the former and the lightness of the wind, was
enabled to do the same. This she accomplished by passing
under the stern of the *Monarca*, as the latter, with colours
rehoisted, was dropping away from the *Tonnant*. In luffing
up to lay the *Monarca* alongside to leeward, the *Bellerophon*,
at about 50 minutes past noon, ran foul of the *Aigle*, the latter's
main yard locking with her fore yard. The British Ship now
fired from both sides, having the *Monarca* on the larboard, and
the *Aigle* on the opposite bow. In a short time three other
Enemy's Ships opened a cannonade upon her, the *Montanez* (we
believe), with her aftermost guns on the larboard quarter, the
French *Swiftsure* on the starboard quarter, and the *Bahama*, with
some of her foremost guns, athwart her stern.

"At about 1 p.m. the *Bellerophon*'s main and mizen topmasts
fell over on the starboard side, and the main topsail and

topgallantsail immediately caught fire with the flash of the guns, assisted by the hand-grenades which the *Aigle*'s people kept throwing from her tops. At 1 h. 5m. p.m. the Master was killed; and at 1 h. 11 m. Captain Cooke. The command now devolved upon Lieutenant William Pryce Cumby. Shortly afterward the *Montanez* dropped out of gun-shot astern, and the *Bahama* and French *Swiftsure* became engaged with the *Colossus*. The musketry from the *Aigle* had by this time played sad havoc upon the *Bellerophon*'s quarterdeck, forecastle, and poop. At 1 h. 40m. p.m. the *Aigle*, who had once or twice vainly attempted to board her opponent, dropped astern, exposed as she fell off to a raking fire, first from the *Bellerophon* herself, and then from the *Revenge*. The *Bellerophon*, now quite in an un- manageable state, fired a few shot at the *Monarca*, who instantly hauled down her colours for the last time, and was taken possession of by the former; as, nearly at the same time, was the *Bahama*, who had previously struck, to relieve herself from the destructive fire of the *Colossus*.

"The *Bellerophon* had her main and mizen topmasts shot away, her fore topmast, all three lower masts, and most of her yards, badly wounded, and her standing and running rigging nearly cut to pieces. In hull also she was much injured, having had several knees and riders shot away, and part of her lower deck ripped up, besides other damage. Her loss consisted of her captain, master (Edward Overton), one midshipman (John Simmons), 20 seamen, and four marines killed; one captain of marines (James Wemyss), her boatswain (Thomas Robinson), one master's mate (Edward Hartley), four midship- men (William N. Jewell, James Stone, Thomas Bant, and George Pearson), 96 seamen, and 20 marines wounded. A great proportion of this heavy loss unfortunately arose from the explosion of a quantity of loose powder spilt about the decks from the cartridges; and which, but for the water that lay around the entrance of the magazine, must have destroyed the ship and all on board of her.

"Although no particular account can be given of the damage or loss sustained by the *Aigle*, it may with certainty be stated, that she suffered greatly in masts, rigging, and hull, and lost in killed and wounded, from the successive fire of the *Bellerophon*,

Revenge, and *Defiance*, nearly two-thirds of her crew, including among the killed her Captain and First Lieutenant, and among the wounded several of her Officers. The loss on board the *Monarca* does not appear to have been recorded; but it must have been severe, from her first action with the *Tonnant*, and from the length of time she was exposed to the close and uninterrupted fire of the *Bellerophon*, one of the best manned, although one of the smallest, 74s in the British Fleet.

"At 1 p.m., or thereabouts, after having, during 10 minutes or so, in her efforts to close, received the fire of two or three Enemy's ships, the *Colossus* ran past the starboard side of the French *Swiftsure*; who had just before bore up, as well to avoid being raked by the *Colossus*, as to bring her larboard guns to bear upon the *Bellerophon*. The density of the smoke on the starboard side hid from view all the Enemy's Ships in that direction, until, having run a short distance to leeward, the *Colossus* found herself close alongside of the *Argonauta*, whose larboard yard-arms locked in her starboard ones. A spirited cannonade now ensued between the two ships, and lasted for about 10 minutes, when the *Argonauta*'s fire became nearly silenced, except from a few of her aftermost guns; a shot from one of which, just as the ships, driven apart by the concussion of the guns, began to settle broadside off, struck Captain Morris a little above the knee. As soon as, by this lateral movement, she had cleared her yards, the *Argonauta* paid off, and went away, receiving into her stern the parting fire of the *Colossus*. The latter, in the meanwhile, was warmly engaged on her larboard quarter, with the French *Swiftsure*, and also with the *Bahama*, who lay close on that ship's larboard bow, and fired at the *Colossus* across the *Swiftsure*'s fore-foot.

"At a few minutes before 3 p.m., having forged ahead, the *Swiftsure* got between the *Bahama* and *Colossus*, and being thus more fully exposed to the latter's well-directed broadsides, soon slackened her fire and dropped astern. The *Colossus* was now enabled to devote her sole attention to the *Bahama*; who, on her mainmast falling, as it presently did, over her engaged side, showed an English jack from the hen-coops on her poop, to denote that she had struck. Meanwhile the French *Swiftsure* endeavoured to bear up under the stern of the *Colossus*; but the latter, wearing more quickly, received a few only of the former's larboard guns, before she poured in her starboard broadside. This brought down the French *Swiftsure*'s mizenmast. At the same time the *Orion*, in passing, gave the French Ship a broadside, which brought down her tottering mainmast; whereupon the *Swiftsure* made signs to the *Colossus* of having surrendered. In hauling up to take possession of her two prizes, the latter lost her wounded mizenmast over the starboard side.

"The mainmast of the *Colossus* was so badly wounded, that she was compelled, during the ensuing night, to cut it away; and her damages altogether were extremely severe. Her only remaining stick, the foremast, had been shot through in several places; two of her anchors and three of her boats had been destroyed, and some of her guns disabled. Four of her starboard lowerdeck ports had also been knocked away by running on board the *Argonauta*, and her hull in every part of it was much shattered. The *Colossus* lost in the action her master (Thomas Scriven), 31 seamen, and eight marines killed; her captain, two lieutenants (George Bully and William Forster), one lieutenant of marines (John Benson), her boatswain (William Adamson), one master's mate (Henry Milbanke), eight midshipmen (William Herringham, Frederick Thistlewayte, Thomas G. Reece, Henry Snellgrove, Rawden M'Lean, George Wharrie, Timothy Renou, and George Denton), 115 seamen, and 31 marines wounded.

"The *Argonaute*, the first broadside-opponent of the *Colossus*, although she lost none of her masts, must have suffered severely in the hull, having had, according to the French accounts, nearly 160 of her crew killed and wounded: she, nevertheless, effected her escape. Some of the French writers are very severe in their strictures upon the conduct of the French *Argonaute*. It appears that the *Hermione* frigate, in compliance with the practice of the French navy, hoisted the signal for ships unengaged to engage, and, finding no attention paid to it, added the number of the *Argonaute*, and kept both signal and pendant flying for one hour. The *Bahama* and French *Swiftsure*, reduced to the state of wrecks, suffered a proportionate loss of men; the first having had nearly 400 killed and wounded, including among the former her captain, and the second very little short of that number.

"Being close astern of the *Colossus* and sailing well, the English *Achille* became, in a few minutes after the former, warmly engaged. Having passed close astern of the *Montanez*, the *Achille* luffed up and engaged that ship to leeward. In less than a quarter of an hour the *Montanez* sheered off, and the *Achille* made sail to succour the *Belleisle*, then lying to leeward totally dismasted, with three Enemy's ships upon her. While on her way to perform this duty, the *Achille* found herself obstructed by the *Argonauta*. The British 74 immediately brought to on the Spanish 80's larboard beam, and a close action ensued, which lasted an hour. The *Argonauta* now attempted to set her mainsail to shoot ahead, but, failing in that, ceased firing, shut her lowerdeck ports, and, as it appeared on board the *Achille*, threw an English jack or ensign over her larboard quarter.

"At this moment two French ships came up, and one of them soon found other employment for the English *Achille* than taking possession of the *Argonauta*. The French *Achille* edged down on her English namesake's larboard quarter, and engaged her in passing to windward; and the *Berwick*, who had been distantly engaged with the *Defence*, ranged up on the English *Achille*'s starboard side, between the latter and the *Argonauta*. The French *Achille* passing on in the direction of the *Belleisle*, and the *Argonauta* dropping to leeward, the English *Achille* and *Berwick* were left in fair single combat. The action continued for upwards of an hour, when the *Berwick* hauled down her colours, and was taken possession of by the *Achille*.

"The masts of the latter, although all standing, were badly wounded, and so was her bowsprit: her hull had also received considerable damage. The loss on board the English *Achille* amounted to one midshipman (Francis John Mugg), six seamen, and six marines killed, and two lieutenants (Parkin Prynn and Josias Bray), one captain and one lieutenant of marines (Palms Westropp and William Leddon), one master's mate (George Pegge), three midshipmen (William H. Staines, William J. Snow, and William Smith Warren), 37 seamen, and 14 marines wounded.

"The *Argonauta*, the English *Achille*'s first steady opponent, appears to have suffered greatly in rigging, hull, and crew, but to have had no spars of any consequence shot away: her loss is represented to have amounted to nearly 400 in killed and wounded, including among the dangerously wounded her captain. It is doubtful if the whole of this damage and loss was inflicted by the English *Achille*: the *Argonauta* must have exchanged some broadsides in passing with other British ships. The *Berwick* was dreadfully cut up in her hull, and her three masts were left in a tottering state. The *Achille*'s officer, who took possession of the ship, counted, upon her decks and in her cockpit and tiers 51 dead bodies, including that of her gallant captain, M. Camas; and the wounded of the *Berwick*, according to the report of her few surviving officers, amounted to nearly 200: her loss in officers was very severe, the quarterdeck having been twice cleared. Nearly the whole of this loss was attributable to the close and unremitting cannonade kept up, for more than an hour, by the English *Achille*. On the other hand, the principal part of the latter's damage and loss was caused by the steady fire and determined opposition of the *Berwick*.

"We quitted the *Victory* at about 1 h. 30m. p.m., or just as Lord Nelson had been carried to the cockpit, mortally wounded from the mizentop of the *Redoutable*. So destructive to the *Victory* was the fire kept up from the *Redoutable*'s tops, as well as from her second deck guns, occasionally pointed upwards, that, within a few minutes of Lord Nelson's fall, several officers and about 40 men, nearly the whole of them upon the third or upper deck, were killed or wounded. A single 18-pounder carronade on the poop, mounted upon an elevating carriage, might very soon have destroyed the *Redoutable*'s mizentop and all that were in it; but the *Victory* had no guns whatever mounted on her poop. The same effect might have been produced upon the fore and main tops by one of the 68-pounder carronades; but their carriages would not give the required elevation. Nor, we believe, could the 68-pounder on the starboard side be even fired a second time upon the decks of the *Redoutable*, owing to some accident that had since befallen it.

"Although, from the loss of the men stationed at them, the 12-pounders of the *Victory* were for the most part abandoned, the larboard guns, her 24 and 32 pounders upon the decks below continued to fire, for a few minutes (until the English

Neptune and ships astern of her intervened), distantly at the starboard quarters of the *Bucentaure* and *Santisima Trinidad*, and the starboard guns, with much more certain effect, right into the hull of the *Redoutable*. 'The starboard guns of the lower and middle decks,' says Dr. Beatty, 'were depressed, and fired with a diminished charge of powder, and three shot each, into the *Redoutable*. This mode of firing was adopted by Lieutenants Williams, King, Yule, and Brown, to obviate the danger of the *Téméraire*'s suffering from the *Victory*'s shot passing through the *Redoutable*; which must have been the case if the usual quantity of powder, and the common elevation, had been given to the guns. A circumstance occurred in this situation, which showed in a most striking manner the cool intrepidity of the officers and men stationed on the lower deck of the *Victory*. When the guns on this deck were run out, their muzzles came into contact with the *Redoutable*'s side; and consequently at every discharge there was reason to fear that the Enemy would take fire, and both the *Victory* and the *Téméraire* be involved in the flames. Here then was seen the astonishing spectacle of the fireman of each gun standing ready with a bucket full of water, which as soon as his gun was discharged he dashed into the Enemy through the holes made in her side by the shot.'

"The respectability of the authority has induced us to give this quotation entire, yet we positively deny that the *Victory*'s guns were fired in the manner there stated. Not only have our inquiries fully satisfied us respecting this fact; but we doubt even if the *Téméraire* had come in contact with the *Redoutable*, at the period to which the statement refers. When, too, the *Téméraire* did lash herself to the *Redoutable*, all effective opposition on the part of the latter had ceased, to the *Victory* at least; and, after firing a few shot, and ascertaining that the *Téméraire* was foul on the *Redoutable*'s starboard side, the *Victory* began to busy herself in getting clear, to seek a more worthy antagonist. This hitherto disputed fact, the details of the *Téméraire*'s proceedings, into which we are now about to enter, will more clearly establish.

"Being an extraordinary fast-sailing line-of-battle ship, the *Victory*, urged as she was, would probably have been, like the *Royal Sovereign* far ahead of the ships in her wake: but that the *Téméraire*, having on board very little water or provisions was, what the sailors call, 'flying light.' After the Téméraire, having closed the Victory, had, instead of leading the column as as first proposed, been directed to take her station astern of the Victory, the dismantled state of the latter from the Enemy's shot, rendered it very difficult for the Téméraire to avoid going ahead of her leader; and to keep astern she was obliged, besides cutting away her studding-sails, occasionally to yaw or make a traverse in her course. Hence the Téméraire shared with the Victory, although by no means to so great an extent, the damage and loss sustained by the head of the weather column from the enemy's heavy and incessant raking fire. Shortly after the Victory had poured her larboard broadside into the Bucentaure's stern, the Téméraire opened her fire at the Neptune and Redoutable. When the Victory put her helm a-port to steer towards the Redoutable, the Téméraire, to keep clear of her leader, was compelled to do the same; receiving, as she passed the Redoutable, a fire that carried away the head of her mizen topmast. When, after striking the Redoutable, the Victory again brought her head to the northward, the Téméraire stood slowly on a short distance to the south-east; and then hauled up to pass through the Enemy's Line. Meanwhile the Victory had, as already stated, dropped alongside the Redoutable, and the two ships were paying off to the eastward.

"Scarcely had she begun to haul up, so as to avoid being raked by the French Neptune, ere the Téméraire discovered, through the smoke, the Redoutable driving towards and almost on board of her. Even had the breeze, now barely sufficient to fill the sails, permitted the Téméraire to manœuvre to clear herself from the Redoutable, the Neptune, who, to avoid getting foul of the Redoutable and Victory, had wore and come to again on the same tack, and at this time lay with her larboard broadside bearing upon the starboard bow of the Téméraire, opened so heavy a raking fire, that in a few minutes the latter's fore yard and main topmast were shot away, and her foremast and bowsprit, particularly the latter, greatly damaged. In this unmanageable state, the Téméraire could do no more than continue to cannonade the Redoutable with her larboard guns. This the former did until, having, as she had done those on the opposite side, shut down her lowerdeck ports, the Redoutable, at

about 1 h. 40m. p.m., fell on board the *Téméraire*, the French
ship's bowsprit passing over the British ship's gangway a little
before the main rigging; and where, in order to have the benefit
of bestowing a raking fire, the crew of the *Téméraire* immediately
lashed it. The raking fire was poured in, and very destructive, as
we shall soon show, did it prove.

"Most of the few effective men, left upon the *Victory*'s upper
deck after the *Redoutable*'s destructive fire formerly noticed,
being employed in carrying their wounded comrades to the
cockpit, Captain Hardy, Captain Adair of the Marines, and
one or two other officers, were nearly all that remained upon
the quarterdeck and poop. The men in the *Redoutable*'s mizentop soon made this known to the officers below; and a considerable portion of the French crew quickly assembled in the
chains and along the gangway of their ship, in order to board
the British three-decker; whose defenceless state they inferred,
not merely from her abandoned upper deck, but from the
temporary silence of her guns on the decks below, occasioned
by a supposition that the *Redoutable*, having discontinued her
fire, was on the eve of surrendering. A party of the *Victory*'s
officers and men quickly ascended from the middle and lower
decks; and, after an interchange of musketry, the French crew,
who, in addition to the unexpected opposition they experienced, found that the curve in the hulls of the two ships
prevented their stepping from one to the other, retired with-
in-board.

"The repulse of this very gallant assault cost the *Victory*
dearly. Captain Adair and 18 men were killed, and one
lieutenant (William Ram, mortally), one midshipman (George
Augustus Westphal), and 20 men wounded. Captain Adair met
his death by a musketball received at the back of the neck, while
standing upon the *Victory*'s gangway encouraging his men, and
several seamen and marines were also killed by the French
musketry; but the lieutenant and midshipman, and four or five
seamen standing near them, were struck by a round shot, or the
splinters it occasioned, which shot had come obliquely through
the quarterdeck, and must have been fired from one of the
Redoutable's maindeck guns pointed upwards in the manner
already described.

"The account which the French give of the origin of this boarding attempt, and of the cause that led to its failure, is as follows: 'In the twinkling of an eye' (alluding to the time when Lord Nelson was carried below), 'the quarterdeck of this ship (the *Victory*) was deserted: the gallant fellows of the *Redoutable* wanted to rush upon it; but the *rentrée* of the two vessels presented an obstacle. In order to obviate this, Captain Lucas directed the main yard of his ship to be lowered, meaning to make of it a bridge whereon to pass on board the *Victory*. At that moment the three-decker *Téméraire* ran foul of the *Redoutable* on the side opposite to that on which the *Victory* lay, pouring in at the same time the whole of her broadside. The effect of this fire was terrible upon the crew of the *Redoutable*, the whole of whom were then assembled upon the forecastle, gangway, and quarterdeck. Nearly 200 were placed *hors de combat*. The brave Captain Lucas, although wounded, remained on deck. The junction of the *Téméraire* giving fresh courage to the crew of the *Victory*, the latter recommenced firing, but soon afterwards ceased in order to disengage herself from the French Ship.'

"Is it likely that a French 74 would attempt to board a British three-decker fast to her on one side, while a second British three-decker was foul of her on the other? We have not a doubt, therefore, that the French account is in this respect correct. In fixing the relative time of these occurrences, we should say that, in about five minutes after Lord Nelson was carried off the deck, or 1 h. 35m. p.m., the boarding indication commenced. Admitting the contest, when the *Téméraire* put an end to it, by lashing the *Redoutable*'s bowsprit to the forepart of her main rigging, and pouring in her destructive raking fire, to have continued five minutes, that would fix the time of the *Téméraire*'s getting foul, as we have already stated it, at 1 h. 40 m. p.m.; and another five minutes may be allowed for the ship to drop fairly alongside.

"Less considerate than either of her antagonists about fire, although in equal if not greater danger from its effects, the *Redoutable* continued throwing hand-grenades from her tops and yardarms ('les grenades pleuvent des hunes du *Redoutable*') some of which, falling on board herself, set fire to her larboard fore chains and starboard fore shrouds. The fire from the fore shrouds presently communicated to the foresail of the *Téméraire*; but, by the active exertions of her forecastle-men, led by the boatswain, the flames on board both ships were presently extinguished. The V*ictory*'s crew, after having put out a fire that had spread itself among some ropes and canvas on the booms, also lent their assistance in extinguishing the flames on board the *Redoutable*, by throwing buckets of water from the gangway upon her chains and forecastle.

"All further hostility having, as well it might, ceased on board the *Redoutable*, Captain Hardy ordered two midshipmen, Messieurs David Ogilvie and Francis E. Collingwood, with the serjeant-major of marines and eight or ten hands, to go on board the French ship, and (not to 'take possession,' for, had that been deemed of any importance, a lieutenant would have been sent, but) to assist in putting out a fire which had just broken out afresh. This party, not being able to step on board for the reason already given, embarked from one of the *Victory*'s stern-ports in the only remaining boat of the two that had been towing astern, and got to the *Redoutable* through one of her stern-ports. As a proof, too, that all hostility had then ceased on board the French ship, the *Victory*'s people were well received. Their boat, we believe, was soon afterwards knocked to pieces by a shot. The other boat had been cut adrift by a shot just as the *Victory* was about to open her fire, and was afterwards picked up with her oars and tackle as complete as when, early in the forenoon, she had been lowered down from the quarter.

"Very soon after these young midshipmen had been despatched, a lieutenant of the *Victory*, looking out of one of her aftermost ports on the starboard side, saw a second French two-decker lying close upon the *Téméraire*'s starboard side; and, as the *Victory*, a few minutes afterwards, was in the act of booming her bows off from the *Redoutable*, the same officer read the name upon the stern of each French ship. The circumstances under which the second French ship came in contact with the *Téméraire*, we shall now proceed to relate.

"In our account of the proceedings of the *Belleisle* and *Mars*, we noticed the hauling off from the former of the French ship *Fougueux*. After quitting the *Belleisle*, the *Fougueux* stood slowly across the wide space between the *Santa Ana* and *Redoutable*, steering a course directly for the starboard beam of the *Téméraire*, then with her head nearly east. The object of the *Fougueux* was probably to pass to windward of the *Téméraire* and rake her; or it might have been (and the French crew were actually assembled on the forecastle in apparent readiness) to board the British three-decker, the appearance of the latter indicating that she was much disabled, and her colours being at this time down, owing to the fall of her gaff. Indeed, as the number of men with which the *Téméraire* had begun the action was only about 660, and as, of the number at this time fit for duty, not perhaps exceeding 550, nearly the whole were below, whither they had been sent by Captain Harvey, that they might not be injured by the hand-grenades constantly thrown from the *Redoutable*'s tops, the *Fougueux* with her 700, or, allowing for a slight loss, 680 men, might have made a serious impression upon the *Téméraire*'s decks.

"While Captain Harvey devoted his attention to the *Redoutable* on the larboard side, the first lieutenant, Thomas Fortescue Kennedy, assembled a portion of the crew on the opposite side, to receive the *Fougueux*. Not having yet discharged her starboard broadside, the *Téméraire* was in perfect readiness there, but delayed firing until the *Fougueux* arrived so close that she could not well escape. At length the latter got within 100 yards. Instantly the *Téméraire*'s broadside opened, and a terrible crash was heard on board the *Fougueux*. Crippled and confused, the French ship, at about 2 h. p.m., ran foul of the *Téméraire*, and was immediately lashed, by her fore rigging, to the latter ship's spare anchor. Lieutenant Kennedy, accompanied by Mr. James Arscott, master's mate, and Mr. Robert Holgate, midshipman, and 20 seamen and six marines, then boarded the *Fougueux* in her larboard main rigging. On the French ship's quarterdeck lay Captain Beaudoin, mortally wounded; and the second captain and other officers were encouraging the men to repel the boarders. In the onset, however, the second captain became very severely wounded; whereupon the French crew suffered themselves to be driven off the quarterdeck by the British, few as they were; and, in 10 minutes from the time of her being boarded by Lieutenant Kennedy and his 28 followers, the *Fougueux* was completely in the possession of the *Téméraire*.

"This occurrence took place at about 2 h. 10m. p.m.; and it was within five minutes afterwards, or at 2 h. 15m. p.m., that the *Victory*, by fire booms and the slight assistance which her helm and sails could afford, disengaged herself from the *Redoutable*. While the *Victory* gradually got her head to the northward, the three fast-locked ships from which she had just parted, the *Redoutable*, *Téméraire*, and *Fougueux*, swang with their heads to the southward.

"Scarcely had the *Victory* broken away from the group, ere the main and mizen masts of the *Redoutable* came down. The mainmast, falling on board the *Téméraire*, carried away the stump of the latter's mizen topmast, broke down the poop-rail, and with its wreck encumbered the whole afterpart of the ship. This accident put an entire stop to the *Redoutable*'s hitherto formidable musketry (even admitting it to have continued till this time, which we doubt), and her only remaining antagonist prepared to take possession. The mainmast of the *Redoutable*, as it lay upon the *Téméraire*'s poop, forming a bridge of easy descent, this was soon accomplished; and, at about 2 h. 20m. p.m., a portion of the British crew, headed by Lieutenant John Wallace, second of the *Téméraire*, stepped on board, and took quiet possession of the gallantly fought *Redoutable*. About the time that this occurrence happened, having got her head well to the southward, the *Téméraire* was enabled to fire a few of her foremost guns on the larboard side, clear of the *Redoutable*'s bows, at the French *Neptune*; whereupon the latter, who also observed the *Leviathan* approaching, ceased her annoyance and bore away.

"Before we enter upon the proceedings of any other Ship, we will give a brief description of the damage and loss sustained by the *Victory* and *Téméraire* and the two French 74's on board of them. The *Victory*'s mizen topmast, as already stated, was shot away; and her fore and main masts and their yards, bow-sprit, jib-boom, main topmast, and cap, and fore and main tops, were badly wounded. All her rigging was cut to pieces, and her spare spars were rendered unfit for use: hull much damaged, particularly in the wales, clamps, and waterways; and some shot had been received between wind and water. Several beams, knees, and riders were injured, and ports and port-timbers knocked off. The starboard cathead was also shot away, and the starboard bower and spare anchor totally disabled.

"The loss on board the *Victory* will show, that the top-cohorns and musketry of the *Redoutable* had made ample amends for the comparative silence of her great guns. Besides Lord Nelson and his secretary, the *Victory* had one captain of marines (Charles W. Adair), one lieutenant (William Ram), two midshipmen (Robert Smith and Alexander Palmer), the captain's clerk (Thomas Whipple), 32 seamen, and 18 marines killed; two lieutenants (John Pasco and George Miller Bligh), two lieutenants of marines (Lewis Buckle Reeves and J. G. Peake), three midshipmen (William Rivers, George Augustus Westphal, and Richard Bulkeley), 59 seamen, and nine marines wounded. This was according to the official account; but 27 additional wounded men reported themselves to the surgeon after the returns had been drawn up. Among this number was included the boatswain, William Wilmet, who, although painfully wounded in the thigh, did not quit his quarters.

"The damages of the *Téméraire* were scarcely less than those of the *Victory*. The foremast had her main topmast, the head of her mizenmast, her fore yard, and her fore and main topsail-yards shot away, her fore and main masts so wounded as to render them unfit to carry sail, and her bowsprit shot through in several places. Her rigging of every sort was cut to pieces, and her starboard cathead and bumpkin were shot away; also the head of her rudder at the water's edge, by the fire of the *Redoutable*, while rounding the latter's stern. Eight feet of the starboard side of the lower deck abreast of the mainmast was also stove in, and the whole of her quarter-galleries on both sides were carried away by the two Ships that had run foul of her.

"The *Téméraire*'s loss amounted to one captain and one lieutenant of marines (Simeon Busigny and John Kingston), her carpenter (Lewis Oades), one midshipman (William Pitts), thirty-five seamen, and eight marines killed; and one lieutenant (James Mould), one lieutenant of marines (Samuel J. Payne), her boatswain (John Brooks), one master's mate (Francis S. Price), one midshipman (John Eastman), fifty-nine seamen, and twelve marines wounded. A part of this heavy loss in killed and wounded arose from the following accident. A stink-pot thrown from the *Redoutable* entered the powder-screen on the quarter-deck, and caused a destructive explosion upon the main-deck. Had it not, indeed, been for the presence of mind of the master at arms, John Toohig, who was quartered in the light-room, the fire would have communicated to the after magazine, and probably have occasioned the loss not only of the *Téméraire*, but of the Ships lashed to her.

"The damages and loss of the *Redoutable*, jammed as she had been betwixt two such formidable antagonists, might well be severe. The fall of her main and mizen masts has already been stated: her fore topmast and bowsprit shared the same fate. Her rudder was destroyed, and her hull shot through in every direction, above and below water. An 18-pounder gun, and a 36-pounder carronade near the stern, had burst, and twenty of her guns, including nine low-deckers, on the side opposite to the *Victory*, lay dismounted. Out of a crew of 643, the *Redoutable* had, according to the French official returns, 300 killed and 222 wounded, including nearly the whole of her officers. Neither the damage nor the loss of the *Fougueux* was by any means so severe as that incurred by the generality of the captured Ships. None of her masts had, at this time, actually fallen, although one or more of them had been badly struck, and her loss could not have well exceeded its reputed amount, 40 in killed and wounded, including among the latter her first lieutenant, and among the former her captain.

"We formerly mentioned that Captain Blackwood went on board the *Téméraire* with the Commander-in-chief's instructions to Captain Harvey. After quitting the latter, Captain Blackwood proceeded to the *Leviathan* and informed Captain Bayntun that Lord Nelson had consented that his Ship should precede the *Victory* in going into action. From her station astern of the *Conqueror*, the *Leviathan* immediately crowded all sail to reach the enviable post assigned her: but, owing to the late hour (about 11 h. 30m.) at which the message was delivered, the *Leviathan* did not get further ahead than just abreast of the *Conqueror*, before the *Victory* was beginning to suffer from the Enemy's fire.

"The necessity of shortening sail for awhile, to facilitate the endeavours of the *Leviathan* to pass ahead of her newly-allotted station, and the almost calm state of the weather after the firing had lasted a short time, made it 1 h. 45m. p.m. before the English *Neptune* became closely engaged. At this time, having with all her endeavours been unable to go ahead, the *Leviathan* had resumed her station in the line, and was close in the wake of the *Neptune*, and a short distance ahead of the *Conqueror*. Hauling up towards the nearest Ship, the English *Neptune* soon found herself close under the stern of the *Bucentaure*. The broadside of the *Neptune*, as she passed on in this direction, shot away the *Bucentaure's* main and mizen masts nearly by the board, and doubtless killed or wounded a great many of her crew. The *Leviathan* poured in her fire within 30 yards of the French Ship's stern, and the *Conqueror* soon afterwards did the same.

"The *Conqueror* then hauled up on the lee quarter and beam of the *Bucentaure*, and shot away her foremast. In a few minutes afterwards the Ship of the Commander-in-chief of the Combined Fleet, whose fate had been previously sealed by the *Victory's* tremendous broadside, hauled down her colours, and was taken possession of by the Conqueror. The Officer in charge of the boat was Captain James Atcherley, of the Marines, who had with him but five hands, a Corporal and two Privates of his corps, and two seamen. On the Captain's stepping upon the *Bucentaure's* quarter-deck, M. Villeneuve and his two Captains presented their swords; but, conceiving that it more properly belonged to Captain Pellew to disarm Officers of their rank, Captain Atcherley declined the honour of receiving them. Having secured the magazine and put the key in his pocket, and placed two of his men as sentries, one at each cabin-door, Captain Atcherley, accompanied by the French Admiral and his two Captains, pulled off, with his three remaining hands, and at length boarded, not the *Conqueror*, who had proceeded in chase, but the *Mars*, her sister-ship; where on account of some mistake about the nature of the message sent by Lieutenant Hennah, the Acting Commander of the *Mars*, to Captain Hardy, the French Officers were ordered to remain.

"Hauling up, after having raked the *Bucentaure*, the *Neptune* soon found herself in a similar position astern of the *Santisima*

Trinidad, whose main and mizen masts came down with a tremendous crash, just as the *Leviathan* was in the act of seconding a fire which her leader had so successfully opened. The English *Neptune* then luffed up alongside the *Santisima Trinidad* to leeward, while the *Conqueror*, with her starboard guns, kept up a distant fire upon her to windward. At about 2h. 30m. p.m. the foremast of the Spanish four-decker shared the fate of her main and mizen masts, and she lay an unmanageable wreck upon the water. At this moment the *Neptune* had her attention suddenly called off by the movement that was making in the Combined van, some of the Ships of which on bearing up, raked her, and caused the principal part of the damage and loss which she sustained in the action.

"The *Africa* 64, having the misfortune to lose sight of her fleet in the night, was, when the firing commenced, broad upon the *Victory*'s larboard beam, and nearly abreast of the van ship of the Combined line. Seeing her danger, Lord Nelson ordered the *Africa*'s signal to be thrown out, to make all possible sail. The intention of this signal appears to have been misunderstood; and instead of using means to run his Ship out of danger, Captain Digby set every sail he could spread to hasten her into it. Passing along, and exchanging broadsides in succession with the Ships of the Combined van, the *Africa*, with much less injury done to her than might have been expected, bore down ahead of the *Santisima Trinidad*.

"Meeting no return to her fire, and seeing no colours hoisted on board the latter, Captain Digby concluded that the four-decker had surrendered, and sent Lieutenant John Smith in a boat to take possession. Upon the lieutenant's reaching the quarterdeck, and asking an officer who advanced to meet him, whether or not the *Santisima Trinidad* had surrendered, the Spaniard replied, 'Non, non,' pointing at the same time to one Spanish and four French Sail of the Line then passing to windward. As, for the want to masts, the *Santisima Trinidad* was settling fast to windward of the two fleets, and he had only a boat's crew with him, Lieutenant Smith quitted the Spanish Ship (the crew of which, singularly enough, permitted him to do so), and returned on board the *Africa*.

"The *Santisima Trinidad* remained without a prize-crew until

5 h. 30m. p.m.; when the *Prince*, by signal, boarded and took her in tow. The *Trinidad*'s loss, although we are unable to particularize it, is described to have been, and no doubt was, extremely severe: she had been exposed to the raking fire, in succession, of four Ships, the *Victory* (distantly and partially), *Neptune*, *Leviathan*, and *Conqueror*; and her hull, in consequence, had been dreadfully shattered, especially about the stern and quarters.

"Before we proceed in our relation of the further part which the *Leviathan* took in the Action, we will briefly state what damages and loss were sustained by the *Neptune*, *Conqueror*, and *Bucentaure*. The *Neptune*'s masts were all more or less wounded, but not dangerously so, and her standing and running rigging somewhat damaged; she had received nine shot between wind and water, and had incurred a loss of 10 seaman killed, her captain's clerk, 30 seamen, and three marines wounded.

"The *Conqueror* had her mizen topmast and main topgallant-mast shot away, her fore and main masts badly wounded, and her rigging of every sort much cut: several shot had also struck her on the larboard side between wind and water. The loss on the part of the *Conqueror*, up to the period of the *Bucentaure*'s surrender (her further loss will be shown presently), was comparatively trifling: she had one seaman killed, and one lieutenant of marines (Thomas Wearing), one lieutenant of the Russian Navy (Philip Mendel), and seven seamen wounded. The damages of the *Bucentaure* in her masts have already been described: her hull also was much cut up; and her loss in killed and wounded, according to the verbal report of her few surviving Officers, amounted to upwards of 400 Officers and men, including among the slightly wounded Admiral Ville-neuve and his Captain.

"Leaving the *Santisima Trinidad* to the care of the English *Neptune*, the *Leviathan* stood on towards the French *Neptune*, then amusing herself in the manner we have related, with now a second French Ship, the *Fougueux*, joined to the *Téméraire*. As the *Leviathan* approached, and before she was in a position to fire a shot, the *Neptune*, at whom the *Téméraire* had just brought some of her foremost guns to bear, wore round, and, in going off before the wind, at least enabled the former to identify, by the name on her stern, the French Ship that chose to fly, the moment an antagonist appeared, who was in a condition to oppose her, although, evidently, not of force enough to maintain the combat with any prospect of success.

"Disappointed here, Captain Bayntun hauled up the larboard tack, and presently observed that all the Ships of the Combined van ahead of the *Santisima Trinidad*, were tacking or wearing, as if to double upon the headmost Ships of the British weather column, and place them betwixt two fires. Sure of finding an opponent among those; and such is the confidence inspired among the Ships of a British Fleet, as sure that, if likely to be overmatched, some friend or other would hasten to her rescue, the *Leviathan* stood on to the north-east.

"A Spanish 74, the *San Augustin*, who was steering south-east, appeared to be desirous to measure her strength with the British 74; and at about 3 p.m., when within 100 yards, put her helm hard a-starboard, in the hope to be able to rake the *Leviathan* ahead. To frustrate a manœuvre so likely to be serious in its effects, the *Leviathan* put her helm hard a-port, and, having fresher way than the *San Augustin*, felt its influence more quickly. The consequence was, that the guns of the British ship were brought to bear before those of her antagonist: and, loaded with three shot each, were discharged, with admirable precision, and at the distance of less than fifty yards, into the starboard quarter of the *San Augustin*. Down went, in an instant, the Spanish Ship's mizenmast, and with it her colours, and feeble was the return she bestowed.

"The probability now was, that, as the *Leviathan* kept forging a-head, and could not, on account of the previously damaged state of her rigging, back her sails, the *San Augustin* would be able to wear under her stern. To prevent this, the *Leviathan*, putting her helm a-starboard, ran on board the *San Augustin*, in such a way, that the latter's jib-boom entangled itself in the former's larboard main rigging, thereby exposing the *San Augustin*'s upper deck to the poop-carronades and marines of the *Leviathan*. A smart and well-directed fire soon drove the Spaniards below; and Lieutenant John Baldwin, third of the *Leviathan*, at the head of a party of seamen and marines, leaped on board the *San Augustin* and carried her without further opposition. The British 74, with her stream-cable, then lashed the prize to herself. Scarcely had the *Leviathan* effected this, ere the *Intrépide*, another fresh Ship from the Combined van, came crowding up, and, after raking the *Leviathan* ahead, ranged along her starboard side; but waited only to exchange a passing fire, as the *Africa* and one or two other British Ships were fast approaching to the assistance of their friend.

"In this spirited, and, for its undisturbed occurrence in a general action, rather singular combat, the *Leviathan*'s damages and loss, although we are not enabled to exhibit them separately, were, it is certain, of trifling amount. Including what she had previously sustained, the *Leviathan* had the main piece of her head shot through, all three masts and bowsprit, and most of her lower and topsail yards wounded, her mizentopsail yard shot away, and a great part of her rigging cut to pieces. She received eight shot between wind and water, and had one long 32 and one long 18 pounder, and one 18-pounder carronade, completely disabled. Her loss amounted to two seamen and two marines killed, one midshipman (J. W. Watson), 17 seamen, and four marines wounded. Besides the loss of her mizenmast, the *San Augustin* had her remaining masts injured, and her hull struck in several places, particularly near the starboard quarter: her loss was represented by her Officers to have amounted to 160 in killed and wounded, including among the latter her Captain, Don Felipe Xado Cagigal.

Being, except the *Leviathan*, the nearest British ship to the *Intrépide*, the *Africa* was the first that brought the latter to action. This, at about 3 h. 20 m. p.m., the *Africa* most gallantly did, and, in spite of her decided inferiority of force, maintained the contest for nearly three quarters of an hour; when the *Orion* came up, and opened a fire upon the *Intrépide*'s starboard quarter. The *Orion* then wore round the French Ship's stern, and, bringing to on the lee bow of the latter, between her and the *Africa*, whose fire, without any disparagement to her, was nearly silenced, maintained so heavy and well-directed a cannonade, that in less than a quarter of an hour the main and mizen masts of the *Intrépide*, already injured by the *Africa*'s fire, fell over his side. The proximity of the *Conqueror*, and the approach of the *Ajax* and *Agamemnon*, left to the *Intrépide* no alternative but to strike her colours. This the French Ship did at 5 p.m., having been greatly damaged in hull as well as masts, and incurred a loss, according to the representation of her Officers, of nearly 200 in killed and wounded.

"The *Africa* had her maintopsail yard shot away, and her bowsprit and three lower masts so badly wounded that none of the latter could afterwards staud. Her remaining masts and yards were also more or less injured; her rigging and sails cut to pieces; and her hull, besides its other serious damage, had received several shot between wind and water. Her loss amounted to twelve seamen and six marines killed; one lieutenant (Matthew Hay), one captain of marines (James Fynmore), two master's mates (Henry West and Abraham Turner), three midshipmen (Frederick White, Philip J. Elmhurst, and John P. Bailey), thirty seamen, and seven marines wounded; a loss which, considering that her complement was only 490 men and boys, and that Captain Digby had voluntarily engaged so superior a force, proves that although but a 64, the *Africa* had performed as gallant a part as any Ship in the British Line. The *Orion*, who came so opportunely to the aid of the *Africa*, had her foremast wounded, and her maintopsail yard and main topgallant-mast shot away. The loss on board the *Orion*, however, amounted to only one seaman killed, and two midshipmen (Charles Tause and Charles P. Cable, both slightly), seventeen seamen, and four marines wounded.

"It was at about 2h. 30m. p.m. that the whole of the Franco-Spanish van, except the *Santisima Trinidad*, who lay dismasted abreast and to leeward of the *Bucentaure*, equally a wreck and either a prize or in the act of becoming one, began to put about, some by staying, others by wearing, in obedience to a signal made by the Commander-in-Chief at 1h. 50m. p.m. to the following purport: "The French Fleet, engaging to windward or to leeward, orders the Ships which from their present position are not engaging, to take such a position as will bring them more quickly into action." 'L'armée navale Française, combattant au vent ou sous le vent, ordre aux vaisseaux qui, par leur position actuelle, ne combattant pas, d'en prendre une quelconque, qui les reporte le plus promptement possible au feu.' It appears that five minutes before, Rear-Admiral Dumanoir had signalled the Commander-in-Chief, that the van had no enemy to contend with.

"According to the Admiral's previous instructions to his Captains, the above signal was to be considered as casting a stigma upon those to whom it was addressed. At all events no immediate attempt was made by the generality of the Ships to comply with the signal, and those that were the most prompt in obeying it were baffled by the calm state of the weather. The *Formidable*, and one or two of the other Ships, had to employ their boats to tow themselves round. Hence the manœuvre was slow, partial, and imperfect. When the ten Ships did at length get on the starboard tack, five (four French and one Spanish), under Rear-Admiral Dumanoir, hauled their wind, and the remaining five kept away, as if to join Admiral Gravina, then to leeward of the rear, in the act of making off.

"It was in the height of all this confusion in the Combined van, that the *Britannia*, *Agamemnon*, *Orion*, and *Ajax* got inter-mingled among the French and Spanish Ships, which had wore and edged away in the manner related. The *Britannia* appears to have been engaged, a short time, with the *San Francisco de Asis*, and subsequently with the *Rayo* three-decker. It was considered on board the *Britannia*, that the Ship they engaged, after the *San Francisco de Asis*, was the French *Neptune*, with 'a tier of guns on her gangway.' Owing to the obscurity occasioned by the smoke, and to the want of wind to blow out the flags, a mistake respecting the colours might easily be made; and certainly the *Neptune* had no guns on her gangway, but was a regular 80, similar to the *Bucentaure*.

"The *Agamemnon* and *Ajax* also exchanged a few broadsides with some of the Ships that had bore up; and the *Orion*, as already stated, was the first, after the *Africa*, that became closely engaged with the *Intrépide*. The latter and the *San Augustin* were the only ships of the five, that seemed to have any other object in view than a retreat. The *San Francisco de Asis* might reasonably have declined closing with the *Britannia*; but the *Héros* appears to have had no three-decker opposed to her, although she probably was one of the Ships that raked the British *Neptune*, after the latter had silenced the *Santisima Trinidad*. The *Héros* had her Captain killed, but sustained no other loss of consequence, and very slight damage. What loss the *Rayo* suffered is not known; but she did undoubtedly incur a loss, and had her masts and rigging tolerably wounded and cut up.

"The *Britannia*, with some slight damage to her masts and still less to her hull, had one lieutenant (Francis Roskruge), eight seamen, and one marine killed; her master (Stephen Trounce), one midshipman (William Grant), thirty-three seamen, and seven marines wounded. The *Ajax* was very slightly damaged, and had only two seamen killed and nine wounded. The principal damage sustained by the *Agamemnon* was a large hole below the quarter, probably from a shot fired by one of M. Dumanoir's Ships. In consequence of this the Ship made four feet water an hour: her loss consisted of only two seamen killed and eight wounded.

"The five French and Spanish Ships which hauled to the wind, after wearing in the manner already stated, were the *Formidable*, commanded by Rear-Admiral Dumanoir, *Duguay-Trouin*, *Mont-Blanc*, *Scipion*, and *Neptuno*. The very British Ships that, from their disabled state, were calculated to offer the least opposition, having little or no sail to force them to leeward, lay nearest to the track of M. Dumanoir's squadron. Among those the *Victory*, *Téméraire*, and *Royal Sovereign* were the most exposed. The *Victory*, with her mizen topmast gone, lay with her head to the northward, having the *Bucentaure*, a mere hulk, a point or two on her weather bow, two or three ships' lengths off, and the *Santisima Trinidad*, another hulk, at a somewhat greater distance on her lee bow. At about three quarters of a mile astern of the *Victory*, or rather upon her weather quarter, lay the *Téméraire* with her two prizes. The head of the *Téméraire*, and of the *Redoutable* also, whose main-mast still held her fast to the former, was pointed to the southward; and her crew were busied in booming off the *Fougueux* from her starboard side, to be ready to salute the French Ships as they passed. The *Royal Sovereign*, with only her foremast standing, lay a short distance astern and to leeward of the *Téméraire*, in the act of being towed clear of her dismasted prize, the *Santa Ana*, by the *Euryalus* frigate.

"Among the first shots fired by M. Dumanoir's Ships, after

they had put about, was one that killed two of the *Conqueror*'s Lieutenants. The manner in which this fatal accident happened, is as extraordinary as it was distressing. Lieutenant William M. St. George, third of the ship, while passing Lieutenant Robert Lloyd, who was first, good-humouredly tapped him on the shoulder, and gave him joy of his approaching epaulet as a Commander. Just as Lieutenant St. George, having moved on a step or two and turned his face round, was in the act of smiling on his friend, a cannon-shot took off the head of the latter, and struck the former senseless on the deck.

"In passing the *Victory*, M. Dumanoir's Squadron, having kept away a little for the purpose, exchanged a few distant and ineffectual shot with her. By the time the van Ship, the *Formidable*, had arrived abreast of the *Téméraire*, the latter had succeeded in clearing her starboard broadside of the *Fougueux*, who now lay athwart the *Téméraire*'s stern, with her head to the eastward, and consequently with her stern exposed to the raking fire of the enemy. One or two broadsides were exchanged between the *Téméraire* and the Ships to windward; and the fire from the latter cut away the main and mizen masts of the *Fougueux*, and killed and wounded some of her people. One shot also shattered the leg of a Midshipman belonging to the *Téméraire*, who had been sent on board the *Redoutable* to assist Lieutenant Wallace, and who died the same evening, after having undergone amputation by the French surgeon.

"A great deal of odium has been cast by the English journals, and even by grave historical works, upon Rear-Admiral Dumanoir, for having fired upon the French and Spanish prizes, in his passage to windward of the Fleets. Admitting the inutility of the act to be an argument (its 'barbarity' is none, because the prisoners ought to have been stationed below) against the propriety of its adoption, it surely was the duty of the French Admiral to fire at, and injure as much as he could, the different British Ships within the reach of his guns. In his letter to the Editor of the Gibraltar Chronicle, whose gross inaccuracy on another point we shall soon have to expose, M. Dumanoir positively denies that he intentionally fired at the prizes; but, how, let us ask, was it possible for the shot to pass clear of them, when, in some instances, they lay within less than their own length of, and in others, absolutely masked, the Ships that had captured them?

"The hauling to windward of M. Dumanoir afforded to the *Minotaur* and *Spartiate* an opportunity which, as the two rearmost Ships of the weather column, they would otherwise have sought in vain. At about 3h. 10m. p.m., having hauled close on the larboard tack, the *Minotaur* and *Spartiate* lay to with their main topsails to the masts, and exchanged broadsides in passing with the *Formidable, Duguay-Trouin, Mont-Blanc*, and *Scipion*, and as the *Neptuno* was considerably astern, succeeded in cutting her off. At 4 p.m. the two British 74s wore, and got close alongside of the Spanish 80; who, after defending herself in the most gallant manner, surrendered at about 5h. 10m. P.M. with the loss of her mizenmast and fore and main topmasts, and with, no doubt, a serious loss of men, although it has not been recorded. Having been captured directly to windward of the *Téméraire* and her two prizes, the *Neptuno* drifted upon and fell on board the former. This gave rise to the extraordinary mistake contained in Lord Collingwood's official despatch, representing that the *Téméraire* had been boarded by a French Ship on one side and a Spaniard on the other.

"The *Minotaur* had her foretopsail yard shot away; and both she and the *Spartiate* had their masts, yards, and rigging in general a good deal damaged. The *Minotaur* had three seamen killed, her boatswain (James Robinson), one midshipman (John Samuel Smith), seventeen seamen, and three marines wounded; and the *Spartiate* had also three seamen killed, and her boatswain (John Clarke), two midshipmen (Henry Bellairs and Edward Knapman), sixteen seamen, and one marine wounded. A great proportion of the loss suffered by these two Ships was no doubt inflicted by the *Neptuno*; who as the *Intrépide* was the last French, was herself the last Spanish Ship that struck to the British on this eventful day. We have still some arrears to bring up in the lee column, a task we shall hasten to execute.

"It was about 2 p.m., when the *Dreadnought* got into action with the *San Juan Nepomuceno*, then surrounded by the *Principe de Asturias, San Justo*, and a French 80 gun Ship, the *Indomptable*. In about 15 minutes the *Dreadnought* ran on board of and captured the *San Juan*; who had previously been engaged by the *Tonnant*, *Bellerophon*, *Defiance*, and some other Ships, and was nearly in a defenceless state. Without, as it would appear, staying to take possession of the Spanish 74, the *Dreadnought* pursued and fired at the Spanish three-decker, but, after the exchange of two or three broadsides, a shot from one of which struck off the left arm of Admiral Gravina, the *Principe de Asturias* made sail and effected her escape.

"The *Dreadnought* had her masts cut with shot, but none carried away: her loss amounted to six seamen and one marine killed; and one lieutenant (James L. Lloyd), two midshipmen (Andrew M'Culloch and James Sabbin), nineteen seamen, and four marines wounded. Besides being dismasted, the *San Juan Nepomuceno* was much shattered in her hull, and sustained a loss, as represented, of nearly 300 in killed and wounded, including among the mortally wounded her gallant Commander.

"Having yawed to starboard to allow the *Dreadnought* to pass on to the Spanish three-decker, then the rearmost Enemy's Ship by two, the *Polyphemus* attempted to haul up again; but, finding the English *Swiftsure* close upon her larboard quarter, she was obliged to wait until the latter passed ahead. It was at about 3h. 25m. p.m. that the English *Swiftsure*, having passed the *Belleisle*'s stern, opened her fire upon the French *Achille*; who, passing along the larboard beam of the *Belleisle*, edged away to the south-east, followed and engaged by the former. The *Swiftsure* presently succeeded in crossing her opponent's stern and in getting to leeward of her; when the *Polyphemus*, who had received a heavy fire from the French *Neptune*, in passing between the latter and the *Belleisle*, advanced on the French *Achille*'s weather quarter. In about forty minutes after the *Swiftsure* had commenced the Action with the *Achille*, the latter, having had her mizenmast and fore yard shot away, and having also caught fire in the fore top, ceased engaging, and, as it appeared to the *Polyphemus*, waved a Union jack at her starboard cathead. The *Polyphemus* then stood away to assist the *Defence* in engaging the *San Ildefonso*, but who struck before the *Polyphemus* got up; and the *Prince* three-decker bore down between the French *Achille* and English *Swiftsure*, just as the latter, considering the *Achille* a beaten Ship, was hauling off to seek a more worthy opponent. But the business of the day, at this end of the line at least, was now nearly over.

"The *Swiftsure* had her mizen topmast shot away, and mizenmast badly wounded, and lost seven seamen and two marines killed, and one midshipman (Alexander Bell Handcock), six seamen, and one marine wounded. The *Polyphemus* had her main and main topmasts badly wounded, her spanker-boom cut through, and one lowerdeck gun disabled, but escaped with the slight loss of two men killed and four wounded.

"While the *Revenge* was attempting to pass through the enemy's line, and just as she had put her helm a-port, to place herself athwart the hawse of the *Aigle*, the latter's jib-boom caught the mizen topsail of the former: and, before the two Ships got clear, the *Revenge* was enabled to pour into the *Aigle*'s bows two deliberate broadsides. The *Revenge* then stood on, and, while hauling up on the larboard tack, received a tremendous fire into her lee quarter from the *Principe de Asturias*; who, in conjunction with three two-deckers, probably the *Neptune*, *Indomptable*, and *San Justo*, nearly fresh Ships from the centre, continued cannonading the *Revenge*, until the *Dreadnought* and *Thunderer* came up and engaged the Spanish three-decker. The latter, who, it appears, would suffer no British Ship to get to leeward of her, soon afterwards bore away, along with the most efficient of the Ships in her company.

"The exposed situation of the *Revenge* had occasioned her damages and loss of men to be very severe. Her bowsprit, three lower masts, main topmast, and gaff were badly wounded: she had received nine shot below the copper; her stern, transoms, and timbers, and several beams, knees, riders, and iron standards, were very much wounded, and so was her hull generally. She had several chain-plates shot away, several of her lower deck ports destroyed, and three of her guns dismounted. With respect to the loss, the *Revenge* had two midshipmen (Thomas Grier and Edward F. Brooks), eighteen seamen; and eight marines killed, and her captain, master (Luke Brokenshaw), one lieutenant (John Berry), one captain of marines (Peter Lily), thirty-eight seamen, and nine marines wounded.

"At about 2h. 30m. p.m. the *Defence* commenced firing at the *Berwick*; who, in less than half an hour, hauled off and was engaged as already stated, by the *Achille*. The *Defence*, shortly afterwards, began engaging the *San Ildefonso*, and, at the end of an hour's action, compelled the Spanish Ship to strike. The *Defence* had her mainmast shot through and wounded in several places, her gaff cut in two, and her lower and topmast rigging much injured; she had also, several hanging knees and chain-plates carried away, one shothole through the knee of the head, and five between wind and water. Her loss amounted to four seamen and three marines killed, and twenty-three seamen and six marines wounded. The *San Ildefonso*, having been engaged by one or two other British Ships before the *Defence* arrived up, had suffered greatly in masts, rigging and hull, and lost a full third of her crew in killed and wounded.

"It was about 3 p.m. when, having bore up to assist the *Revenge*, the *Thunderer* wore athwart the hawse of the *Principe de Asturias*, and having raked her distantly, brought to on the starboard tack. In about five minutes the French *Neptune* came to the assistance of the Spanish three-decker (into whom the *Dreadnought* was now firing), and engaged the *Thunderer* for a short time; when these two ships, with most of the others near them, bore up and made off. The *Thunderer*'s main and mizen masts and bowsprit had a shot in each, but otherwise her damages were not material. Her loss amounted to two seamen and two marines killed, and one master's mate (John Snell), one midshipman (Alexander Galloway), nine seamen, and one marine wounded. The *Principe de Asturias*, at the time she bore up to escape, had been partially engaged by the *Revenge* and *Defiance*, and had received two broadsides from the *Prince*, in addition to the contest she had previously maintained with the *Dreadnought* and other British Ships: hence her damages and loss were comparatively severe. None of the Spanish three-decker's masts appear to have been shot away, but that all were more or less damaged may be inferred from the fact, that her main and mizen masts were unable to withstand the gale that ensued. The loss sustained by the *Principe de Asturias* amounted to a lieutenant and 40 men killed, and 107 men badly wounded, including Admiral Gravina himself, as already mentioned, in the left arm (which was afterwards amputated, but too late to save his life), and some other officers.

"Finding her rigging and sails too much cut to enable her to follow the *Principe de Asturias*, the *Defiance* stood for the *Aigle*, whose crippled state had prevented her from making sail. At about 3 p.m. the *Defiance* ran alongside of the *Aigle*, lashed the latter to herself, boarded her with little resistance, got possession of the poop and quarter-deck, hauled down the French colours, and hoisted the English in their stead; when, suddenly, so destructive a fire of musketry was opened upon the boarders from the forecastle, waist and tops of the *Aigle*, that the British, before they had been well five minutes in possession of their prize, were glad to quit her and escape back to their Ship.

"As soon as the lashings were cut loose, the *Defiance* sheered off to a half-pistol-shot distance, and there kept up so well-directed a cannonade that, in less than twenty-five minutes, the *Aigle*, the fire from whose great guns had also been nobly maintained, called for quarter, and was presently taken quiet possession of. The *Defiance* afterwards took possession of the *San Juan Nepomuceno*; which Ship, besides her crippled state from the previous attacks she had sustained, had already surrendered to the *Dreadnought*. On the coming up, therefore, of the latter Ship, Captain Durham sent the *San Juan*'s Captain and Officers to her.

"The *Defiance* had her bowsprit and fore and main masts shot through in the centre of each, also her mizenmast, three topmasts, jib and driver booms, and gaff wounded: her rigging and sails were likewise much cut, and her hull struck with shot in several places. She had one lieutenant (Thomas Simens), her boatswain (William Forster), one midshipman (James Williamson), eight seamen, six marines killed, and her captain (slightly), two master's mates (James Spratt and Robert Browne), two midshipmen (John Hodge and Edmund Andrew Chapman), thirty-nine seamen and nine marines wounded. The *Aigle*, although her principal masts do not appear to have been shot away, had received several shot through them, and was otherwise much disabled. Her hull was pierced in every direction, and her starboard quarter nearly beaten in. The *Aigle* had been successively engaged by six or seven British Ships, and had conducted herself in the most gallant manner. Her loss amounted to about 270 in killed and wounded, including several of her Officers.

"Of the nineteen Ships composing the Combined Rear, eleven have been captured, and seven have quitted the line and run to leeward; thus leaving one Ship only, the French *Achille*, whose fate remains to be shown. This Ship, in her successive encounters with the English *Achille*, *Belleisle*, *Swiftsure*, and *Polyphemus*, had lost her mizenmast, maintopmast, and foreyard, and having since, owing in all probability to her swivels or musketry there, caught fire in her fore top, was without the means of extinguishing the flames on account of the destruction of her engine by the Enemy's shot. The only alternative left was to cut away the mast. At 4h. 30m. p.m., while the crew were preparing to do this, so that it might fall clear of the Ship, a broadside from the *Prince* cut the mast in two at about its centre; and the wreck, with its flaming top, fell directly upon the boats in the waist. These soon caught fire, and so in succession did the decks below.

"After the discharge of one or two broadsides, the *Prince* discovered the accident that had befallen her antagonist, and, wearing, hove to, and in company with the *Swiftsure*, sent her boats to save as many as possible of the French *Achille*'s crew: in which laudable attempt, soon afterwards, the *Pickle Schooner* and *Entreprenante Cutter* zealously employed themselves. This was a dangerous service, on account of the French Ship's guns, when heated, discharging their contents. The *Swiftsure*'s boats had two or three men killed and wounded in consequence. The *Achille* had already suffered a heavy loss in killed and wounded, including among the latter her Captain and the principal part of her Officers; leaving not a doubt, that the Ship had most gallantly conducted herself throughout the engagement.

"It was about 5h. 45m. p.m., that the *Achille* exploded, and with her perished her then Commanding Officer, Enseigne de vaisseau Charles-Alexandre Cauchard, and a great portion of her crew. It may be, as the French say, that the *Achille* at this time had her colours flying; but the Ship certainly had, two hours before, made signs of submission, and was, in consequence, spared by the British Ship (*Polyphemus*) then in action with her. The damages of the *Prince* consisted of a shot in her bowsprit, three shots in her foremast, and the same in her mizenmast: but she experienced the singular good fortune, as a Ship of this Fleet, not to have a man of her crew injured.

"We have now, according to the best information in our power, gone through the details of each British Ship's proceedings in the Battle of Trafalgar. Should justice not have been done to the exertions of any particular Ship on this glorious occasion, we hope it will be attributed, rather to the confused manner in which the attack, the latter part of it especially, was carried on, than to any deficiency of research in us. How far the published accounts on either side are calculated to guide the historian, has already in part appeared, and will be more fully shown when some of those accounts pass under review. As to the accounts furnished exclusively for this work by individuals present in the battle, much as we, and through us the public, owe to them, they are, in many instances, imperfect, obscure, and even contradictory. Nor can it be wondered at, considering how each Officer's attention must have been absorbed in the immediate duties of his station; and how few yards, beyond the side of his own Ship, the smoke of so many combatants would permit him to see.

"According to the official returns the aggregate loss in killed and wounded on the part of the British amounted to 1690; of which amount about six-sevenths, or 1452, fell to the share of fourteen out of the twenty-seven Ships in the Fleet. With few exceptions, the Ships so suffering were in the van of their respective columns. This was a consequence of the peculiar mode of attack adopted by Lord Nelson, coupled with the fall of the breeze after the firing had begun. For instance, the leading Ships of each column as they approached within gun-shot of the Combined Fleet, were exposed to the deliberate and uninterrupted fire of seven or eight Ships drawn up in a line a-head, without being able, until nearly on board of them, to bring a gun to bear in return. The moment the former did begin to engage, the French and Spanish Ships closed for mutual support; whereby the latter not only prevented each other from firing at such of the British Ships as were still bearing down, but became too seriously occupied with close antagonists, to bestow much attention upon distant ones.

APPENDIX II

Naval Strategy and Tactics at the time of Trafalgar by Admiral Sir Cyprian Bridge G.C.B.

Read to the Institution of Naval Architects, July 19th 1905

In taking account of the conditions of the Trafalgar epoch we have to note two distinct but, of course, closely related matters. These are the strategic plan of the enemy and the strategic plan adopted to meet it by the British. The former of these was described in the House of Commons by William Pitt at the beginning of the war in words which may be used without change at the present time. On May 16, 1803, the war, which had been interrupted by the unstable Peace of Amiens, was definitely resumed. The struggle was now to be a war, not so much between the United Kingdom and the French nation as between the United Kingdom and the great Napoleon wielding more than the resources of France alone. Speaking a week after the declaration of war, Pitt said that any expectation of success which the enemy might have must be based on the supposition that he could break the spirit or weaken the determination of the country by harassing us with the perpetual apprehension of descents on our coasts; or else that our resources could be impaired and our credit undermined by the effects of an expensive and protracted war. More briefly stated, the hostile plan was to invade the United

Kingdom, ruin our maritime trade, and expel us from our over-sea possessions, especially in the East, from which it was supposed our wealth was chiefly derived. The plan was comprehensive, but not easily concealed. What we had to do was to prevent the invasion of the United Kingdom and defend our trade and our outlying territories. As not one of the hostile objects could be attained except by making a maritime expedition of some kind, that is to say, by an expedition which had to cross restricted or extensive areas of *water*, it necessarily followed that our most effective method of defence was the keeping open of our sea communications. It became necessary for us to make such arrangements that the maritime paths by which a hostile expedition could approach our home-coasts, or hostile cruisers molest our sea-borne trade, or hostile squadrons move to the attack of our trans-marine dependencies – that all these paths should be so defended by our Navy that either the enemy would not venture to traverse them or, if he did, that he could be driven off.

Short as it is, time at my disposal permits me to give a few details. It was fully recognized that defence of the United Kingdom against invasion could not be secured by naval means alone. As in the times of Queen Elizabeth, so in those of George III, no seaman of reputation contended that a sufficient land force could be dispensed with. Our ablest seamen always held that small hostile expeditions could be prepared in secret and might be able to slip through the most complete lines of defence that we could hope to maintain. It was not discovered or alleged till the twentieth century that the crew of a dinghy could not land in this country in the face of the Navy. Therefore an essential feature of our defensive strategy was the provision of land forces in such numbers that an invader would have no chance of succeeding except he came in strength so great that his preparations could not be concealed and his expedition could not cross the water unseen.

As our Mercantile Marine was to be found in nearly every sea, though in greater accumulation in some areas than in others, its defence against the assaults of an enemy could only be ensured by the virtual ubiquity of our cruising force. This, of course, involved the necessity of employing a large number of cruisers, and of arranging the distribution of them in accordance with the relative amount and value of the traffic to be protected from molestation in different parts of the ocean. It may be mentioned here that the term "cruiser," at the time with which we are dealing, was not limited to frigates and smaller classes of vessel. It included also ships of the line, it being the old belief of the British Navy, justified by the experience of the many campaigns and consecrated by the approval of our greatest admirals, that the value of a ship of war was directly proportionate to her capacity for cruising and keeping the sea. If the ocean paths used by our merchant ships – the trade routes or sea communications of the United Kingdom with friendly or neutral markets and areas of production – could be kept open by our Navy, that is, made so secure that our trade could traverse them with so little risk of molestation that it could continue to be carried on, it resulted as a matter of course that no sustained attack could be made on our outlying territory. Where this was possible it was where we had failed to keep open the route or line of communications, in which case the particular trade following it was, at least temporarily, destroyed, and the territory to which the route led was either cut off or seized. Naturally, when this was perceived, efforts were made to reopen and keep open the endangered or interrupted communication line.

Napoleon, notwithstanding his super-eminent genius, made some extraordinary mistakes about warfare on the sea. The explanation of this has been given by a highly distinguished French admiral. The Great Emperor, he says, was wanting in exact appreciation of the difficulties of naval operations. He never understood that the naval officer – alone of all men in the world—must be master of two distinct professions. The naval officer must be as completely a seaman as an officer in any mercantile marine; and, in addition to this, he must be as accomplished in the use of the material of war entrusted to his charge as the members of any armed force in the world. The Emperor's plan for the invasion of the United Kingdom was conceived on a grand scale. A great army, eventually 130,000 strong, was collected on the coast of North-Eastern France, with its headquarters at Boulogne. The numerical strength of this army is worth attention. By far the larger part of it was to have made the first descent on our territory; the remainder was to be a reserve to follow as quickly as possible. It has been doubted if Napoleon really meant to invade this country, the suggestion being that his collection of an army on the shores of the Straits of Dover and the English Channel was merely a "blind" to cover another intended movement. The overwhelming weight of authoritative opinion is in favour of the view that the project of invasion was real. It is highly significant that he considered so large a number of troops necessary. It could not have been governed by any estimate of the naval obstruction to be encountered during the sea passage of the expedition, but only by the amount of the land force likely to be met if the disembarkation on our shores could be effected. The numerical strength in troops which Napoleon thought necessary compelled him to make preparations on so great a scale that concealment became quite impossible. Consequently an important part of his plan was disclosed to us betimes, and the threatened locality indicated to us within comparatively narrow limits of precision.

Notwithstanding his failure to appreciate all the difficulties of naval warfare, the Great Emperor had grasped one of its leading principles. Before the Peace of Amiens, indeed before his campaign in Egypt, and even his imposing triumphs in Italy, he had seen that the invasion of the United Kingdom was impracticable without first obtaining the command of the sea. His strategic plan, therefore, included arrangements to secure this. The details of the plan were changed from time to time as conditions altered; but the main object was adhered to until the final abandonment of the whole scheme under pressure of circumstances as embodied in Nelson and his victorious brothers-in-arms. The gunboats, transport boats, and other small craft, which to the number of many hundreds filled the ports of North-Eastern France and the Netherlands, were not the only naval components of the expedition. Fleets of line-of-battle ships were essential parts of it, and on their effective action the success of the scheme was largely made to depend. This feature remained unaltered in principle when, less than twelve months before Trafalgar, Spain took part in the war as Napoleon's ally, and brought him a great reinforcement of ships and important assistance in money.

We should not fail to notice that, before he considered himself strong enough to undertake the invasion of the United Kingdom, Napoleon found it necessary to have at his disposal the resources of other countries besides France, notwithstanding that by herself France had a population more than 60 per cent greater than that of England. By the alliance with Spain he had added largely to the resources on which he could draw. Moreover, his strategic position was geographically much improved. With the exception of that of Portugal, the coast of Western Continental Europe, from the Texel to Leghorn, and somewhat later to Taranto also, was united in hostility to us. This complicated the strategic problem which the British Navy had to solve, as it increased the number of points to be watched; and it facilitated the junction of Napoleon's Mediterranean naval forces with those assembled in his Atlantic ports by supplying him with allied ports of refuge and refit on Spanish territory; such as Cartagena or Cadiz; between Toulon and the Bay of Biscay. Napoleon, therefore, enforced upon us by the most convincing of all arguments the necessity of maintaining the British Navy at the "two-power standard" at least. The lesson had been taught us long before by Philip II, who did not venture on an attempt at invading this country till he was master of the resources of the whole Iberian peninsula as well as of those of the Spanish dominions in Italy, in the Burgundian heritage, and in the distant regions across the Atlantic Ocean.

At several ports on the long stretch of coast of which he was now the master, Napoleon equipped fleets that were to unite and win for him the command of the sea during a period long enough to permit the unobstructed passage of his invading army across the water which separated the starting points of his expedition from the United Kingdom. Command of the sea to be won by a powerful naval combination was thus an essential element in Napoleon's strategy in the time of Trafalgar. It was not in deciding what was essential that this soldier of stupendous ability erred: it was in choosing the method of gaining the essential that he went wrong. The British strategy adopted in opposition to that of Napoleon was based on the acquisition and preservation of the command of the sea. Formulated and carried into effect by seamen, it differed in some important features from his. We may leave out of sight for the moment the special arrangements made in the English Channel to oppose the movements of Napoleon's flotillas of gunboats, transport boats, amid other small craft. The British strategy at the time of Trafalgar, as far as it was concerned with opposition to Napoleon's sea-going fleets, may be succinctly described as stationing off each of the ports in which the enemy's forces were lying a fleet or squadron of suitable strength. Though some of our admirals, notably Nelson himself, objected to the application of the term "blockade" to their plans, the hostile ships were to this extent blockaded, that if they should come out they would find outside their port a British force sufficient to drive them in again or even to defeat them thoroughly and destroy them, beating them and thus having done with them, and not simply shutting them up in harbour, was what was desired by our admirals. This necessitated a close watch on the hostile ports; and how consistently that was maintained let the history of Cornwallis' command off Brest and of Nelson's off Toulon suffice to tell us.

The junction of two or more of Napoleon's fleets would have ensured over almost any single British fleet a numerical superiority that would have rendered the defeat or retirement of the latter almost certain. To meet this condition the British strategy contemplated the falling back, if necessary, of one of our detachments on another, which might be carried further, and junction with a third detachment be effected. By this step we should preserve, if not a numerical superiority over the enemy, at least so near an equality of force as to render his defeat probable and his serious maltreatment, even if undefeated, a certainty. The strategic problem before our Navy was, however, not quite so easy as this might make it seem. The enemy's concentration might be attempted either towards Brest or towards Toulon. In the latter case, a superior force might fall upon our Mediterranean fleet before our watching ships in the Atlantic could discover the escape of the enemy's ships from the Atlantic port or could follow and come up with them. Against the probability of this was to be set the reluctance of Napoleon to carry out an eccentric operation which a concentration off Toulon would necessitate, when the essence of his scheme was to concentrate in a position from which he could obtain naval control of the English Channel.

After the addition of the Spanish Navy to his own, Napoleon to some extent modified his strategic arrangements. The essential feature of the scheme remained unaltered. It was to effect the junction of the different parts of his naval force and thereupon to dominate the situation, by evading the several British fleets or detachments which were watching his. Before Spain joined him in the war his intention was that his escaping fleets should go out into the Atlantic, behind the backs, as it were, of the British ships, and then make for the English Channel. When he had the aid of Spain the point of junction was to be in the West Indies.

The remarkable thing about this was the evident belief that the command of the sea might be won without fighting for it; won, too, from the British Navy which was ready, and indeed wished to fight. We now see that Napoleon's naval strategy in the time of Trafalgar, whilst it aimed at gaining command of the sea, was based on what has been called evasion. The fundamental principle of the British naval strategy of that time was quite different. So far from thinking that the contest could be settled without one or more battles, the British admirals, though nominally blockading his ports, gave the enemy every facility for coming out in order that they might be able to bring him to action. Napoleon, on the contrary, declared that a battle would be useless, and distinctly ordered his officers not to fight one. Could it be that, when pitted against admirals whose accurate conception of the conditions of naval warfare had been over and over again tested during the hostilities ended by the Peace of Amiens, Napoleon still trusted to the efficacy of methods which had proved so successful when he was out-maneuvering and intimidating the generals who opposed him in North Italy? We can only explain his attitude in the campaign of Trafalgar by attributing to him an expectation that the British seamen of his day, tried as they had been in the fire of many years of war, would succumb to his methods as readily as the military formalists of Central Europe. Napoleon had at his disposal between 70 and 80 French, Dutch, and Spanish ships of the line, of which some 67 were available at the beginning of the Trafalgar campaign. In January, 1805, besides other ships of the class in distant waters or specially employed, we – on our side – had 80 ships of the line in commission. A knowledge of this will enable us to form some idea of the chances of success that would have attended Napoleon's concentration if it had been effected. To protect the passage of his invading expedition across the English Channel he did not depend only on concentrating his more distant fleets. In the Texel there were, besides smaller vessels, 9 sail of the line. Thus the Emperor did what we may be sure any future intending invader will not fail to do, viz., he provided his expedition with a respectable naval escort. The British naval officers of the day, who knew what war was, made arrangements to deal with this escort. Lord Keith, who commanded in the Downs, had under him 6 sail of the line in addition to many frigates and sloops; and there were 5 more line-of-battle ships ready at Spithead if required.

There had been a demand in the country that the defence of our shores against an invading expedition should be entrusted to gunboats, and what may be called coastal small craft and boats. This was resisted by the naval officers. Nelson had already said, "Our first defence is close to the enemy's ports," thus agreeing with a long line of eminent British seamen in their view of our strategy. Lord St. Vincent said that "Our great reliance is on the vigilance and activity of our cruisers at sea, any reduction in the number of which by applying them to guard our ports, inlets, and beaches would, in my judgment, tend to our destruction." These are memorable words, which we should do well to ponder in these days. The Government of the day insisted on having the coastal boats; but St. Vincent succeeded in postponing the preparation of them till the cruising ships had been manned. His plan of defence has been described by his biographer as "a triple line of barricade; 50-gun ships, frigates, sloops of war, and gun-vessels upon the coast of the enemy; in the Downs opposite France another squadron, but of powerful ships of the line, continually disposable, to support the former or attack any force of the enemy which, it might be imagined possible, might slip through the squadron hanging over the coast; and a force on the beach on all the shores of the English ports, to render assurance doubly sure." This last item was the one that St. Vincent had been compelled to adopt, and he was careful that it should be, in addition to those measures of defence in the efficacy of which he and his brother seamen believed. Concerning it his biographer makes the following remark "It is to be noted that Lord St. Vincent did not contemplate repelling an invasion of gunboats by gunboats," etc. He objected to the force of sea-fencibles, or "long-shore organization", because he considered it more useful to have the sea-going ships manned. Speaking of this coastal defence scheme, he said: "It would be a good bone for the officers to pick, but a very dear one for the country."

The defence of our ocean trade entered largely into the strategy of the time. An important part was played by our fleets and groups of line-of-battle ships which gave usually indirect, but sometimes direct, protection to our own merchant vessels, and also to neutral vessels carrying commodities to or from British ports. The strategy of the time, the correctness of which was confirmed by long belligerent experience, rejected the employment of a restricted number of powerful cruisers, and relied upon the practical ubiquity of the defending ships, which ubiquity was rendered possible by the employment of very numerous craft of moderate size. This can be seen in the lists of successive years. In January, 1803, the number of cruising frigates in commission was 107, and of sloops and smaller vessels 139, the total being 246. In 1805 the numbers were – Frigates, 108; sloops, etc., 181; with a total of 289. In 1805 the figures had grown to 129 frigates, 416 sloops, &c., the total being 545. Most of these were employed in defending commerce. We all know how completely Napoleon's project of invading the United Kingdom was frustrated. It is less well known that the measures for defending our sea-borne trade, indicated by the figures, just given, were triumphantly successful. Our Mercantile Marine increased during the war, a sure proof that it had been effectually defended. Consequently we may accept it as established beyond the possibility of refutation that branch of our naval strategy at the time of Trafalgar which was concerned with the defence of our trade was rightly conceived and properly carried into effect.

As has been stated already, the defence of our sea-borne trade, being in practice the keeping open of our ocean lines of communication, carried with it the protection, in part at any rate, of our transmarine territories. Napoleon held pertinaciously to the belief that British prosperity was chiefly due to our position in India. We owe it to Captain Mahan that we now know that the eminent American Fulton – a name of interest to the members of this Institution – told Pitt of the belief held abroad that "the fountains of British wealth are in India and China." In the great scheme of naval concentration, which the Emperor devised, seizure of British Colonies in the West Indies had a definite place. We kept in that quarter, and varied as necessary a force capable of dealing with a naval raid as well as guarding the neighbouring lines of communication. In 1803 we had 4 ships of the line in the West Indian area. In 1804 we had 6 of the same class; and in 1805, while the line-of-battle-ships were reduced to 4, the number of frigates was increased from 9 to 25. Whether our Government divined Napoleon's designs on India or not, it took measures to protect our interests there. In January, 1804, we had on the Cape of Good Hope and the East Indies Stations, both together, 6 sail of the line, 3 smaller twodeckers, 6 frigates, and 6 sloops, or 21 ships of war in all. This would have been sufficient to repel a raiding attack made in some strength. By the beginning of 1805 our East Indies force had been increased; and in the year 1805 itself we raised it to a strength of 41 ships in all, of which 9 were of the line and 17 were frigates. Had, therefore, any of the hostile ships managed to get to the East Indies from the Atlantic or the Mediterranean ports, in which they were being watched by our navy, their chances of succeeding in their object would have been small indeed.

When we enter the domain of tactics strictly so called, that is to say, when we discuss the proceedings of naval forces whether single ships, squadrons, or fleets, in hostile contact with one another, we find the time of Trafalgar full of instructive episodes. Even with the most recent experience of naval warfare vividly present to our minds, we can still regard Nelson as the greatest of tacticians. Naval tactics may be roughly divided into two great classes or sections, viz., the tactics of groups of ships, that is to say, fleet actions; and the tactics of what the historian James calls "single ship actions," that is to say, fights between two individual ships. In the former the achievements of Nelson stand out with incomparable brilliancy. It would be impossible to describe his method fully except in a rather lengthy treatise. We may, however, say that Nelson was an innovator, and that his tactical principles and methods have been generally misunderstood down to this very day. If ever there was an admiral who was opposed to an unthinking, headlong rush at an enemy it was he. Yet this is the character that he still bears in the conception of many. He was, in truth, an industrious and patient student of tactics, having studied them in what in these days we should call a scientific spirit, at an early period, when there was but little reason to expect that he would ever be in a position to put to a practical test the knowledge that he had acquired and the ideas that he had formed. He saw that the old battle formation in single line ahead was insufficient if you wanted as he himself always did – to gain an overwhelming victory. He also saw that, though an improvement on the old formation, Lord Howe's innovation of the single line abreast was still a good deal short of tactical perfection. Therefore, he devised what he called, with pardonable elation, the "Nelson touch", the attack in successive lines so directed as to overwhelm one part of the enemy's fleet, whilst the other part was prevented from coming to the assistance of the first, and was in its turn overwhelmed or broken up. His object was to bring a larger number of his own ships against a smaller number of the enemy's. He would by this method destroy the part attacked, suffering in the process so little damage himself that with his whole force he would be able to deal effectively with the hostile remnant if it ventured to try conclusions with him. It is of the utmost importance that we should thoroughly understand Nelson's fundamental tactical principle, viz., the bringing of a larger number of ships to fight against a smaller number of the enemy's. There is not, I believe, in the whole of the records of Nelson's opinions and actions a single expression tending to show that tactical efficiency was considered by him to be due to superiority in size of individual ships of the same class or – as far as *materiel* was concerned—to anything but superior numbers, of course at the critical point. He did not require, and did not have, more ships in his own fleet than the whole of those in the fleet of the enemy. What he wanted was to bring to the point of impact, when the fight began, a larger number of ships than were to be found in that part of the enemy's line.

I believe that I am right in saying that, from the date of Salamis downwards, history records no decisive naval victory in which the victorious fleet has not succeeded in concentrating against a relatively weak point in its enemy's formation a greater number of its own ships. I know of nothing to show that this has not been the rule throughout the ages of which detailed history furnishes us with any memorial no matter what the class of ship, what the type of weapon, what the mode of propulsion. The rule certainly prevailed in the battle of August 10 last off Port Arthur, though it was not so overwhelmingly decisive as some others. We do not yet know enough of the recent sea fight in the Straits of Tsushima to be able to describe it in detail; but we do know that at least some of the Russian ships were defeated or destroyed by a combination of Japanese ships against them.

Looking back at the tactics in the time of Trafalgar, we may see that the history of them confirms the experience of earlier wars, viz., that victory does not necessarily fall to the side which has the biggest ships. It is a well-known fact of naval history that generally the French ships were larger and the Spanish much larger than the British ships of corresponding classes. This superiority in size certainly did not carry with it victory in action. On the other hand, British ships were generally bigger than the Dutch ships with which they fought; and it is of great significance that at Camperdown the victory was due not to superiority in the size of individual ships, but, as shown by the different lists of killed and wounded, to the act of bringing a larger number against a smaller. It remains to be seen how far the occurrences in the battle of the Japan Sea will support or be opposed to this conclusion; but it may be said that there is nothing tending to upset it in the previous history of the present war in the Far East.

I do not know how far I am justified in expatiating on this point; but, as it may help to bring the strategy and tactics of the Trafalgar epoch into practical relation with the stately science of which in our day this Institution is, as it were, the mother-shrine and metropolitical temple, you may allow me to dwell upon it a little longer. The object aimed at by those who favour great size of individual ships is not, of course, magnitude alone. It is to turn out a ship which shall be more powerful than an individual antagonist. All recent development of man-of-war construction has taken the form of producing, or at any rate trying to produce, a more powerful ship than those of earlier date, or belonging to a rival navy. I know the issues that such statements are likely to raise; and I ask you, as naval architects, to bear with me patiently when I say what I am going to say. It is this: If you devise for the ship so produced the tactical system for which she is specially adapted you must, in order to be logical, base your system on her power of defeating her particular antagonist. Consequently, you must abandon the principle of concentration of superior numbers against your enemy; and, what is more, must be prepared to maintain that such concentration on his part against yourself would be ineffectual. This will compel a reversion to tactical methods, which made a fleet action a series of duels between pairs of combatants, and – a thing to be pondered on seriously – never enabled anyone to win a decisive victory on the sea. The position will not be made more logical if you demand both superior size and also superior numbers, because if you adopt the tactical system appropriate to one of the things demanded, you will rule out the other. You cannot employ two different and opposed tactical systems.

It is not necessary to the line of argument above indicated to ignore the merits of the battleship class. Like their predecessors, the ships of the line, it is really battleships which in a naval war dominate the situation. We saw that it was so at the time of Trafalgar, and we see that it has been so in the war at present in progress, at all events throughout the 1904 campaign. The experience of naval war, down to the close of that in which Trafalgar was the most impressive event, led to the virtual abandonment of ships of the line above and below a certain class. The 64-gun ships and smaller two-deckers had greatly diminished in number, and repetitions of them grew more and more rare. It was the same with the three deckers, which, as the late Admiral Colomb pointed out, continued to be built, though in reduced numbers, not so much for their tactical efficiency as for the convenient manner in which they met the demands for the accommodation required in flag-ships.

The tactical condition which the naval architects of the Trafalgar period had to meet was the employment of an increased number of two-deckers of the medium classes.

A fleet of ships of the line as long as it could keep the sea, that is until it had to retreat into port before a stronger fleet, controlled a certain area of water. Within that area smaller men-of-war as well as friendly merchant ships were secure from attack. As the fleet moved about, so the area moved with it. Skilful disposition and manoeuvring added largely to the extent of sea within which the maritime interests that the fleet was meant to protect would be safe. It seems reasonable to expect that it will be the same with modern fleets of suitable battleships.

The tactics of "single ship actions" at the time of Trafalgar were based upon pure seamanship backed up by good gunnery. The better a captain handled his ship the more likely he was to beat his antagonist. Superior speed, where it existed, was used to "gain the weather gage," not in order to get a suitable range for the faster ship's guns, but to compel her enemy to fight. Superior speed was also used to run away, capacity to do which was not then, and ought not to be now, reckoned a merit in a ship expressly constructed for fighting, not fleeing. It is some-times claimed in these days that superior speed will enable a modern ship to keep at a distance from her opponent which will be the best range for her own guns. It has not been explained why a range which best suits her guns should not be equally favourable for the guns of her opponent; unless, indeed, the latter is assumed to be weakly armed, in which case the distance at which the faster ship might engage her would be a matter of comparative indifference. There is nothing in the tactics of the time of Trafalgar to make it appear that – when a fight had once begun—superior speed, of course within moderate limits, conferred any considerable tactical advantage in "single ship actions," and still less in general or fleet actions.

Taking up a position ahead or astern of a hostile ship so as to be able to rake her was not facilitated by originally superior speed so much as by the more damaged state of the ship to be raked. Raking, as a rule, occurring rather late in an action.

A remarkable result of long experience of war made itself clearly apparent in the era of Trafalgar. I have already alluded to the tendency to restrict the construction of line-of-battle ships to those of the medium classes. The same thing may be noticed in the case of the frigates. Those of 44, 40, and 28 guns relatively or absolutely diminished in number; whilst the number of the 38-gun, 36-gun, and 32-gun frigates increased. The officers who had personal experience of many campaigns were able to impress on the naval architects of the day the necessity of recognising the sharp distinction that really exists between what we should now call the "battleship" and what we should now call the "cruiser." In the earlier time there were ships which were intermediate between the ship of the line and the frigate. These were the two deckers of 56, 54, 50, 44, and even 40 guns. They had long been regarded as not "fit to lie in a line," and they were never counted in the frigate classes. They seemed to have held a nondescript position, for no one knew exactly how to employ them in war any more than we now know exactly how to employ our armoured cruisers, as to which it is not settled whether they are fit for general actions or should be confined to commerce defending or other cruiser service. The two-deckers just mentioned were looked upon by the date of Trafalgar as forming an unnecessary class of fighting ships. Some were employed, chiefly because they existed, on special service; but they were being replaced by true battleships on one side and true frigates on the other.

In conclusion, I would venture to say that the strategical and tactical lessons taught by a long series of naval campaigns had been mastered by our Navy by the time of the Trafalgar campaign. The effect of those lessons showed itself in our ship building policy, and has been placed on permanent record in the history of maritime achievement and of the adaptation of material means to belligerent ends.

Reprinted from *Royal Navy During the Napoleonic Era* website, http://home.gci.net

APPENDIX III

Tables of Battlefleet Tonnages and Strength, 1790–1815 and the Complete List of Ships in the Royal Navy in April 1794

Battlefleet Tonnages of
The Major Powers 1790–1815

The figures represent effective useable tonnage (in thousands of tons)

	Britain	France	Holland	Spain	Denmark	Sweden	Russia (Baltic)	Russia (Black Sea)	USA
1790	334	231	87	188	71	31	114	14	
1795	312	180	51	203	70	26	114	24	
1800	330	136	35	176	67	29	114	31	
1805	360	129	33	104	49	25	123	32	
1810	413	148	31	77	4	27	85	30	
1815	358	179	52	47	4	27	92	47	11

Taken from J. Glete, *Navies and Nations: Warships, Navies and State Building in Europe and America, 1500–1850*, Stockholm, 1993

Strength of the Royal Navy, 1794 compared with 1814

			1794			1814		
Rate	Guns	Average tonnage	In full com- mission	Reserve or repair	Rele- gated	In full com- mission	Reserve or repair	Rele- gated
First 3 decks	100/120	2,500	5	1	none	7	none	2
Second 3 decks	98	2,200	9	7	3	5	3	4
Third 2 decks	64/80	1,750	71	24	22	87	16	80
Fourth 2 decks	50	1,100	8	4	7	8	2	9
Fifth 2 decks	44	900	12	3	3	2	none	1
Fifth Frigates	32/44	900	66	3	4	121	11	45
Sixth Frigates	28	600	22	2	4	none	none	4
Sixth Postship	20/24	500	10	2	2	25	4	11
Unrated vessels	4/18	70/450	76	3	7	360	6	46

Reprinted from *The Frigates*, James Henderson, Adlard Coles, 1970

On pages 353–365 is an approximately alphabetical list of ships in the Royal as of April 1794, derived from "Steel's original and Correct List of the Royal Navy".

Understanding the list:

Status:
O-Ordinary
C-In commission
B-Building

Ship:
* means captured from, with "B" = Batavian,
"F" = France, "E" = Spain.

Other abbreviations:

ASSp – Armed Storeship		Lug – Lugger	
AT – Armed Transport		PS – Prison Ship	
Bp – Bomb		Sch – Schooner	
Bg – Brig		Sp – Sloop	
Corv – Corvette		SS – Storeship	
Cut – Cutter		Sur Sp – Surveying Ship	
FS – Fireship		Ten – Tender	
GS – Guardship		Yt – Yacht	
Gy – Galley		– Hired	
HS – Hospital Ship (& rigged as brig)			

Locations:

Ch	= Chatham	N	= Nore
Cnl	= Channel	Po	= Portsmouth
Cv	= on convoy to	Py	= Plymouth
Df	= Deptford	Sh	= Sheerness
EI	= East Indies	Spit	= Spithead
G	= Gibraltar	WI	= West Indies
J	= Jamaica	Wo	= Woolwich
M	= Mediterranean		

Status	Ship	Guns	Locations	Year Built
O	Atlas	98	Py repairing	1782
C	Albion	74	Ch	1763
C	Alcide	74	M	1779
C	Alexander	74	Cnl	1773
C	Alfred	74	With Admiral Bowyer	1778
C	Arrogant	74	N	1761
C	Audacious	74	Spit	1785
C	Africa	64	Spit	1781
C	Agememnon	64	M	1781
C	America	64	Spit	1777
O	Anson	64	Ch serviceable	1743
O	Ardent	64	M	1783
C	Argonaut*F	64	Py refitting	1782
C	Asia	64	Cv to WI	1764

Status	Ship	Guns	Locations	Year Built
C	Adamant	50	Cv to WI	1779
B	Antelope	50	Sh	–
C	Assistance	50	Cv to M	1781
O	Acteon	44	Po	1779
C	Adventure	44	Spit	1784
C	Argo	44	Cv to St Helena	1781
C	Assurance	44	M	1780
O	Apollo	38	Df fitting	1794
C	Arethusa	38	With Admiral Macbride	1781
C	Artois	38	Df fitting	1794
C	L'Aigle *F	36	M	1782
C	Active	32	Ireland	1780
O	Aeolus	32	Ch repairing	1758
C	L'Aimable *F	32	M	1782
C	Alarm	32	WI	1758
O	Amazon	32	Py repairing	1773
C	Amphion	32	Spit	1780
C	Andromache	32	Ireland	1781
O	Andromeda	32	Py fitting	1784
C	Aquilon	32	G	1786
C	Astrea	32	Cv to M	1781
C	Alligator	28	WI	1786
C	Aurora	28	Bristol Channel	1777
C	Ariadne	20	M	1776
O	Albicore, Sp	16	N	1793
O	Alert, Sp	16	Cnl	1793
O	Ariel, Sp	16	Po	1779
O	Atlanta, Sp	14	Po	1776
O	Alecto, FS	12	Po	1779
O	Aetna, Bb	8	Wo repairing	1781
C	Assistant, Ten	8	Df	1791
C	Britannia	100	M	1762
C	Barfleur	98	Cnl	1768
C	Boyne	98	WI	1790
O	Blenheim	90	Py	1761
C	Bedford	74	M	1775

C	Bellerophon	74	Spit	1786
Status	Ship	Guns	Locations	Year Built
C	Bellona	74	Spit	1760
C	Berwick	74	M	1779
O	Bombay Castle	74	Py repairing	1782
C	Brunswick	74	With Admiral Bowyer	1790
C	Belliqueux	64	Cv to WI	1780
O	Bienfaisant	64	Py repairing	1759
O	Bristol	50	Ch Church ship	1775
C	Beaulieu	40	WI	1791
O	Belle Poule, *F	36	Ch repairing	1779
C	Blanche	32	WI	1786
C	Blonde	32	WI	1787
C	Boston	32	Cv to Newfoundland	1762
O	Boreas, SS	28	Sh	1774
C	Brilliant	28	Cnl	1779
C	Bien Aime, ASSp	20	EI	1793
C	Bonetta, Sp	16	Po	1779
O	Brisk, Sp	16	Po	1784
C	Bulldog, Sp	14	Africa	1782
O	Brazen, Cut	14	Py	1781
C	Birbice, Sch	?	WI	?
C	Black Joke, Lug	10	Spit	1793
C	Cambridge, GS	80	Py	1750
C	Caesar	80	Cnl	1793
C	Canada	74	Po	1766
C	Captain	74	M	1787
O	Carnatic	74	Py repairing	1783
B	Centaur	74	Wo	?
C	Colossus	74	Po	1787
O	Conqueror	74	Ch repairing	1775
C	Courageux	74	M	1761
C	Culloden	74	Py	1783
O	Cumberland	74	Ch	1774
O	Chichester, R	74	Py	1753
C	Le Caton, HS, *F	64	Py	1782
O	Crown	64	Po	1782

Status	Ship	Guns	Locations	Year Built
C	Centurion	50	EI	1774
C	Chatham	50	Py Convalescent ship	1758
C	Charon	44	Spit	1783
C	Chichester, SS	44	Po fitting	1785
C	Concorde, *F	36	Po	1783
C	Crescent	36	With Admiral Macbride	1784
C	Castor	32	Ostend	1785
C	Ceres	32	WI	1781
C	Cleopatra	32	Po	1780
C	Carysfort	28	St George's Channel	1767
C	Circe	28	Cnl	1785
C	Cyclops	28	M	1779
O	Champion	24	Wo serviceable	1779
O	Camel, ASSp	24	Wo	1782
C	Camilla	20	Py fitting	1776
B	Cerberus	?	Southampton	?
O	Cygnet, Sp	18	Po	1776
O	Calypso, Sp	16	Po	1783
C	Cormorant, Sp	16	Cnl	1794
C	Childers, Sp	14	Df	1778
C	Comet, FS	14	Spit	1783
C	Conflagration, FS	14	M	1783
C	Cockatrice, Cut	14	Po	1782
C	Catherine, Yt	8	Df	1720
O	Chatham, Yt	8	Ch	1741
C	Chatham, Ten	?	EI	1790
B	Dreadnought	98	Po	—
O	Duke	98	Py repairing	1777
C	Defence	74	With Admiral Macbride	1763
O	Defiance	74	Ch refitting	1783
C	Diadem	64	M	1782
C	Dictator	64	to Africa	1783
O	Director	64	Ch	1784
C	Diomede	44	EI	1781
C	Dolphin, HS	44	M	1781
O	Dover	44	Po	1784

Status	Ship	Guns	Locations	Year Built
O	Diamond	38	Df fitting	1791
O	Diana	38	Df fitting	1794
C	Daedalas	32	Virginia	1780
C	Druid	32	Cruising	1783
C	Dido	28	M	1784
C	Daphne	20	Cv to Downs from Py	1776
C	Dorset, Yt	10	Dublin	1753
C	Dromedary, SS	24	WI	1779
C+	Drake, Sp	14	Sh	1779
C	Discovery, Sp	10	Nootka Sound	1790
C+	Daedalus, SS	?	Botany Bay	—
C	Deptford, Ten	8	On impress service	1788
O	Edgar	74	Ch	1773
C	Egmont	74	M	1766
O	Elephant	74	Po	1789
O	Elizabeth	74	Po	1768
C	Excellent	74	Po	1786
O	Eagle	64	Ch repairing	1777
O	Essex, R	64	Po	1763
O	Europe	64	Py repairing	1769
C	Europa	50	J	1782
C	Expedition	44	On ordnance service	1781
C	Experiment	44	WI	1780
C	Enterprise	28	Tower to receive men	1774
C	Eurydice	24	Spit	1784
C	La Eclair *F	20	M	1793
C	Echo, Sp	16	Coasting convoy	1784
C	L'Espion, Sp *F	16	Py	1793
C	Expedition, Cut	10	Cnl	1775
C	Experiment, Lug	10	Cruising	—
O	Formidable	98	Py repairing	1777
B	Foudroyant	80	Py	—
O	Fame	74	Py	1759
C	Fortitude	74	M	1780
O	Fortunee, PS *F	40	Langstone	1779
C	Flora	36	With Admiral Macbride	1780

C	Fox	32	G	1780
Status	Ship	Guns	Locations	Year
				Built
C	Fairy, Sp	16	Africa	1778
C	Favourite, Sp	16	Df fitting	1794
C	Fly, Sp	16	Cruising	1776
C+	Fortune, Sp	16	Cruising	1778
C	Fury, Sp	16	Cruising	1790
C+	Falcon, Sp	14	Cnl	1782
C	Ferret, Sp	14	Cnl	1784
O	Flirt, Sp	14	Df	–
C	Flying Fifth, Sch	?	J	–
C	Glory	98	With Admiral Bowyer	1788
C	Gibraltar *E	80	Spit	1780
C	Ganges	74	Py refitting	1782
O	Goliath	74	Po repairing	1781
O	Grafton	74	Po serviceable	1771
O	Grampus	50	Df repairing	1782
C	Gladiator, HS	44	Po	1783
C	Gorgon	44	M	1784
O	Greyhound	32	Limehouse repairing	1783
C	Grana, HS *E	28	Ch	1781
C	Le Goelan, *F	14	J	1793
B	Hibernia	110	PY	–
C	Hannibal	74	Py, refitting	1786
C	Hector	74	With Admiral Macbride	1779
C	Hero, PS	74	R. Medway	1753
C	Hebe, *F	38	Cnl.	1782
C	Hermione	32	J	1782
C	Heroine	32	EI	1783
C	Hind	28	G	1785
C	Hussar	28	Halifax	1784
C	Hawke, Sp	16	Cnl	1793
O	Hazard, Sp	16	Ch	1794
C	Hornet, Sp.	16	Df fitting	1794
C	Hound, Sp	16	J	1790
C+	Helena, Sp	14	Spit	1778
C	Impregnable	90	Spit	1786

| C | Illustrious | 74 | M | 1789 |
Status	Ship	Guns	Locations	Year Built
C	Invincible	74	Cruising	1765
C	Irresistable	74	WI	1782
O	Indefatigable	64	Po serviceable	1784
C	Inflexible, SS	64	Spit	1780
C	Intrepid	64	Py for J	1770
O	Isis	50	Sh	1774
C	L'Imperieuse *F	40	G	1793
C	Inconstant	36	M	1783
C	Iphigenia	32	J	1780
C	Iris	32	N	1783
C	Inspector, Sp	16	Wl	1782
C	Incendiary, FS	14	Py refitting	1782
O	Jupiter	50	Sh. repairing	1778
B	Jason	38	Df	–
C	Juno	32	M	1780
C	King's Fisher, Sp	18	Cruising	1782
O	Kite, Cut	14	Po	1778
O	London	98	Po	1766
C	Leviathan	74	Spit	1790
C	Lion	64	To China Sept 1792	1777
O	Leander	50	Po	1780
C	Leopard, GS	50	Downs	1790
C	Latona	38	Cnl	1781
C	Leda	36	M	1783
C	Lowestoffe	32	M	1762
B	Lively	32	Northam	–
C	Lapwing	28	Wo fitting	1785
C	Lizard	28	Lisbon	1757
C	Lark, Sp	16	Wo fitting	1794
O	Lynx, Sp	16	Wo serviceable	1794
C	Liberty, Cut	16	Cruising	1779
C	Lutin *F	16	Newfoundland	1793
C	Lutine, Bb	?	M	–
O	Magnificent	74	Po serviceable	1766
C	Majestic	74	With Admiral Rowley	1785

C	Marlborough	74	Spit	1767
Status	Ship	Guns	Locations	Year Built
B	Mars	74	Df	–
C	Minotaur	74	Cnl	1793
C	Monarch	74	Cnl	1765
C	Montague	74	With Admiral Bowyer	1779
C	Magnanirne	64	Py repairing	1780
O	Modeste, R *F	64	Po	1759
O	Monmouth	64	Po repairing	1773
O	Medway, R	60	Py	1755
O	Medusa, GS	50	Cork	1785
C	La Modeste *F	40	M	1793
C	Minerva	38	EI	1780
C	Melampus	36	With Admiral Macbride	1785
C	Magiciene *F	32	WI	1781
C	Meleager	32	M	1785
C	Mermaid	32	Sh	1785
O	Maidstone	28	Sh repairing	1758
O	Medea	28	Po reparing	1778
O	Mercury	28	Po	1780
C	Myrmidon, Slopship	20	Py	1780
O	Merlin, Sp	20	Sh repairing	1777
C	Martin, Sp	14	Cruising	1789
C	Megaera, FS	14	Spit	1782
C	Mutine, Cut *F	14	Cnl	1778
C	Mary, Yt	10	Df repairing	1723
C	Medina, Yt	10	Isle of Wight	1771
C	Marie Antoinette, Sch *F	10	J	1793
B	Neptune	98	Df	–
O	Namur	90	Py	1756
O	Nassau	64	Py repairing	1785
C	Nonsuch	64	Ch	1774
C	La Nymphe *F	36	With Admiral Macbride	1780
C	Niger	32	Spit	1759
C	Nemesis	28	M	1780
C	Narcisus	20	Df fitting	1781
C	Nautilus, Sp	16	WI	1784

| C | Nimble, Cut | 14 | North Sea | 1781 |
Status	Ship	Guns	Locations	Year Built
B	Ocean	98	Wo	–
C	Orion	74	Cnl	1787
C	L'Orseau *F	36	Spit	1793
C	Orpheus	32	EI	1780
C+	Orestes, Sp *Bat	18	Spit	1781
C+	Otter, Sp	14	Sh	1782
O	Prince George	98	Ch serviceable	1772
C	Princess Royal	98	M	1773
B	Prince of Wales	98	Po	–
O	Prince	98	Po	1788
C	Le Pegase, HS *F	74	Po	1782
C	Powerful	74	J	1783
O	Polyphemus	64	Ch serviceable	1782
O	Prothee *F	64	Po repairing	1780
O	Prudent	64	Py repairing	1768
O	Prince Edward, R *Bat	60	Ch	1781
O	Portland	50	Po repairing	1770
O	Princess Caroline, R *Bat	50	Sh	1781
C	Phaeton	38	Cnl	1782
O	La Prudente *F	38	Po serviceable	1779
O	Perserverence	36	Po	1781
O	Phoenix	36	Wo	1783
C	Pallas	32	Cnl	1794
C	Pearl	32	Milford	1762
C	Penelope	32	J	1783
C	Pegasus	28	Spit	1779
C	Pomona	28	Spit	1778
C	La Prompte *F	28	Po	1793
C	Proserpine	28	Spit	1777
C	Porcupine	24	Py	1779
O	Prosperity, ASSp, R	22	Sh	1782
C	Perseus	20	Py refitting	1776
O	Peterell, Sp	16	Ch fitting	1794
C	Providence, Sp	16	Wo	1791
B	Pylades, Sp	16	Rotherhithe	–

Status	Ship	Guns	Locations	Year Built
C	Pluto	14	Newfoundland	1782
C	Pilote, Cut *F	14	Cruising	1778
O	Portsmouth, Yt	8	Po serviceable	1755
O	Princess Augusta, Yt	8	Df	1710
C	Placentia, Sp	?	Newfoundland	1790
C	Queen Charlotte	100	Spit	1790
C	Queen	98	Spit	1769
C	Quebec	32	Madeira	1781
C	Royal George	100	Cnl	1788
C	Royal Sovereign	100	Spit	1786
C	Royal William	84	Spit	1719
C	Ramillies	74	With Admiral Bowyer	1785
C	Resolution	74	With Admiral Macbride	1770
C	Robust	74	Po refitting	1764
O	Royal Oak	74	Po repairing	1769
C	Russell	74	Cnl	1764
C	Raisonable	64	Po	1768
O	Repulse	64	Po serviceable	1780
C	Ruby	64	Spit	1775
O	Rippon, R	60	Py	1758
O	Renown	50	Ch repairing	1774
C	Romney	50	M	1762
O	Rainbow, R	44	Wo	1761
C	Regulus	44	Spit	1785
C	Resistance	44	EI	1782
C	Roebuck	44	WI	1774
O	La Reunion *F	38	Po	1793
C	Romulus	36	G	1785
C	Resource	28	WI	1778
C	Rose	28	WI	1783
C	Redoubt, Floating battery	20	Ostend	1793
O	Le Robert *F	20	Py refitting	1794
O	Racehorse, Sp	16	Sh	1783
O	Ranger, Sp	16	Df	1794
B	Rattler, Sp	16	Northam	–
C	Rattlesnake, Sp	16	WI	1791

C	Ranger, Cut	14	Cnl	1787
Status	Ship	Guns	Locations	Year Built
C	Rattler, Cut	14	Py	–
C	Resolution, Cut	14	Cnl	1779
O	Royal Charlotte, Yt	10	Df	1749
C	St George	98	M	1785
C	Sandwich, GS	98	N	1759
C	Saturn	74	Po refitting	1786
C	Suffolk	74	Spit	1765
O	Sultan	74	Po repairing	1775
C	Swiftsure, GS	74	Cork	1787
C	St Albans	64	Cv to Wl	1764
C	Sampson	64	Cv to St Helena	1781
C	Sceptre	64	Wl	1781
O	Scipio	64	Ch fitting for a HS	1782
O	Standard	64	Py repairing	1782
C	Stately	64	Po refitting	1784
O	Salisbury	50	Po	1769
O	Serapis	44	Ch serviceable	1781
C	Severn	44	Py refitting	1786
C	Sheerness	44	North Sea	1787
B	Sea Horse	38	Rotherhithe	–
O	Santa Leocadia *E	36	Wo repairing	1781
C	Santa Margarita *E	36	WI	1779
C	Sole Bay	32	WI	1785
C	Southampton	32	Cnl	1757
B	Stag	32	Ch	–
C	Success	32	WI	1781
C	Syren	32	Py refitting	1782
C	Sybil	28	Df fitting	1779
C	Squirrel	24	St George's Channel	1785
C	Sphynx	20	Sh	1775
C	Savage, Sp	16	Cruising	1778
C	Scorpion, Sp	16	Cv to WI	1785
C+	Scourge, Sp	16	N	1779
C	Serpent, Sp	16	Cnl	1789
C	Shark, Sp	16	Po	1780

Status	Ship	Guns	Locations	Year Built
O+	Swallow, Sp	16	Po	1781
C	Swift, Sp	16	Po for EI	1793
C	Sea Flower, Cut	16	WI	1782
C+	Scour, Sp	14	G	1781
C+	Speedy, Sp	14	G	1782
C	Swan, Sp	14	Cv to WI	1767
C	Spitfire, Sp	14	Cruising	1782
C	Speedwell, Cut	14	Spit	1780
C	Sprightly, Cut	14	Cnl	1778
O	Sultana, Cut	14	Py	1780
C	Spider, Cut *F	12	Cnl	1782
C	Spitfire, Sch	8	J	1793
B	Téméraire	98	Ch	–
C	Terrible	74	M	1785
C	Theseus	74	Ch	1786
C	Thunderer	74	Ch fitting	1783
C	Tremendous	74	With Admiral Bowyer	1784
O	Triumph	74	Po repairing	1764
O	Trident	64	Po serviceable	1768
B	Tiger	50	Po	–
C	Trusty	50	Cork	1782
C	Thetis	38	Cnl	1782
C	Thalis	36	Po	1782
C	Terpsichore	32	WI	1786
C	Tartar	28	M	1756
C	Thisbe	28	Spit	1783
C	Triton	28	Po fitting	1773
O	Termagent, Sp	18	Sh	1781
O	La Trompeuse *F	18	Py	1794
C	Thorn, Sp	16	NN	1779
C	Trespassy, SS	?	Newfoundland	1790
O	Trimmer, Sp *F	16	Sh	1782
C	Tisiphone, Sp	12	M	1781
O	Tyral, Cut	12	Cnl	1781
C	Terror, Bb	8	Spit	1779
C	Union, HS	90	Sh	1756

Status	Ship	Guns	Locations	Year Built
C	Ulysses	44	WI	1779
B	Unicorn	32	Ch	–
B	Ville de Paris	110	Ch	–
C	Victory	100	M	1765
C	Valiant	74	Cnl	1759
C	Vanguard	74	WI	1787
O	Venerable	74	Ch serviceable	1784
C	Vengeance	74	WI	1774
C	Victorious	74	Ch fitting	1785
C	Veteran	64	WI	1787
O	Vigilant	64	Po serviceable	1774
C	Venus	32	With Admiral Rowley	1758
C	Vestal	28	North Sea	1779
O	Viper *F	18	?	1794
C	Vulture, Sp (Slopship)	14	Po	1776
C	Viper, Cut	12	Cnl	1780
C	Vesuvius, Bb	8	WI	1776
C	Windsor Castle	98	M	1790
O	Warrior	74	Po serviceable	1781
O	Warspite, R	74	Po	1758
C	Warwick, R	50	Ch	1767
C	Woolwich	44	WI	1785
C	Winchelsea	32	WI	1764
O+	Wasp, Sp	16	Sh	1782
C+	Weazle, Sp	12	Cnl	1783
C	Woolwich, Ten	10	On impress service	1788
O	William & Mary, Yt	8	Df	1694
O	Yarmouth, R	64	Py	1754
O	Zealous	74	CH serviceable	1786
C	Zebra, Sp	16	WI	1780

Reprinted from:
Navies of the Napoleonic Era, Pivka, Otta von, David and Charles Ltd, 1980.

A History of HMS *Victory*

Successive Ships bearing the name of "*Victory*," have existed in the English Navy ever since the year 1570, but *the* "*Victory*" – Nelson's "*Victory*" – is comparatively of modern date, she having been built about the year 1765. She has always been a celebrated Ship, and commanded by distinguished men. In 1778 she bore the flag of Keppel, in his memorable battle with the French on the 27th of May, which led to a vexatious Court-Martial. She successively carried the flags of Sir Peter Parker, Lord Howe, Lord Hood, and (in the glorious victory off Cape St. Vincent) of Admiral Sir John Jervis, afterwards Earl St. Vincent. It is not a little remarkable, that it was on the quarter-deck of that very Ship wherein he was destined to achieve a still greater triumph, and to seal his fame with his blood, that Nelson, after the Battle, was received by Sir John, who took him in his arms, and said he could never sufficiently thank him for his assistance. In 1806 [December 1805] the *Victory* was paid off. She was re-commissioned in 1808, and remained in Service till 1812; but during that period she did nothing worthy of particular notice. After the Battle of St. Vincent's she was used, or, rather, *mis*-used, as a prison hospital-ship! and "who would have thought (says the United Service Journal, October 1841) that it was once proposed to break up, or cut down, the *Victory*! Yet so it was; and it has but recently come to our knowledge that the well-timed remonstrances of a popular, and, we may add, in this instance, patriotic writer (printed in the Brighton Gazette, and copied into many other newspapers, chiefly those published at the Outports,) first called attention to this nautical sacrilege, and mainly aided to avert it." "This Ship, we had almost said this *sacred* Ship, is now lying in Portsmouth harbour; and it must be the wish of every Englishman's heart that she may be preserved as long as one plank of her will hold to another." On the anniversary of Trafalgar, 1844, THE QUEEN, on her visit to Portsmouth, passed near the *Victory* commanded by Captain George Moubray, who served as First Lieutenant of the *Polyphemus*, at Trafalgar, and noticing that she was decorated with Flags, and her mast-heads adorned with laurel, inquired the cause; and on being informed, immediately expressed Her intention of going on board. Her Majesty, accompanied by Prince Albert, accordingly went over the Ship. On being shown the spot where Nelson received his death wound, Her Majesty read aloud the affecting inscription –

"Here Nelson fell"

and plucked from the wreath of laurel in which it was enshrined two of its leaves, and carefully treasured them as a precious memento of the Hero. Her Majesty then went over to the pooprail, where, over the steering-wheel, is inscribed in letters of gold the words of the memorable signal,

"England expects every man will do his duty"

This inscription was also adorned with laurels and flowers. With marked emphasis, Her Majesty repeated the words. Her Majesty and Prince Albert looked around from the poop for a few moments, and then the Queen desired to be shown where Nelson died. The Royal party proceeded to the cabin, in which the very spot is marked by a funeral urn (in paint), surmounted by Nelson's Flag, and on its top, encircled in a wreath, the words,

"Here Nelson died"

There was a pause here for several minutes, and it was remarked that Her Majesty was again much affected by the reflections which such a scene awakened."

It is satisfactory to add, that for many years the command of the *Victory* has been most properly given to Officers who had served at Trafalgar, viz.: to Captain William Wilmott Henderson, C. B., who was a Midshipman of the *Belleisle*; Captain George Moubray, who was First Lieutenant of the *Polyphemus*; and now, to Captain John Pasco, who was wounded on board of her, when Lord Nelson's Flag-Lieutenant, at Trafalgar.

From *The Dispatches and Letters of Lord Nelson*, Sir Nicholas Harris Nicolas, Vol. III, 1846

APPENDIX IV

Life & Death in the Royal Navy, 1793–1811: Some statistics, tables, regulations and documents

Allowance of Provisions
from Regulations and Instructions, 1808

Day	Bisket lbs.	Beer gals.	Beef lbs.	Pork lbs.	Pease pints	Oatmeal pints	Sugar ozs.	Butter ozs.	Cheese ozs.
Sunday	1	1	–	1	0.5	–	–	–	–
Monday	1	1	–	–	–	0.5	2	2	4
Tuesday	1	1	2	–	–	–	–	–	–
Wednesday	1	1	–	–	0.5	0.5	2	2	4
Thursday	1	1	–	1	0.5	–	–	–	–
Friday	1	1	–	–	0.5	0.5	2	2	4
Saturday	1	1	2	–	–	–	–	–	–
Weekly Total	7	7	4	2	2	1.5	6	6	12

The men ate in messes, usually consisting of eight men.

Causes of Death
Fatal Casualties in the Royal Navy in 1810

Cause of Death	Number	Percentage
By Disease	2592	50.0
By Individual Accident	1630	31.5
By Foundering, Wreck, Fire, Explosion	530	10.2
By the Enemy, killed in action	281	5.4
By the Enemy, died of wounds	150	2.9
All Causes	5183	100

British and Enemy Casualties
In the Six Major Victories

Battle	British			Enemy estimated			
	killed	wounded	total	killed	wounded	total	prisoners
First of June 1794	287	811	1098	1500	2000	3500	3500
Cape St. Vincent 1797	73	227	300	430	570	1000	3157
Camperdown 1797	203	622	825	540	620	1160	3775
The Nile 1798	218	677	895	1400	600	2000	3225
Copenhagen 1801	253	688	941	540	620	1160	3775
Trafalgar 1805	449	1241	1690	4408	2545	6953	7000
Total	1438	4266	5749	9068	7245	16313	22657

Table from Lewis, *A Social History of the Navy 1793–1815*

Gratuities to the Relations of Officers and Others Killed in Action

1. To a widow, her husband's full pay for a year.
2. Orphans, each the one-third proportion of a widow; posthumous children are esteemed orphans.
3. Orphans married are not entitled to any bounty.
4. If there is no widow, a mother, if a widow and above fifty years of age, is entitled to a widow's share.
5. The relations of officers of fire-ships are entitled to the same bounty as those of officers of like rank in fourth rates.
6. Captains are to set down the names of the killed at the end of the muster book, and on what occasion.
7. This bounty extends to those who are killed in tenders, in boats, or on shore, as well as to those on board the ships; also to those who are killed in action with pirates, or in engaging British ships through mistake. They who die of their wounds after battle are all equally entitled with those killed in action.

—*The Naval Chronicle*, 1799

Petition of the Seamen to the Admiralty, 18 April 1797

Written by delegates of the mutineers at Spithead

To the Right Honourable the Lords Commissioners of the
     Admiralty.
MY LORDS,

We, the seamen of his majesty's navy, take the liberty of addressing your lordships in an humble petition, shewing the many hardships and oppressions we have laboured under for many years, and which, we hope, your lordships will redress as soon as possible. We flatter ourselves that your lordships, together with the nation in general, will acknowledge our worth and good services, both in the American war, as well as the present; for which good service your lordships petitioners do unanimously agree in opinion, that their worth to the nation, and laborious industry in defence of their country, deserve some better encouragement than that we meet with at present, or from any we have experienced. We, your petitioners, do not boast our good services, for any other purpose than that of putting you and the nation in mind of the respect due to us, nor do we ever intend to deviate from our former character; so far from any thing of that kind, or that an Englishman or men should turn their coats, we likewise agree in opinion, that we should suffer double the hardships we have hitherto experienced, before we would wish the crown of England to be in the least imposed upon by that of any other power in the world; we therefore beg leave to inform your lordships of the grievances which we at present labour under.

We, your humble petitioners, relying that your lordships will take into early consideration the grievances of which we complain, and do not in the least doubt but your lordships will comply with our desires, which are every way reasonable.

The first grievance we have to complain of, is, that our wages are too low, and ought to be raised, that we might be the better able to support our wives and families in a manner comfortable, and whom we are in duty bound to support, as far as our wages will allow; which, we trust, will be looked into by your lordships and the honourable house of commons in parliament assembled.

We, your petitioners, beg that your lordships will take into consideration the grievances of which we complain, and now lay before you.

First, That our provisions be raised to the weight of sixteen ounces to the pound, and of a better quality; and that our measures may be the same as those used in the commercial trade of this country.

Secondly, That your petitioners request your honours will be pleased to observe, there should be no flour served while we are in harbour, in any port whatever, under the command of the British flag; and also, that there might be granted a sufficient quantity of vegetables, of such kind as may be the most plentiful in the ports to which we go; which we grievously complain and lay under the want of.

Thirdly, That your lordships will be pleased seriously to look into the state of the sick on board his majesty's ships, that they may be better attended to; and that they may have the use of such necessaries as are allowed for them in time of sickness; and that these necessaries be not on any account embezzled.

Fourthly, That your lordships will be so kind as to look into this affair, which is nowise unreasonable; and that we may be looked upon as a number of men standing in defence of our country; and that we may in somewise have grant and opportunity to taste the sweets of liberty on shore, when in any harbour, and when we have completed the duty of our ship, after our return from sea: And that no man may encroach upon his liberty, there shall be a boundary limited, and those trespassing any further, without a written order from the commanding officer, shall be punished according to the rules of the navy; which is a natural request, and congenial to the heart of man, and certainly to us, that you make the boast of being the guardians of the land.

Fifthly, That if any man is wounded in action, his pay may be continued till he is cured and discharged; and if any ship has any real grievances to complain of, we hope your lordships will readily redress them, as far as in your power, to prevent disturbances.

It is also unanimously agreed by the fleet, that, from this day, no grievances shall be received, in order to convince the nation at large, that we know when to cease to ask, as well as to begin, and that we ask nothing but what is moderate, and may be granted without detriment to the nation, or any injury to the service.

Given on board the *Queen Charlotte*, by the delegates of the fleet, the 18th day of April 1797.

The Floating Republic, Manwaring, G.E., and Bonamy Dobree, 1935

The Suppression of the Mutiny at Nore 1797

The Report from the Annual Register

The suppression of the disturbances among the seamen at Portsmouth, without recurring to violent measures, and by granting their petitions, occasioned universal satisfaction, and it was hoped that the causes of their discontent being thus effectually removed, no further complaints would arise to spread alarm throughout the nation. But these reasonable expectations were in a short time wholly disappointed by a fresh mutiny that broke out in the fleet at the Nore, on the twenty-second of May.

The crews on that day took possession of their respective ships, elected delegates to preside over them, and to draw up a statement of their demands, and transmit them to the lords of the admiralty . . .

The principal person at the head of this mutiny was one Richard Parker, a man of good natural parts, and some education, and of a remarkably bold and resolute character. Admiral Buckner, the commanding officer at the Nore, was directed by the lords of the admiralty to inform the seamen, that their demands were totally inconsistent with the good order and regulations necessary to be observed in the navy, and could not for that reason be complied with; but that on returning to their duty, they would receive the king's pardon for their breach of obedience. To this offer Parker replied by a declaration, that the seamen had unanimously determined to keep possession of the fleet, until the lords of the admiralty had repaired to the Nore, and redressed the grievances which had been laid before them. . . . [Eventually] Parker was seized and imprisoned, and after a solemn trial, that lasted three days, on board of the *Neptune*, he was sentenced to death. He suffered with great coolness and intrepidity, acknowledging the justice of his sentence, and expressing his hope, that mercy might be extended to his associates. But it was judged necessary to make public examples of the principal and most guilty, who were accordingly tried, and, after full proof of their criminality, condemned and executed. Others were ordered to be whipped; but a considerable number remained under sentence of death till after the great victory obtained, over the Dutch fleet, by Admiral Duncan: when his majesty sent a general pardon to those unhappy men; who were, at that period, confined on board a prison ship in the river Thames.

Impressment: A Memoir, 1811

Robert Hay

In 1793 the paper strength of the Royal Navy was 45,000 men; by 1801 it had risen to 135,000; by 1812 it was 145,000. Some of the influx was composed of volunteers attracted by patriotism or the proffered bounty of £70, some of it was the result of the Quota Act – whereby parishes were forced to raise a certain number of men for the senior service – but most of the increase in naval manpower came from impressment. Under the auspices of the Impress Service, press-gangs operated in fifty-one ports in Britain and Ireland, forcibly taking into service any mariners between the ages of eighteen and fifty-five unlucky enough to cross their path and not be exempted by their rank or their trade. (Landlubbers in their entirety were for-mally exempted from impressment although this was more honoured in the breach than the observance, to the chagrin of captains heading to sea with clueless and seasick landsmen). Most pressed men were taken from merchant ships, but the press gang also operated ashore. Robert Hay, a 22-year-old seamen, was press-ganged in London in 1811.

I was when crossing Towerhill accosted by a person in seamen's dress who tapped me on the shoulder enquiring in a familiar and technical strain "What ship?" I assumed an air of gravity and surprise and told him I presumed he was under some mistake as I was not connected with shipping. The fellow, however, was too well acquainted with his business to be thus easily put off. He gave a whistle and in a moment I was in the hands of six or eight ruffians who I immediately dreaded and soon found to be a press gang. They dragged me hurriedly along through several streets amid bitter execrations bestowed on them, expressions of sympathy directed towards me and landed me in one of their houses of rendezvous. I was imme-diately carried into the presence of the Lieutenant of the gang, who questioned me as to my profession, whither I had ever been to sea, and what business had taken me to Towerhill. I made some evasive answers to these interrogations and did not acknowledge having been at sea: but my hands being examined and found hard with work, and perhaps a little discoloured with tar, overset all my hesitating affirmations and I was remanded for further examination.

Some of the gang then offered me Spirits and attempted to comfort me under my misfortune, but like the friends of Job, miserable comforters were they all. The very scoundrel who first laid hold of me put on a sympathising look and observed what a pity it was to be pressed when almost within sight of the mast of the Scotch Smacks. Such sympathy from such a source was well calculated to exasperate my feelings, but to think of revenge was folly and I had patiently to listen to their mock pity.

I trembled exceedingly in the fear that they would inspect my small bundle, for in it there were a pair of numbered stockings,* which would not only have made them suppose I had been at sea, but would have given them good reason to think I had been in a war ship. I contrived, however, to slip them out unobserved and concealed them behind one of the benches and thus had my fears a little moderated.

In a short time I was reconducted for further examination before the Lieutenant, who told me as I was in his hands and would assuredly be kept I might as well make a frank confession of my circumstances, it would save time and insure me better treatment. What could I do? I might indeed have continued sullen and silent, but whither such procedure might or might not have procured me worse treatment, one thing I knew it would not restore me to liberty. I therefore acknowledged that I had been a voyage to the West Indies and had come home Carpenter of a ship. His eye seemed to brighten at this intelligence. "I am glad of that, my lad," said he, "we are very much in want of Carpenters. Step along with these men and they will give you a passage on board." I was then led back the way I came by the fellow who first seized me, put aboard of a pinnace at Tower Wharf and by midday was securely lodged on board the *Enterprise*.

As soon as the boat reached the ship I was sent down into the great cabin, in various parts of which tables were placed covered with green cloth, loaded with papers and surrounded

* Purser's issue.

with men well dressed and powdered. Such silence prevailed and such solemn gravity was displayed in every countenance that I was struck with awe and dread. The tables were so placed as to give the whole of those seated at them a fair opportunity of narrowly scrutinizing every unhappy wretch that was brought in. No sooner did I enter the cabin door than every eye was darted on me. Mine were cast down and fearing there might be some of the inquisitors who knew me I scarcely dared to raise them all the time I remained in the cabin.

A short sketch of what had passed between the press officer and myself had been communicated to the examining officer, for when I was ushered into his presence he thus addressed me:

"Well, young man, I understand you are a carpenter by trade."

"Yes, sir."

"And you have been at sea?"

"One voyage, sir."

"Are you willing to join the King's Service?"

"No, sir."

"Why?"

"Because I get much better wages in the merchant service and should I be unable to agree with the Captain I am at Liberty to leave him at the end of the voyage."

"As to wages," said he, "the chance of prize money is quite an equivalent and obedience and respect shown to your officers are all that is necessary to insure you good treatment. Besides," continued he, "you may in time be promoted to be carpenter of a line of Battle ship when your wages will be higher than in the merchant service, and should any accident happen to you, you will be provided for."

I argued under great disadvantage. My interrogator was like a judge on the bench; I like a criminal at the bar, and I had not fortitude to make any reply.

"Take my advice, my lad," continued he, "and enter the service cheerfully, you will then have a bounty, and be in a fair way for promotion. If you continue to refuse, remember you are aboard (cogent reasoning), you will be kept as a pressed man and treated accordingly."

I falteringly replied that I could not think of engaging in any service voluntarily when I knew of a better situation elsewhere. He said no more, but making a motion with his hand I was seized by two marines, hurried along towards the main hatchway with these words thundered in my ears, "A pressed man to go below." What injustice and mockery, thought I, first to have that best of blessings, liberty, snatched from me and then insulted by a seeming offer of allowing me to act with freedom! But my doom was fixed and I was thrust down among five or six score of miserable beings, who like myself had been kidnapped, and immured in the confined and unwholesome dungeon of a press room.

Here I had full leisure for reflection, but my reflection was very far from being of the agreeable kind. A few hours before I had entered London possessed of Liberty and buoyed up with animating hope. Now, I was a slave immured in a dungeon and surrounded by despair. I had proceeded from Hyde Park Corner in as direct a line as lanes and alleys would admit and had just fallen directly into those merciless hands I so anxiously wished to avoid. Such is the blindness of human nature! We are often on the very brink of a precipice when we think ourselves in the utmost safety and dream not of impending danger.

By some mismanagement on the part of the pursers stewart [d], I was left all that day without food and would have been so the second day also, for I had not yet assumed courage to make application, but that two or three of the most humane of the seamen, noticing me, took me into their mess, and applied for my allowance of provisions. With the exception of these few I was generally treated with ridicule and contempt. Seamen who have been pressed together into one ship have usually a great affection for one another. Their trade, their habits, their misfortunes are the same and they become endeared to each other by a similarity of sufferings; but my landward appearance placed me in some measure beyond the pale of sympathy. I was styled by way of distinction and ridicule "the Gentleman", and was considered a priviledged butt for the shafts of nautical witt and banter to be levelled at. I must allow this did not affect me greatly. I knew that I myself had often joined in the same strain of Irony against those who had been brought on board the *Salvador* in landsmans' clothing, and I was now merely getting paid in my own coin. Hence, however, I resolved never again to mock at the sufferings more especially when I had no other reason for such conduct than a difference of occupation or professional habits. I soon became accustomed to the jokes and when any of these nautical punsters brandished their knife and threatened to unbend my ringtail and water sail (the name of the sails set abaft the spanker and below the spanker boom), I calmly tucked up my skirts and tucking them up behind buttoned my coat closely so that they could not accomplish their purpose without coming in front to disengage the button, by which I would have been put upon my guard. I was forced to observe this precaution every night otherwise I would soon have been stumped.

Once or twice a day a limited number were permitted to go on deck to breath the fresh air, but from the surly manner in which we were treated it was easy to observe that it was not for our pleasure this indulgence was granted, but to preserve our healths, which would have soon been greatly endangered had not a little fresh air been occasionally mixed with the pestiferous breaths and pestilential vapours of the press room. I remained in this ship something more than a week, when she became so crowded as to render the removal of a considerable number a measure of necessity. I, among a considerable number of others, was put aboard of a cutter when we were very closely confined, never seeing anything on our passage down the river but the sky divided into minute squares by the gratings which covered our dungeon.

We arrived at the Nore shortly after dusk and were immediately put on board the *Ceres*, guardship. I rejoiced at its being dark when we were taken aboard because I thus escaped the prying observation of four or five hundred gazers among whom I thought it probable that some one or other would know me. The following day I got blended with a motley crowd and was less taken notice of than I would have been at my first entrance.

Here I considered it folly to dress any longer in my landsmans habillements. I therefore purchased a secondhand jacket, trowsers and check shirt, in which I equipped myself and packed up my long coat, breeches, vest, white neckcloth, etc., lest I should on some future occasion require their services. What became of them will be seen in the sequel.

Next morning my acquaintances were greatly surprised to see how completely I had been metamorphosed. Not only was my external appearance greatly changed, but my manners were still more so. Hitherto I had preserved the greatest taciturnity. I knew that had I talked much sea phrases would have slipped and I thought it as well that my behaviour and my discourse should correspond with my appearance. Hence credit was given me for far more wisdom, learning and politeness than I possessed. How easy then is it to be thought wise? It is merely to preserve silence and though we may not thereby give an opportunity of displaying our wisdom and wit we with great ease can conceal our ignorance and folly.

I now became somewhat loquacious, probably in order to make up former lee way, and as I could with great volubility string together the technical terms of seamanship, I was soon on a footing with the rest. Next day my shipmates being in a humorous mood, I flourished my knife over my head, offered a quart of grog to any one who would point me out the gentleman as I was determined to close reef him. This was as good to them as if it had been sterling wit. They all burst out a laughing, considered me a shrewd fellow and henceforth rated my nautical abilities as much too high as they before had my learning and politeness. Not one of my shipmates knew my name, except one that was pressed shortly after myself who called me by name as soon as he came aboard, and who was no other than one of my shipmates in the *Edward*. One of those who seized the boat and pulled ashore in spite of the Captains remonstrances and threats. Bill, Tom, Dick, Bob, Jack came all alike familiar to me and when I knew I was spoken to I answered to all of them promiscuously.

In this ship we had liberty to go on deck at all hours and were therefore much more comfortable than when on board the *Enterprise* or cutter. Our distance from the shore being only about 6 or 8 miles, the land was seen very clearly and many an anxious, earnest look did I take of it. Frequently would I feast my eyes for hours together gazing on it, and my imagination in forming schemes how to gain it. No hopes or at least very distant ones could be entertained of success. The distance from the shore was in itself no small barrier, but what made the attempt most hazardous, there was only one point of land where there was any probability of making a landing at all. This was on a small Island, I think called Grain. But how was this point to be gained in the dark? If I went to the right I would be taken up the Thames and carried to sea at the return of the tide. If I went to the left I would be carried in amongst the ships in Sheerness, where I would be sure to be observed, and either picked up by some of the war boats, or shot by some of the sentinels on duty.

But even suppose the point gained. Still insuperable difficulties seemed to present themselves. How could I escape observation in my wet seamans clothes? How could I pass from that Island to the main? How could I travel anywhere without being intercepted? But were even all these obstacles surmountable, how was it possible to escape from the ship guarded as she was by Midshipmen, quartermasters, ships corporals and marines? On a review of all these circumstances any attempt to escape seemed impracticable, but as the thoughts of it were easily enough indulged in I was constantly meditating on the subject.

Amongst those who were pressed about the same time as myself was a man a few years older than I, a native of Hartley, by the name of John Patterson. I often observed him casting many a wishfull look to the shore, and often heard him utter a half suppressed sigh as he turned his eyes from it. He doubtless had observed my conduct also, for he frequently looked very earnestly at me as we had occasion to pass each other. We soon came on speaking terms, and from that time forth seemed to enjoy much pleasure in each other's company. Still, however, we abstained from introducing a subject in which it was evident enough both of us had very closely at heart. It was not till after a good many days acquaintanceship had elapsed and many conversations on indifferent topics held that we ventured to open our minds to each other. This was done slowly and with great precaution at first, but soon finding how much our sentiments were in unison we dismissed reserve and became inseperable. From this time almost the

whole subject of our thoughts and conversation was the means
of escape. All the various ways in which there was the least
probability of success were calmly and deliberately discussed,
and the arguments for and against them duly weighed.
Whatever view we took of the matter, obstacles seemingly
insurmountable presented themselves to our view, and had the
prize been anything less than the recovery of our liberty, we
would have dispaired of success.

"He," says the proverb, "who thinks an object unattainable
makes it so." So we resolved to think our escape within the
bounds of possibility. Our first consideration was, How were we
to get clear of the ship and reach the shore? We at length
confined our attention solely to these points, resolved to make
the attempt and leave the rest to providence.

Our first step was to procure some bladders which we easily
prevailed with one of the men belonging to the ships boats to
purchase. We then tore up some old shirts and made them into
long narrow bags, large enough to hold a bladder when full
blown, and of sufficient length to go round the body below the
arm pits. Straps were attached to pass over each shoulder, and
one to pass between the legs in order to keep all in a proper
position. We had seven bladders in whole, of which Patterson
had three large and I four small – our quantity of wind would
be about the same, but my four distributing the wind more
regularly round the body afterwards proved the most como-
dious.

At this time the ship was very full of hands insomuch that
there were not room for all hands to sleep below. A considerable
number therefore slept in the waist hammock nettings. A place
on the upper deck projecting a small bit beyond the ships side,
where the greater number of beds and hammocks were stowed
during the day. As both the sides and top of this place were
covered with tarpaulins, we slept in it comfortable enough.

In this station did Patterson and I nightly place ourselves to
watch a favourable opportunity of escape. We left our beds to
the care of our messmates below, tied our bags of bladders in
our coverlets to resemble a bed and free of all suspicion repaired
to the hammock netting. Many nights passed away after our
resolutions were taken and our preparations made before we

were enabled to make the attempt. Some nights the tide did not suit, some it was too light, and some a very strict sentinel was on duty. Still, however, we adhered to our resolutions and our perseverance, as will be seen in the sequel, was crowned with success.

About the tenth or twelfth of October 1811, for I do not remember the precise date, conditions seemed to bid fair for our purpose. The weather was dark and lowering, the wind blew pretty fresh and to all appearance promised a wet night. What was of still greater consequence the tide exactly suited us. As the unfavourable, or I should rather say favourable, state of the weather continued till nightfall we resolved to attempt our project. Before dusk, we purchased and drank two or three glasses of rum each that we might stand the cold, bade adieu to a couple of our bosom confidants and then repaired to our station in the hammock netting.

When the evening drum beat a little before eight o'clock everything seemed favourable. The drum and the storm made noise enough to prevent our movements being heard, and the sentinel who paced the gangway was muffled closely up in his great coat.

When it came to the point my friend Patterson felt strongly inclined to draw back. All the dangers which we had before so amply discussed were again enumerated and amplified. With the same earnestness did I expatiate on the evils of slavery and enumerate the advantages that would result from our success. And how was success to be gained without exertion! My reasoning at last succeeded, and, fearing his resolution might forsake him after I was in the water, I prevailed on him to descend first.

When he gained the water the end of the rope got entangled about his foot and he gave a plunge to clear it. I trembled. The sound, increased as it was by my fears, seemed like the plunging of a grampus, but the noise was drowned by the surrounding storm. As soon as he was clear of the rope I slid softly down and slipped into the water without the smallest noise. I glided smoothly along close by the ship's side not daring to strike out lest my motion should be observed. I kept touching the ship's side with my hands as I floated along, and had thus an idea about how fast the tide carried me along. After I thought myself clear enough of the ship, I struck out and in a minute or two regained my companion. I found him very ill. In his strugle to clear himself of the rope he had swallowed some salt water which made him sick and when I overtook him I found him vomiting. I felt very unhappy on his account and soothed and encouraged him by all the means in my power. After his vomiting had ceased he grew better, and side by side we proceeded cheerily along. I had practised the art of swimming much more than my companion and could therefore proceed with much more ease and expedition. I amused myself with swimming round him relating anecdotes, chaunting in a low voice a verse or two of a song, etc., in encouraging him to put forth his strength. When he became fatigued we took each other by the hand and drifted slowly along until we recovered strength to put forth farther exertion.

When two or three miles from the ship we were excessively alarmed by the sound of human voices, apparently near at hand and almost immediately observed a boat from the shore standing toward the ship we had quitted. From our relative position we saw she must pass us within a few fathoms. We were overwhelmed with dread and terror. We expected nothing else than to be picked up and taken back where we would have met with the most rigorous punishment and would probably have been put in iron besides as long as we remained in harbour. We dared not to swim out of her way lest the motion should have betrayed us, so that we had no other resource but remain motionless and trust to providence. As she approached our alarm increased. We strove to sink beneath the surface, but were prevented by the buoyancy of our bladders. Fortunately she was rather to windward and the belly of the sail hanging over the lee gunnel in some measure sheltered us from the observation of those on board. What was also in our favour the crew seemed intent on some subject of debate as a continued and indistinct sound proceeded from the boat as long as she was distinguishable. It may here be asked, had we no apprehension of steering a wrong course? We had none. We possessed a most excellent compass. This was no other than the large comet of 1811. We had frequently observed that it lay precisely over the point of land we wished to gain. We therefore shaped our course direct for it and it proved a faithful guide.*

After many a trial to feel ground, Patterson exclaimed with the joy and in the words of Archimedes, "I have found it, I have found it!" I was almost afraid to try lest I should be disappointed, but seeing him at rest I let down my feet and found ground at little more than half a fathom. We found the shore very shelving, for when we first felt the ground we could scarcely observe any traces of the land. I think we had to walk about three quarters of a mile before we gained the beach and fatiguing walking we found it. On reaching the beach we threw ourselves on our knees to return our united thanks to that being who had brought us deliverance from the mighty waters, and to implore future guidance, strength and fortitude to support us under whatever trials we might still have to endure.

When we had advanced a few paces, we saw a light and by crossing a field or two soon gained it. It proceeded from a pretty large house standing alone. A board resembling a sign was fixed over the door, but we could not see whither it bore any inscription. On knocking at the door a person appeared at the window from which the light proceeded and demanded our business. We dared not tell him our true circumstances, but feigned a story of distress. It however made no impression on him. He told us in a surly tone to be gone, that it was past midnight and that he was determined not to open his door at such an unseasonable hour for any person whatever. We then tried another house whence a light issued, but with no better success. How comfortable would a glass or two of rum have been to us shivering as we were with cold and wetness? but a glass of rum we could not obtain.

We left these houses to retrace our steps to where we landed, but missed our way. We soon however gained the beach at a different and at a much better place. It seemed to be a snug little cove in which a considerable number of small boats were lying. The project on which we mainly depended previous to leaving the ship was to seize a boat and pull over to the Essex shore whence we could go to Maldon by land. Patterson had

* The comet of 1811 was brilliant for many weeks in the Northern Hemisphere, being specially conspicuous in the autumn of that year.

been at Maldon and knew several of the captains of coal vessels belonging to the North of England, which traded there, so that we expected if we could reach that place in safety it would not be difficult to procure a passage to the Northward. When we saw so many boats lying so oportunely, we were overjoyed and already anticipated the completion of our projects. After searching through a great number of them we found one seemingly Dutch built that had a small sail and a couple of oars aboard. This was just what we wanted. We slipped her painter and as the wind was southerly we set sail and stood as near as we could guess North East. From being so long wet we were very cold, but getting our oars out and pulling vigorously we soon brought ourselves into a state of agreeable warmth.

About an hour before day break we touched ground with our oars, on which we hauled a little more to the eastward resolving to get as far along shore as possible before dawn. We heard the *Ceres* fire her morning gun and had the happiness of seeing her hull down. It was our intention to land before sun rise and we made several attempts at this, but the shore was so shelving that we could no where get within half a mile of the shore. We therefore continued edging along shore as near as the depth of water would admit. We saw a good many vessels resembling light colliers bound to the Northwards, but we could not think of venturing to pull out to any of them lest they should betray us. We could easily have coasted it along to Blackwater river and have got in to Maldon with our boat, but we were detterred from this by considering that our appearance would have rendered us suspected, besides when day broke we saw our sail was merely a man of war's hammock, and this made our appearance still more suspicious. After a great many attempts during the morning and forenoon made to land, we, about midday, were fortunate enough to discover a small creek just wide enough to receive our boat. The water in it, being pretty deep, she did not ground untill her stern took the land, so that we were enabled to land without wetting our shoes. What became of the boat we never heard, but as we left her in a very snug berth and well moored, and as her owner's name was painted on the inside of her stern, we hoped, and doubted not, that the owner would ultimately recover her.

After passing a small earthen mound erected to keep the sea from breaking into the adjoining fields, we found ourselves on a delightful meadow. The sun was shining in meridian splendour, scarcely a cloud was to be seen in the wide expanse, the mild Zephyrs, as they skimmed along the fragrant meadow or over those fields which showed they had recently richly contributed to the support of man, seemed to whisper congratulations in our ear. We had just escaped from thralldom and were begining to taste the dawning sweets of that blessing so highly valued by Britons. Everything around us tended to exhilerate our spirits and we gave unrestrained scope to our feelings. Had any sober man seen us he would have undoubtedly questioned the soundness of our intellects. We leapt, we run, we rolled, we tumbled, we shouted, we gambolled in all the excess of joy and exultation, and it was not till several minutes elapsed that we could so far restrain the ebulitions of our joy as to permit us to set out on our journey. Observing a farm house at some distance we made up to it and found only one woman at home. The truth cannot always be told, nor could it be told here. We were compelled to fabricate a story of our shipwreck which we did with as few falsehoods as the case would admit. But sh! how much more difficult is it to scramble along the mazy paths of falsehood and prevarication than in the broad plain and open way of integrity and truth. With whatever care a falsehood may be fabricated it is supported with the utmost difficulty. A thousand questions may be put which the utmost human ingenuity could not have anticipated and a thousand falsehoods have to be uttered in support and confirmation of the first. The higher we rear the baseless structure, the more tottering it becomes, till at length it falls with a mighty crash and entombs its shuffling fabricators beneath its massy ruins.

The woman into whose house we went was of a mild and kindly disposition, more inclined to pity and releive than to doubt and question. She herself had a son who followed the seafaring business and who had been several times wrecked, so that she felt towards all those who suffered the same misfortune a kind of maternal sympathy. She set before us what a well stored pantry and dairy could afford, pressed us to partake heartily, which we were both able and willing to do, and at parting she would accept of no payment. "Keep your money, my lads," said she, beaming a look of kindness on us, "you have yet a long way to go (we had told her we were for the North) and you know not what you may yet need. May God bless you and deliver you from all your dangers, as he has from this last one." The gratitude excited in our breasts by this genuine treat of English hospitality, blended with the joy we felt at the recovery of our liberty, excited in us the most delightful emotions. Emotions which the greatest monarch on earth, possessed of unlimited power, abounding in riches, surrounded by flatterers, and wallowing in sensual pleasure, might well envy. We learned at this house that we were about 12 miles from Maldon, for which place, after taking an affectionate leave of our kind hostess, we set out. A luxuriant store of bramble berries by the roadside and a desire to avoid entering Maldon with day light induced us to linger a little by the way so that we did not reach Maldon till after dusk. We readily procured a bed to which after supper we immediately retired and soon made up for last night's lee way.

From *Landsman Hay: The Memoirs of Robert Hay 1785–1847*, (ed.) M.D. Hay, Rupert Hart-Davis, 1952

Inside the Wooden Walls I: an Ordinary Seaman's Memoir of Life in the Georgian Royal Navy

William Robinson

. . . we began to feel discipline with all its horrors. Our crew were divided into two watches, starboard and larboard. When one was on deck the other was below: for instance, the starboard watch would come on at eight o'clock at night, which is called eight-bells; at half-past is called one bell, and so on; every half-hour is a bell, as the hour-glass is turned, and the messenger sent to strike the bell, which is generally affixed near the fore-hatchway. It now becomes the duty of the officer on deck to see that the log-line is run out, to ascertain how many knots the ship goes an hour, which is entered in the log-book, with any other occurrence which may take place during the watch. At twelve o'clock, or eight-bells in the first watch, the boatswain's mate calls out lustily, "*Larboard watch, a-hoy*." This is called the middle watch, and when on deck, the other watch go below to their hammocks, till eight-bells, which is four o'clock in the morning. They then come on deck again, pull off their shoes and stockings, turn up their trowsers to above their knees, and commence *holy-stoning* the deck, as it is termed, (for Jack is sometimes a little impious in the way of his sayings.) – Here the men suffer from being obliged to kneel down on the wetted deck, and a gravelly sort of sand strewed over it. To perform this work they kneel with their bare knees, rubbing the deck with a stone and the sand, the grit of which is very injurious. In this manner the watch continues till about four-bells, or six o'clock; they then begin to wash and swab the decks till seven-bells, and at eight-bells the boatswain's mate pipes to breakfast. This meal consists of burgoo, made of coarse oatmeal and water; others will have Scotch coffee, which is burnt bread boiled in some water, and sweetened with sugar. This is generally cooked in a hook-pot in the galley, where there is a range. Nearly all the crew have one of these pots, a spoon, and a knife; for these are things indispensable: there are also basons, plates, &c. which are kept in each mess, which generally consists of eight persons, whose berth is between two of the guns on the lower deck, where there is a board placed, which swings with the rolling of the ship, and answers for a table. It sometimes happens that a lurch will dash all the crockery to pieces; they are then obliged to eat out of wooden or tin utensils, until they come into harbour, where they get another supply. At half-past eight o'clock, or one-bell in the forenoon watch, the larboard goes on deck, and the starboard remains below. Here again the *holy-stones* or *hand-bibles* as they are called by the crew, are used, and sometimes iron scrapers. After the lower deck has been wetted with swabs, these scrapers are used to take the rough dirt off. Whilst this is going on, the cooks from each mess are employed in cleaning the utensils and preparing for dinner, at the same time the watch are working the ship, and doing what is wanting to be done on deck.

About eleven o'clock, or six-bells, when any of the men are in irons, or on the black list, the boatswain or mate are ordered to call all hands; the culprits are then brought forward by the master at arms, who is a warrant officer, and acts the part of John Ketch, when required: he likewise has the prisoners in his custody, until they are put in irons, under any charge. All hands being now mustered, the captain orders the man to strip; he is then seized to a grating by the wrists and knees; his crime is then mentioned, and the prisoner may plead, but, in nineteen cases out of twenty, he is flogged for the most trifling offence or neglect, such as not hearing the watch called at night, not doing any thing properly on deck or aloft, which he might happen to be sent to do, when, perhaps, he has been doing the best he could, and at the same time ignorant of having done wrong, until he is pounced on, and put in irons. So much for the legal process.

After punishment, the boatswain's mate pipes to dinner, it being eight-bells, or twelve o'clock; and this is the pleasantest part of the day, as at one-bell the fifer is called to play "*Nancy Dawson*," or some other lively tune, a well-known signal that the grog is ready to be served out. It is the duty of the cook from each mess to fetch and serve it out to his messmates, of which every man and boy is allowed a pint, that is, one gill of rum and three of water, to which is added lemon acid, sweetened with sugar. Here I must remark, that the cook comes in for the perquisites of office, by reserving to himself an extra portion of grog, which is called the over-plus, and generally comes to the double of a man's allowance. Thus the cook can take upon himself to be the man of consequence, for he has the opportunity of inviting a friend to partake of a glass, or of paying any little debt he may have contracted. It may not be known to every one that it is grog which pays debts, and not money, in a man of war. Notwithstanding the cook's apparently preeminent situation, yet, on some occasions, he is subject to censure or punishment by his messmates, for not attending to the dinner properly, or for suffering the utensils of his department to be in a dirty condition. Justice, in these cases, is awarded by packing a jury of cooks from the different messes, for it falls to the lot of each man in a mess to act as cook in his turn. The mode or precept by which this jury is summoned is by hoisting a mess swab or beating a tin dish between decks forward, which serves as a proclamation to call the court together, when the case is fully heard and decided upon.

At two-bells in the afternoon, or one o'clock, the starboard watch goes on deck, and remains working the ship, pointing the ropes, or doing any duty that may be required until the eight-bells strike, when the boatswain's mate pipes to supper. This consists of half a pint of wine, or a pint of grog to each man, with biscuit and cheese, or butter . . .

From *Jack Nastyface: Nautical Economy*, William Robinson, 1836

Inside the Wooden Walls II: an Ordinary Seaman's Memoir of Life in the Georgian Royal Navy on the West Indies Station

Aaron Thomas, HMS Lapwing

Religion:
"There is no Clergyman there, no canonical man to bury their dead, or Christian their Children. No man to Join together in holy Wedlock or Church weomen. and yet most of the islander are good people. They are a fine set of looking persons. Very Tractable, and all might be easyly made true followers of God. The men & weomen are hale looking but generally very lank in their bodies, they live on Yams, Sweet Potatoes, and the roots which their Island produceth, their wants are few & their supplies are many. On Sundays they have nothing to do, but visit each other, had they a Holy man amongst them *His House* would be the general redevoze for all of the Island on Sunday."

"Ashore at St. Kitts this day, the Captain waited an hour for *all the* Boats Crew. – He swore he would flog the Coxwain and all of them, when they were found; pray where have you all been, says the Captain; We have *all been to Church* says the Coxwain, – I will Church you all says the Captain when you get aboard. – But the Captain took no notice of it, further than remarking to Capt Brown that he was very angry with them, but the extreme novelty of a Boats Crew, being absent from the Boat, and found *in a Church*; instead of a Grog Shop; was so *new*. so *singular*, and so uncommon a *thing*; – That their answer melted his rath, into complete forgiveness."

Corporal Punishment:
"Saturday 13 October. Captain Harvey paid much attention to the circumstances of the Robery last night. The theife Thomson accused many people, of Robing Mr Taylor before, – In Thompsons Pillow was found a Bag, containing 6 Joes, secreted there; being the produce of his former plundering, With money of Thomsons in other people hands, and the money in the Bag, it was proved that he had about 15 Joes, and all except Three; was plunder. a poor french Boy about Twenty days Back, lost 8 Dollars in little Bag from under his head, as he laid asleep, and the money which was found in Thomsons Pillow Case, was enclosed in this Identical Bag, which the Boy owned, as soon as he saw it.

At 10 a.m Thomsons arms was lashed; the Ships Company formed a Lane all around the Waiste of the Ship, every man being provided with a Nettle, 2 Marines faced him with each a Bayonet pointed at the Theife, a Cord was thrown over the prisoners body, the ends of which were held behind by Two Quartermasters, Things being thus ordered he run the Gauntlet, every man striking him as he passed; the noise of which I thought at the time, resembled Reapers at work, when cuting Corn. After passing once round, he fainted and & droped down. – The Surgeon threw some Hartshorn in his face, and he was ordered into Irons, to receive more punishment when his back recovers."

Disease:
"At half past Seven p.m. Peter Bird a Seaman Aged Twenty Three departed this life. He had been ill of a Flux about nine days. – About three months ago this young man showed me a Letter which he had from his Mother he also told me, that his mind was fixed upon young weoman in London: who he *intended to Marry*, when the war was over adding I am but a young man, and she will forgive me for leaving her as I did. – So I see this poor youth, was boasting in his strength, but the Lord has told us of this folly, by taking one away from amongst us, who has been in the Ship more than 4 years, and during all that period, has never been in the Sick List untill nine days before his death."

"I am sorry to inform you, quella our Bastimento is very sickly, several of our hale, healthy looking Lads, have died suddenly of fevers, within these 9 days. We have sent a number to the Hospital, where some have died also. My old Ship the *Concord*, is now refiting in English Harbor Antigua, She has been there about 4 weeks, since which time she has buryed 27 men, and has 98 sick in the Hospital at this time."

"Took another live Gigger from out of the under part of my second Toe, of my left foot. It is a foolish thing to be to proud. We all know that grubs & worms destroy our Carcases when dead, but in this climate the Gigger worm eats its way under our Skin, lays his Eggs there, without our knowledge, until its young ones, by it motions give us uneasyness. We then look at the place and see a loathsome wound in which is 90, or 130 live insects. The wound must be cut open, and all the insects taken clean out, or else its effects will be fatal. From this Insects creeping alive, under the Skin of my two fear, I have not them both laped up in rags. The Giggers by getting into the feet of Soldiers, have stoped the military progress of many good General in the West Indies. It is said that a Gigger, at a certain period of his age will fly: it must be so, or how do they get about ones breasts & c. One of our men a few days ago, had one taken out of his private parts in the Cockput. in which were 85 eggs."

"The Black Negro Girls have the Pox amongst them, as well as our white Ladies in England. There is at this time Eleven Venerals in the List. Silvia the Spaniard. Farthing & Hassels cases are uncommonly virulent and malignant. The only good, the unhappy Captain Cook did in visiting the North & South Pacific Ocean; was to *give the Pox*; to the Inhabitants of *every Island* where the Adventure & Resolution watered at as when these 2 Ships left Maderia in August 1772. Each had several veneral patients on board which arose from the amours which the English Sailors had; with the Portuguese Puttani, in Funchal."

Alcohol consumption:
"Punished the Boy Skipper on his Backside with 12 Lashes for giving yesterday half a Gill of Rum to Gater the Marine for

washing his Cloaths. – There is something particular in this case. The Boys are allowed their Rum and if they drink it, they often get drunk with it, therefore it is understood, they may give it to persons who wash & mind for them: And many Boys in some Ships sell their Liquor. But this particular Boy was floged for giving his Liquor away to a Marine who had done work for him. So that by floging this Lad, it is the same as giving out orders, for all the Boys to drink their own allowance, and thereby get drunk with it. The best that can be said of it is; that it will encourage intoxication."

"William Woodcock had half a Dozen Lashes, for being the person, who requested Elder to bring off the Quart of Gin;

NB at the Gangway the Captain declared to Elder, that he would flog him, untill he confessed who the Bladder of Gin belonged to, – Elder took 2 Dozen, and then he confessed it was Woodcock, who the Gin was for.

CONTRAST. The Captain got drunk – so drunk that he fell three times off his Horse – I myself at Breakfast heard him say 'I drank too much wine yesterday: I would give Sixpence had I not drank so much.' Yet this man who got so drunk as to fall 3 times off his Horse; gave 30 lashes on the bare backs of 2 men, for attempting to obtain the possession of one Quart of Gin."

Morals:
"What a Desolute life does man lead in the West Indias. The Blacks never marry. But have intercourse one with another promiscuously. All the white men; Planters as well as merchants: have connection with their female Negros. As to the black Girls themselves, any white or Creole man may have commerce with them, so very little difficulty is there on this head, that it is as easy to lye with them, as it is to convey a glass of wine to your mouth, when you have it in your hand. A white Sailor may go amongst the Hutts upon an Esstate, where there is 70 female Negros and he will not find the smallest opposition to his will, but will be courted to stop amongst them."

"Capt Renolds of the *Etrusco* was ordered to carry home a Lady, who was going from England to the East Indias to see her Husband. At St Helens she heard of her Husbands death. She took a passage from Spence back to England again, & in the Passage back was captured by french Privateer, & carried to Guadulupe, she got her Liberty was ordered to go home in the *Etrusco* but Renolds said he would not take her unless she slept with him all the passage."

Prize-Taking:

"Sunday 26th. off Fort Royal Bay at daylight saw a small strange Sail, which bore down towards us, but when she came near enough to reconoitre, she hauled her wind, & made sail from us; at 6 a.m. we made sail in Chace, at 7 she hoisted french Colours, worked her Sweeps, and made every effort to escape. We fired – Grape, and round shot at her until 30 minutes past Eight; when she struck her colours, and shortened Sail. She proved to be *la Fortune* french Schooner of 6 swivels (4 of which she threw overboard in Chace) and 22 men, from Guadulupe, but last from Descada. – Got the Prisonors aboard, gave the Prize a Tow Rope, and made sale for fort Royal Bay. – This small Schooner in her last Cruize took, a prize when each man shared 2,500 Dollars each. – This Schooner will not fetch more than 40 Joes at Martinico, but the French Prisonors say, was she at Basseterre in Guadulupe, she would sell for 150 Joes, because they are just the size Vessels which the French want to anoy our commerce with. The Captain of the Schooner says, that this little Schooner will fetch more money in Guadulupe then a Ship of 300 Ton. – so much do they run on Privateering."

"There is more Prize money made in the West Indias than there is at home, but to counterbalance this advantage one Guinea in England, will go as far as two Guineas in the West Indias."

"Monday the 18th of March 1799 At 8 a.m. gave Chace to a Strange Sail at 2 p.m. came up with the Chace, she proved to be a Sweedish Schooner from Cyane to St. Batholomew, laden with Cotton, Drugs & live Turtles. She had four french Passengers aboard, and a small part of the Cargo, no doubt was french property, but the trouble of taking her in, Condemnation, Admiralty & Expences, would a made it a poor Prize, so the Captains thought it best to let her go on, on her voyage."

Social hierarchy:

"In my present situation, I can speak and walke with whom I like, but had I laid hold of the public situation which you hint at; I could not a done so, for had I spoken to persons in an inferior rank to myself, my Brother officers, would have said, that I acted deregoratory to my Character. Saint James, in his Epistle to his Bretheren says, Chapter 2 Verse 9. 'If he have respects to persons, ye commit sin; and are convinced of the Law, as transgressors.' Now was I a Purser, the moment I became one, I must bid advice, to ever *saying* a civil word, or ever giving a *civil* look, to any one of the men before the Mast, in presence of a superior Officer, for it is held in the Navy, to be a proof, of something shocking & bad, to speake to the men with civillity, and if you do, do it: your promotion is damed. Now for my own part, I never am more happier, than when conversing with my inferiors, for from them I learn more of life, than I do by conversing with Officers, whose general talke is to abuse high & low, or every body whom they know. Besides let my Ideas be what they will, I can never give, but on general sentiment at the Wardroom, or Gunroom table, and at the Captains Table, I must set 3 hours, to hear him talke of *himself*, and must *never* contradict a word he utters, but nod *yes* to everything he says, and do not you think this forced tacitity, is paying very dear, for a plate of Mutton, a Tumbler of Porter & Six glasses of wine."

From Thomas's journal 1788–9, reprinted from the University of Miami Library website, www.library miami edu/archives/thomas

APPENDIX V

The Early Life and Career of Nelson
Robert Southey

Horatio, son of Edmund and Catherine Nelson, was born September 29, 1758, in the parsonage-house of Burnham Thorpe, a village in the county of Norfolk, of which his father was rector. His mother was a daughter of Dr. Suckling, prebendary of Westminster, whose grandmother was sister of Sir Robert Walpole, and this child was named after his godfather, the first Lord Walpole. Mrs. Nelson died in 1767, leaving eight out of eleven children. Her brother, Captain Maurice Suckling, of the navy visited the widower upon this event, and promised to take care of one of the boys. Three years afterwards, when Horatio was only twelve years of age, being at home during the Christmas holidays, he read in the county newspaper that his uncle was appointed to the *Raisonnable*, of sixty-four guns. "Do, William," said he to a brother who was a year and a half older than himself, "write to my father, and tell him that I should like to go to sea with uncle Maurice." Mr. Nelson was then at Bath, whither he had gone for the recovery of his health: his circumstances were straitened, and he had no prospect of ever seeing them bettered: he knew that it was the wish of providing for himself by which Horatio was chiefly actuated, and did not oppose his resolution; he understood also the boy's character, and had always said, that in whatever station he might be placed, he would climb if possible to the very top of the tree. Captain Suckling was written to. "What," said he in his answer, "has poor Horatio done, who is so weak, that he, above all the rest, should be sent to rough it out at sea? – But let him come; and the first time we go into action, a cannon-ball may knock off his head, and provide for him at once."

It is manifest from these words that Horatio was not the boy whom his uncle would have chosen to bring up in his own profession. He was never of a strong body; and the ague, which at that time was one of the most common diseases in England, had greatly reduced his strength; yet he had already given proofs of that resolute heart and nobleness of mind which, during his whole career of labour and of glory, so eminently distinguished him. When a mere child, he strayed a-birds'-nesting from his grandmother's house in company with a cowboy: the dinner-hour elapsed; he was absent, and could not be found; and the alarm of the family became very great, for they apprehended that he might have been carried off by gipsies. At length, after search had been made for him in various directions, he was discovered alone, sitting composedly by the side of a brook which he could not get over. "I wonder, child," said the old lady when she saw him, "that hunger and fear did not drive you home." "Fear! grandmama:" replied the future hero, "I never saw fear: – what is it?" Once, after the winter holidays, when he and his brother William had set off on horseback to return to school, they came back, because there had been a fall of snow; and William, who did not much like the journey, said it was too deep for them to venture on. "If that be the case," said the father, "you certainly shall not go; but make another attempt, and I will leave it to your honour. If the road is dangerous you may return: but remember, boys, I leave it to your honour!" The snow was deep enough to have afforded them a reasonable excuse; but Horatio was not to be prevailed upon to turn back. "We must go on," said he: "remember, brother, it was left to our honour!" – There were some fine pears growing in the schoolmaster's garden, which the boys regarded as lawful booty, and in the highest degree tempting;

but the boldest among them were afraid to venture for the prize. Horatio volunteered upon this service: he was lowered down at night from the bedroom window by some sheets, plundered the tree, was drawn up with the pears, and then distributed them among his school-fellows without reserving any for himself. "He only took them," he said, "because every other boy was afraid."

Early on a cold and dark spring morning Mr. Nelson's servant arrived at this school, at North Walsham, with the expected summons for Horatio to join his ship. The parting from his brother William, who had been for so many years his playmate and bed-fellow, was a painful effort, and was the beginning of those privations which are the sailor's lot through life. He accompanied his father to London. The *Raisonnable* was lying in the Medway. He was put into the Chatham stage, and on its arrival was set down with the rest of the passengers, and left to find his way on board as he could. After wandering about in the cold, without being able to reach the ship, an officer observed the forlorn appearance of the boy, questioned him; and happening to be acquainted with his uncle, took him home and gave him some refreshments. When he got on board, Captain Suckling was not in the ship, nor had any person been apprised of the boy's coming. He paced the deck the whole remainder of the day without being noticed by any one; and it was not till the second day that somebody, as he expressed it, "took compassion on him." The pain which is felt when we are first transplanted from our native soil—when the living branch is cut from the parent tree is one of the most poignant which we have to endure through life. There are after-griefs which wound more deeply, which leave behind them scars never to be effaced, which bruise the spirit, and sometimes break the heart; but never do we feel so keenly the want of love, the necessity of being loved, and the sense of utter desertion, as when we first leave the haven of home, and are, as it were, pushed off upon the stream of life. Added to these feelings, the sea-boy has to endure physical hardships, and the privation of every comfort, even of sleep. Nelson had a feeble body and an affectionate heart, and he remembered through life his first days of wretchedness in the service.

The *Raisonnable* having been commissioned on account of the dispute respecting the Falkland Islands, was paid off as soon as the difference with the court of Spain was accommodated, and Captain Suckling was removed to the *Triumph*, seventy-four, then stationed as a guard-ship in the Thames. This was considered as too inactive a life for a boy, and Nelson was therefore sent a voyage to the West Indies in a merchantship, commanded by Mr. John Rathbone, an excellent seaman, who had served as master's mate under Captain Suckling in the Dreadnought. He returned a practical seaman, but with a hatred of the king's service, and a saying then common among the sailors—"Aft the most honour; forward the better man." Rathbone had probably been disappointed and disgusted in the navy; and, with no unfriendly intentions, warned Nelson against a profession which he himself had found hopeless. His uncle received him on board the *Triumph* on his return, and discovering his dislike to the navy, took the best means of reconciling him to it. He held it out as a reward that, if he attended well to his navigation, he should go in the cutter and decked long-boat, which was attached to the commanding-officer's ship at Chatham. Thus he became a good pilot for vessels of that description from Chatham to the Tower, and down the Swin Channel to the North Foreland, and acquired a confidence among rocks and sands of which he often felt the value.

Nelson had not been many months on board the *Triumph*, when his love of enterprise was excited by hearing that two ships were fitting out for a voyage of discovery towards the North Pole. In consequence of the difficulties which were expected on such a service, these vessels were to take out effective men instead of the usual number of boys. This, however, did not deter him from soliciting to be received, and, by his uncle's interest, he was admitted as coxswain under Captain Lutwidge, second in command. The voyage was undertaken in compliance with an application from the Royal Society. The Hon. Captain Constantine John Phipps, eldest son of Lord Mulgrave, volunteered his services. The *Racehorse* and *Carcass* bombs were selected as the strongest ships, and, therefore, best adapted for such a voyage; and they were taken into dock and strengthened, to render them as secure as possible against the ice. Two masters of Greenlandmen were employed as pilots for each ship. No expedition was ever more carefully fitted out; and the First Lord of the Admiralty, Lord Sandwich, with a laudable solicitude, went on board himself, before their departure, to see that everything had been completed to the wish of the officers. The ships were provided with a simple and excellent apparatus for distilling fresh from salt water, the invention of Dr. Irving, who accompanied the expedition. It consisted merely in fitting a tube to the ship's kettle, and applying a wet mop to the surface as the vapour was passing. By these means, from thirty-four to forty gallons were produced every day.

They sailed from the Nore on the 4th of June. On the 6th of July they were in latitude 79d 56m 39s; longitude 9d 43m 30s E. The next day, about the place where most of the old discoverers had been stopped, the *Racehorse* was beset with ice; but they hove her through with ice-anchors. Captain Phipps continued ranging along the ice, northward and westward, till the 24th; he then tried to the eastward. On the 30th he was in latitude 80d 13m; longitude 18d 48m E. among the islands and in the ice, with no appearance of an opening for the ships. The weather was exceedingly fine, mild, and unusually clear. Here they were becalmed in a large bay, with three apparent openings between the islands which formed it; but everywhere, as far as they could see, surrounded with ice. There was not a breath of air, the water was perfectly smooth, the ice covered with snow, low and even, except a few broken pieces near the edge; and the pools of water in the middle of the ice-fields just crusted over with young ice. On the next day the ice closed upon them, and no opening was to be seen anywhere, except a hole, or lake as it might be called, of about a mile and a half in circumference, where the ships lay fast to the ice with their ice-anchors. From these ice-fields they filled their casks with water, which was very pure and soft. The men were playing on the ice all day; but the Greenland pilots, who were further than they had ever been before, and considered that the season was far advancing, were alarmed at being thus beset.

The next day there was not the smallest opening; the ships

were within less than two lengths of each other, separated by ice, and neither having room to turn. The ice, which the day before had been flat and almost level with the water's edge, was now in many places forced higher than the mainyard by the pieces squeezing together. A day of thick fog followed: it was succeeded by clear weather; but the passage by which the ships had entered from the westward was closed, and no open water was in sight, either in that or any other quarter. By the pilots' advice the men were set to cut a passage, and warp through the small openings to the westward. They sawed through pieces of ice twelve feet thick; and this labour continued the whole day, during which their utmost efforts did not move the ships above three hundred yards; while they were driven, together with the ice, far to the N.E. and E. by the current. Sometimes a field of several acres square would be lifted up between two larger islands, and incorporated with them; and thus these larger pieces continued to grow by aggregation. Another day passed, and there seemed no probability of getting the ships out without a strong E. or N.E. wind. The season was far advanced, and every hour lessened the chance of extricating themselves. Young as he was, Nelson was appointed to command one of the boats which were sent out to explore a passage into the open water. It was the means of saving a boat belonging to the *Racehorse* from a singular but imminent danger. Some of the officers had fired at and wounded a walrus. As no other animal has so human-like an expression in its countenance, so also is there none that seems to possess more of the passions of humanity. The wounded animal dived immediately, and brought up a number of its companions; and they all joined in an attack upon the boat. They wrested an oar from one of the men; and it was with the utmost difficulty that the crew could prevent them from staving or upsetting her, till the *Carcass*'s boat came up; and the walruses, finding their enemies thus reinforced, dispersed. Young Nelson exposed himself in a more daring manner. One night, during the mid-watch, he stole from the ship with one of his comrades, taking advantage of a rising fog, and set off over the ice in pursuit of a bear. It was not long before they were missed. The fog thickened, and Captain Lutwidge and his officers became exceedingly alarmed for their safety. Between three and four in the morning the weather cleared, and the two adventurers were seen, at a considerable distance from the ship, attacking a huge bear. The signal for them to return was immediately made; Nelson's comrade called upon him to obey it, but in vain; his musket had flashed in the pan; their ammunition was expended; and a chasm in the ice, which divided him from the bear, probably preserved his life. "Never mind," he cried; "do but let me get a blow at this devil with the butt-end of my musket, and we shall have him." Captain Lutwidge, however, seeing his danger, fired a gun, which had the desired effect of frightening the beast; and the boy then returned, somewhat afraid of the consequences of his trespass. The captain reprimanded him sternly for conduct so unworthy of the office which he filled, and desired to know what motive he could have for hunting a bear. "Sir," said he, pouting his lip, as he was wont to do when agitated, "I wished to kill the bear, that I might carry the skin to my father."

A party were now sent to an island, about twelve miles off (named Walden's Island in the charts, from the midshipman who was intrusted with this service), to see where the open water lay. They came back with information that the ice, though close all about them, was open to the westward, round the point by which they came in. They said also, that upon the island they had had a fresh east wind. This intelligence considerably abated the hopes of the crew; for where they lay it had been almost calm, and their main dependence had been upon the effect of an easterly wind in clearing the bay. There was but one alternative: either to wait the event of the weather upon the ships, or to betake themselves to the boats. The likelihood that it might be necessary to sacrifice the ships had been foreseen. The boats accordingly were adapted, both in number and size, to transport, in case of emergency, the whole crew; and there were Dutch whalers upon the coast, in which they could all be conveyed to Europe. As for wintering where they were, that dreadful experiment had been already tried too often. No time was to be lost; the ships had driven into shoal water, having but fourteen fathoms. Should they, or the ice to which they were fast, take the ground, they must inevitably be lost; and at this time they were driving fast toward some rocks on the N.E. Captain Phipps sent for the officers of both ships, and told them his intention of preparing the boats for going away. They were immediately hoisted out, and the fitting begun. Canvas bread-bags were made, in case it should be necessary suddenly to desert the vessels; and men were sent with the lead and line to N. and E., to sound wherever they found cracks in the ice, that they might have notice before the ice took the ground; for in that case the ships must instantly have been crushed or overset.

On the 7th of August they began to haul the boats over the ice, Nelson having command of a four-oared cutter. The men behaved excellently well, like true British seamen: they seemed reconciled to the thought of leaving the ships, and had full confidence in their officers. About noon, the ice appeared rather more open near the vessels; and as the wind was easterly, though there was but little of it, the sails were set, and they got about a mile to the westward. They moved very slowly, and were not now nearly so far to the westward as when they were first beset. However, all sail was kept upon them, to force them through whenever the ice slacked the least. Whatever exertions were made, it could not be possible to get the boats to the water's edge before the 14th; and if the situation of the ships should not alter by that time, it would not be justifiable to stay longer by them. The commander therefore resolved to carry on both attempts together, moving the boats constantly, and taking every opportunity of getting the ships through. A party was sent out next day to the westward to examine the state of the ice: they returned with tidings that it was very heavy and close, consisting chiefly of large fields. The ships, however, moved something, and the ice itself was drifting westward. There was a thick fog, so that it was impossible to ascertain what advantage had been gained. It continued on the 9th; but the ships were moved a little through some very small openings: the mist cleared off in the afternoon, and it was then perceived that they had driven much more than could have been expected to the westward, and that the ice itself had driven still further. In the course of the day they got past the boats, and took them on board again. On the morrow the wind sprang up to the N.N.E. All sail was set, and the ships forced their way through a great deal of very heavy ice. They frequently struck, and with such force that one stroke broke the shank of the *Racehorse*'s best bower-anchor, but the vessels made way; and by noon they had cleared the ice, and were out at sea. The next day they anchored in Smeerenberg Harbour, close to that island of which the westernmost point is called Hakluyt's Headland, in honour of the great promoter and compiler of our English voyages of discovery.

Here they remained a few days, that the men might rest after their fatigue. No insect was to be seen in this dreary country, nor any species of reptile – not even the common earth-worm. Large bodies of ice, called icebergs, filled up the valleys between high mountains, so dark as, when contrasted with the snow, to appear black. The colour of the ice was a lively light green. Opposite to the place where they fixed their observatory was one of these icebergs, above three hundred feet high; its side toward the sea was nearly perpendicular, and a stream of water issued from it. Large pieces frequently broke off and rolled down into the sea. There was no thunder nor lightning during the whole time they were in these latitudes. The sky was generally loaded with hard white clouds, from which it was never entirely free even in the clearest weather. They always knew when they were approaching the ice long before they saw it, by a bright appearance near the horizon, which the Greenlandmen called the blink of the ice. The season was now so far advanced that nothing more could have been attempted, if indeed anything had been left untried; but the summer had been unusually favourable, and they had carefully surveyed the wall of ice, extending for more than twenty degrees between the latitudes of 80d and 81d, without the smallest appearance of any opening.

The ships were paid off shortly after their return to England; and Nelson was then placed by his uncle with Captain Farmer, in the *Seahorse*, of twenty guns, then going out to the East Indies in the squadron under Sir Edward Hughes. He was stationed in the foretop at watch and watch. His good conduct attracted the attention of the master (afterwards Captain Surridge), in whose watch he was; and upon his recommendation the captain rated him as midshipman. At this time his countenance was florid, and his appearance rather stout and athletic; but when he had been about eighteen months in India, he felt the effects of that climate, so perilous to European constitutions. The disease baffled all power of medicine; he was reduced almost to a skeleton; the use of his limbs was for some time entirely lost; and the only hope that remained was from a voyage home. Accordingly he was brought home by Captain Pigot, in the *Dolphin*; and had it not been for the attentive and careful kindness of that officer on the way, Nelson would never have lived to reach his native shores. He had formed an acquaintance with Sir Charles Pole, Sir Thomas Troubridge, and other distinguished officers, then, like himself, beginning their career: he had left them pursuing that career in full enjoyment of health and hope, and was returning, from a country in which all things were to him new and interesting, with a body broken down by sickness, and spirits which had sunk with his strength. Long afterwards, when the name of Nelson was known as widely as that of England itself, he spoke of the feelings which he at this time endured. "I felt impressed," said he, "with a feeling that I should never rise in my profession. My mind was staggered with a view of the difficulties I had to surmount and the little interest I possessed. I could discover no means of reaching the object of my ambition. After a long and gloomy reverie, in which I almost wished myself overboard, a sudden glow of patriotism was kindled within me, and presented my king and country as my patron. 'Well then,' I exclaimed, 'I will be a hero! and, confiding in Providence, I will brave every danger!'"

Long afterwards Nelson loved to speak of the feelings of that moment; and from that time, he often said, a radiant orb was suspended in his mind's eye, which urged him onward to renown. The state of mind in which these feelings began, is what the mystics mean by their season of darkness and desertion. If the animal spirits fail, they represent it as an actual temptation. The enthusiasm of Nelson's nature had taken a different direction, but its essence was the same. He knew to what the previous state of dejection was to be attributed; that an enfeebled body, and a mind depressed, had cast this shade over his soul; but he always seemed willing to believe that the sunshine which succeeded bore with it a prophetic glory, and that the light which led him on was "light from heaven."

His interest, however, was far better than he imagined, During his absence, Captain Suckling had been made Comptroller of the Navy; his health had materially improved upon the voyage; and as soon as the *Dolphin* was paid off, he was appointed acting lieutenant in the *Worcester*, sixty-four, Captain Mark Robinson, then going out with convoy to Gibraltar. Soon after his return, on the 8th of April 1777, he passed his examination for a lieutenancy. Captain Suckling sat at the head of the board; and when the examination had ended, in a manner highly honourable to Nelson, rose from his seat, and introduced him to the examining captains as his nephew. They expressed their wonder that he had not informed them of this relationship before; he replied that he did not wish the younker to be favoured; he knew his nephew would pass a good examination, and he had not been deceived. The next day Nelson received his commission as second lieutenant of the *Lowestoffe* frigate, Captain William Locker, then fitting out for Jamaica.

American and French privateers, under American colours, were at that time harassing our trade in the West Indies: even a frigate was not sufficiently active for Nelson, and he repeatedly got appointed to the command of one of the *Lowestoffe*'s tenders. During one of their cruises the *Lowestoffe* captured an American letter-of-marque: it was blowing a gale, and a heavy sea running. The first lieutenant being ordered to board the prize, went below to put on his hanger. It happened to be mislaid; and while he was seeking it, Captain Locker came on deck. Perceiving the boat still alongside, and in danger every moment of being swamped, and being extremely anxious that the privateer should be instantly taken in charge, because he feared that It would otherwise founder, he exclaimed, "Have I no officer in the ship who can board the prize?" Nelson did not offer himself immediately, waiting, with his usual sense of propriety, for the first lieutenant's return; but hearing the master volunteer, he jumped into the boat, saying, "It is my turn now; and if I come back, it is yours." The American, who had carried a heavy press of sail in hope of escaping, was so completely water-logged that the *Lowestoffe*'s boat went in on deck and out again with the sea

About this time he lost his uncle. Captain Locker, however, who had perceived the excellent qualities of Nelson, and formed a friendship for him which continued during his life, recommended him warmly to Sir Peter Parker, then commander-in-chief upon that station. In consequence of this recommendation he was removed into the *Bristol* flag-ship, and Lieutenant Cuthbert Collingwood succeeded him in the *Lowestoffe*. Sir Peter Parker was the friend of both, and thus it happened that whenever Nelson got a step in rank, Collingwood succeeded him. The former soon became first lieutenant, and on the 8th of December 1778 was appointed commander of the *Badger* brig; Collingwood taking his place in the *Bristol*. While the *Badger* was lying in Montego Bay, Jamaica, the *Glasgow* of twenty guns came in and anchored there, and in two hours was in flames, the steward having set fire to her while stealing rum out of the after-hold. Her crew were leaping into the water, when Nelson came up in his boats, made them throw their powder overboard and point their guns upward; and by his presence of mind and personal exertions prevented the loss of life which would otherwise have ensued. On the 11th of June 1779 he was made post into the *Hinchinbrook*, of twenty-eight guns, an enemy's merchantman, sheathed with wood, which had been taken into the service. Collingwood was then made commander into the *Badger*. A short time after he left the *Lowestoffe*, that ship, with a small squadron, stormed the fort of St. Fernando de Omoa, on the south side of the Bay of Honduras, and captured some register ships which were lying under its guns. Two hundred and fifty quintals of quicksilver and three millions of piastres were the reward of this enterprise; and it is characteristic of Nelson that the chance by which he missed a share in such a prize is never mentioned in any of his letters; nor is it likely that it ever excited even a momentary feeling of vexation.

Nelson was fortunate in possessing good interest at the time when it could be most serviceable to him: his promotion had been almost as rapid as it could be; and before he had attained the age of twenty-one he had gained that rank which brought all the honours of the service within his reach. No opportunity, indeed, had yet been given him of distinguishing himself; but he was thoroughly master of his profession, and his zeal and ability were acknowledged wherever he was known. Count d'Estaing, with a fleet of one hundred and twenty-five sail, men of war and transports, and a reputed force of five-and twenty thousand men, threatened Jamaica from St. Domingo. Nelson offered his services to the Admiral and to Governor-General Dalling, and was appointed to command the batteries of Fort Charles, at Port Royal. Not more than seven thousand men could be mustered for the defence of the island, – a number wholly inadequate to resist the force which threatened them. Of this Nelson was so well aware, that when he wrote to his friends in England, he told them they must not be surprised to hear of his learning to speak French. D'Estaing, however, was either not aware of his own superiority, or not equal to the command with which he was intrusted: he attempted nothing with his formidable armament; and General Dalling was thus left to execute a project which he had formed against the Spanish colonies.

This project was, to take Fort San Juan on the river of that name, which flows from Lake Nicaragua into the Atlantic; make himself master of the lake itself, and of the cities of Granada and Leon; and thus cut off the communication of the Spaniards between their northern and southern possessions in America. Here it is that a canal between the two seas may most easily be formed—a work more important in its conse-quences than any which has ever yet been effected by human power. Lord George Germaine, at that time secretary of state for the American Department, approved the plan; and as discontents at that time were known to prevail in the Nuevo Reyno, in Popayan, and in Peru, the more sanguine part of the English began to dream of acquiring an empire in one part of America, more extensive than that which they were on the point of losing in another. General Dalling's plans were well formed; but the history and the nature of the country had not been studied as accurately as its geography: the difficulties which occurred in fitting out the expedition delayed it till the season was too far advanced; and the men were thus sent to adventure themselves, not so much against an enemy, whom they would have beaten, as against a climate which would do the enemy's work.

Early in the year 1780, five hundred men destined for this service were convoyed by Nelson from Port Royal to Cape Gracias a Dios, in Honduras. Not a native was to be seen when they landed: they had been taught that the English came with no other intent than that of enslaving them, and sending them to Jamaica. After a while, however, one of them ventured down, confiding in his knowledge of one of the party; and by his means the neighbouring tribes were conciliated with presents, and brought in. The troops were encamped on a swampy and unwholesome plain, where they were joined by a party of the 79th regiment from Black River, who were already in a deplorable state of sickness. Having remained here a month, they proceeded, anchoring frequently, along the Mosquito shore, to collect their Indian allies, who were to furnish proper boats for the river, and to accompany them. They reached the river San Juan, March 24th; and here, according to his orders, Nelson's services were to terminate; but not a man in the expedition had ever been up the river, or knew the distance of any fortification from its mouth; and he not being one who would turn back when so much was to be done, resolved to carry the soldiers up. About two hundred, therefore, were embarked in the Mosquito shore craft and in two of the *Hinchinbrook*'s boats, and they began their voyage. It was the latter end of the dry season, the worst time for such an expedition; the river was consequently low. Indians were sent forward through narrow channels between shoals and sand-banks, and the men were frequently obliged to quit the boats and exert their utmost strength to drag or thrust them along. This labour continued for several days; when they came into deeper water, they had then currents and rapids to contend with, which would have been insurmountable but for the skill of the Indians in such difficulties. The brunt of the labour was borne by them and by the sailors – men never accustomed to stand aloof when any exertion of strength or hardihood is required. The soldiers, less accustomed to rely upon themselves, were of little use. But all equally endured the violent heat of the sun, rendered more intense by being reflected from the white shoals; while the high woods, on both sides of the river, were frequently so close as to prevent any refreshing circulation of air; and during the night all were equally exposed to the heavy and unwholesome dews.

On the 9th of April they reached an island in the river, called San Bartolomeo, which the Spaniards had fortified, as an outpost, with a small semicircular battery, mounting nine or ten swivels, and manned with sixteen or eighteen men. It commanded the river in a rapid and difficult part of the navigation. Nelson, at the head of a few of his seamen, leaped upon the beach. The ground upon which he sprung was so muddy that he had some difficulty in extricating himself, and lost his shoes: bare-footed, however, he advanced, and, in his own phrase, boarded the battery. In this resolute attempt he was bravely supported by Despard, at that time a captain in the army, afterward unhappily executed for his schemes of revolutionary treason. The castle of San Tuan is situated about 16 miles higher up; the stores and ammunition, however, were landed a few miles below the castle, and the men had to march through woods almost impassable. One of the men was bitten under the eye by a snake which darted upon him from the bough of a tree. He was unable to proceed from the violence of the pain; and when, after a short while, some of his comrades were sent back to assist him, he was dead, and the body already putrid. Nelson himself narrowly escaped a similar fate. He had ordered his hammock to be slung under some trees, being excessively fatigued, and was sleeping, when a monitory lizard passed across his face. The Indians happily observed the reptile; and knowing what it indicated, awoke him. He started up, and found one of the deadliest serpents of the country coiled up at his feet. He suffered from poison of another kind; for drinking at a spring in which some boughs of the manchineel had been thrown, the effects were so severe as, in the opinion of some of his friends, to inflict a lasting injury upon his constitution.

The castle of San Juan is 32 miles below the point where the river issues from the Lake of Nicaragua, and 69 from its mouth. Boats reach the sea from thence in a day and a-half; but their navigation back, even when unladen, is the labour of nine days. The English appeared before it on the 11th, two days after they had taken San Bartolomeo. Nelson's advice was, that it should instantly be carried by assault; but Nelson was not the commander; and it was thought proper to observe all the formalities of a siege. Ten days were wasted before this could be commenced. It was a work more of fatigue than of danger; but fatigue was more to be dreaded than the enemy; the rains set in; and could the garrison have held out a little longer, diseases would have rid them of their invaders. Even the Indians sunk under it, the victims of unusual exertion, and of their own excesses. The place surrendered on the 24th. But victory procured to the conquerors none of that relief which had been expected; the castle was worse than a prison; and it contained nothing which could contribute to the recovery of the sick, or the preservation of those who were yet unaffected. The huts which served for hospitals were surrounded with filth, and with the putrefying hides of slaughtered cattle – almost sufficient of themselves to have engendered pestilence; and when at last orders were given to erect a convenient hospital, the contagion had become so general that there were none who could work at it; for besides the few who were able to perform garrison duty, there were not orderly men enough to assist the sick. Added to these evils, there was the want of all needful remedies; for though the expedition had been amply provided with hospital stores, river craft enough had not been procured for transporting the requisite baggage; and when much was to be left behind, provision for sickness was that which of all things men in health would be most ready to leave. Now, when these medicines were required, the river was swollen, and so turbulent that its upward navigation was almost impracticable. At length even the task of burying the dead was more than the living could perform, and the bodies were tossed into the stream, or left for beasts of prey, and for the gallinazos – those dreadful carrion birds, which do not always wait for death before they begin their work. Five months the English persisted in what may be called this war against nature; they then left a few men, who seemed proof against the climate, to retain the castle till the Spaniards should choose to retake it and make them prisoners.

The rest abandoned their baleful conquest. Eighteen hundred men were sent to different posts upon this wretched expedition: not more than three hundred and eighty ever returned. The *Hinchinbrook*'s complement consisted of two hundred men; eighty-seven took to their beds in one night, and of the whole crew not more than ten survived.

The transports' men all died, and some of the ships, having none left to take care of them, sunk in the harbour: but transport ships were not wanted, for the troops which they had brought were no more: they had fallen, not by the hand of an enemy, but by the deadly influence of the climate.

Nelson himself was saved by a timely removal. In a few days after the commencement of the siege he was seized with the prevailing dysentery; meantime Captain Glover (son of the author of *Leonidas*) died, and Nelson was appointed to succeed him in the Janus, of forty-four guns; Collingwood being then made post into the *Hinchinbrook*. He returned to the harbour the day before San Juan surrendered, and immediately sailed for Jamaica in the sloop which brought the news of his appointment. He was, however, so greatly reduced by the disorder, that when they reached Port Royal he was carried ashore in his cot; and finding himself, after a partial amendment, unable to retain the command of his new ship, he was compelled to ask leave to return to England, as the only means of recovery. Captain (afterwards Admiral) Cornwallis took him home in the *Lion*; and to his fare and kindness Nelson believed himself indebted for his life. He went immediately to Bath, in a miserable state; so helpless that he was carried to and from his bed; and the act of moving him produced the most violent pain. In three months he recovered, and immediately hastened to London, and applied for employment. After an interval of about four months he was appointed to the *Albemarle*, of twenty-eight guns, a French merchantman which had been purchased from the captors for the king's service.

His health was not yet thoroughly re-established; and while he was employed in getting his ship ready, he again became so ill. as hardly to be able to keep out of bed. Yet in this state, still suffering from the fatal effect of a West Indian climate, as if it might almost be supposed, he said, to try his constitution, he was sent to the North Seas, and kept there the whole winter. The asperity with which he mentioned this so many years afterwards evinces how deeply he resented a mode of conduct equally cruel to the individual and detrimental to the service. It was during the armed neutrality; and when they anchored off Elsinore, the Danish Admiral sent on board, desiring to be informed what ships had arrived, and to have their force written down. "The *Albemarle*," said Nelson to the messenger, "is one of his Britannic Majesty's ships: you are at liberty, sir, to count the guns as you go down the side; and you may assure the Danish Admiral that, if necessary, they shall all be well served." During this voyage he gained a considerable knowledge of the Danish coast and its soundings, greatly to the advantage of his country in after-times. The *Albemarle* was not a good ship, and was several times nearly overset in consequence of the masts having been made much too long for her. On her return to England they were shortened, and some other improvements made at Nelson's suggestion. Still he always insisted that her first owners, the French, had taught her to run away, as she was never a good sailer except when going directly before the wind.

On their return to the Downs, while he was ashore visiting the senior officer, there came on so heavy a gale that almost all the vessels drove, and a store-ship came athwart-hawse of the *Albemarle*. Nelson feared she would drive on the Goodwin Sands; he ran to the beach; but even the Deal boatmen thought it impossible to get on board, such was the violence of the storm. At length some of the most intrepid offered to make the attempt for fifteen guineas; and to the astonishment and fear of all the beholders, he embarked during the height of the tempest. With great difficulty and imminent danger he succeeded in reaching her. She lost her bowsprit and foremast, but escaped further injury. He was now ordered to Quebec, where his surgeon told him he would certainly be laid up by the climate. Many of his friends urged him to represent this to Admiral Keppel; but having received his orders from Lord Sandwich, there appeared to him an indelicacy in applying to his successor to have them altered.

Accordingly he sailed for Canada. During her first cruise on that station the *Albemarle* captured a fishing schooner which contained in her cargo nearly all the property that her master possessed, and the poor fellow had a large family at home, anxiously expecting him. Nelson employed him as a pilot in Boston Bay, then restored him the schooner and cargo, and gave him a certificate to secure him against being captured by any other vessel. The man came off afterwards to the *Albemarle*, at the hazard of his life, with a present of sheep, poultry, and fresh provisions. A most valuable supply it proved, for the scurvy was raging on board: this was in the middle of August, and the ship's company had not had a fresh meal since the beginning of April. The certificate was preserved at Boston in memory of an act of unusual generosity; and now that the fame of Nelson has given interest to everything connected with his name, it is regarded as a relic. The *Albemarle* had a narrow escape upon this cruise. Four French sail of the line and a frigate, which had come out of Boston harbour, gave chase to her; and Nelson, perceiving that they beat him in sailing, boldly ran among the numerous shoals of St. George's Bank, confiding in his own skill in pilotage. Captain Salter, in the *Sta. Margaretta*, had escaped the French fleet by a similar manoeuvre not long before. The frigate alone continued warily to pursue him; but as soon as he perceived that this enemy was unsupported, he shortened sail and hove to; upon which the Frenchman thought it advisable to give over the pursuit, and sail in quest of his consorts.

At Quebec Nelson became acquainted with Alexander Davison, by whose interference he was prevented from making what would have been called an imprudent marriage. The *Albemarle* was about to leave the station, her captain had taken leave of his friends, and was gone down the river to the place of anchorage; when the next morning, as Davison was walking on the beach, to his surprise he saw Nelson coming back in his boat. Upon inquiring the cause of this reappearance, Nelson took his arm to walk towards the town, and told him that he found it utterly impossible to leave Quebec without again seeing the woman whose society had contributed so much to his happiness there, and offering her his hand. "If you do," said his friend, "your ruin must inevitably follow." "Then let it follow," cried Nelson, "for I am resolved to do it" "And I," replied Davison, "am resolved you shall not." Nelson, however, upon this occasion, was less resolute than his friend, and suffered himself to be led back to the boat.

The *Albemarle* was under orders to convoy a fleet of transports to New York. "A very pretty job" said her captain, "at this late season of the year" (October was far advanced), "for our sails are at this moment frozen to the yards." On his arrival at Sandy Hook, he waited on the commander-in-chief, Admiral Digby, who told him he was come on a fine station for making prize-money. "Yes, sir," Nelson made answer, "but the West Indies is the station for honour." Lord Hood, with a detachment of Rodney's victorious fleet, was at that time at Sandy Hook: he had been intimate with Captain Suckling; and Nelson, who was desirous of nothing but honour, requested him to ask for the *Albemarle*, that he might go to that station where it was most likely to be obtained. Admiral Digby reluctantly parted with him. His professional merit was already well known; and Lord Hood, on introducing him to Prince William Henry, as the Duke of Clarence was then called, told the prince, if he wished to ask any questions respecting naval tactics, Captain Nelson could give him as much information as any officer in the fleet. The Duke—who, to his own honour, became from that time the firm friend of Nelson—describes him as appearing the merest boy of a captain he had ever seen, dressed in a full laced uniform, an old-fashioned waistcoat with long flaps, and his lank unpowdered hair tied in a stiff Hessian tail of extraordinary length; making altogether so remarkable a figure, that, says the duke, "I had never seen anything like it before, nor could I imagine who he was, nor what he came about. But his address and conversation were irresistibly pleasing; and when he spoke on professional subjects, it was with an enthusiasm that showed he was no common being."

It was expected that the French would attempt some of the passages between the Bahamas; and Lord Hood, thinking of this, said to Nelson, "I suppose, sir, from the length of time you were cruising among the Bahama Keys, you must be a good pilot there." He replied, with that constant readiness to render justice to every man which was so conspicuous in all his conduct through life, that he was well acquainted with them himself, but that in that respect his second lieutenant was far his superior. The French got into Puerto Cabello, on the coast of Venezuela. Nelson was cruising between that port and La Guapra, under French colours, for the purpose of obtaining information; when a king's launch, belonging to the Spaniards, passed near, and being hailed in French, came alongside without suspicion, and answered all questions that were asked concerning the number and force of the enemy's ships. The crew, however, were not a little surprised when they were taken on board and found themselves prisoners. One of the party went by the name of the Count de Deux-Ponts. He was, however, a prince of the German empire, and brother to the heir of the Electorate of Bavaria: his companions were French officers of distinction, and men of science, who had been collecting specimens in the various branches of natural history. Nelson, having entertained them with the best his table could afford, told them they were at liberty to depart with their boat, and all that it contained: he only required them to promise that they would consider themselves as prisoners if the commander-in-chief should refuse to acquiesce in their being thus liberated: a circumstance which was not likely to happen. Tidings soon arrived that the preliminaries of peace had been signed; and the *Albemarle* returned to England and was paid off. Nelson's first business, after he got to London, even before he went to see his relations, was to attempt to get the wages due to his men for the various ships in which they had served during the war. "The disgust of seamen to the navy," he said, "was all owing to the infernal plan of turning them over from ship to ship; so that men could not be attached to their officers, nor the officers care the least about the men." Yet he himself was so beloved by his men that his whole ship's company offered, if he could get a ship, to enter for her immediately. He was now, for the first time, presented at court. After going through this ceremony, he dined with his friend Davison at Lincoln's Inn. As soon as he entered the chambers, he threw off what he called his iron-bound coat;

and, putting himself at ease in a dressing gown, passed the
remainder of the day in talking over all that had befallen
them since they parted on the shore of the River St. Lawrence.

CHAPTER II
1784–1793

Nelson goes to France—Reappointed to the *Boreas* at the
Leeward Islands in the *Boreas*—His firm conduct concerning
the American Interlopers and the Contractors—Marries and
returns to England—Is on the point of quitting the Service in
Disgust—Manner of Life while unemployed—Appointed to the
Agamemnon on the breaking out of the War of the French
Revolution.

"I have closed the war," said Nelson in one of his letters,
"without a fortune; but there is not a speck in my character.
True honour, I hope, predominates in my mind far above
riches." He did not apply for a ship, because he was not wealthy
enough to live on board in the manner which was then become
customary. Finding it, therefore, prudent to economise on his
half-pay during the peace, he went to France, in company with
Captain Macnamara of the navy, and took lodgings at St.
Omer's. The death of his favourite sister, Anne, who died in
consequence of going out of the ball-room at Bath when heated
with dancing, affected his father so much that it had nearly
occasioned him to return in a few weeks. Time, however, and
reason and religion, overcame this grief in the old man; and
Nelson continued at St. Omer's long enough to fall in love with
the daughter of an English clergyman. This second attachment
appears to have been less ardent than the first, for upon
weighing the evils of a straitened income to a married man,
he thought it better to leave France, assigning to his friends
something in his accounts as the cause. This prevented him from
accepting an invitation from the Count of Deux-Ponts to visit
him at Paris, couched in the handsomest terms of acknowledgment for the treatment which he had received on board the
Albermarle.

The self-constraint which Nelson exerted in subduing this

attachment made him naturally desire to be at sea; and when, upon visiting Lord Howe at the Admiralty, he was asked if he wished to be employed, he made answer that he did. Accordingly in March, he was appointed to the *Boreas*, twenty-eight guns, going to the Leeward Islands as a cruiser on the peace establishment. Lady Hughes and her family went out with him to Admiral Sir Richard Hughes, who commanded on that station. His ship was full of young midshipmen, of whom there were not less than thirty on board; and happy were they whose lot it was to be placed with such a captain. If he perceived that a boy was afraid at first going aloft, he would say to him in a friendly manner, "Well, sir, I am going a race to the mast-head, and beg that I may meet you there." The poor little fellow instantly began to climb, and got up how he could,—Nelson never noticed in what manner, but when they met in the top, spoke cheerfully to him, and would say how much any person was to be pitied who fancied that getting up was either dangerous or difficult. Every day he went into the school-room to see that they were pursuing their nautical studies; and at noon he was always the first on deck with his quadrant. Whenever he paid a visit of ceremony, some of these youths accompanied him; and when he went to dine with the governor at Barbadoes, he took one of them in his hand, and presented him, saying, "Your Excellency must excuse me for bringing one of my midshipmen. I make it a rule to introduce them to all the good company I can, as they have few to look up to, besides myself, during the time they are at sea."

When Nelson arrived in the West Indies, he found himself senior captain, and consequently second in command on that station. Satisfactory as this was, it soon involved him in a dispute with the admiral, which a man less zealous for the service might have avoided. He found the *Latona* in English Harbour, Antigua, with a broad pendant hoisted; and upon inquiring the reason, was presented with a written order from Sir R. Hughes, requiring and directing him to obey the orders of Resident Commissioner Moutray during the time he might have occasion to remain there; the said resident commissioner being in consequence, authorised to hoist a broad pendant on board any of his Majesty's ships in that port that he might think proper. Nelson was never at a loss how to act in any emergency.

"I know of no superior officers," said he, "besides the Lords Commissioners of the Admiralty, and my seniors on the post list." Concluding, therefore, that it was not consistent with the service for a resident commissioner, who held only a civil situation, to hoist a broad pendant, the moment that he had anchored he sent an order to the captain of the *Latona* to strike it, and return it to the dock-yard. He went on shore the same day, dined with the commissioner, to show him that he was actuated by no other motive than a sense of duty, and gave him the first intelligence that his pendant had been struck. Sir Richard sent an account of this to the Admiralty; but the case could admit of no doubt, and Captain Nelson's conduct was approved.

He displayed the same promptitude on another occasion. While the *Boreas*, after the hurricane months were over, was riding at anchor in Nevis Roads, a French frigate passed to leeward, close along shore. Nelson had obtained information that this ship was sent from Martinico, with two general officers and some engineers on board, to make a survey of our sugar islands. This purpose he was determined to prevent them from executing, and therefore he gave orders to follow them. The next day he came up with them at anchor in the roads of St. Eustatia, and anchored at about two cables' length on the frigate's quarter. Being afterwards invited by the Dutch governor to meet the French officers at dinner, he seized that occasion of assuring the French captain that, understanding it was his intention to honour the British possessions with a visit, he had taken the earliest opportunity in his power to accompany him, in his Majesty's ship the *Boreas*, in order that such attention might be paid to the officers of his Most Christian Majesty as every Englishman in the islands would be proud to show. The French, with equal courtesy, protested against giving him this trouble; especially, they said, as they intended merely to cruise round the islands without landing on any. But Nelson, with the utmost politeness, insisted upon paying them this compliment, followed them close in spite of all their attempts to elude his vigilance, and never lost sight of them;

till, finding it impossible either to deceive or escape him, they gave up their treacherous purpose in despair, and beat up for Martinico.

A business of more serious import soon engaged his attention. The Americans were at this time trading with our islands, taking advantage of the register of their ships, which had been issued while they were British subjects. Nelson knew that, by the Navigation Act, no foreigners, directly or indirectly, are permitted to carry on any trade with these possessions. He knew, also, that the Americans had made themselves foreigners with regard to England; they had disregarded the ties of blood and language when they acquired the independence which they had been led on to claim, unhappily for themselves before they were fit for it; and he was resolved that they should derive no profit from those ties now. Foreigners they had made themselves, and as foreigners they were to be treated. "If once," said he, "they are admitted to any kind of intercourse with our islands, the views of the loyalists, in settling at Nova Scotia, are entirely done away; and when we are again embroiled in a French war, the Americans will first become the carriers of these colonies, and then have possession of them. Here they come, sell their cargoes for ready money, go to Martinico, buy molasses, and so round and round. The loyalist cannot do this, and consequently must sell a little dearer. The residents here are Americans by connection and by interest, and are inimical to Great Britain. They are as great rebels as ever were in America, had they the power to show it." In November, when the squadron, having arrived at Barbadoes, was to separate, with no other orders than those for examining anchorages, and the usual inquiries concerning wood and water, Nelson asked his friend Collingwood, then captain of the *Mediator*, whose opinions he knew upon the subject, to accompany him to the commander-in-chief, whom he then respectfully asked, whether they were not to attend to the commerce of the country, and see that the Navigation Act was respected—that appearing to him to be the intent of keeping men-of-war upon this station in time of peace? Sir Richard Hughes replied, he had no particular orders, neither had the Admiralty sent him any Acts of Parliament. But Nelson made answer, that the Navigation Act was included in the statutes of the Admiralty, with which every captain was furnished, and that Act was directed to admirals, captains, &c., to see it carried into execution. Sir Richard said he had never seen the book. Upon this Nelson produced the statutes, read the words of the Act, and apparently convinced the commander-in-chief, that men-of-war, as he said, "were sent abroad for some other purpose than to be made a show of." Accordingly orders were given to enforce the Navigation Act.

Major-General Sir Thomas Shirley was at this time governor of the Leeward Islands; and when Nelson waited on him, to inform him how he intended to act, and upon what grounds, he replied, that "old generals were not in the habit of taking advice from young gentlemen." "Sir," said the young officer, with that confidence in himself which never carried him too far, and always was equal to the occasion, "I am as old as the prime minister of England, and I think myself as capable of commanding one of his Majesty's ships as that minister is of governing the state." He was resolved to do his duty, whatever might be the opinion or conduct of others; and when he arrived upon his station at St. Kitt's, he sent away all the Americans, not choosing to seize them before they had been well apprised that the Act would be carried into effect, lest it might seem as if a trap had been laid for them. The Americans, though they prudently decamped from St. Kitt's, were emboldened by the support they met with, and resolved to resist his orders, alleging that king's ships had no legal power to seize them without having deputations from the customs. The planters were to a man against him; the governors and the presidents of the different islands, with only a single exception, gave him no support; and the admiral, afraid to act on either side, yet wishing to oblige the planters, sent him a note, advising him to be guided by the wishes of the president of the council. There was no danger in disregarding this, as it came unofficially, and in the form of advice. But scarcely a month after he had shown Sir Richard Hughes the law, and, as he supposed, satisfied him concerning it, he received an order from him, stating that he had now obtained good advice upon the point, and the Americans were not to be hindered from coming, and having free egress and regress, if the governor chose to permit them. An order to the same purport had been sent round to the different governors and presidents; and General Shirley and others informed him, in an authoritative manner, that they chose to admit American ships, as the commander-in-chief had left the decision to them. These persons, in his own words, he soon "trimmed up, and silenced;" but it was a more delicate business to deal with the admiral: "I must either," said he, "disobey my orders, or disobey Acts of Parliament. I determined upon the former, trusting to the uprightness of my intentions, and believing that my country would not let me be ruined for protecting her commerce." With this determination he wrote to Sir Richard; appealed again to the plain, literal, unequivocal sense of the Navigation Act; and in respectful language told him, he felt it his duty to decline obeying these orders till he had an opportunity of seeing and conversing with him. Sir Richard's first feeling was that of anger, and he was about to supersede Nelson; but having mentioned the affair to his captain, that officer told him he believed all the squadron thought the orders illegal, and therefore did not know how far they were bound to obey them. It was impossible, therefore, to bring Nelson to a court-martial, composed of men who agreed with him in opinion upon the point in dispute; and luckily, though the admiral wanted vigour of mind to decide upon what was right, he was not obstinate in wrong, and had even generosity enough in his nature to thank Nelson afterwards for having shown him his error.

Collingwood in the *Mediator*, and his brother, Wilfred Collingwood, in the *Rattler*, actively co-operated with Nelson. The custom-houses were informed that after a certain day all foreign vessels found in the ports would be seized; and many were, in consequence, seized, and condemned in the Admiralty Court. When the *Boreas* arrived at Nevis, she found four American vessels deeply laden, and what are called the island colours flying—white, with a red cross. They were ordered to hoist their proper flag, and depart within 48 hours; but they refused to obey, denying that they were Americans. Some of their crews were then examined in Nelson's cabin, where the Judge of

Admiralty happened to be present. The case was plain; they confessed that they were Americans, and that the ships, hull and cargo, were wholly American property; upon which he seized them. This raised a storm: the planters, the custom-house, and the governor, were all against him. Subscriptions were opened, and presently filled, for the purpose of carrying on the cause in behalf of the American captains; and the admiral, whose flag was at that time in the roads, stood neutral. But the Americans and their abettors were not content with defensive law. The marines, whom he had sent to secure the ships, had prevented some of the masters from going ashore; and those persons, by whose depositions it appeared that the vessels and cargoes were American property, declared that they had given their testimony under bodily fear, for that a man with a drawn sword in his hand had stood over them the whole time. A rascally lawyer, whom the party employed, suggested this story; and as the sentry at the cabin door was a man with a drawn sword, the Americans made no scruple of swearing to this ridiculous falsehood, and commencing prosecutions against him accordingly. They laid their damages at the enormous amount of £40,000; and Nelson was obliged to keep close on board his own ship, lest he should be arrested for a sum for which it would have been impossible to find bail. The marshal frequently came on board to arrest him, but was always prevented by the address of the first lieutenant, Mr. Wallis. Had he been taken, such was the temper of the people that it was certain he would have been cast for the whole sum. One of his officers, one day, in speaking of the restraint which he was thus compelled to suffer, happened to use the word *pity*! "Pity!" exclaimed Nelson: "Pity! did you say? I shall live, sir, to be envied! and to that point I shall always direct my course." Eight weeks remained in this state of duresse. During that time the trial respecting the detained ships came on in the court of Admiralty. He went on shore under a protection for the day from the judge; but, notwithstanding this, the marshal was called upon to take that opportunity of arresting him, and the merchants promised to indemnify him for so doing. The judge, however, did his duty, and threatened to send the marshal to prison if he attempted to violate the protection of the court. Mr.

Herbert, the president of Nevis, behaved with singular generosity upon this occasion. Though no man was a greater sufferer by the measures which Nelson had pursued, he offered in court to become his bail for £10,000 if he chose to suffer the arrest. The lawyer whom he had chosen proved to be an able as well as an honest man; and notwithstanding the opinions and pleadings of most of the counsel of the different islands, who maintained that ships of war were not justified in seizing American vessels without a deputation from the customs, the law was so explicit, the case so clear, and Nelson pleaded his own cause so well, that the four ships were condemned. During the progress of this business he sent a memorial home to the king, in consequence of which orders were issued that he should be defended at the expense of the crown. And upon the representation which he made at the same time to the Secretary of State, and the suggestions with which he accompanied it, the Register Act was framed. The sanction of Government, and the approbation of his conduct which it implied, were highly gratifying to him; but he was offended, and not without just cause, that the Treasury should have transmitted thanks to the commander-in-chief for his activity and zeal in protecting the commerce of Great Britain. "Had they known all," said he, "I do not think they would have bestowed thanks in that quarter, and neglected me. I feel much hurt that, after the loss of health and risk of fortune, another should be thanked for what I did against his orders. I either deserved to be sent out of the service, or at least to have had some little notice taken of what I had done. They have thought it worthy of notice, and yet have neglected me. If this is the reward for a faithful discharge of my duty, I shall be careful, and never stand forward again. But I have done my duty, and have nothing to accuse myself of."

The anxiety which he had suffered from the harassing uncertainties of law is apparent from these expressions. He had, however, something to console him, for he was at this time wooing the niece of his friend the president, then in her eighteenth year, the widow of Dr. Nisbet, a physician. She had one child, a son, by name Josiah, who was three years old. One day Mr. Herbert, who had hastened half-dressed to receive Nelson, exclaimed, on returning to his dressing-room, "Good God! if I did not find that great little man, of whom everybody is so afraid, playing in the next room, under the dining-table, with Mrs. Nisbet's child!" A few days afterwards Mrs. Nisbet herself was first introduced to him, and thanked him for the partiality which he had shown to her little boy. Her manners were mild and winning; and the captain, whose heart was easily susceptible of attachment, found no such imperious necessity for subduing his inclinations as had twice before withheld him from marrying. They were married on March 11, 1787: Prince William Henry, who had come out to the West Indies the preceding winter, being present, by his own desire, to give away the bride. Mr. Herbert, her uncle, was at this time so much displeased with his only daughter, that he had resolved to disinherit her, and leave his whole fortune, which was very great, to his niece. But Nelson, whose nature was too noble to let him profit by an act of injustice, interfered, and succeeded in reconciling the president to his child.

"Yesterday," said one of his naval friends the day after the wedding, "the navy lost one of its greatest ornaments by Nelson's marriage. It is a national loss that such an officer should marry: had it not been for this, Nelson would have become the greatest man in the service." The man was rightly estimated; but he who delivered this opinion did not understand the effect of domestic love and duty upon a mind of the true heroic stamp.

"We are often separate," said Nelson, in a letter to Mrs. Nisbet a few months before their marriage; "but our affections are not by any means on that account diminished. Our country has the first demand for our services; and private convenience or happiness must ever give way to the public good. Duty is the great business of a sea officer: all private considerations must give way to it, however painful." "Have you not often heard," says he in another letter, "that salt water and absence always wash away love? Now I am such a heretic as not to believe that article, for, behold, every morning I have had six pails of salt water poured upon my head, and instead of finding what seamen say to be true, it goes on so contrary to the prescription, that you may, perhaps, see me before the fixed time." More frequently his correspondence breathed a deeper strain.

"To write letters to you," says he, "is the next greatest pleasure I feel to receiving them from you. What I experience when I read such as I am sure are the pure sentiments of your heart, my poor pen cannot express; nor, indeed, would I give much for any pen or head which could express feelings of that kind. Absent from you, I feel no pleasure: it is you who are everything to me. Without you, I care not for this world; for I have found, lately, nothing in it but vexation and trouble. These are my present sentiments. God Almighty grant they may never change! Nor do I think they will. Indeed there is, as far as human knowledge can judge, a moral certainty that they cannot; for it must be real affection that brings us together, not interest or compulsion." Such were the feelings, and such the sense of duty, with which Nelson became a husband.

During his stay upon this station he had ample opportunity of observing the scandalous practices of the contractors, prize-agents, and other persons in the West Indies connected with the naval service. When he was first left with the command, and bills were brought him to sign for money which was owing for goods purchased for the navy, he required the original voucher, that he might examine whether those goods had been really purchased at the market price; but to produce vouchers would not have been convenient, and therefore was not the custom. Upon this Nelson wrote to Sir Charles Middleton, then Comptroller of the Navy, representing the abuses which were likely to be practised in this manner. The answer which he received seemed to imply that the old forms were thought sufficient; and thus, having no alternative, he was compelled, with his eyes open, to submit to a practice originating in fraudulent intentions. Soon afterwards two Antigua merchants informed him that they were privy to great frauds which had been committed upon government in various departments; at Antigua, to the amount of nearly £500,000; at Lucie, £300,000; at Barbadoes, £250,000; at Jamaica, upwards of a million. The informers were both shrewd sensible men of business; they did not affect to be actuated by a sense of justice, but required a percentage upon so much as government should actually recover through their means. Nelson examined the books and papers which they produced, and was convinced that government had been most infamously plundered. Vouchers, he found, in that country, were no check whatever: the principle was, that "a thing was always worth what it would bring;" and the merchants were in the habit of signing vouchers for each other, without even the appearance of looking at the articles. These accounts he sent home to the different departments which had been defrauded; but the peculators were too powerful, and they succeeded not merely in impeding inquiry, but even in raising prejudices against Nelson at the Board of Admiralty, which it was many years before he could subdue.

Owing probably, to these prejudices, and the influence of the peculators, he was treated, on his return to England, in a manner which had nearly driven him from the service. During the three years that the *Boreas* had remained upon a station which is usually so fatal, not a single officer or man of her whole complement had died. This almost unexampled instance of good health, though mostly, no doubt, imputable to a healthy season, must in some measure, also, be ascribed to the wise conduct of the captain. He never suffered the ships to remain more than three or four weeks at a time at any of the islands; and when the hurricane months confined him to English Harbour, he encouraged all kinds of useful amusements—music, dancing, and cudgelling among the men; theatricals among the officers; anything which could employ their attention, and keep their spirits cheerful. The *Boreas* arrived in England in June. Nelson, who had many times been supposed to be consumptive when in the West Indies, and perhaps was saved from consumption by that climate, was still in a precarious state of health; and the raw wet weather of one of our ungenial summers brought on cold, and sore throat, and fever; yet his vessel was kept at the Nore from the end of June till the end of November, serving as a slop and receiving ship. This unworthy treatment, which more probably proceeded from inattention than from neglect, excited in Nelson the strongest indignation. During the whole five months he seldom or never quitted the ship, but carried on the duty with strict and sullen attention. On the morning when orders were received to prepare the *Boreas* for being paid off, he expressed his joy to the senior officer in the Medway, saying, "It will release me for

ever from an ungrateful service; for it is my firm and unalterable
determination never again to set my foot on board a king's ship.
Immediately after my arrival in town I shall wait on the First
Lord of the Admiralty, and resign my commission." The officer
to whom he thus communicated his intentions behaved in the
wisest and most friendly manner; for finding it in vain to
dissuade him in his present state of feeling, he secretly interfered
with the First Lord to save him from a step so injurious to
himself, little foreseeing how deeply the welfare and honour of
England were at that moment at stake. This interference
produced a letter from Lord Howe the day before the ship
was paid off, intimating a wish to see Captain Nelson as soon as
he arrived in town; when, being pleased with his conversation,
and perfectly convinced, by what was then explained to him, of
the propriety of his conduct, he desired that he might present
him to the king on the first levee-day; and the gracious manner
in which Nelson was then received effectually removed his
resentment.

Prejudices had been, in like manner, excited against his
friend, Prince William Henry. "Nothing is wanting, sir," said
Nelson, in one of his letters, "to make you the darling of the
English nation but truth. Sorry am I to say, much to the
contrary has been dispersed." This was not flattery, for Nelson
was no flatterer. The letter in which this passage occurs shows in
how wise and noble a manner he dealt with the prince. One of
his royal highness's officers had applied for a court-martial
upon a point in which he was unquestionably wrong. His royal
highness, however, while he supported his own character and
authority, prevented the trial, which must have been injurious
to a brave and deserving man. "Now that you are parted," said
Nelson, "pardon me, my prince, when I presume to recommend
that he may stand in your royal favour as if he had never sailed
with you, and that at some future day you will serve him. There
only wants this to place your conduct in the highest point of
view. None of us are without failings—his was being rather too
hasty; but that, put in competition with his being a good officer,
will not, I am bold to say, be taken in the scale against him.
More able friends than myself your royal highness may easily
find, and of more consequence in the state; but one more

attached and affectionate is not so easily met with: Princes seldom, very seldom, find a disinterested person to communicate their thoughts to: I do not pretend to be that person; but of this be assured, by a man who, I trust, never did a dishonourable act, that I am interested only that your royal highness should be the greatest and best man this country ever produced."

Encouraged by the conduct of Lord Howe, and by his reception at court, Nelson renewed his attack upon the peculators with fresh spirit. He had interviews with Mr. Rose, Mr. Pitt, and Sir Charles Middleton, to all of whom he satisfactorily proved his charges. In consequence, it is said, these very extensive public frauds were at length put in a proper train to be provided against in future; his representations were attended to; and every step which he recommended was adopted; the investigation was put into a proper course, which ended in the detection and punishment of some of the culprits; an immense saving was made to government, and thus its attention was directed to similar peculations in other arts of the colonies. But it is said also that no mark of commendation seems to have been bestowed upon Nelson for his exertion. It has been justly remarked that the spirit of the navy cannot be preserved so effectually by the liberal honours bestowed on officers when they are worn out in the service, as by an attention to those who, like Nelson at this part of his life, have only their integrity and zeal to bring them into notice. A junior officer, who had been left with the command at Jamaica, received an additional allowance, for which Nelson had applied in vain. Double pay was allowed to every artificer and seaman employed in the naval yard: Nelson had superintended the whole business of that yard with the most rigid exactness, and he complained that he was neglected. "It was most true," he said, "that the trouble which he took to detect the fraudulent practices then carried on was no more than his duty; but he little thought that the expenses attending his frequent journeys to St. John's upon that duty (a distance of twelve miles) would have fallen upon his pay as captain of the *Boreas*." Nevertheless, the sense of what he thought unworthy usage did not diminish his zeal. "I," said he, "must buffet the waves in search of—

What? Alas! that they called honour is thought of no more. My fortune, God knows, has grown worse for the service; so much for serving my country! But the devil, ever willing to tempt the virtuous, has made me offer, if any ships should be sent to destroy his Majesty of Morocco's ports, to be there; and I have some reason to think that, should any more come of it, my humble services will be accepted. I have invariably laid down, and followed close, a plan of what ought to be uppermost in the breast of an officer,—that it is much better to serve an ungrateful country than to give up his own fame. Posterity will do him justice. A uniform course of honour and integrity seldom fails of bringing a man to the goal of fame at last."

The design against the Barbary pirates, like all other designs against them, was laid aside; and Nelson took his wife to his father's parsonage, meaning only to pay him a visit before they went to France; a project which he had formed for the sake of acquiring a competent knowledge of the French language. But his father could not bear to lose him thus unnecessarily. Mr. Nelson had long been an invalid, suffering under paralytic and asthmatic affections, which, for several hours after he rose in the morning, scarcely permitted him to speak. He had been given over by his physicians for this complaint nearly forty years before his death; and was, for many of his latter years, obliged to spend all his winters at Bath. The sight of his son, he declared, had given him new life. "But, Horatio," said he, "it would have been better that I had not been thus cheered, if I am so soon to be bereaved of you again. Let me, my good son, see you whilst I can. My age and infirmities increase, and I shall not last long."

To such an appeal there could be no reply. Nelson took up his abode at the parsonage, and amused himself with the sports and occupations of the country. Sometimes he busied himself with farming the glebe; sometimes spent the greater part of the day in the garden, where he would dig as if for the mere pleasure of wearying himself. Sometimes he went a birds'-nesting, like a boy; and in these expeditions Mrs. Nelson always, by his expressed desire, accompanied him. Coursing was his favourite amusement. Shooting, as he practised it, was far too dangerous for his companions; for he carried his gun upon the full cock, as if he were going to board an enemy; and the moment a bird rose, he let fly without ever putting the fowling-piece to his shoulder. It is not, therefore, extraordinary that his having once shot a partridge should be remembered by his family among the remarkable events of his life.

But his time did not pass away thus without some vexatious cares to ruffle it. The affair of the American ships was not yet over, and he was again pestered with threats of prosecution. "I have written them word," said he, "that I will have nothing to do with them, and they must act as they think proper. Government, I suppose, will do what is right, and not leave me in the lurch. We have heard enough lately of the consequences of the Navigation Act to this country. They may take my person; but if sixpence would save me from a prosecution, I would not give it." It was his great ambition at this time to possess a pony; and having resolved to purchase one, he went to a fair for that purpose. During his absence two men abruptly entered the parsonage and inquired for him: they then asked for Mrs. Nelson; and after they had made her repeatedly declare that she was really and truly the captain's wife, presented her with a writ, or notification, on the part of the American captains, who now laid their damages at £20,000, and they charged her to give it to her husband on his return. Nelson, having bought his pony, came home with it in high spirits. He called out his wife to admire the purchase and listen to all its excellences: nor was it till his glee had in some measure subsided that the paper could be presented to him. His indignation was excessive; and in the apprehension that he should be exposed to the anxieties of the suit and the ruinous consequences which might ensue, he exclaimed, "This affront I did not deserve! But I'll be trifled with no longer. I will write immediately to the Treasury, and if government will not support me, I am resolved to leave the country." Accordingly, he informed the Treasury that, if a satisfactory answer were not sent him by return of post, he should take refuge in France. To this he expected he should be driven, and for this he arranged everything with his characteristic rapidity of decision. It was settled that he should depart immediately, and Mrs. Nelson follow, under the care of his elder brother Maurice, ten days after him. But the answer which he received from government quieted his fears: it stated that Captain Nelson was a very good officer, and needed to be under no apprehension, for he would assuredly be supported.

Here his disquietude upon this subject seems to have ended. Still he was not at ease; he wanted employment, and was mortified that his applications for it produced no effect. "Not being a man of fortune," he said, "was a crime which he was unable to get over, and therefore none of the great cared about him." Repeatedly he requested the Admiralty that they would not leave him to rust in indolence. During the armament which was made upon occasion of the dispute concerning Nootka Sound, he renewed his application; and his steady friend, Prince William, who had then been created Duke of Clarence, recommended him to Lord Chatham. The failure of this recommendation wounded him so keenly that he again thought of retiring from the service in disgust; a resolution from which nothing but the urgent remonstrances of Lord Hood induced him to desist. Hearing that the *Raisonnable*, in which he had commenced his career, was to be commissioned, he asked for her. This also was in vain; and a coolness ensued, on his part, toward Lord Hood, because that excellent officer did not use his influence with Lord Chatham upon this occasion. Lord Hood, however, had certainly sufficient reasons for not interfering; for he ever continued his steady friend. In the winter of 1792, when we were on the eve of the revolutionary war, Nelson once more offered his services, earnestly requested a ship, and added, that if their lordships should be pleased to appoint him to a cockle-boat he should feel satisfied. He was answered in the usual official form: "Sir, I have received your letter of the 5th instant, expressing your readiness to serve, and have read the same to my Lords Commissioners of the Admiralty." On the 12th of December he received this dry acknowledgment. The fresh mortification did not, however, affect him long; for, by the joint interest of the Duke and Lord Hood, he was appointed, on the 30th of January following, to the *Agamemnon*, of sixty-four guns.

CHAPTER III
1793–1795

The *Agamemnon* sent to the Mediteranean—Commencement of Nelson's aquaintance with Sir W. Hamilton—He is sent to Corsica, to cooperate with Paoli—State of Affairs in that island—Nelson undertakes the Siege of Bastia, and reduces it—Takes a distinguished part in the Siege of Calvi, where he loses an eye—Admiral Hotham's action—The *Agamemnon* ordered to Genoa, to co-operate with the Austrian and Sardinian Forces—Cross misconduct of the Austrian General.

"There are three things, young gentleman," said Nelson to one of his midshipmen, "which you are constantly to bear in mind. First, you must always implicitly obey orders, without attempting to form any opinion of your own respecting their propriety; secondly, you must consider every man your enemy who speaks ill of your king; and, thirdly, you must hate a Frenchman as you do the devil." With these feelings he engaged in the war. Josiah, his son-in-law, went with him as a midshipman.

The *Agamemnon* was ordered to the Mediterranean under Lord Hood. The fleet arrived in those seas at a time when the south of France would willingly have formed itself into a separate republic, under the protection of England. But good principles had been at that time perilously abused by ignorant and profligate men; and, in its fear and hatred of democracy, the English Government abhorred whatever was republican. Lord Hood could not take advantage of the fair occasion which presented itself; and which, if it had been seized with vigour, might have ended in dividing France:—but he negotiated with the people of Toulon, to take possession provisionally of their port and city; which, fatally for themselves, was done. Before the British fleet entered, Nelson was sent with despatches to Sir William Hamilton, our envoy at the Court of Naples. Sir William, after his first interview with him, told Lady Hamilton he was about to introduce a little man to her, who could not boast of being very handsome; but such a man as, he believed, would one day astonish the world. "I have never before," he continued, "entertained an officer at my house; but I am determined to bring him here. Let him be put in the room prepared for Prince Augustus." Thus that acquaintance began which ended in the destruction of Nelson's domestic happiness. It seemed to threaten no such consequences at its commencement. He spoke of Lady Hamilton, in a letter to his wife, as a young woman of amiable manners, who did honour to the station to which she had been raised; and he remarked, that she had been exceedingly kind to Josiah. The activity with which the envoy exerted himself in procuring troops from Naples, to assist in garrisoning Toulon, so delighted him, that he is said to have exclaimed, "Sir William, you are a man after my own heart!—you do business in my own way:" and then to have added, "I am now only a captain; but I will, if I live, be at the top of the tree." Here, also, that acquaintance with the Neapolitan court commenced, which led to the only blot upon Nelson's public character. The king, who was sincere at that time in his enmity to the French, called the English the saviours of Italy, and of his dominions in particular. He paid the most flattering attentions to Nelson, made him dine with him, and seated him at his right hand.

Having accomplished this mission, Nelson received orders to join Commodore Linzee at Tunis. On the way, five sail of the enemy were discovered off the coast of Sardinia, and he chased them. They proved to be three forty-four gun frigates, with a corvette of twenty-four and a brig of twelve. The *Agamemnon* had only 345 men at quarters, having landed part of her crew at Toulon, and others being absent in prizes. He came near enough one of the frigates to engage her, but at great disadvantage, the Frenchman manoeuvring well and sailing greatly better. A running fight of three hours ensued, during which the other ships, which were at some distance, made all speed to come up. By this time the enemy was almost silenced, when a favourable change of wind enabled her to get out of reach of the *Agamemnon*'s guns; and that ship had received so much damage in the rigging that she could not follow her. Nelson, conceiving that this was but the forerunner of a far more serious engagement, called his officers together, and asked them if the ship was fit to go into action against such a superior force without some small refit and refreshment for the men. Their answer was, that she certainly was not. He then gave these orders;—"Veer the ship, and lay her head to the westward: let some of the best men be employed in refitting the rigging, and the carpenter in getting crows and capstan-bars to prevent our wounded spars from coming down: and get the wine up for the people, with some bread, for it may be half an hour good before we are again in action." But when the French came up, their comrade made signals of distress, and they all hoisted out their boats to go to her assistance, leaving the *Agamemnon* unmolested.

Nelson found Commodore Linzee at Tunis, where he had been sent to expostulate with the Dey upon the impolicy of his supporting the revolutionary government of France. Nelson represented to him the atrocity of that government. Such arguments were of little avail in Barbary; and when the Dey was told that the French had put their sovereign to death, he drily replied, that "Nothing could be more heinous; and yet, if historians told the truth, the English had once done the same." This answer had doubtless been suggested by the French about him: they had completely gained the ascendancy, and all negotiation on our part proved fruitless. Shortly afterward, Nelson was detached with a small squadron, to co-operate with General Paoli and the Anti-Gallican party in Corsica.

Some thirty years before this time the heroic patriotism of the Corsicans, and of their leader Paoli, had been the admiration of England. The history of these brave people is but a melancholy tale. The island which they inhabit has been abundantly blessed by nature; it has many excellent harbours; and though the malaria, or pestilential atmosphere, which is so deadly in many parts of Italy and of the Italian islands, prevails on the eastern coast, the greater part of the country is mountainous and healthy. It is about 150 miles long, and from 40 to 50 broad; in circumference, some 320; a country large enough, and sufficiently distant from the nearest shores, to have subsisted as an independent state, if the welfare and happiness of the human race had ever been considered as the end and aim of policy. The Moors, the Pisans, the kings of Aragon, and the Genoese, successively attempted, and each for a time effected its conquest. The yoke of the Genoese continued longest, and was the heaviest. These petty tyrants ruled with an iron rod; and when at any time a patriot rose to resist their oppressions, if they failed to subdue him by force they resorted to assassination. At the commencement of the last century they quelled one revolt by the aid of German auxiliaries, whom the Emperor Charles VI sent against a people who had never offended him, and who were fighting for whatever is most dear to man. In 1734 the war was renewed; and Theodore, a Westphalian baron, then appeared upon the stage. In that age men were not accustomed to see adventurers play for kingdoms, and Theodore became the common talk of Europe. He had served in the French armies; and having afterwards been noticed both by Ripperda and Alberoni, their example, perhaps, inflamed a spirit as ambitious and as unprincipled as their own. He employed the whole of his means in raising money and procuring arms; then wrote to the leaders of the Corsican patriots, to offer them considerable assistance, if they would erect Corsica into an independent kingdom, and elect him king. When he landed among them, they were struck with his stately person, his dignified manners, and imposing talents. They believed the magnificent promises of foreign assistance which he held out, and elected him king accordingly. Had his means been as he represented them, they could not have acted more wisely than in thus at once fixing the government of their country, and putting an end to those rivalries among the leading families, which had so often proved pernicious to the public weal. He struck money, conferred titles, blocked up the fortified towns which were held by the Genoese, and amused the people with promises of assistance for about eight months: then, perceiving that they cooled in their affections towards him in proportion as their expectations were disappointed, he left the island, under the plea of expediting himself the succours which he had so long awaited. Such was his address, that he prevailed upon several rich merchants in Holland, particularly the Jews, to trust him with cannon and warlike stores to a great amount. They shipped these under the charge of a supercargo. Theodore returned with this supercargo to Corsica, and put him to death on his arrival, as the shortest way of settling the account. The remainder of his life was a series of deserved afflictions. He threw in the stores which he had thus fraudulently obtained; but he did not dare to land, for Genoa had now called in the French to their assistance, and a price had been set upon his head. His dreams of royalty were now at an end; he took refuge in London, contracted debts, and was thrown into the King's Bench. After lingering there many years, he was released under an act of insolvency, in consequence of which he made over the kingdom of Corsica for the use of his creditors, and died shortly after his deliverance.

The French, who have never acted a generous part in the history of the world, readily entered into the views of the Genoese, which accorded with their own policy: for such was their ascendancy at Genoa, that in subduing Corsica for these allies, they were in fact subduing it for themselves. They entered into the contest, therefore, with their usual vigour, and their usual cruelty. It was in vain that the Corsicans addressed a most affecting memorial to the court of Versailles; that remorseless government persisted in its flagitious project. They poured in troops; dressed a part of them like the people of the country, by which means they deceived and destroyed many of the patriots; cut down the standing corn, the vines, and the olives; set fire to the villages, and hung all the most able and active men who fell into their hands. A war of this kind may be carried on with success against a country so small and so thinly peopled as Corsica. Having reduced the island to perfect servitude, which they called peace, the French withdrew their forces. As soon as they were gone, men, women, and boys rose at once against their oppressors. The circumstances of the times were now favourable to them; and some British ships, acting as allies of Sardinia, bombarded Bastia and San Fiorenzo, and delivered them into the hands of the patriots. This service was long remembered with gratitude: the impression made upon our own countrymen was less favourable. They had witnessed the heartburnings of rival chiefs, and the dissensions among the patriots; and perceiving the state of barbarism to which continual oppression, and habits of lawless turbulence, had reduced the nation, did not recollect that the vices of the people were owing to their unhappy circumstances, but that the virtues which they displayed arose from their own nature. This feeling, perhaps, influenced the British court, when, in 1746, Corsica offered to put herself under the protection of Great Britain: an answer was returned, expressing satisfaction at such a communication, hoping that the Corsicans would preserve the same sentiments, but signifying also that the present was not the time for such a measure.

These brave islanders then formed a government for themselves, under two leaders, Gaffori and Matra, who had the title of protectors. The latter is represented as a partisan of Genoa, favouring the views of the oppressors of his country by the most treasonable means. Gaffori was a hero worthy of old times. His eloquence was long remembered with admiration. A band of assassins was once advancing against him; he heard of their approach, went out to meet them; and, with a serene dignity which overawed them, requested them to hear him. He then spake to them so forcibly of the distresses of their country, her intolerable wrongs, and the hopes and views of their brethren in arms, that the very men who had been hired to murder him, fell at his feet, implored his forgiveness, and joined his banner. While he was besieging the Genoese in Corte, a part of the garrison perceiving the nurse with his eldest son, then an infant in arms, straying at a little distance from the camp, suddenly sallied out and seized them. The use they made of their persons was in conformity to their usual execrable conduct. When Gaffori advanced to batter the walls, they held up the child directly over that part of the wall at which the guns were pointed. The Corsicans stopped: but Gaffori stood at their head, and ordered them to continue the fire. Providentially the child escaped, and lived to relate, with becoming feeling, a fact so honourable to his father. That father conducted the affairs of the island till 1753, when he was assassinated by some wretches, set on, it is believed, by Genoa, but certainly pensioned by that abominable government after the deed. He left the country in such a state that it was enabled to continue the war two years after his death without a leader: the Corsicans then found one worthy of their cause in Pasquale de Paoli.

Paoli's father was one of the patriots who effected their escape from Corsica when the French reduced it to obedience. He retired to Naples, and brought up his youngest son in the Neapolitan service. The Corsicans heard of young Paoli's abilities, and solicited him to come over to his native country, and take the command. He did not hesitate long: his father, who was too far advanced in years to take an active part himself, encouraged him to go; and when they separated, the old man fell on his neck, and kissed him, and gave him his blessing. "My son," said he, "perhaps I may never see you more; but in my mind I shall ever be present with you. Your design is great and noble; and I doubt not but God will bless you in it. I shall devote to your cause the little remainder of my life in offering up my prayers for your success." When Paoli assumed the command, he found all things in confusion: he formed a democratical government, of which he was chosen chief: restored the authority of the laws; established a university; and took such measures, both for repressing abuses and moulding the rising generation, that, if France had not interfered, upon its wicked and detestable principle of usurpation, Corsica might at this day have been as free, and flourishing and happy a commonwealth as any of the Grecian states in the days of their prosperity. The Genoese were at this time driven out of their fortified towns, and must in a short time have been expelled. France was indebted some millions of livres to Genoa: it was not convenient to pay this money; so the French minister proposed to the Genoese, that she should discharge the debt by sending six battalions to serve in Corsica for four years. The indignation which this conduct excited in all generous hearts was forcibly expressed by Rousseau, who, with all his errors, was seldom deficient in feeling for the wrongs of humanity. "You Frenchmen" said he, writing to one of that people, "are a thoroughly servile nation, thoroughly sold to tyranny, thoroughly cruel and relentless in persecuting the unhappy. If you knew of a freeman at the other end of the world, I believe you would go thither for the mere pleasure of extirpating him."

The immediate object of the French happened to be purely mercenary: they wanted to clear off their debt to Genoa; and as the presence of their troops in the island effected this, they aimed at doing the people no farther mischief. Would that the conduct of England had been at this time free from reproach! but a proclamation was issued by the English government, after the peace of Paris, prohibiting any intercourse with the rebels of Corsica. Paoli said he did not expect this from Great Britain.

This great man was deservedly proud of his country. "I defy Rome, Sparta, or Thebes," he would say, "to show me thirty years of such patriotism as Corsica can boast!" Availing himself of the respite which the inactivity of the French and the weakness of the Genoese allowed, he prosecuted his plans of civilising the people. He used to say, that though he had an unspeakable pride in the prospect of the fame to which he aspired; yet if he could but render his countrymen happy, he could be content to be forgotten. His own importance he never affected to undervalue. "We are now to our country," said he, "like the prophet Elisha stretched over the dead child of the Shunamite,—eye to eye, nose to nose, mouth to mouth. It begins to recover warmth, and to revive: I hope it will yet regain full health and vigour."

But when the four years were expired, France purchased the sovereignty of Corsica from the Genoese for forty millions of livres; as if the Genoese had been entitled to sell it; as if any bargain and sale could justify one country in taking possession of another against the will of the inhabitants, and butchering all who oppose the usurpation! Among the enormities which France has committed, this action seems but as a speck; yet the foulest murderer that ever suffered by the hand of the executioner has infinitely less guilt upon his soul than the statesman who concluded this treaty, and the monarch who sanctioned and confirmed it. A desperate and glorious resistance was made, but it was in vain; no power interposed in behalf of these injured islanders, and the French poured in as many troops as were required. They offered to confirm Paoli in the supreme authority, only on condition that he would hold it under their government. His answer was, that "the rocks which surrounded him should melt away before he would betray a cause which he held in common with the poorest Corsican." This people then set a price upon his head. During two campaigns he kept them at bay: they overpowered him at length; he was driven to the shore, and having escaped on shipboard, took refuge in England. It is said that Lord Shelburne resigned his seat in the cabinet because the ministry looked on without attempting to prevent France from succeeding in this abominable and important act of aggrandizement.

In one respect, however, our country acted as became her. Paoli was welcomed with the honours which he deserved, a pension of £1200 was immediately granted him, and provision was liberally made for his elder brother and his nephew.

Paoli remained about twenty years in England, enjoying the friendship of the wise and the admiration of the good. But when the French Revolution began, it seemed as if the restoration of Corsica was at hand. The whole country, as if animated by one spirit, rose and demanded liberty; and the National Assembly passed a decree recognising the island as a department of France, and therefore entitled to all the privileges of the new French constitution. This satisfied the Corsicans, which it ought not to have done; and Paoli, in whom the ardour of youth was passed, seeing that his countrymen were contented, and believing that they were about to enjoy a state of freedom, naturally wished to return to his native country. He resigned his pension in the year 1790, and appeared at the bar of the Assembly with the Corsican deputies, when they took the oath of fidelity to France. But the course of events in France soon dispelled those hopes of a new and better order of things, which Paoli, in common with so many of the friends of human-kind, had indulged; and perceiving, after the execution of the king, that a civil war was about to ensue, of which no man could foresee the issue, he prepared to break the connection between Corsica and the French Republic. The convention suspecting such a design, and perhaps occasioning it by their suspicions, ordered him to their bar. That way he well knew led to the guillotine; and returning a respectful answer, he declared that he would never be found wanting in his duty, but pleaded age and infirmity as a reason for disobeying the summons. Their second order was more summary; and the French troops, who were in Corsica, aided by those of the natives, who were either influenced by hereditary party feelings, or who were sincere in Jacobinism, took the field against him. But the people were with him. He repaired to Corte, the capital of the island, and was again invested with the authority which he had held in the noonday of his fame. The convention upon this denounced him as a rebel, and set a price upon his head. It was not the first time that France had proscribed Paoli.

Paoli now opened a correspondence with Lord Hood, promising, if the English would make an attack upon St. Fiorenzo from the sea, he would at the same time attack it by land. This promise he was unable to perform; and Commodore Linzee, who, in reliance upon it, was sent upon this service, was repulsed with some loss. Lord Hood, who had now been compelled to evacuate Toulon, suspected Paoli of intentionally deceiving him. This was an injurious suspicion. Shortly afterwards he dispatched Lieutenant-Colonel (afterward Sir John) Moore and Major Koehler to confer with him upon a plan of operations. Sir Gilbert Elliot accompanied them; and it was agreed that, in consideration of the succours, both military and naval, which his Britannic Majesty should afford for the purpose of expelling the French, the island of Corsica should be delivered into the immediate possession of his Majesty, and bind itself to acquiesce in any settlement he might approve of concerning its government, and its future relation with Great Britain. While this negotiation was going on, Nelson cruised off the island with a small squadron, to prevent the enemy from throwing in supplies. Close to St. Fiorenzo the French had a storehouse of flour near their only mill: he watched an opportunity, and landed 120 men, who threw the flour into the sea, burnt the mill, and re-embarked before 1000 men, who were sent against him, could occasion them the loss of a single man. While he exerted himself thus, keeping out all supplies, intercepting despatches, attacking their outposts and forts, and cutting out vessels from the bay,—a species of warfare which depresses the spirit of an enemy even more than it injures them, because of the sense of individual superiority which it indicates in the assailants—troops were landed, and St. Fiorenzo was besieged. The French finding themselves unable to maintain their post sunk one of their frigates, burnt another, and retreated to Bastia. Lord Hood submitted to General Dundas, who commanded the land forces, a plan for the reduction of this place: the general declined co-operating, thinking the attempt impracticable without a reinforcement of 2000 men, which he expected from Gibraltar. Upon this Lord Hood determined to reduce it with the naval force under his command; and leaving part of his fleet off Toulon, he came with the rest to Bastia.

He showed a proper sense of respect for Nelson's services, and of confidence in his talents, by taking care not to bring with him any older captain. A few days before their arrival, Nelson had had what he called a brush with the enemy. "If I had had with me 500 troops," he said, "to a certainty I should have stormed the town; and I believe it might have been carried. Armies go so slow that seamen think they never mean to get forward; but I daresay they act on a surer principle, although we seldom fail." During this partial action our army appeared upon the heights; and having reconnoitered the place, returned to St. Fiorenzo. "What the general could have seen to make a retreat necessary," said Nelson, "I cannot comprehend. A thousand men would certainly take Bastia: with five hundred and the *Agamemnon* I would attempt it. My seamen are now what British seamen ought to be—almost invincible. They really mind shot no more than peas." General Dundas had not the same confidence. "After mature consideration," he said in a letter to Lord Hood," and a personal inspection for several days of all circumstances, local as well as others, I consider the siege of Bastia, with our present means and force, to be a most visionary and rash attempt; such as no officer would be justified in undertaking." Lord Hood replied that nothing would be more gratifying to his feelings than to have the whole responsibility upon himself; and that he was ready and willing to undertake the reduction of the place at his own risk with the force and means at present there. General D'Aubant, who succeeded at this time to the command of the army, coincided in opinion with his predecessor, and did not think it right to furnish his lordship with a single soldier, cannon, or any stores. Lord Hood could only obtain a few artillerymen; and ordering on board that part of the troops who, having been embarked as marines, "were borne on the ships" books as part of their respective complements, he began the siege with 1183 soldiers, artillerymen, and marines, and 250 sailors. "We are but few," said Nelson, "but of the right sort; our general at St. Fiorenzo not giving us one of the five regiments he has there lying idle."

These men were landed on the 4th of April, under Lieutenant-Colonel Villettes and Nelson, who had now acquired from the army the title of brigadier. Guns were dragged by the sailors up heights where it appeared almost impossible to convey them—a work of the greatest difficulty, and which Nelson said could never, in his opinion, have been accomplished by any but British seamen. The soldiers, though less dexterous in such service, because not accustomed, like sailors, to habitual dexterity behaved with equal spirit. "Their zeal," said the brigadier, "is almost unexampled. There is not a man but considers himself as personally interested in the event, and deserted by the general. It has, I am persuaded, made them equal to double their numbers." This is one proof, of many, that for our soldiers to equal our seamen, it is only necessary for them to be equally well commanded. They have the same heart and soul, as well as the same flesh and blood. Too much may, indeed, be exacted from them in a retreat; but set their face toward a foe, and there is nothing within the reach of human achievement which they cannot perform. The French had improved the leisure which our military commander had allowed them; and before Lord Hood commenced his operations, he had the mortification of seeing that the enemy were every day erecting new works, strengthening old ones, and rendering the attempt more difficult. La Combe St. Michel, the commissioner from the national convention, who was in the city, replied in these terms to the summons of the British admiral—"I have hot shot for your ships, and bayonets for your troops. When two-thirds of our men are killed, I will then trust to the generosity of the English." The siege, however, was not sustained with the firmness which such a reply seemed to augur. On the 19th of May a treaty of capitulation was begun; that same evening the troops from St. Fiorenzo made their appearance on the hills; and, on the following morning, General d'Aubant arrived with the whole army to take possession of Bastia.

The event of the siege had justified the confidence of the sailors; but they themselves excused the opinion of the generals when they saw what they had done. "I am all astonishment," said Nelson, "when I reflect on what we have achieved; 1000 regulars, 1500 national guards, and a large party of Corsican troops, 4000 in all, laying down their arms to 1200 soldiers, marines, and seamen! I always was of opinion, have ever acted up to it, and never had any reason to repent it, that one

Englishman was equal to three Frenchmen. Had this been an English town, I am sure it would not have been taken by them." When it had been resolved to attack the place, the enemy were supposed to be far inferior in number; and it was not till the whole had been arranged, and the siege publicly undertaken, that Nelson received certain information of the great superiority of the garrison. This intelligence he kept secret, fearing lest, if so fair a pretext were afforded, the attempt would be abandoned. "My own honour," said he to his wife, "Lord Hood's honour, and the honour of our country, must have been sacrificed had I mentioned what I knew; therefore you will believe what must have been my feelings during the whole siege, when I had often proposals made to me to write to Lord Hood to raise it." Those very persons who thus advised him, were rewarded for their conduct at the siege of Bastia: Nelson, by whom it may truly be affirmed that Bastia was taken, received no reward. Lord Hood's thanks to him, both public and private, were, as he himself said, the handsomest which man could give; but his signal merits were not so mentioned in the despatches as to make them sufficiently known to the nation, nor to obtain for him from government those honours to which they so amply entitled him. This could only have arisen from the haste in which the despatches were written; certainly not from any deliberate purpose, for Lord Hood was uniformly his steady and sincere friend.

One of the cartel's ships, which carried the garrison of Bastia to Toulon, brought back intelligence that the French were about to sail from that port;—such exertions had they made to repair the damage done at the evacuation, and to fit out a fleet. The intelligence was speedily verified. Lord Hood sailed in quest of them toward the islands of Hieres. The *Agamemnon* was with him. "I pray God," said Nelson, writing to his wife, "that we may meet their fleet. If any accident should happen to me, I am sure my conduct will be such as will entitle you to the royal favour; not that I have the least idea but I shall return to you, and full of honour: if not, the Lord's will be done. My name shall never be a disgrace to those who may belong to me. The little I have, I have given to you, except a small annuity—I wish it was more; but I have never got a farthing dishonestly: it descends from clean hands. Whatever fate awaits me, I pray God to bless you, and preserve you, for your son's sake." With a mind thus prepared, and thus confident, his hopes and wishes seemed on the point of being gratified, when the enemy were discovered close under the land, near St. Tropez. The wind fell, and prevented Lord Hood from getting between them and the shore, as he designed: boats came out from Antibes and other places to their assistance, and towed them within the shoals in Gourjean Roads, where they were protected by the batteries on isles St. Honore and St. Marguerite, and on Cape Garousse. Here the English admiral planned a new mode of attack, meaning to double on five of the nearest ships; but the wind again died away, and it was found that they had anchored in compact order, guarding the only passage for large ships. There was no way of effecting this passage, except by towing or warping the vessels; and this rendered the attempt impracticable. For this time the enemy escaped; but Nelson bore in mind the admirable plan of attack which Lord Hood had devised, and there came a day when they felt its tremendous effects.

The *Agamemnon* was now despatched to co-operate at the siege of Calvi with General Sir Charles Stuart; an officer who, unfortunately for his country, never had an adequate field allotted him for the display of those eminent talents which were, to all who knew him, so conspicuous. Nelson had less responsibility here than at Bastia; and was acting with a man after his own heart, who was never sparing of himself, and slept every night in the advanced battery. But the service was not less hard than that of the former siege. "We will fag ourselves to death," said he to Lord Hood, "before any blame shall lie at our doors. I trust it will not be forgotten, that twenty-five pieces of heavy ordnance have been dragged to the different batteries, mounted, and, all but three, fought by seamen, except one artilleryman to point the guns." The climate proved more destructive than the service; for this was during the lion sun, as they call our season of the dog-days. Of 2000 men, above half were sick, and the rest like so many phantoms. Nelson described himself as the reed among the oaks, bowing before the storm when they were laid low by it. "All the prevailing disorders have attacked me," said he, "but I have not strength enough for them to fasten on." The loss from the enemy was not great; but Nelson received a serious injury: a shot struck the ground near him, and drove the sand and small gravel into one of his eyes. He spoke of it slightly at the time: writing the same day to Lord Hood, he only said that he had got a little hurt that morning, not much; and the next day, he said, he should be able to attend his duty in the evening. In fact, he suffered it to confine him only one day; but the sight was lost.

After the fall of Calvi, his services were, by a strange omission, altogether overlooked; and his name was not even mentioned in the list of wounded. This was no ways imputable to the admiral, for he sent home to government Nelson's journal of the siege, that they might fully understand the nature of his indefatigable and unequalled exertions. If those exertions were not rewarded in the conspicuous manner which they deserved, the fault was in the administration of the day, not in Lord Hood. Nelson felt himself neglected. "One hundred and ten days," said he, "I have been actually engaged at sea and on shore against the enemy; three actions against ships, two against Bastia in my ship, four boat actions, and two villages taken, and twelve sail of vessels burnt. I do not know that any one has done more. I have had the comfort to be always applauded by my Commander-in-Chief, but never to be rewarded; and, what is more mortifying, for services in which I have been wounded, others have been praised, who, at the same time, were actually in bed, far from the scene of action. They have not done me justice. But never mind, I'll have a Gazette of my own." How amply was this second-sight of glory realised!

The health of his ship's company had now, in his own words, been miserably torn to pieces by as hard service as a ship's crew ever performed: 150 were in their beds when he left Calvi; of them he lost 54 and believed that the constitutions of the rest were entirely destroyed. He was now sent with despatches to Mr. Drake, at Genoa, and had his first interview with the Doge. The French had, at this time, taken possession of Vado Bay, in the Genoese territory; and Nelson foresaw that, if their thoughts were bent on the invasion of Italy, they would accomplish it the ensuing spring. "The allied powers," he said, "were jealous of each other; and none but England was hearty in the cause." His wish was for peace on fair terms, because England he thought was draining herself to maintain allies who would not fight for themselves. Lord Hood had now returned to England, and the command devolved on Admiral Hotham. The affairs of the Mediterranean wore at this time a gloomy aspect. The arts, as well as the arms of the enemy, were gaining the ascendancy there. Tuscany concluded peace relying upon the faith of France, which was, in fact, placing itself at her mercy. Corsica was in danger. We had taken that island for ourselves, annexed it formally to the crown of Great Britain, and given it a constitution as free as our own. This was done with the consent of the majority of the inhabitants; and no transaction between two countries was ever more fairly or legitimately conducted: yet our conduct was unwise;—the island is large enough to form an independent state, and such we should have made it, under our protection, as long as protection might be needed; the Corsicans would then have felt as a nation; but when one party had given up the country to England, the natural consequence was that the other looked to France. The question proposed to the people was, to which would they belong? Our language and our religion were against us; our unaccommodating manners, it is to be feared, still more so. The French were better politicians. In intrigue they have ever been unrivalled; and it now became apparent that, in spite of old wrongs, which ought never to have been forgotten nor forgiven, their partisans were daily acquiring strength. It is part of the policy of France, and a wise policy it is, to impress upon other powers the opinion of its strength, by lofty language: and by threatening before it strikes; a system which, while it keeps up the spirit of its allies, and perpetually stimulates their hopes, tends also to dismay its enemies. Corsica was now loudly threatened. "The French, who had not yet been taught to feel their own inferiority upon the seas, braved us in contempt upon that element." They had a superior fleet in the Mediterranean, and they sent it out with express orders to seek the English and engage them. Accordingly, the Toulon fleet, consisting of seventeen ships of the line and five smaller vessels, put to sea. Admiral Hotham received this information at Leghorn, and sailed immediately in search of them. He had with him fourteen sail of the line, and one Neapolitan seventy-four;

but his ships were only half-manned, containing but 7650 men, whereas the enemy had 16,900. He soon came in sight of them: a general action was expected; and Nelson, as was his custom on such occasions, wrote a hasty letter to his wife, as that which might possibly contain his last farewell. "The lives of all," said he, "are in the hand of Him who knows best whether to preserve mine or not; my character and good name are in my own keeping."

But however confident the French government might be of their naval superiority, the officers had no such feeling; and after manoeuvring for a day in sight of the English fleet, they suffered themselves to be chased. One of their ships, the *Ça ira*, of eighty-four guns, carried away her main and fore top-masts. The *Inconstant* frigate fired at the disabled ship, but received so many shot that she was obliged to leave her. Soon afterwards a French frigate took the *Ça ira* in tow; and the *Sans-Culottes*, one hundred and twenty, and the *Jean Barras*, seventy-four, kept about gunshot distance on her weather bow. The *Agamemnon* stood towards her, having no ship of the line to support her within several miles. As she drew near, the *Ça ira* fired her stern guns so truly, that not a shot missed some part of the ship; and latterly, the masts were struck by every shot. It had been Nelson's intention not to fire before he touched her stern; but seeing how impossible it was that he should be supported, and how certainly the *Agamemnon* must be severely cut up if her masts were disabled, he altered his plan according to the occasion. As soon, therefore, as he was within a hundred yards of her stern, he ordered the helm to be put a-starboard, and the driver and after-sails to be brailed up and shivered; and, as the ship fell off, gave the enemy her whole broadside. They instantly braced up the after-yards, put the helm a-port, and stood after her again. This manoeuvre he practised for two hours and a quarter, never allowing the *Ça ira* to get a single gun from either side to bear on him; and when the French fired their after-guns now, it was no longer with coolness and precision, for every shot went far ahead. By this time her sails were hanging in tatters, her mizen-top-mast, mizen-top-sail, and cross-jack-yards shot away. But the frigate which had her in tow hove in stays, and got her round. Both these French ships now brought their guns to bear, and opened their fire. The *Agamemnon* passed them within half-pistol shot; almost every shot passed over her, for the French had elevated their guns for the rigging, and for distant firing, and did not think of altering the elevation. As soon as the *Agamemnon*'s after-guns ceased to bear, she hove in stays, keeping a constant fire as she came round; and being worked, said Nelson, with as much exactness as if she had been turning into Spithead. On getting round, he saw that the *Sans-Culottes*, which had wore, with many of the enemy's ships, was under his lee bow, and standing to leeward. The admiral, at the same time, made the signal for the van ships to join him. Upon this Nelson bore away, and prepared to set all sail; and the enemy, having saved their ship, hauled close to the wind, and opened upon him a distant and ineffectual fire. Only seven of the *Agamemnon*'s men were hurt—a thing which Nelson himself remarked as wonderful: her sails and rigging were very much cut, and she had many shots in her hull, and some between wind and water. The *Ça ira* lost 110 men that day, and was so cut up that she could not get a top-mast aloft during the night.

At daylight on the following morning, the English ships were taken aback with a fine breeze at N.W., while the enemy's fleet kept the southerly wind. The body of their fleet was about five miles distant; the *Ça ira* and the *Censeur*, seventy-four, which had her in tow, about three and a half. All sail was made to cut these ships off; and as the French attempted to save them, a partial action was brought on. The *Agamemnon* was again engaged with her yesterday's antagonist; but she had to fight on both sides of the ship at the same time. The *Ça ira* and the *Censeur* fought most gallantly: the first lost nearly 300 men, in addition to her former loss; the last, 350. Both at length struck; and Lieutenant Andrews, of the *Agamemnon*, brother to the lady to whom Nelson had become attached in France, and, in Nelson's own words, "as gallant an officer as ever stepped a quarter-deck," hoisted English colours on board them both. The rest of the enemy's ships' behaved very ill. As soon as these vessels had struck, Nelson went to Admiral Hotham and proposed that the two prizes should be left with the *Illustrious* and *Courageux*, which had been crippled in the action, and with four frigates, and that the rest of the fleet should pursue the enemy, and follow up the advantage to the utmost. But his reply was—"We must be contented: we have done very well."—"Now," said Nelson," had we taken ten sail, and allowed the eleventh to escape, when it had been possible to have got at her, I could never have called it well done. Goodall backed me; I got him to write to the admiral; but it would not do. We should have had such a day as, I believe, the annals of England never produced." In this letter the character of Nelson fully manifests itself. "I wish" said he, "to be an admiral, and in the command of the English fleet: I should very soon either do much, or be ruined: my disposition cannot bear tame and slow measures. Sure I am, had I commanded on the 14th, that either the whole French fleet would have graced my triumph, or I should have been in a confounded scrape." What the event would have been, he knew from his prophetic feelings and his own consciousness of power; and we also know it now, for Aboukir and Trafalgar have told it.

The *Ça ira* and *Censeur* probably defended themselves with more obstinacy in this action, from a persuasion that, if they struck, no quarter would be given; because they had fired red-hot shot, and had also a preparation sent, as they said, by the convention from Paris, which seems to have been of the nature of the Greek fire; for it became liquid when it was discharged, and water would not extinguish its flames. This combustible was concealed with great care in the captured ships; like the red-hot shot, it had been found useless in battle. Admiral Hotham's action saved Corsica for the time; but the victory had been incomplete, and the arrival at Toulon of six sail of the line, two frigates, and two cutters from Brest, gave the French a superiority which, had they known how to use it, would materially have endangered the British Mediterranean fleet. That fleet had been greatly neglected at the Admiralty during Lord Chatham's administration: and it did not, for some time, feel the beneficial effect of his removal. Lord Hood had gone home to represent the real state of affairs, and solicit reinforcements adequate to the exigencies of the time, and the importance of the scene of action. But that fatal error of under-proportioning the force to the service; that ruinous economy, which, by sparing a little, renders all that is spent useless, infected the British councils; and Lord Hood, not being able to obtain such reinforcements as he knew were necessary, resigned the command. "Surely," said Nelson, "the people at home have forgotten us." Another Neapolitan seventy-four joined Admiral Hotham, and Nelson observed with sorrow that this was a matter of exultation to an English fleet. When the store-ships and victuallers from Gibraltar arrived, their escape from the enemy was thought wonderful; and yet, had they not escaped, "the game," said Nelson, "was up here. At this moment our operations are at a stand for want of ships to support the Austrians in getting possession of the sea-coast of the king of Sardinia; and behold our admiral does not feel himself equal to show himself, much less to give assistance in their operations." It was reported that the French were again out with 18 or 20 sail. The combined British and Neapolitan were but sixteen; should the enemy be only eighteen, Nelson made no doubt of a complete victory; but if they were twenty, he said, it was not to be expected; and a battle, without complete victory, would have been destruction, because another mast was not to be got on that side of Gibraltar. At length Admiral Man arrived with a squadron from England. "What they can mean by sending him with only five sail of the line," said Nelson, "is truly astonishing; but all men are alike, and we in this country do not find any amendment or alteration from the old Board of Admiralty. They should know that half the ships in the fleet require to go to England; and that long ago they ought to have reinforced us."

About this time Nelson was made colonel of marines; a mark of approbation which he had long wished for rather than expected. It came in good season, for his spirits were oppressed by the thought that his services had not been acknowledged as they deserved; and it abated the resentful feeling which would else have been excited by the answer to an application to the War-office. During his four months' land service in Corsica, he had lost all his ship furniture, owing to the movements of a camp. Upon this he wrote to the Secretary at War, briefly stating what his services on shore had been, and saying, he trusted it was not asking an improper thing to request that the same allowance might be made to him which would be made to a land officer of his rank, which, situated as he was, would be that of a brigadier-general: if this could not be accorded, he hoped that his additional expenses would be paid him. The answer which he received was, that "no pay had ever been issued under the direction of the War-office to officers of the navy serving with the army on shore."

He now entered upon a new line of service. The Austrian and Sardinian armies, under General de Vins, required a British squadron to co-operate with them in driving the French from the Riviera di Genoa; and as Nelson had been so much in the habit of soldiering, it was immediately fixed that the brigadier should go. He sailed from St. Fiorenzo on this destination; but fell in, off Cape del Mele, with the enemy's fleet, who immediately gave his squadron chase. The chase lasted four-and-twenty hours; and, owing to the fickleness of the wind, the British ships were sometimes hard pressed; but the want of skill on the part of the French gave Nelson many advantages. Nelson bent his way back to St. Fiorenzo, where the fleet, which was in the midst of watering and refitting, had, for seven hours, the mortification of seeing him almost in possession of the enemy, before the wind would allow them to put out to his assistance. The French, however, at evening, went off, not choosing to approach nearer the shore. During the night, Admiral Hotham, by great exertions, got under weigh; and, having sought the enemy four days, came in sight of them on the fifth. Baffling winds and vexatious calms, so common in the Mediterranean, rendered it impossible to close with them; only a partial action could be brought on; and then the firing made a perfect calm. The French being to windward, drew inshore; and the English fleet was becalmed six or seven miles to the westward. *L'Alcide*, of seventy-four guns, struck; but before she could be taken possession of, a box of combustibles in her fore-top took fire, and the unhappy crew experienced how far more perilous their inventions were to themselves than to their enemies. So rapid was the conflagration, that the French in their official account say, the hull, the masts, and sails, all seemed to take fire at the same moment; and though the English boats were put out to the assistance of the poor wretches on board, not more than 200 could be saved. The *Agamemnon*, and Captain Rowley in the *Cumberland*, were just getting into close action a second time, when the admiral called them off, the wind now blowing directly into the Gulf of Frejus, where the enemy anchored after the evening closed.

Nelson now proceeded to his station with eight sail of frigates under his command. Arriving at Genoa, he had a conference with Mr. Drake, the British envoy to that state; the result of which was, that the object of the British must be to put an entire stop to all trade between Genoa, France, and the places occupied by the French troops; for unless this trade were stopped, it would be scarcely possible for the allied armies to hold their situation, and impossible for them to make any progress in driving the enemy out of the Riviera di Genoa. Mr. Drake was of opinion that even Nice might fall for want of supplies, if the trade with Genoa were cut off. This sort of blockade Nelson could not carry on without great risk to himself. A captain in the navy, as he represented to the envoy, is liable to prosecution for detention and damages. This danger was increased by an order which had then lately been issued; by which, when a neutral ship was detained, a complete specification of her cargo was directed to be sent to the secretary of the Admiralty, and no legal process instituted against her till the pleasure of that board should be communicated. This was requiring an impossibility. The cargoes of ships detained upon this station, consisting chiefly of corn, would be spoiled long before the orders of the Admiralty could be known; and then, if they should happen to release the vessel, the owners would look to the captain for damages. Even the only precaution which could be taken against this danger, involved another danger not less to be apprehended: for if the captain should direct the cargo to be taken out, the freight paid for, and the vessel released, the agent employed might prove fraudulent, and become bankrupt; and in that case the captain became responsible. Such things had happened: Nelson therefore required, as the only means for carrying on that service, which was judged essential to the common cause, without exposing the officers to ruin, that the British envoy should appoint agents to pay the freight, release the vessels, sell the cargo, and hold the amount till process was had upon it: government thus securing its officers. "I am acting," said Nelson. "not only without the orders of my commander-in-chief, but, in some measure, contrary to him. However, I have not only the support of his Majesty's ministers, both at Turin and Genoa, but a consciousness that I am doing what is right and proper for the service of our king and country. Political courage, in an officer abroad, is as highly necessary as military courage."

This quality, which is as much rarer than military courage as it is more valuable, and without which the soldier's bravery is often of little avail, Nelson possessed in an eminent degree. His representations were attended to as they deserved. Admiral Hotham commended him for what he had done; and the attention of government was awakened to the injury which the cause of the allies continually suffered from the frauds of neutral vessels. "What changes in my life of activity!" said the indefatigable man. "Here I am, having commenced a co-operation with an old Austrian general, almost fancying myself charging at the head of a troop of horse! I do not write less than from ten to twenty letters every day; which, with the Austrian general and aides-de-camp, and my own little squadron, fully employ my time. This I like; active service or none." It was Nelson's mind which supported his feeble body through these exertions. He was at this time almost blind, and wrote with very great pain. "Poor *Agamemnon*" he sometimes said, "was as nearly worn out as her captain; and both must soon be laid up to repair."

When Nelson first saw General de Vins, he thought him an able man, who was willing to act with vigour. The general charged his inactivity upon the Piedmontese and Neapolitans, whom, he said, nothing could induce to act; and he concerted a plan with Nelson for embarking a part of the Austrian army, and landing it in the rear of the French. But the English commodore soon began to suspect that the Austrian general was little disposed to any active operations. In the hope of spurring him on, he wrote to him, telling him that he had surveyed the coast to the W. as far as Nice, and would undertake to embark 4,000 or 5,000 men, with their arms and a few days' provisions, on board the squadron, and land them within two miles of St. Remo, with their field-pieces. Respecting further provisions for the Austrian army, he would provide convoys, that they should arrive in safety; and if a re-embarkation should be found necessary, he would cover it with the squadron. The possession of St. Remo, as headquarters for magazines of every kind, would enable the Austrian general to turn his army to the eastward or westward. The enemy at Oneglia would be cut off from provisions, and men could be landed to attack that place whenever it was judged necessary. St. Remo was the only place between Vado and Ville Franche where the squadron could lie in safety, and anchor in almost all winds. The bay was not so good as Vado for large ships; but it had a mole, which Vado had not, where all small vessels could lie, and load and unload their cargoes. This bay being in possession of the allies, Nice could be completely blockaded by sea. General de Vins affecting, in his reply, to consider that Nelson's proposal had no other end than that of obtaining the bay of St. Remo as a station for the ships, told him, what he well knew, and had expressed before, that Vado Bay was a better anchorage; nevertheless, if Monsieur le Commandant Nelson was well assured that part of the fleet could winter there, there was no risk to which he would not expose himself with pleasure, for the sake of procuring a safe station for the vessels of his Britannic Majesty. Nelson soon assured the Austrian commander that this was not the object of his memorial. He now began to suspect that both the Austrian Court and their general had other ends in view than the cause of the allies. "This army," said he, "is slow beyond all description; and I begin to think that the Emperor is anxious to touch another £4,000,000 of English money. As for the German generals, war is their trade, and peace is ruin to them; therefore we cannot expect that they should have any wish to finish the war. The politics of courts are so mean, that private people would be ashamed to act in the same way; all is trick and finesse, to which the common cause is sacrificed. The general wants a loop-hole; it has for some time appeared to me that he means to go no further than his present position, and to lay the miscarriage of the enterprise against Nice, which has always been held out as the great object of his army, to the non-co-operation of the British fleet and of the Sardinians."

To prevent this plea, Nelson again addressed De Vins, requesting only to know the time, and the number of troops ready to embark; then he would, he said, dispatch a ship to Admiral Hotham, requesting transports, having no doubt of obtaining them, and trusting that the plan would be successful to its fullest extent. Nelson thought at the time that, if the whole fleet were offered him for transports, he would find some other excuse; and Mr. Drake, who was now appointed to reside at the Austrian headquarters, entertained the same idea of the general's sincerity. It was not, however, put so clearly to the proof as it ought to have been. He replied that, as soon as Nelson could declare himself ready with the vessels necessary for conveying 10,000 men, with their artillery and baggage, he would put the army in motion. But Nelson was not enabled to do this: Admiral Hotham, who was highly meritorious in leaving such a man so much at his own discretion, pursued a cautious system, ill according with the bold and comprehensive views of Nelson, who continually regretted Lord Hood, saying that the nation had suffered much by his resignation of the Mediterranean command. The plan which had been concerted, he said, would astonish the French, and perhaps the English.

There was no unity in the views of the allied powers, no cordiality in their co-operation, no energy in their councils. The neutral powers assisted France more effectually than the allies assisted each other. The Genoese ports were at this time filled with French privateers, which swarmed out every night, and covered the gulf; and French vessels were allowed to tow out of the port of Genoa itself, board vessels which were coming in, and then return into the mole. This was allowed without a remonstrance; while, though Nelson abstained most carefully from offering any offence to the Genoese territory or flag, complaints were so repeatedly made against his squadron, that, he says, it seemed a trial who should be tired first; they of complaining, or he of answering their complaints. But the question of neutrality was soon at an end. An Austrian commissary was travelling from Genoa towards Vado; it was known that he was to sleep at Voltri, and that he had £10,000 with him

– a booty which the French minister in that city, and the captain of a French frigate in that port, considered as far more important than the word of honour of the one, the duties of the other, and the laws of neutrality. The boats of the frigate went out with some privateers, landed, robbed the commissary, and brought back the money to Genoa. The next day men were publicly enlisted in that city for the French army: 700 men were embarked, with 7,000 stand of arms, on board the frigates and other vessels, who were to land between Voltri and Savona. There a detachment from the French army was to join them, and the Genoese peasantry were to be invited to insurrection – a measure for which everything had been prepared. The night of the 13th was fixed for the sailing of this expedition; the Austrians called loudly for Nelson to prevent it; and he, on the evening of the 13th, arrived at Genoa. His presence checked the plan: the frigate, knowing her deserts, got within the merchant-ships, in the inner mole; and the Genoese government did not now even demand of Nelson respect to the neutral port, knowing that they had allowed, if not connived at, a flagrant breach of neutrality, and expecting the answer which he was prepared to return, that it was useless and impossible for him to respect it longer.

But though this movement produced the immediate effect which was designed, it led to ill consequences, which Nelson foresaw, but for want of sufficient force was unable to prevent. His squadron was too small for the service which it had to perform. He required two seventy-fours and eight or ten frigates and sloops; but when he demanded this reinforcement, Admiral Hotham had left the command. Sir Hyde Parker had succeeded till the new commander should arrive; and he immediately reduced it to almost nothing, leaving him only one frigate and a brig. This was a fatal error. While the Austrian and Sardinian troops, whether from the imbecility or the treachery of their leaders, remained inactive, the French were preparing for the invasion of Italy. Not many days before Nelson was thus summoned to Genoa, he chased a large convoy into Alassio. Twelve vessels he had formerly destroyed in that port, though 2,000 French troops occupied the town. This former attack had made them take new measures of defence; and there were now above 100 sail of victuallers, gun-boats, and ships of war. Nelson represented to the Admiral how important it was to destroy these vessels; and offered, with his squadron of frigates, and the *Culloden* and *Courageux*, to lead himself in the *Agamemnon*, and take or destroy the whole. The attempt was not permitted; but it was Nelson's belief that, if it had been made, it would have prevented the attack upon the Austrian army, which took place almost immediately afterwards.

General de Vins demanded satisfaction of the Genoese government for the seizure of his commissary; and then, without waiting for their reply, took possession of some empty magazines of the French, and pushed his sentinels to the very gates of Genoa. Had he done so at first, he would have found the magazines full; but, timed as the measure was, and useless as it was to the cause of the allies, it was in character with the whole of the Austrian general's conduct; and it is no small proof of the dexterity with which he served the enemy, that in such circumstances he could so act with Genoa as to contrive to put himself in the wrong. Nelson was at this time, according to his own expression, placed in a cleft stick. Mr. Drake, the Austrian minister, and the Austrian general, all joined in requiring him not to leave Genoa; if he left that port unguarded, they said, not only the imperial troops at St. Pier d'Arena and Voltri would be lost, but the French plan for taking post between Voltri and Savona would certainly succeed; if the Austrians should be worsted in the advanced posts, the retreat of the Bocchetta would be cut off; and if this happened, the loss of the army would be imputed to him, for having left Genoa. On the other hand, he knew that if he were not at Pietra, the enemy's gunboats would harass the left flank of the Austrians, who, if they were defeated, as was to be expected, from the spirit of all their operations, would, very probably, lay their defeat to the want of assistance from the *Agamemnon*. Had the force for which Nelson applied been given him, he could have attended to both objects; and had he been permitted to attack the convoy in Alassio, he would have disconcerted the plans of the French, in spite of the Austrian general. He had foreseen the danger, and pointed out how it might be prevented; but the means of preventing it were withheld. The attack was made as he foresaw; and the gunboats brought their fire to bear upon the Austrians. It so happened, however, that the left flank, which was exposed to them, was the only part of the army that behaved well: this division stood its ground till the centre and the right wing fled, and then retreated in a soldierlike manner. General de Vins gave up the command in the middle of the battle, pleading ill health. "From that moment," says Nelson, "not a soldier stayed at his post: it was the devil take the hindmost. Many thousands ran away who had never seen the enemy; some of them thirty miles from the advanced posts. Had I not, though I own, against my inclination, been kept at Genoa, from 8,000 to 10,000 men would have been taken prisoners, and, amongst the number, General de Vins himself; but by this means the pass of the Bocchetta was kept open. The purser of the ship, who was at Vado, ran with the Austrians eighteen miles without stopping; the men without arms, officers without soldiers, women without assistance. The oldest officers say they never heard of so complete a defeat, and certainly without any reason. Thus has ended my campaign. We have established the French republic: which but for us, I verily believe, would never have been settled by such a volatile, changeable people. I hate a Frenchman: they are equally objects of my detestation whether royalists or republicans: in some points, I believe, the latter are the best." Nelson had a lieutenant and two midshipmen taken at Vado: they told him, in their letter, that few of the French soldiers were more than three or four and twenty years old, a great many not more than fourteen, and all were nearly naked; they were sure, they said, his barge's crew could have beat a hundred of them; and that, had he himself seen them, he would not have thought, if the world had been covered with such people, that they could have beaten the Austrian army.

The defeat of General de Vins gave the enemy possession of the Genoese coast from Savona to Voltri, and it deprived the Austrians of their direct communication with the English fleet. The *Agamemnon*, therefore, could no longer be useful on this station, and Nelson sailed for Leghorn to refit. When his ship went into dock, there was not a mast, yard, sail, or any part of the rigging, but what stood in need of repair, having been cut to pieces with shot. The hull was so damaged that it had for some time been secured by cables, which were served or thrapped round it.

CHAPTER IV
1796–1797

Sir J. Jervis takes the Command—Genoa joins the French—Bounaparte begins his Career—Evacuation of Corsica—Nelson hoists his broad Pennant in the *Minerve*—Action with the *Sabina*—Battle off Cape St. Vincent—Nelson commands the inner Squadron at the Blockade of Cadiz—Boat Action in the Bay of Cadiz—Expedition against Teneriffe—Nelson loses an Arm—His Sufferings in England, and Recovery.

Sir John Jervis had now arrived to take the command of the Mediterranean fleet. The *Agamemnon* having, as her captain said, been made as fit for sea as a rotten ship could be, Nelson sailed from Leghorn, and joined the admiral in Fiorenzo Bay. "I found him," said he, "anxious to know many things which I was a good deal surprised to find had not been communicated to him by others in the fleet; and it would appear that he was so well satisfied with my opinion of what is likely to happen, and the means of prevention to be taken, that he had no reserve with me respecting his information and ideas of what is likely to be done." The manner in which Nelson was received is said to have excited some envy. One captain observed to him: "You did just as you pleased in Lord Hood's time, the same in Admiral Hotham's, and now again with Sir John Jervis: it makes no difference to you who is commander-in-chief." A higher compliment could not have been paid to any commander-in-chief than to say of him that he understood the merits of Nelson, and left him, as far as possible, to act upon his own judgment.

Sir John Jervis offered him the *St George*, ninety, or the *Zealous*, seventy-four, and asked if he should have any objection to serve under him with his flag. He replied, that if the *Agamemnon* were ordered home, and his flag were not arrived, he should, on many accounts, wish to return to England; still, if the war continued, he should be very proud of hoisting his flag under Sir John's command, "We cannot spare you," said Sir

John, "either as captain or admiral." Accordingly, he resumed his station in the Gulf of Genoa. The French had not followed up their successes in that quarter with their usual celerity. Scherer, who commanded there, owed his advancement to any other cause than his merit: he was a favourite of the directory; but for the present, through the influence of Barras, he was removed from a command for which his incapacity was afterwards clearly proved, and Buonaparte was appointed to succeed him. Buonaparte had given indications of his military talents at Toulon, and of his remorseless nature at Paris; but the extent either of his ability or his wickedness was at this time known to none, and perhaps not even suspected by himself.

Nelson supposed, from the information which he had obtained, that one column of the French army would take possession of Port Especia; either penetrating through the Genoese territory, or proceeding coast-ways in light vessels; our ships of war not being able to approach the coast, because of the shallowness of the water. To prevent this, he said; two things were necessary: the possession of Vado Bay, and the taking of Port Especia; if either of these points were secured, Italy would be safe from any attack of the French by sea. General Beaulieu, who had now superseded De Vins in the command of the allied Austrian and Sardinian army, sent his nephew and aide-de-camp to communicate with Nelson, and inquire whether he could anchor in any other place than Vado Bay. Nelson replied, that Vado was the only place where the British fleet could lie in safety, but all places would suit his squadron; and wherever the general came to the sea-coast, there he should find it. The Austrian repeatedly asked, if there was not a risk of losing the squadron? and was constantly answered, that if these ships should be lost, the admiral would find others. But all plans of co-operation with the Austrians were soon frustrated by the battle of Montenotte. Beaulieu ordered an attack to be made upon the post of Voltri. It was made twelve hours before the time which he had fixed, and before he arrived to direct it. In consequence, the French were enabled to effect their retreat, and fall back to Montenotte, thus giving the troops there a decisive superiority in number over the division which attacked them. This drew on the defeat of the Austrians. Buonaparte, with a celerity which had never before been witnessed in modern war, pursued his advantages; and, in the course of a fortnight, dictated to the court of Turin terms of peace, or rather of submission; by which all the strongest places of Piedmont were put into his hands.

On one occasion, and only on one, Nelson was able to impede the progress of this new conqueror. Six vessels, laden with cannon and ordnance-stores for the siege of Mantua, sailed from Toulon for St. Pier d'Arena. Assisted by Captain Cockburn, in the *Meleager*, he drove them under a battery; pursued them, silenced the batteries, and captured the whole. Military books, plans and maps of Italy, with the different points marked upon them where former battles had been fought, sent by the directory for Buonaparte's use, were found in the convoy. The loss of this artillery was one of the chief causes which compelled the French to raise the siege of Mantua; but there was too much treachery, and too much imbecility, both in the councils and armies of the allied powers, for Austria to improve this momentary success. Buonaparte perceived that the conquest of Italy was within his reach; treaties, and the rights of neutral or of friendly powers, were as little regarded by him as by the government for which he acted. In open contempt of both he entered Tuscany, and took possession of Leghorn. In consequence of this movement, Nelson blockaded that port, and landed a British force in the Isle of Elba, to secure Porto Ferrajo. Soon afterwards he took the Island of Capraja, which had formerly belonged to Corsica, being less than forty miles distant from it; a distance, however, short as it was, which enabled the Genoese to retain it, after their infamous sale of Corsica to France. Genoa had now taken part with France: its government had long covertly assisted the French, and now willingly yielded to the first compulsory menace which required them to exclude the English from their ports. Capraja was seized in consequence; but this act of vigour was not followed up as it ought to have been. England at that time depended too much upon the feeble governments of the Continent, and too little upon itself. It was determined by the British cabinet to evacuate Corsica, as soon as Spain should form an offensive alliance with France. This event, which, from the moment that Spain had been compelled to make peace, was clearly foreseen, had now taken place; and orders for the evacuation of the island were immediately sent out. It was impolitic to annex this island to the British dominions; but having done so, it was disgraceful thus to abandon it. The disgrace would have been spared, and every advantage which could have been derived from the possession of the island secured, if the people had at first been left to form a government for themselves, and protected by us in the enjoyment of their independence.

The viceroy, Sir Gilbert Elliott, deeply felt the impolicy and ignominy of this evacuation. The fleet also was ordered to leave the Mediterranean. This resolution was so contrary to the last instructions which had been received, that Nelson exclaimed, "Do his majesty's ministers know their own minds? They at home," said he, "do not know what this fleet is capable of performing—anything and everything. Much as I shall rejoice to see England, I lament our present orders in sackcloth and ashes, so dishonourable to the dignity of England, whose fleets are equal to meet the world in arms; and of all the fleets I ever saw, I never beheld one, in point of officers and men, equal to Sir John Jervis's, who is a commander-in-chief able to lead them to glory." Sir Gilbert Elliott believed that the great body of the Corsicans were perfectly satisfied, as they had good reason to be, with the British Government, sensible of its advantages, and attached to it. However this may have been, when they found that the English intended to evacuate the island, they naturally and necessarily sent to make their peace with the French. The partisans of France found none to oppose them. A committee of thirty took upon them the government of Bastia, and sequestrated all the British property; armed Corsicans mounted guard at every place, and a plan was laid for seizing the viceroy. Nelson, who was appointed to superintend the evacuation, frustrated these projects. At a time when every one else despaired of saving stores, cannon, provisions, or property of any kind, and a privateer was moored across the mole-head to prevent all boats from passing, he sent word to the committee, that if the slightest opposition were made to the embarkment and removal of British property, he would batter the town down. The privateer pointed her guns at the officer who carried this message, and muskets were levelled against his boats from the mole-head. Upon this Captain Sutton, of the *Egmont*, pulling out his watch, gave them a quarter of an hour to deliberate upon their answer. In five minutes after the expiration of that time, the ships, he said, would open their fire. Upon this the very sentinels scampered off, and every vessel came out of the mole. A shipowner complained to the commodore that the municipality refused to let him take his goods out of the custom-house. Nelson directed him to say, that unless they were instantly delivered, he would open his fire. The committee turned pale, and, without answering a word, gave him the keys. Their last attempt was to levy a duty upon the things that were re-embarked. He sent them word, that he would pay them a disagreeable visit, if there were any more complaints. The committee then finding that they had to deal with a man who knew his own power, and was determined to make the British name respected, desisted from the insolent conduct which they had assumed; and it was acknowledged that Bastia never had been so quiet and orderly since the English were in possession of it. This was on the 14th of October; during the five following days the work of embarkation was carried on, the private property was saved, and public stores to the amount of £200,000. The French, favoured by the Spanish fleet, which was at that time within twelve leagues of Bastia, pushed over troops from Leghorn, who landed near Cape Corse on the 18th; and on the 20th, at one in the morning, entered the citadel, an hour only after the British had spiked the guns and evacuated it. Nelson embarked at daybreak, being the last person who left the shore; having thus, as he said, seen the first and the last of Corsica. Provoked at the conduct of the municipality, and the disposition which the populace had shown to profit by the confusion, he turned towards the shore, as he stepped into his boat, and exclaimed: "Now, John Corse, follow the natural bent of your detestable character —plunder and revenge." This, however, was not Nelson's deliberate opinion of the people of Corsica; he knew that their vices were the natural consequences of internal anarchy and foreign oppression, such as the same causes would produce in any people; and when he saw, that of all those who took leave of the viceroy there was not one who parted from him without tears, he acknowledged that they manifestly acted not from dislike of the English, but from fear of the French. England then might, with more reason, reproach her own rulers for pusillanimity than the Corsicans for ingratitude.

Having thus ably effected this humiliating service, Nelson was ordered to hoist his broad pendant on board the *Minerve* frigate, Captain George Cockburn, and with the *Blanche* under his command, proceed to Porto Ferrajo, and superintend the evacuation of that place also. On his way, he fell in with two Spanish frigates, the *Sabina* and the *Ceres*. The *Minerve* engaged the former, which was commanded by D. Jacobo Stuart, a descendent of the Duke of Berwick. After an action of three hours, during which the Spaniards lost 164 men, the *Sabina* struck. The Spanish captain, who was the only surviving officer, had hardly been conveyed on board the *Minerve*, when another enemy's frigate came up, compelled her to cast off the prize, and brought her a second time into action. After half an hour's trial of strength, this new antagonist wore and hauled off; but a Spanish squadron of two ships of the line and two frigates came in sight. The *Blanche*, from which the *Ceres* had got off, was far to windward, and the *Minerve* escaped only by the anxiety of the enemy to recover their own ship. As soon as Nelson reached Porto Ferrajo he sent his prisoner in a flag of truce to Carthagena, having returned him his sword; this he did in honour of the gallantry which D. Jacobo had displayed, and not without some feeling of respect for his ancestry. "I felt it," said he, "consonant to the dignity of my country and I always act as I feel right, without regard to custom; he was reputed the best officer in Spain, and his men were worthy of such a commander." By the same flag of truce he sent back all the Spanish prisoners at Porto Ferrajo; in exchange for whom he received his own men who had been taken in the prize.

General de Burgh, who commanded at the Isle of Elba, did not think himself authorised to abandon the place till he had received specific instructions from England to that effect; professing that he was unable to decide between the contradictory orders of government, or to guess at what their present intentions might be; but he said, his only motive for urging delay in this measure arose from a desire that his own conduct might be properly sanctioned, not from any opinion that Porto Ferrajo ought to be retained. But Naples having made peace, Sir John Jervis considered his business with Italy as concluded; and the protection of Portugal was the point to which he was now instructed to attend. Nelson, therefore, whose orders were perfectly clear and explicit, withdrew the whole naval establishment from that station, leaving the transports victualled, and so arranged that all the troops and stores could be embarked in three days. He was now about to leave the Mediterranean. Mr. Drake, who had been our minister at Genoa, expressed to him, on this occasion, the very high opinion which the allies entertained of his conspicuous merit; adding, that it was impossible for any one, who had the honour of co-operating with him, not to admire the activity, talents, and zeal which he had so eminently and constantly displayed. In fact, during this long course of services in the Mediterranean, the whole of his conduct had exhibited the same zeal, the same indefatigable energy, the same intuitive judgment, the same prompt and unerring decision which characterised his after-career of glory. His name was as yet hardly known to the English public; but it was feared and respected throughout Italy. A letter came to him, directed "Horatio Nelson, Genoa;" and the writer, when he was asked how he could direct it so vaguely, replied, "Sir, there is but one Horatio Nelson in the world." At Genoa, in particular, where he had so long been stationed, and where the nature of his duty first led him to continual disputes with the government, and afterwards compelled him to stop the trade of the port, he was equally respected by the doge and by the people; for, while he maintained the rights and interests of Great Britain with becoming firmness, he tempered the exercise of power with courtesy and humanity wherever duty would permit. "Had all my actions," said he, writing at this time to his wife, "been gazetted, not one fortnight would have passed, during the whole war, without a letter from me. One day or other I will have a long Gazette to myself. I feel that such an opportunity will be given me. I cannot, if I am in the field of glory, be kept out of sight; wherever there is anything to be done, there Providence is sure to direct my steps."

These hopes and anticipations were soon to be fulfilled. Nelson's mind had long been irritated and depressed by the fear that a general action would take place before he could join the fleet. At length he sailed from Porto Ferrajo with a convoy for Gibraltar; and having reached that place, proceeded to the westward in search of the admiral. Off the mouth of the Straits he fell in with the Spanish fleet; and on the 13th of February reaching the station off Cape St. Vincent, communicated this intelligence to Sir John Jervis. He was now directed to shift his broad pendant on board the *Captain*, seventy-four, Captain R.W. Miller; and before sunset the signal was made to prepare for action, and to keep, during the night, in close order. At daybreak the enemy were in sight. The British force consisted of two ships of one hundred guns, two of ninety-eight, two of ninety, eight of seventy-four, and one sixty-four; fifteen of the line in all; with four frigates, a sloop, and a cutter. The Spaniards had one four-decker, of one hundred and thirty-six guns; six three-deckers, of one hundred and twelve; two eighty-four, eighteen seventy-four—in all, twenty-seven ships of the line, with ten frigates and a brig. Their admiral, D. Joseph de Cordova, had learnt from an American on the 5th, that the English had only nine ships, which was indeed the case when his informer had seen them; for a reinforcement of five ships from England, under Admiral Parker, had not then joined, and the *Culloden* had parted company. Upon this information the Spanish commander, instead of going into Cadiz, as was his intention when he sailed from Carthagena, determined to seek an enemy so inferior in force; and relying, with fatal confidence, upon the American account, he suffered his ships to remain too far dispersed, and in some disorder. When the morning of the 14th broke, and discovered the English fleet, a fog for some time concealed their number. That fleet had heard their signal-guns during the night, the weather being fine though thick and hazy; soon after daylight they were seen very much scattered, while the British ships were in a compact little body. The look-out ship of the Spaniards, fancying that her signal was disregarded because so little notice seemed to be taken of it, made another signal, that the English force consisted of forty sail of the line. The captain afterwards said he did this to rouse the admiral; it had the effect of perplexing him and alarming the whole fleet. The absurdity of such an act shows what was the state of the Spanish navy under that miserable government by which Spain was so long oppressed and degraded, and finally betrayed. In reality, the general incapacity of the naval officers was so well known, that in a pasquinade, which about this time appeared at Madrid, wherein the different orders of the state were advertised for sale, the greater part of the sea-officers, with all their equipments, were offered as a gift; and it was added, that any person who would please to take them, should receive a handsome gratuity. When the probability that Spain would take part in the war, as an ally of France, was first contemplated, Nelson said that their fleet, if it were no better than when it acted in alliance with us, would "soon be done for."

Before the enemy could form a regular order of battle, Sir J. Jervis, by carrying a press of sail, came up with them, passed through their fleet, then tacked, and thus cut off nine of their ships from the main body. These ships attempted to form on the larboard tack, either with a design of passing through the British line, or to leeward of it, and thus rejoining their friends. Only one of them succeeded in this attempt; and that only because she was so covered with smoke that her intention was not discovered till she had reached the rear: the others were so warmly received, that they put about, took to flight, and did not appear again in the action to its close. The admiral was now able to direct his attention to the enemy's main body, which was still superior in number to his whole fleet, and greatly so in weight of metal. He made signal to tack in succession. Nelson, whose station was in the rear of the British line, perceived that the Spaniards were bearing up before the wind, with an intention of forming their line, going large, and joining their separated ships, or else of getting off without an engagement. To prevent either of these schemes, he disobeyed the signal without a moment's hesitation: and ordered his ship to be wore. This at once brought him into action with the *Santísima Trinidad*, one hundred and thirty-six; the *San Joseph*, one hundred and twelve; the *Salvador Del Mundo*, one hundred and twelve; the *San Nicolas*, eighty; the *San Isidor*, seventy-four, another seventy-four, and another first-rate. Troubridge, in the *Culloden*, immediately joined, and most nobly supported him; and for nearly an hour did the *Culloden* and *Captain* maintain what Nelson called "this apparently, but not really unequal contest;"—such was the advantage of skill and discipline, and the confidence which brave men derive from them. The *Blenheim* then passing between them and the enemy, gave them a respite, and poured in her fire upon the Spaniards. The *Salvador Del Mundo* and *San Isidro* dropped astern, and were fired into in a masterly style by the *Excellent*, Captain Collingwood. The *San Isidro* struck; and Nelson thought that the *Salvador* struck also. "But Collingwood," says he, "disdaining the parade of taking possession of beaten enemies, most gallantly pushed up, with every sail set, to save his old friend and messmate, who was to appearance in a critical situation;" for the *Captain* was at this time actually fired upon by three first-rates—by the *San Nicolas*, and by a seventy-four, within about pistol-shot of that vessel. The *Blenheim* was ahead, the *Culloden* crippled and astern. Collingwood ranged up, and hauling up his mainsail just astern, passed within ten feet of the *San Nicolas*, giving her a most tremendous fire, then passed on for the *Santisíma Trinidad*. The *San Nicolas* luffing up, the *San Joseph* fell on board her, and Nelson resumed his station abreast of them, and close alongside. The *Captain* was now incapable of further service, either in the line or in chase: she had lost her foretop-mast; not a sail, shroud, or rope was left, and her wheel was shot away. Nelson therefore directed Captain Miller to put the helm a-starboard, and calling for the boarders, ordered them to board.

Captain Berry, who had lately been Nelson's first lieutenant, was the first man who leaped into the enemy's mizen chains. Miller, when in the very act of going, was ordered by Nelson to remain. Berry was supported from the spritsail-yard, which locked in the *San Nicolas*'s main rigging. A soldier of the 69th broke the upper quarter-gallery window, and jumped in, followed by the commodore himself and by the others as fast as possible. The cabin doors were fastened, and the Spanish officers fired their pistols at them through the window; the doors were soon forced, and the Spanish brigadier fell while retreating to the quarter-deck. Nelson pushed on, and found Berry in possession of the poop, and the Spanish ensign hauling down. He passed on to the forecastle, where he met two or three Spanish officers, and received their swords. The English were now in full possession of every part of the ship, when a fire of pistols and musketry opened upon them from the admiral's stern-gallery of the *San Joseph*. Nelson having placed sentinels at the different ladders, and ordered Captain Miller to send more men into the prize, gave orders for boarding that ship from the *San Nicolas*. It was done in an instant, he himself leading the way, and exclaiming, "Westminster Abbey or victory!" Berry assisted him into the main chains; and at that moment a Spanish officer looked over the quarter-deck rail, and said they surrendered. It was not long before he was on the quarter-deck, where the Spanish captain presented to him his sword, and told him the admiral was below dying of his wounds. There, on the quarter-deck of an enemy's first-rate, he received the swords of the officers, giving them, as they were delivered, one by one to William Fearney, one of his old *Agamemnon*'s, who, with the utmost coolness, put them under his arm, "bundling them up," in the lively expression of Collingwood, "with as much composure as he would have made a faggot, though twenty-two sail of their line were still within gunshot." One of his sailors came up, and with an Englishman's feeling took him by the hand, saying he might not soon have such another place to do it in, and he was heartily glad to see him there. Twenty-four of the *Captain*'s men were killed, and fifty-six wounded; a fourth part of the loss sustained by the whole squadron falling upon this ship. Nelson received only a few bruises.

The Spaniards had still eighteen or nineteen ships which had suffered little or no injury: that part of the fleet which had been separated from the main body in the morning was now coming up, and Sir John Jervis made signal to bring to. His ships could not have formed without abandoning those which they had captured, and running to leeward: the *Captain* was lying a perfect wreck on board her two prizes; and many of the other vessels were so shattered in their masts and rigging as to be wholly unmanageable. The Spanish admiral meantime, according to his official account, being altogether undecided in his own opinion respecting the state of the fleet, inquired of his captains whether it was proper to renew the action; nine of them answered explicitly that it was not; others replied that it was expedient to delay the business. The *Pelayo* and the *Prince Conquistador* were the only ships that were for fighting.

As soon as the action was discontinued, Nelson went on board the admiral's ship. Sir John Jervis received him on the quarter-deck, took him in his arms, and said he could not sufficiently thank him. For this victory the commander-in-chief was rewarded with the title of Earl St. Vincent. Nelson, who before the action was known in England had been advanced to the rank of rear-admiral, had the Order of the Bath given him. The sword of the Spanish rear-admiral, which Sir John Jervis insisted upon his keeping, he presented to the Mayor and Corporation of Norwich, saying that he knew no place where it could give him or his family more pleasure to have it kept than in the capital city of the county where he was born. The freedom of that city was voted him on this occasion. But of all the numerous congratulations which he received, none could have affected him with deeper delight than that which came from his venerable father. "I thank my God," said this excellent man, "with all the power of a grateful soul, for the mercies he has most graciously bestowed on me in preserving you. Not only my few acquaintance here, but the people in general, met me at every corner with such handsome words, that I was obliged to retire from the public eye. The height of glory to which your professional judgment, united with a proper degree of bravery, guarded by Providence, has raised you, few sons, my dear child, attain to, and fewer fathers live to see. Tears of joy have involuntarily trickled down my furrowed cheeks: who could stand the force of such general congratulation? The name and services of Nelson have sounded through this city of Bath—from the common ballad-singer to the public theatre." The good old man concluded by telling him that the field of glory, in which he had so long been conspicuous, was still open, and by giving him his blessing.

Sir Horatio, who had now hoisted his flag as rear-admiral of the blue, was sent to bring away the troops from Porto Ferrajo; having performed this, he shifted his flag to the *Theseus*. That ship, had taken part in the mutiny in England, and being just arrived from home, some danger was apprehended from the temper of the men. This was one reason why Nelson was removed to her. He had not been on board many weeks before a paper, signed in the name of all the ship's company, was dropped on the quarter-deck, containing these words: "Success attend Admiral Nelson! God bless Captain Miller! We thank them for the officers they have placed over us. We are happy and comfortable, and will shed every drop of blood in our veins to support them; and the name of the *Theseus* shall be immortalised as high as her captain's." Wherever Nelson commanded, the men soon became attached to him; in ten days' time he would have restored the most mutinous ship in the navy to order. Whenever an officer fails to win the affections of those who are under his command, he may be assured that the fault is chiefly in himself.

While Sir Horatio was in the *Theseus*, he was employed in the command of the inner squadron at the blockade of Cadiz. During this service, the most perilous action occurred in which he was ever engaged. Making a night attack upon the Spanish gun-boats, his barge was attacked by an armed launch, under their commander, D. Miguel Tregoyen, carrying 26 men. Nelson had with him only his ten bargemen, Captain Freemantle, and his coxswain, John Sykes, an old and faithful follower, who twice saved the life of his admiral by parrying the blows that were aimed at him, and at last actually interposed his own head to receive the blow of a Spanish sabre, which he could not by any other means avert; thus dearly was Nelson beloved. This was a desperate service—hand to hand with swords; and Nelson always considered that his personal courage was more conspicuous on this occasion than on any other during his whole life. Notwithstanding the great disproportion of numbers, 18 of the enemy were killed, all the rest wounded, and their launch taken. Nelson would have asked for a lieutenancy for Sykes, if he had served long enough; his manner and conduct, he observed, were so entirely above his situation, that Nature certainly intended him for a gentleman; but though he recovered from the dangerous wound which he received in this act of heroic attachment, he did not live to profit by the gratitude and friendship of his commander.

Twelve days after this rencontre, Nelson sailed at the head of an expedition against Teneriffe. A report had prevailed a few months before, that the viceroy of Mexico, with the treasure ships, had put into that island. This had led Nelson to meditate the plan of an attack upon it, which he communicated to Earl St. Vincent. He was perfectly aware of the difficulties of the attempt. "I do not," said he, "reckon myself equal to Blake; but, if I recollect right, he was more obliged to the wind coming off the land than to any exertions of his own. The approach by sea to the anchoring-place is under very high land, passing three valleys; therefore the wind is either in from the sea, or squally with calms from the mountains:" and he perceived that if the Spanish ships were won, the object would still be frustrated if the wind did not come off shore. The land force, he thought, would render success certain; and there were the troops from Elba, with all necessary stores and artillery, already embarked. "But here," said he, "soldiers must be consulted; and I know, from experience, they have not the same boldness in undertaking a political measure that we have: we look to the benefit of our country, and risk our own fame every day to serve her; a soldier obeys his orders, and no more." Nelson's experience at Corsica justified him in this harsh opinion: he did not live to see the glorious days of the British army under Wellington. The army from Elba, consisting of 3,700 men, would do the business, he said, in three days, probably in much less time; and he would undertake, with a very small squadron, to perform the naval part; for though the shore was not easy of access, the transports might run in and land the troops in one day.

The report concerning the viceroy was unfounded: but a homeward-bound Manilla ship put into Santa Cruz at this time, and the expedition was determined upon. It was not fitted out upon the scale which Nelson had proposed. Four ships of the line, three frigates, and the *Fox* cutter, formed the squadron; and he was allowed to choose such ships and officers as he thought proper. No troops were embarked; the seamen and marines of the squadron being thought sufficient. His orders were, to make a vigorous attack; but on no account to land in person, unless his presence should be absolutely necessary. The plan was, that the boats should land in the night, between the fort on the N.E. side of Santa Cruz bay and the town, make themselves masters of that fort, and then send a summons to the governor. By midnight, the three frigates, having the force on board which was intended for this debarkation, approached within three miles of the place; but owing to a strong gale of wind in the offing, and a strong current against them in-shore, they were not able to get within a mile of the landing-place before daybreak; and then they were seen, and their intention discovered. Troubridge and Bowen, with Captain Oldfield, of the marines, went upon this to consult with the admiral what was to be done; and it was resolved that they should attempt to get possession of the heights above the fort. The frigates accordingly landed their men; and Nelson stood in with the line-of-battle ships, meaning to batter the fort for the purpose of distracting the attention of the garrison. A calm and contrary current hindered him from getting within a league of the shore; and the heights were by this time so secured, and manned with such a force, as to be judged impracticable. Thus foiled in his plans by circumstances of wind and tide, he still considered it a point of honour that some attempt should be made. This was on the 22nd of July: he re-embarked his men that night, got the ships on the 24th to anchor about two miles north of the town, and made show as if he intended to attack the heights. At six in the evening signal was made for the boats to prepare to proceed on the service as previously ordered.

When this was done, Nelson addressed a letter to the commander-in-chief—the last which was ever written with his right hand. "I shall not," said he, "enter on the subject, why we are not in possession of Santa Cruz. Your partiality will give credit, that all has hitherto been done which was possible, but without effect. This night I, humble as I am, command the whole destined to land under the batteries of the town; and to-morrow my head will probably be crowned either with laurel or cypress. I have only to recommend Josiah Nisbet to you and my country. The Duke of Clarence, should I fall, will, I am confident, take a lively interest for my son-in-law, on his name being mentioned." Perfectly aware how desperate a service this was likely to prove, before he left the *Theseus* he called Lieutenant Nisbet, who had the watch on deck, into the cabin, that he might assist in arranging and burning his mother's letters. Perceiving that the young man was armed, he earnestly begged him to remain behind. "Should we both fall, Josiah," said he, "what will become of your poor mother! The care of the *Theseus* falls to you: stay, therefore, and take charge of her." Nisbet replied: "Sir, the ship must take care of herself: I will go with you to-night, if I never go again."

He met his captains at supper on board the *Seahorse*, Captain Freemantle, whose wife, whom he had lately married in the Mediterranean, presided at table. At eleven o'clock the boats, containing between 600 and 700 men, with 180 on board the *Fox* cutter, and from 70 to 80 in a boat which had been taken the day before, proceeded in six divisions toward the town, conducted by all the captains of the squadron, except Freemantle and Bowen, who attended with Nelson to regulate and lead the way to the attack. They were to land on the mole, and thence hasten as fast as possible into the great square; then form and proceed as should be found expedient. They were not discovered till about half-past one o'clock, when, being within half gun-shot of the landing-place, Nelson directed the boats to cast off from each other, give a huzza, and push for the shore. But the Spaniards were exceedingly well prepared; the alarm-bells answered the huzza, and a fire of thirty or forty pieces of cannon, with musketry from one end of the town to the other, opened upon the invaders. Nothing, however, could check the intrepidity with which they advanced. The night was exceedingly dark: most of the boats missed the mole and went on shore through a raging surf, which stove all to the left of it. The Admiral, Freemantle, Thompson, Bowen, and four or five other boats, found the mole: they stormed it instantly, and carried it, though it was defended, as they imagined, by 400 or 500 men. Its guns, which were six-and-twenty pounders, were spiked; but such a heavy fire of musketry and grape was kept up from the citadel and the houses at the head of the mole, that the assailants could not advance, and nearly all of them were killed or wounded.

In the act of stepping out of the boat, Nelson received a shot through the right elbow, and fell; but as he fell he caught the sword, which he had just drawn, in his left hand, determined never to part with it while he lived, for it had belonged to his uncle, Captain Suckling, and he valued it like a relic. Nisbet, who was close to him, placed him at the bottom of the boat, and laid his hat over the shattered arm, lest the sight of the blood, which gushed out in great abundance, should increase his faintness. He then examined the wound, and taking some silk handkerchiefs from his neck, bound them round tight above the lacerated vessels. Had it not been for this presence of mind in his son-in-law, Nelson must have perished. One of his bargemen, by name Level, tore his shirt into shreds, and made a sling with them for the broken limb. They then collected five other seamen, by whose assistance they succeeded at length in getting the boat afloat; for it had grounded with the falling tide. Nisbet took one of the oars and ordered the steersman to go close under the guns of the battery, that they might be safe from its tremendous fire. Hearing his voice, Nelson roused himself, and desired to be lifted up in the boat that he might look about him. Nisbet raised him up; but nothing could be seen except the firing of the guns on shore, and what could be discerned by their flashes upon a stormy sea. In a few minutes a general shriek was heard from the crew of the *Fox*, which had received a shot under water, and went down. Ninety-seven men were lost in her: 83 were saved, many by Nelson himself, whose exertions on this occasion greatly increased the pain and danger of his wound. The first ship which the boat could reach happened to be the *Seahorse*; but nothing could induce him to go on board, though he was assured that if they attempted to row to another ship it might be at the risk of his life. "I had rather suffer death," he replied, "than alarm Mrs. Freemantle, by letting her see me in this state, when I can give her no tidings whatever of her husband." They pushed on for the *Theseus*. When they came alongside he peremptorily refused all assistance in getting on board, so impatient was he that the boat should return, in hopes that it might save a few more from the *Fox*. He desired to have only a single rope thrown over the side, which he twisted round his left hand, saying "Let me alone; I have yet my legs left and one arm. Tell the surgeon to make haste and get his instruments. I know I must lose my right arm, so the sooner it is off the better." The spirit which he displayed in jumping up the ship's side astonished everybody.

Freemantle had been severely wounded in the right arm soon after the admiral. He was fortunate enough to find a boat on the beach, and got instantly to his ship. Thompson was wounded: Bowen killed, to the great regret of Nelson: as was also one of his own officers, Lieutenant Weatherhead, who had followed him from the *Agamemnon*, and whom he greatly and deservedly esteemed. Troubridge, meantime, fortunately for his party, missed the mole in the darkness, but pushed on shore under the batteries, close to the south end of the citadel. Captain Waller, of the *Emerald*, and two or three other boats, landed at the same time. The surf was so high that many others put back. The boats were instantly filled with water and stove against the rocks; and most of the ammunition in the men's pouches was wetted. Having collected a few men they pushed on to the great square, hoping there to find the admiral and the rest of the force. The ladders were all lost, so that they could make no immediate attempt on the citadel; but they sent a sergeant with two of the town's-people to summon it: this messenger never returned; and Troubridge having waited about an hour in painful expectation of his friends, marched to join Captains Hood and Miller, who had effected their landing to the south-west. They then endeavoured to procure some intelligence of the admiral and the rest of the officers, but without success. By daybreak they had gathered together about eighty marines, eighty pikemen, and one hundred and eighty small-arm sea-men; all the survivors of those who had made good their landing. They obtained some ammunition from the prisoners whom they had taken, and marched on to try what could be done at the citadel without ladders. They found all the streets commanded by field-pieces, and several thousand Spaniards, with about a hundred French, under arms, approaching by every avenue. Finding himself without provisions, the powder wet, and no possibility of obtaining either stores or reinforce-ments from the ships, the boats being lost, Troubridge with great presence of mind, sent Captain Samuel Hood with a flag of truce to the governor to say he was prepared to burn the town, and would instantly set fire to it if the Spaniards ap-proached one inch nearer. This, however, if he were compelled to do it, he should do with regret, for he had no wish to injure

the inhabitants; and he was ready to treat upon these terms—
that the British troops should re-embark, with all their arms of
every kind, and take their own boats, if they were saved, or be
provided with such others as might be wanting; they, on their
part, engaging that the squadron should not molest the town, or
any of the Canary Islands: all prisoners on both sides to be given
up. When these terms were proposed the governor made
answer, that the English ought to surrender as prisoners of
war; but Captain Hood replied, he was instructed to say, that if
the terms were not accepted in five minutes, Captain Troubridge would set the town on fire and attack the Spaniards at
the point of the bayonet. Satisfied with his success, which was
indeed sufficiently complete, and respecting, like a brave and
honourable man, the gallantry of his enemy, the Spaniard
acceded to the proposal, found boats to re-embark them, their
own having all been dashed to pieces in landing, and before
they parted gave every man a loaf and a pint of wine.

"And here," says Nelson in his journal, "it is right we should
notice the noble and generous conduct of Don Juan Antonio
Gutierrez, the Spanish governor. The moment the terms were
agreed to, he directed our wounded men to be received into the
hospitals, and all our people to be supplied with the best
provisions that could be procured; and made it known that
the ships were at liberty to send on shore and purchase whatever refreshments they were in want of during the time they
might be off the island." A youth, by name Don Bernardo
Collagon, stripped himself of his shirt to make bandages for one
of those Englishmen against whom, not an hour before, he had
been engaged in battle. Nelson wrote to thank the governor for
the humanity which he had displayed. Presents were inter-
changed between them. Sir Horatio offered to take charge of his
despatches for the Spanish Government, and thus actually
became the first messenger to Spain of his own defeat.

The total loss of the English in killed, wounded, and
drowned, amounted to 250. Nelson made no mention of his
own wound in his official despatches; but in a private letter to
Lord St. Vincent – the first which he wrote with his left hand –
he shows himself to have been deeply affected by the failure of
this enterprise. "I am become," he said, "a burthen to my

friends, and useless to my country; but by my last letter you will perceive my anxiety for the promotion of my son-in-law, Josiah Nisbet. When I leave your command I become dead to the world – I go hence, and am no more seen. If from poor Bowen's loss, you think it proper to oblige me, I rest confident you will do it. The boy is under obligations to me, but he repaid me by bringing me from the mole of Santa Cruz. I hope you will be able to give me a frigate to convey the remains of my carcass to England." "A left-handed admiral," he said in a subsequent letter, "will never again be considered as useful; therefore the sooner I get to a very humble cottage the better, and make room for a sounder man to serve the state." His first letter to Lady Nelson was written under the same opinion, but in a more cheerful strain. "It was the chance of war," said he, "and I have great reason to be thankful: and I know it will add much to your pleasure to find that Josiah, under God's providence, was principally instrumental in saving my life. I shall not be surprised if I am neglected and forgotten: probably I shall no longer be considered as useful; however, I shall feel rich if I continue to enjoy your affection. I beg neither you nor my father will think much of this mishap; my mind has long been made up to such an event."

His son-in-law, according to his wish, was immediately promoted; and honours enough to heal his wounded spirit awaited him in England. Letters were addressed to him by the first lord of the Admiralty, and by his steady friend the Duke of Clarence, to congratulate him on his return, covered as he was with glory. He assured the Duke, in his reply, that not a scrap of that ardour with which he had hitherto served his king had been shot away. The freedom of the cities of Bristol and London were transmitted to him; he was invested with the Order of the Bath, and received a pension of £3000 a-year. The memorial which, as a matter of form, he was called upon to present on this occasion, exhibited an extraordinary catalogue of services performed during the war. It stated that he had been in four actions with the fleets of the enemy, and in three actions with boats employed in cutting out of harbour, in destroying vessels, and in taking three towns. He had served on shore with the army four months, and commanded the batteries at the sieges of Basti and Calvi: he had assisted at the capture of seven sail of the line, six frigates, four corvettes, and eleven privateers: taken and destroyed near fifty sail of merchant vessels, and actually been engaged against the enemy upwards of a hundred and twenty times, in which service he had lost his right eye and right arm, and been severely wounded and bruised in his body.

His sufferings from the lost limb were long and painful. A nerve had been taken up in one of the ligatures at the time of the operation; and the ligature, according to the practice of the French surgeons, was of silk instead of waxed thread; this produced a constant irritation and discharge; and the ends of the ligature being pulled every day, in hopes of bringing it away, occasioned fresh agony. He had scarcely any intermission of pain, day or night, for three months after his return to England. Lady Nelson, at his earnest request, attended the dressing of his arm, till she had acquired sufficient resolution and skill to dress it herself. One night, during this state of suffering, after a day of constant pain, Nelson retired early to bed, in hope of enloymg some respite by means of laudanum. He was at that time lodging in Bond Street, and the family were soon disturbed by a mob knocking loudly and violently at the door. The news of Duncan's victory had been made public, and the house was not illuminated. But when the mob were told that Admiral Nelson lay there in bed, badly wounded, the foremost of them made answer: "You shall hear no more from us to-night:" and in fact, the feeling of respect and sympathy was communicated from one to another with such effect that, under the confusion of such a night, the house was not molested again.

About the end of November, after a night of sound sleep, he found the arm nearly free from pain. The surgeon was immediately sent for to examine it; and the ligature came away with the slightest touch. From that time it began to heal. As soon as he thought his health established, he sent the following form of thanksgiving to the minister of St. George's, Hanover Square:—"An officer desires to return thanks to Almighty God for his perfect recovery from a severe wound, and also for the many mercies bestowed on him."

Not having been in England till now, since he lost his eye, he went to receive a year's pay as smart money; but could not obtain payment, because he had neglected to bring a certificate from a surgeon that the sight was actually destroyed. A little irritated that this form should be insisted upon, because, though the fact was not apparent, he thought it was sufficiently notorious, he procured a certificate at the same time for the loss of his arm; saying, they might just as well doubt one as the other. This put him in good humour with himself, and with the clerk who had offended him. On his return to the office, the clerk, finding it was only the annual pay of a captain, observed, he thought it had been more. "Oh!" replied Nelson, "this is only for an eye. In a few days I shall come for an arm; and in a little time longer, God knows, most probably for a leg." Accordingly he soon afterwards went, and with perfect good humour exhibited the certificate of the loss of his arm.

From *Life of Nelson*, Robert Southey, 1813

SOURCES

Prelude

1 Quoted in Edgar Vincent, *Nelson: Love & Fame*, (Yale University Press, 2003).
2 *ibid.*
3 Quoted in Christopher Hibbert, *Nelson: A Personal History*, (Viking, 1994).
4 *ibid.*
5 William Dillon, (ed. Michael A. Lewis), *A Narrative of My Adventures*, (Navy Records Society, 1953).
6 M.C, An Old Agamemnon, "Nelson at Bastia" in *United Services Journal*, February 1841, No. 147.
7 John Drinkwater Bethune, *A Narrative of the Battle of St. Vincent; with Anecdotes of Nelson, Before and After that Battle*, 1840.
8 E.H. Moorhouse, *Letters of the English Seamen*, (Chapman & Hall, 1910).
9 William Hoste, *Memoirs & Letters*, 1833
10 Quoted in Vincent *op cit*.
11 *ibid.*
12 Geoffrey Rawson (ed.), *Nelson's Letters*, (J.M. Dent & Son, 1960).
13 *ibid.*
14 *ibid.*
15 *ibid.*
16 *ibid.*
17 *ibid.*
18 *ibid.*
19 *ibid.*
20 *ibid.*
21 *ibid.*
22 *ibid.*
23 *ibid.*
24 *ibid.*
25 *ibid.*

26 *ibid.*
27 *ibid.*
28 Sir Nicholas Harris Nicolas, *The Dispatches and Letters of Lord Nelson*, Vol. III, January 1798—August 1799, (Henry Colburn, 1845).
29 *ibid.*
30 *ibid.*
31 Quoted in E. Fraser, *Sailors Whom Nelson Led*, (Methuen, 1913).
32 Nicholas, Vol. III *op cit.*
33 Quoted in E. Fraser, *Sailors Whom Nelson Led, op cit.*
34 Nicholas, Vol. III *op cit.*
35 Rawson *op cit.*
36 *ibid.*
37 *ibid.*
38 *ibid.*
39 *ibid.*
40 *ibid.*
41 *ibid.*
42 *ibid.*
43 *ibid.*
44 *ibid.*
45 Nicholas Vol. III *op cit.*
46 *ibid.*
47 Quoted in Terry Coleman, *Nelson: The Man and the Legend*, (Bloomsbury, 2001).
48 Nicholas Vol III *op cit.*
49 Sir Nicholas Harris Nicolas, *The Dispatches and Letters of Lord Nelson*, Vol. IV, (Henry Colburn, 1845).
50 *ibid.*
51 S.T. Jackson, *Logs of the Great Sea Fights*, (Navy Records Society, 1899–1900).
52 Quoted in Hibbert *op cit.*

The Long Watch

1 Christopher Hibbert, *Nelson: A Personal History*, (Viking, 1994).
2 *ibid.*
3 W. Badcock (aka W.S. Lovell), *Personal Narrative of Events from 1799–1815*, (W. Allen, 1879).
4 Quoted in Hibbert *op cit.*
5 William Beatty, *The Death of Lord Nelson, 21 October 1805*
6 Quoted in P. Padfield, *Nelson's War*, (Hart-Davis MacGibbon, 1976).
7 Quoted in John Terraine, *Trafalgar*, (Sidgwick & Jackson, 1976).
8 Quoted in Jon E. Lewis, *The Mammoth Book of How It Happened: Britain*, (Robinson, 2001)
9 Sir Nicholas Harris Nicolas, *The Dispatches and Letters of Lord Nelson*, Vol. II, August 1805—October 1805, (Henry Colburn, 1845).
10 *ibid.*
11 *ibid.*

12 *ibid.*
13 *ibid.*
14 *ibid.*
15 *ibid.*
16 *ibid.*
17 *ibid.*
18 *ibid.*
19 *ibid.*
20 *ibid.*
21 *ibid.*
22 *ibid.*
23 *ibid.*
24 *ibid.*
25 *ibid.*
26 *ibid.*
27 *ibid.*
28 *ibid.*
29 *ibid.*
30 *ibid.*
31 *ibid.*
32 *ibid.*
33 *ibid.*
34 E Fraser, *The Enemy at Trafalgar* (Hodder & Stoughton, 1900)

England's Glory
 1 William Beatty, *The Death of Lord Nelson, 21 October 1805* (Edward Arbor, 1807)
 2 Sir Nicholas Harris Nicolas, *The Dispatches and Letters of Lord Nelson,* Vol IV (Henry Colburn, 1845)
 3 *ibid*
 4 *ibid*
 5 Quoted in John Terraine, *Trafalgar* (Sidgwick & Jackson, 1976)
 6 *ibid*
 7 E Fraser, *The Enemy at Trafalgar* (Hodder & Stoughton, 1900)
 8 Quoted in Terraine *op cit*
 9 E Fraser, *The Sailors Whom Nelson Led* (Methuen, 1913)
10 *ibid*
11 Fraser, *The Enemy at Trafalgar op cit*
12 EH Moorhouse, *Letters of the English Seamen* (Chapman & Hall, 1910)
13 Quoted in Terraine *op cit*
14 Quoted in Terraine *op cit*
15 Fraser, *The Enemy at Trafalgar op cit*
16 Nicolas *op cit*
17 Fraser, *The Enemy at Trafalgar op cit*
18 Fraser, *The Enemy at Trafalgar op cit*
19 Fraser, *The Enemy at Trafalgar op cit*

20 Nicolas *op cit*
21 Fraser, *The Enemy at Trafalgar op cit*
22 Nicolas *op cit*
23 Fraser, *The Enemy at Trafalgar op cit*
24 Fraser, *The Enemy at Trafalgar op cit*
25 Nicolas *op cit*
26 Nicolas *op cit*
27 Fraser, *The Enemy at Trafalgar op cit*
28 Fraser, *The Enemy at Trafalgar op cit*
29 Nicolas *op cit*
30 Quoted in Terraine *op cit*
31 Beatty, *op cit*
32 Quoted in Terraine *op cit*
33 Quoted in Terraine *op cit*
34 Fraser, *The Enemy at Trafalgar op cit*
35 Fraser, *The Enemy at Trafalgar op cit*
36 Nicolas *op cit*
37 Fraser, *The Enemy at Trafalgar op cit*
38 Quoted in Terraine *op cit*

Aftermath
1 Sir Nicholas Harris Nicolas, *The Letters and Dispatches of Lord Nelson*, Vol IV (Henry Colburn, 1845)
2 *ibid*
3 *ibid*
4 EH Moorhouse, *Letters of the English Seamen* (Chapman & Hall, 1910)
5 *ibid*
6 *ibid*
7 E Fraser, *The Enemy at Trafalgar* (Hodder & Stoughton, 1900)
8 ibid
9 ibid
10 ibid
11 Nicolas *op cit*
12 Nicolas *op cit*
13 Nicolas *op cit*
14 Nicolas *op cit*
15 Nicolas *op cit*
16 Nicolas *op cit*
17 Nicolas *op cit*
18 Samuel Taylor Coleridge, *Collected Letters of Samuel Taylor Coleridge*, Vol II, Earl Leslie Griggs (ed), (Clarendon Press, 1956)
19 Quoted in Christopher Hibbert, *Nelson: A Personal History*, (Viking, 1994)
20 Nicolas *op cit*
21 Moorhouse *op cit*
22 Sir Nicholas Harris Nicolas, *The Letters and Dispatches of Lord Nelson*, Vol VII (Henry Colburn, 1846)

SELECT BIBLIOGRAPHY

General

Brodie, Bernard, *A Guide to Naval Strategy*, (Greenwood Press, 1977)
———*Sea Warfare in the Machine Age*, (Princeton University Press, 1941)
Callender, Geoffrey, *The Naval Side of British History*, (Christophers, 1924)
Corbett, Julian, *England in the Seven Years War*, (Longmans, 1907)
Creswell, John, *British Admirals of the Eighteenth Century: Tactics in Battle*, (Allen & Unwin, 1972)
Dugan, James, *The Great Mutiny*, (Deutsch, 1966)
Fremantle, Anne (ed.), *The Wynne Diaries*, 3 vols, (Oxford University Press, 1935)
Gardiner, Leslie. *The British Admiralty*, (W. Blackwood, 1968)
Glete, Jan, *Navies and Nations: Warships, Navies and State Building in Europe and America 1500–1860*, (Almqvist & Wiksell International, 1993)
Hattendorf, J.B. et al, *British Naval Documents, 1204–1960*, (Scolar Press, 1993)
Henderson, James, *The Frigates: An Account of the Lesser Warships of the Wars from 1793 to 1815*, (Adlard Coles, 1970)
Hill, Richard, *The Oxford Illustrated History of the Royal Navy*, (Oxford University Press, 1965)
Jackson, T. Sturges, *Logs of the Great Sea Fights 1794–1805*, (Navy Records Society, 1900-1)
James, William, *The Naval History of Great Britain 1793–1830*, 6 vols, (Richard Bentley, 1859)
Keegan, John, *The Price of Admiralty*, (Hutchinson, 1988)
Kennedy, Paul M., *The Rise and Fall of British Naval Mastery*, (Allen Lane, 1976)
Lambert, Andrew, *War at Sea in the Age of Sail*, (Weidenfeld & Nicolson military, 2000)
Landstrom, B., *Sailing Ships*, (Allen & Unwin, 1978)
Lavery, Brian, *The Ship of the Line: The Development of the Battlefleet 1650–1850*, vol I, (Conway Maritime, 1983)

Lewis, Jon. E. (ed), *The Mammoth Book of Life Before the Mast*, (Robinson, 2001)

Lewis, Michael, *England's Sea Officers: The Story of the Naval Profession*, (Allen & Unwin, 1948)

———*The History of the British Navy*, (Penguin Books, 1962)

———*A Social History of the Navy, 1793–1815*, (Allen & Unwin, 1960)

Lloyd, Christopher, *The British Seaman 1200–1860: A Social Survey*, (Collins, 1968)

———*St. Vincent and Camperdown*, (Batsford, 1963)

Lyon, David, *Sea Battles in Close-Up: The Age of Nelson*, (Ian Allan Ltd, 1996)

Mahan, A. T., *Influence of Sea Power 1890–1905*, (Sampson Low, 1989)

Manwaring, G.E. and Bonamy, Dobree, *The Floating Republic*, (Harcourt Brace, 1935)

Miller, Nathan, *Broadsides: The Age of Fighting Sail 1775–1815*, (John Wiley & Sons Inc., 2000)

Moorhouse, E.H., *Letters of the English Seamen*, (Chapman & Hall, 1910)

Morris, Roger, *The Royal Dockyards During the Revolutionary and Napoleonic Wars*, (Leicester University Press, 1983)

Parkinson, C. Northcote, *Britannia Rules: The Classic Age of Naval History 1793–1815*, (Weidenfeld & Nicolson, 1977)

Pivka, Otto von, *Navies of the Napoleonic Era*, (David & Charles Hippocrene Books, 1980)

Robinson, William, *Jack Nastyface: Memoirs of a Seaman*, (Wayland, 1973)

Rodger, N.A.M., *The Wooden World: Anatomy of the Georgian Navy*, (HarperCollins, 1986)

Stark, Suzanne J., *Female Tars: Women Aboard Ship in the Age of Sail*, (Constable, 1996)

Tunstall, Brian and Nicholas, Tracy, *Naval Warfare in the Age of Sail: The Evolution of Fighting Tactics 1650–1815*, (Naval Institute Press, 1991)

Nelson and Trafalgar

Allen, Joseph, *The Life of Viscount Nelson*, (George Routledge & Sons, 1853)

Beatty, W., *The Death of Nelson*, (Athenaeum, 1985)

Bennett, G., *The Battle of Trafalgar*, (Batsford, 1977)

———*Nelson the Commander*, (Scribner, 1972)

Beresford, Charles and Wilson, H.W., *Nelson and His Times*, (Harmsworth, 1897–8)

Blake, Nicholas and Lawrence, Richard, *The Illustrated Companion to Nelson's Navy*, (Stackpole Books, 2000)

Bradford, Emle, *Nelson: The Essential Hero*, (Macmillan, 1977)

Broadley, A.M. and Bartelot, R.G., *Nelson's Hardy: His Life, Letters and Friends*, (John Murray, 1909)

Bryant, Arthur, *Nelson*, (Collins, 1970)

Callender, Geoffrey, *The Story of HMS Victory*, (Philip Allan, 1929)

SELECT BIBLIOGRAPHY 491

Capes, Renalt, *Poseidon: A Personal Study of Admiral Lord Nelson*, (Sidgwick & Jackson, 1947)

Clarke, James and McArthur, John, *The Life of Admiral Lord Nelson*, 2 vols, (T. Cadell and W. Davies, 1809)

Coleman, Terry, *Nelson: The Man and the Legend*, (Bloomsbury, 2001)

Corbett, Julian, *The Campaign of Trafalgar*, (Longmans, Green & Co., 1910)

———*Fighting Instructions: Nelson's Tactical Memoranda*, vol 29, (Publications of the Navy Records Society, 1905)

Davies, David, *Nelson's Navy: English Fighting Ships, 1793–1815*, (Stackpole Books, 1997)

Eyre, Matcham M., *The Nelsons of Burnham Thorpe*, (John Lane, The Bodley Head, 1911)

Fenwick, Kenneth, HMS *Victory*, (Cassell & Co. Ltd, 1959)

Fitchett, W.H., *Nelson and His Captains*, (Smith, Elder, 1902)

Forester, C.S., *The Age of Fighting Sail*, (Doubleday, 1956)

———*Nelson: A Biography*, (John Lane, The Bodley Head, 1929)

Fraser, E., *The Sailors Whom Nelson Led*, (Methuen, 1913)

Gardiner, Richard, *The Campaign of Trafalgar 1803–1805*, (Chatham, 1997)

———*Nelson Against Napoleon*, (Chatham, 1997)

Gerin, Winifred, *Horatia Nelson*, (Clarendon Press, 1970)

Grenfell, Russell, *Nelson the Sailor*, (The Macmillan Company, 1950)

Harbron, J.D., *Trafalgar and the Spanish Navy*, (Naval Institute Press, 1988)

Hardwick, Mollie, *Emma, Lady Hamilton: A Study*, (Holt, Rinehart & Winston, 1969)

Hattersley, Roy, *Nelson*, (Weidenfeld & Nicolson, 1974)

Hewitt, James (ed), *Eyewitnesses to Nelson's Battles*, (Osprey, 1972)

Hibbert, Christopher, *Nelson: A Personal History*, (Viking, 1994)

Hough, Richard, *Nelson: A Biography*, (Park Lane Press, 1980)

Howarth, David, *Trafalgar: The Nelson Touch*, (Collins, 1969)

Keate, E.M., *Nelson's Wife*, (Cassell, 1939)

Kennedy, Ludovic, *Nelson's Band of Brothers*, (Odhams Press Ltd, 1951)

Kerr, Mark, *The Sailor's Nelson*, (Hurst & Blackett, 1932)

Kircheisen, Friedrich M., *Nelson: The Establishment of British World Dominion*, (Hutchinson, 1931)

Lavery, Brian, *Nelson and the Nile: The Mediterranean Campaign of 1798*, (Chatham Publishing, 1998)

———*Nelson's Navy: Ships, Men and Organisation 1793–1815*, (Naval Institute Press, 1989)

Legg, Stuart, *Trafalgar: An Eyewitness Account of a Great Battle*, (John Day Co., 1966)

Longridge, C.N., *The Anatomy of Nelson's Ships*, (Argus, 1994)

Mackenzie, Robert H., *The Trafalgar Roll: The Ships and the Officers*, (Naval Institute Press, 1989)

Mahan, A.T., *The Life of Nelson: The Embodiment of the Sea Power of Great Britain*, 2 vols, (Little Brown and Company, 1897, 1899)

Maine, Rene, *Trafalgar: Napoleon's Naval Waterloo*, (Charles Scribner's Sons, 1957)

Nicolas, Nicholas, *The Dispatches and Letters of Lord Nelson*, 7 vols, (Henry Colburn, 1844-6)

Oman, Carola, *Nelson*, (Hodder & Stoughton, 1947)

Padfield, Peter, *Nelson's War*, (Hart-Davis MacGibbon, 1976)

Parsons, George Samuel, *Nelsonian Reminiscences, Leaves from Memory's Log: A Dramatic Eye-Witness Account of the War at Sea 1795–1810*, (Saunders and Otley, 1843)

Pettogrew, Thomas, *Memoirs of the Life of Nelson*, 2 vols, (Boone, 1849)

Pocock, Tom, *Horatio Nelson*, (Weidenfeld & Nicolson Illustrated, 1988)

———*The Young Nelson in the Americas*, (Collins, 1980)

Pope, Dudley, *England Expects*, (Weidenfeld & Nicolson, 1959)

———*The Great Gamble: Nelson at Copenhagen*, (Weidenfeld & Nicolson, 1972)

———*Life in Nelson's Navy*, (HarperCollins, 1981)

Rawson, Geoffrey (ed), *Nelson's Letters*, (J.M. Dent & Son, 1960)

Russell, Jack, *Nelson and the Hamiltons*, (Simon & Schuster, 1969)

Schom, Alan, *Trafalgar: Countdown to Battle 1803–1805*, (Atheneum, 1990)

Sherrard, O.A., *A Life of Emma Hamilton*, (Sidgwick & Jackson, 1927)

Southey, Robert, *The Life of Horatio Lord Nelson*, (Murray, 1813)

Terraine, John, *Trafalgar*, (Sidgwick & Jackson, 1976)

Tours, Hugh, *The Life and Letters of Emma Hamilton*, (Gollancz, 1963)

Tracy, Nicholas, *Nelson's Battles: The Art of Victory in the Age of Sail*, (Chatham Publishing, 1996)

Walder, David, *Nelson*, (Hamish Hamilton, 1978)

Warner, O., *Emma Hamilton and Sir William*, (Chatto & Windus, 1960)

———*Nelson's Battles*, (Batsford, 1965)

———*A Portrait of Lord Nelson*, (The Reprint Society, 1958)

———*Trafalgar*, (Pan, 1959)

White, Colin (ed), *1797: Nelson's Year of Destiny*, (Sutton Publishing, 1998)

———*The Nelson Companion*, (Sutton Publishing, 1995)

Wilkinson, Clennell, *Life of Nelson*, (Harrap, 1931)